Rabelais and His World

Indiana University Press
Bloomington and Indianapolis

Rabelais and His World

BY MIKHAIL BAKHTIN   TRANSLATED BY HELENE ISWOLSKY

This book is a publication of

Indiana University Press
601 North Morton Street
Bloomington, IN 47404-3797 USA

http://www.indiana.edu/~iupress

Telephone orders 800-842-6796
Fax orders 812-855-7931
Orders by e-mail iuporder@indiana.edu

Rabelais and His World is translated from *Tvorchestvo Fransua Rable,* Moscow, Khudozhestvennia literatura, 1965.

The extracts from *Gargantua and Pantagruel* are from The Heritage Press edition, translated by Jacques LeClercq, reproduced by permission of The George Macy Companies, Inc., copyright 1936, renewed 1964.

The paper used in this publication meets the minimum requirements of American National Standard for Information Sciences—Permanence of Paper for Printed Library Materials, ANSI Z39.48-1984.

Manufactured in the United States of America

Library of Congress Cataloging-in-Publication Data

Bakhtin, M. M. (Mikhail Mikhaĭlovich), 1895–1975.
   Rabelais and his world.
   Translation of: Tvorchestvo Fransua Rable i narodnaĭa kul'tura srednevekov'ia i Renessansa.
   Includes index.
   1. Rabelais, François, ca. 1490–1553?—Criticism and interpretation.   2. Europe—popular culture.   3. Civilization, Medieval.   4. Renaissance.   5. Fiction.
6. Carnival.   I. Title.
PQ1694.B313   1984   843'.3   84-47792
ISBN 978-0-253-34830-2
ISBN 978-0-253-20341-0 (pbk.)

20   13

CONTENTS

FOREWORD *Krystyna Pomorska*   vii

PROLOGUE *Michael Holquist*   xiii

INTRODUCTION   1

ONE *Rabelais in the History of Laughter*   59

TWO *The Language of the Marketplace in Rabelais*   145

THREE *Popular-Festive Forms and Images in Rabelais*   196

FOUR *Banquet Imagery in Rabelais*   278

FIVE *The Grotesque Image of the Body and Its Sources*   303

SIX *Images of the Material Bodily Lower Stratum*   368

SEVEN *Rabelais' Images and His Time*   437

INDEX   475

When *Rabelais and His World,* Mikhail Bakhtin's first book to be published in English, appeared in 1968,[1] the author was totally unknown in the West. Moreover, his name, his biography, and his authorship were a mystery even in his native Russia. Today, Bakhtin (1895–1975) is internationally acclaimed in the world of letters and the humanities generally. His biography is gradually becoming better known as scholars from both East and West discover information and reconstruct the data. His books, previously neglected or unkown, are being republished, such as the one introduced here. What accounts for the new popularity of this theoretician who

wrote his pioneering works half a century ago and whose deep
concern was a subject as "enigmatic" as literature? In response, we
must look to his fundamental ideas about art, its ontology, and its
context. His roots in the intellectual life of the turn of the century,
Bakhtin insisted that art is oriented toward communication.
"Form" in art, thus conceived, is particularly active in expressing
and conveying a system of values, a function that follows from the
very nature of communication as an exchange of meaningful messages. In such statements,[2] Bakhtin recognizes the duality of every
sign in art, where all content is formal and every form exists
because of its content. In other words, "form" is active in any structure as a specific aspect of a "message."

Even more striking are Bakhtin's ideas concerning the role of
semiosis outside the domain of art, or, as he put it, in the organization of life itself. In opposition to interpretations of life as inert
"chaos" that is transformed into organized "form" by art, Bakhtin
claims that life itself (traditionally considered "content") is organized by human acts of behavior and cognition (*postupok i poz-
nanie*) and is therefore already charged with a system of values at
the moment it enters into an artistic structure. Art only transforms
this organized "material" into a *new* system whose distinction is
to mark *new* values. Bakhtin's semiotic orientation and his pioneering modernity of thought are grounded in his accounting for
human behavior as *communication* and, *eo ipso,* his recognition
of the goal-directedness of all human messages.

As a philosopher and literary scholar, Bakhtin had a "language
obsession" as Michael Holquist calls it, or, as we might also say, a
perfect understanding of language as a system; he managed to use
language comprehended as a *model* for his analysis of art, specifically the art of the novel. Besides his revolutionary book on
Dostoevsky, his essay "Discourse in the Novel"[3] ("Slovo v romane"),
written in 1934–35, belongs among the fundamental works on
verbal art today. In it Bakhtin argues first and foremost against the
outdated yet persistent idea of the "randomness" in the organization of the novel in contrast to poetry. He proved this assertion by
demonstrating in his works the particular transformations of

language necessary to produce the genre labeled the "novel." In contradistinction to poetry, Bakhtin defines the novel as a "multiplicity of styles" *(mnozhestvo stilei)* in their mutual echoing, or as *the word constantly reinvolved in a dialogue* (which he calls *romannoe slovo*—the "novelistic word"). Behind each reply in this dialogue stands a "speaking man," and therefore the word in the novel is always socially charged and thus necessarily polemical. There is no one-voiced novel, and, consequently, every novel by its very nature is polemical.

Another of Bakhtin's outstanding ideas connecting him with modern semiotics is his discovery that *quoted speech (chuzhaia rech')* permeates all our language activities in both practical and artistic communication. Bakhtin reveals the constant presence of this phenomenon in a vast number of examples from all areas of life: literature, ethics, politics, law, and inner speech. He points to the fact that we are actually dealing with someone else's words more often than with our own. Either we remember and respond to someone else's words (in the case of ethics); or we represent them in order to argue, disagree, or defend them (in the case of law); or, finally, we carry on an inner dialogue, responding to someone's words (including our own). In each case someone else's speech makes it possible to generate our own and thus becomes an indispensable factor in the creative power of language.

A further domain of Bakhtin's interest, and the source of his methodology, is folk culture. Even more than language and semiotics,[4] his concern with folk culture derives from the Russian tradition of his youth. Just as the Montpellier school of Rabelais's time promoted the importance and developed various theories of laughter, so Russian scholars in the early 1920s, including Zelenin, Trubetzkoy, Jakobson, Bogatyrev, and Propp, emphasized the importance of the "lower" strata of culture as opposed to the uniform, official "high culture." The prohibition of laughter and the comical in the epoch prior to the Renaissance parallels the rejection of "subcultures" in the years prior to the Second World War. As Trubetzkoy showed in his unjustly neglected book, *Europe and Mankind (Evropa i chelovechestvo),*[5] this cultural "centrism" pertains not only to a social but also to an ethnic hierarchy. The danger of European cultural "centrism," the recognition of the multiplicity of cultural strata, their relative hierarchy, and their "dialogue" occupied Trubetzkoy all his life.[6] The same is true of Bakhtin, as manifested in his works from the study on Dostoevsky (1929) to the Rabelais book (1965). This interest ties the author of *Rabelais and His World* to modern anthropology in America and in Europe.

Bakhtin's ideas concerning folk culture, with carnival as its indispensable component, are integral to his theory of art. The inherent features of carnival that he underscores are its emphatic and purposeful "heterglossia" (*raznogolosost'*) and its multiplicity of styles (*mnogostil'nost'*). Thus, the carnival principle corresponds to and is indeed a part of the novelistic principle itself. One may say that just as dialogization is the *sine qua non* for the novel structure, so carnivalization is the condition for the ultimate "structure of life" that is formed by "behavior and cognition." Since the novel represents the very essence of life, it includes the carnivalesque in its properly transformed shape. In his book on Dostoevsky, Bakhtin notes that "In carnival . . . the new mode of man's relation to man is elaborated."[7] One of the essential aspects of this relation is the "unmasking" and disclosing of the unvarnished truth under the veil of false claims and arbitrary ranks. Now, the role of dialogue—both historically and functionally, in language as a system as well as in the novel as a structure—is exactly the same. Bakhtin repeatedly points to the Socratian dialogue as a prototype of the discursive mechanism for revealing the truth. Dialogue so conceived is opposed to the "authoritarian word" (*avtoritarnoe slovo*) in the same way as carnival is opposed to official culture. The "authoritarian word" does not allow any other type of speech to approach and interfere with it. Devoid of any zones of cooperation with other types of words, the "authoritarian word" thus excludes dialogue. Similarly, any official culture that considers itself the only respectable model dismisses all other cultural strata as invalid or harmful.

Long before he published his book on Rabelais, Bakhtin had

defined in the most exact terms the principle and the presence of the carnivalesque in his native literary heritage.[8] However, the presence of carnival in Russian literature had been noted before Bakhtin, and a number of earlier critics and scholars had tried to approach and grasp this phenomenon. The nineteenth-century critic Vissarion Belinsky's renowned characterization of Gogol's universe as "laughter through tears" was probably the first observation of this kind. The particular place and character of humor in Russian literature has been a subject of discussion ever since. Some scholars have claimed that humor, in the western sense, is precluded from Russian literature, with the exception of works by authors of non-Russian, especially southern, origin, such as Gogol, Mayakovsky, or Bulgakov. Some critics, notably Chizhevsky and, especially, Trubetzkoy, discussed the specific character of Dostoevsky's humor,[9] and came close to perceiving its essence; yet they did not attain Bakhtin's depth and exactitude.

The official prohibition of certain kinds of laughter, irony, and satire was imposed upon the writers of Russia after the revolution. It is eloquent that in the 1930s Anatoly Lunacharsky, the Commissar of Enlightenment, himself wrote on the subject and organized a special government commission to study satiric genres. The fate of Mayakovsky, Bulgakov, and Zoshchenko—the prominent continuers of the Gogolian and Dostoevskian tradition—testifies to the Soviet state's rejection of free satire and concern with national self-irony, a situation similar to that prevailing during the Reformation. In defiance of this prohibition, both Rabelais and Bakhtin cultivated laughter, aware that laughter, like language, is uniquely characteristic of the human species.

Krystyna Pomorska

NOTES

1. Translated from the Russian by Hélène Iswolsky, foreword by Krystyna Pomorska (Cambridge: MIT Press, 1968).

2. *Voprosy literatury i estetiki* (Moscow: Khudozhestvennaia literatura, 1975).

3. In *The Dialogic Imagination: Four Essays by M. M. Bakhtin*, ed. Michael Holquist (Austin: University of Texas Press, 1981), pp. 259–422.
4. See V. N. Voloshinov, *Marksizm i filosofiia iazyka* (Leningrad, 1930); *Marxism and the Philosophy of Language* (New York, 1973).
5. (Sofia, 1920); German edition, *Europa und die Menschheit* (Munich: Drei Masken Verlag, 1922).
6. See his *K probleme russkogo samopoznaniia* (Evraziiskoe knigoizdatel'stvo, 1927).
7. *Problemy poetiki Dostoevskogo* (Moscow, 1963), p. 164, my translation.
8. In *Problemy poetiki Dostoevskogo*.
9. See I. I. Lapshin, "Komicheskoe v proizvedeniiakh Dostoevskogo," in *O Dostoevskom*, ed. A. L. Bem (Prague, 1933).

Although the word "intelligentsia" is originally Russian, it was best defined by Karl Mannheim when, in *Ideology And Utopia,* he wrote, "In every society there are social groups whose special task it is to provide an interpretation of the world for that society. We call these the 'intelligentsia.' "[1] So large a task is difficult at any time, but there are periods when events threaten to outstrip any capacity to interpret them. The Chinese had in mind periods of this kind when they politely wished their friends, "May you not live in interesting times." The Russian revolution was just such an interesting time. The political discrowning it accomplished was merely the most obvious of several simultaneous inversions for which "1917" has become a homogenizing metaphor. Those who lived through it were willy nilly thrown into the work of history. No one was allowed the luxury of a spectator's role. Those who normally seek the safety and anonymity of the gallery, such as peasants, workers, and—perhaps especially—intellectuals, to watch the kings, generals, prophets, and other public figures who occupy center stage go forward to volunteer their blood at Hegel's "slaughter bench of history," discovered they could not sit back and eat popcorn—or read books. The revolution gave a particularly Russian twist to Joyce's line, "Here comes everybody."

The unique species of historical event we call a revolution occurs when everything changes at once, not excluding the very categories used for gauging and shaping change. During the first decades of this century the whole Russian cultural system experienced an identity crisis. The generations that lived through those years had to work out for themselves fresh categories by which the utterly new and bewildering universe into which they had been thrust would let itself be known. It is in the nature of revolutions that no one can be an experienced citizen of the new order they bring into being. Those who fought for change, as well as those who resisted it, are confronted with the postlapsarian mandate to live their lives without a usable past.

Among the many things Mikhail Bakhtin attempts to accomplish in *Rabelais and His World* is the job he, as a Russian intellectual of his time, was called upon by history to undertake: to interpret the world for his society. In the Rabelais book Bakhtin works through his own experience of revolution to provide conceptual categories for the aid of others finding themselves in a similar gap between cosmologies. In common with everything Bakhtin wrote, this book is double-voiced: it is doing two things— at least two—simultaneously, for the multitude of shattered unities we call revolution brings forth texts with peculiar forms of unity. At one level *Rabelais and His World* is a parable and guidebook for its times, inexplicable without reference to the close connection between the circumstances of its own production and Soviet intellectual and political history. At another level, directed to scholars anywhere at any time, it is a contribution to historical poetics with theoretical implications not limited by its origin in a particular time and place. These two levels are reflected in the contrast between the book's cool official reception in the Soviet Union and its extraordinary popularity in the West. The two differing attitudes could be easily (in 1984, in the midst of what seemed increasingly to be a Cold War II, all *too* easily) explained away as yet another demonstration of "our" openness versus "their" closedness. But to do so is to misperceive much of the book's distinctiveness. Soviets who objected—and still object—to the book see in it a dimension that foreign scholars often miss as they hastily note obvious parallels between Bakhtin's scathing references to the Catholic church in the sixteenth century and Stalinism in the twentieth before focusing their attention on theoretical issues raised by the book. Soviet critics are wrong, of course, to limit the book's significance to a peculiarly Soviet reality. And we would be wrong to do the same thing. But not to perceive that significance in its full complexity is another way to undervalue the historical relevance of *Rabelais and His World.* For above and beyond the obvious differences between Bakhtin and Rabelais, the Russian critic and the French novelist have one fundamental feature in common: each created a special kind of open text that they explored as a means for inscribing themselves into their times.

Both Rabelais and Bakhtin knew that they were living in an unusual period, a time when virtually everything taken for granted in less troubled ages lost its certainty, was plunged into contest and flux. Unlike Dickens in his famous opening to *A Tale of Two Cities,* Bakhtin knew that all historical epochs are *not* essentially the same. There were periods, such as his own, when certain generations were presented with unusual dangers and unique opportunities. He was deeply responsive to the Renaissance because he saw in it an age similar to his own in its revolutionary consequences and its acute sense of one world's death and another world's being born. Thus, although Bakhtin is typically very modest, he nevertheless feels justified in claiming that in his book Rabelais, after four hundred years of incomprehension, is finally understood. He bases this extravagant claim on what can only be called the unique similarity of *Rabelais and His World* and *Gargantua*. Each springs from an age of revolution and each enacts a peculiarly open sense of the text. Bakhtin, unlike many others who have dealt with *Gargantua*, can hear Rabelais laughing because Bakhtin knows how Rabelais wrote his book and, in fact, writes one very much like it. *Rabelais and His World* is, of course, *about* the subversive openness of the Rabelaisian novel, but it is also a subversively open book itself.

For example, in the fourth book of *Gargantua* the tale is told of Master Villon, a rogue who wishes to organize a travestied passion play. All that is lacking is a costume for the character who is to play the role of God the Father. The local sacristan, shocked by what Villon intends, refuses to lend any church vestments for so devilish a purpose. The prankster Villon takes revenge by staging a rehearsal just as the sacristan rides by: the actors create enough commotion to frighten the churchman's horse; the sacristan is dragged along the ground until only the stump of his foot is left in a stirrup. Bakhtin makes of this tale a structural metaphor for what Rabelais does throughout his mischeivous novel: just as Villon, the character, derides and destroys the humorless representative of the Church through his parody of a play, so Rabelais, the author, seeks to destroy the forces of stasis and official ideology through his parody of a novel. As Bakhtin says, "In his novel, and by means of his novel, Rabelais behaves exactly as did Villon. . . . He uses the popular-festive system of images . . . to inflict a severe punishment on his foe, the Gothic age" (p. 268).

This passage is one of the loopholes Bakhtin always left open in his works: what he is saying about the relation of Rabelais to Villon describes very accurately Bakhtin's own relation to Rabelais. Bakhtin, like Rabelais, explores throughout his book the interface between a stasis imposed from above and a desire for change from below, between old and new, official and unofficial. In treating the specific ways Rabelais sought holes in the walls between what was held to be punishable and what unpunishable in the 1530s, Bakhtin seeks gaps in those borders in the 1930s.

One of the specific topics explored in the book is the peculiarity of the novel among other literary genres. This theme had a particular urgency in the 1930s because the novel had become the primary focus of the government's efforts to bring Soviet intellectual institutions into line. In 1932 all authors, no matter what their style or politics, were forced to join the new Union of Writers. Two years later there was a concerted effort to cap this institutional unity with a stylistic unity based on the Socialist Realist novel: one leader, one party, one aesthetic. As part of the campaign in 1934 to advance Socialist Realism, the Communist Academy organized a series of discussions on the nature of the novel, considered the most important genre for defining the new obligatory style. Transcripts of these discussions, in which a number of leading intellectuals, including George Lukacs, then resident in the Soviet Union, participated, were published in 1935 in the major theoretical journal, *The Literary Critic*. It was not by chance that Bakhtin's new concern with the genre of the novel dated precisely from 1934–1935.

Although now widely known as a theorist of the novel, Bakhtin actually had done very little work in that area before the thirties, with, of course, the exception of his 1929 book on Dostoevsky.[2] The overwhelming majority of his publications in the 1920s not only were devoted to topics other than the novel, they were not primarily literary criticism at all. Only after 1934, the year in which he began on the series of studies that culminated in *Rabelais and His World*, did novels become a major preoccupation for Bakhtin. He was, in effect, proposing his vision of the novel genre as a celebration of linguistic and stylistic variety as a counter to tight canonical formulas for the novel (and for other genres and even media, such as films or painting) proposed by official spokesmen for the Soviet government. The "grotesque realism" of which so much is made in this book is a point-by-point inversion of categories used in the thirties to define Socialist Realism.

In the Rabelais book Bakhtin also initiated a specific dialogue with the man who presided over the foundation of Soviet culture, the Commissar of Enlightenment, Anatoly Lunacharsky. Shortly before his death in 1933, Lunacharsky had set up a government commission to study satiric genres and was himself at work on a book called *The Social Role of Laughter*. Two years earlier he had addressed the Academy of Sciences on the historical importance of satire, especially its connection with folk festivals such as carnival. Published in 1935, this speech had a galvanizing effect on Bakhtin, who was at that point still in exile in Kazakhstan. Lunacharsky, after all, had written a positive review of Bakhtin's Dostoevsky book, which had helped lighten Bakhtin's original sentence after his arrest in 1929; and Lunacharsky's basic argument, that carnival was a kind of safety valve for passions the common people might otherwise direct to revolution, flew directly in the face of the evidence Bakhtin was then compiling for his first sketches of the Rabelais book.

Bakhtin's carnival, surely the most productive concept in this book, is not only not an impediment to revolutionary change, it is revolution itself. Carnival must not be confused with mere holiday or, least of all, with self-serving festivals fostered by governments, secular or theocratic. The sanction for carnival derives ultimately not from a calendar prescribed by church or state, but from a force that preexists priests and kings and to whose superior power they are actually deferring when they appear to be licensing carnival.

The discussion of carnival inevitably raised another topic of heated debate in the 1930s, the nature of the anonymous mass, the folk, in history. *Rabelais and His World* is a hymn to the common man; at times it makes excessive claims for the people. But Bakhtin's utopian vision of the folk was not the only one abroad at the time, and in order to appreciate it for what it was, we should remember it was only one side of a dialogue about the nature of the folk. Needless to say, Bakhtin was the unofficial side. The official side was represented by the immensely powerful doyen of Soviet culture, Maxim Gorky. At the fatal first All-Union Congress of Writers in 1934, it was Gorky who urged the assembled "culture workers" to model their positive heroes on the heroes of folklore.

We can date from that occasion a rapid Stalinization of Russian folklore: the folk artists of Palekh were commissioned to paint new enamels in their traditional style, with Lenin and Stalin appearing on the firebirds and flying steeds that had previously carried the bogatyrs of the Russian epic. Bewildered bards from the tundra were imported to Moscow and set to creating new epics celebrating tractor drivers and Arctic pilots. Films starring Stalin's favorite actress, Lyubov Orlova, showed ersatz peasants from the country triumphing over Westernized city slickers in All-Union talent contests which were held in a stylized Moscow depicted in these films as a second Kitezh, the underwater wonder city visited by Sadko in the ancient bylina.

Bakhtin's image of the folk is also open to the charge of idealization, but he employs his most glowing colors to highlight attributes of the folk precisely and diametrically opposed to those celebrated in Soviet *folklorico*. His folk are blasphemous rather than adoring, cunning rather than intelligent; they are coarse, dirty, and rampantly physical, reveling in oceans of strong drink, poods of sausage, and endless coupling of bodies. In the prim world of Stalinist Biedermeier, that world of lace curtains, showily displayed water carafes, and militant propriety, Bakhtin's claim that the folk not only picked their noses and farted, but enjoyed doing so, seemed particularly unregenerate. The opposition is not merely between two different concepts of the common man, but between two fundamentally opposed worldviews with nothing in common except that each finds its most comprehensive metaphor in "the folk."

The question arises, if this book is so clearly at odds with official culture in its own time and place, how did it ever get published? The answer is—it almost did not. Bakhtin brought together the many notebooks he had filled on Rabelais throughout the late thirties into a single text in 1940 and submitted it as a thesis to the Gorky Institute of World Literature in Moscow. The defense of the thesis was delayed by a number of factors, primarily the outbreak of war. When, in 1947, Bakhtin finally received notification that he should appear to defend the dissertation, the tone of the letter from the State Commission on Degrees made it chillingly clear that defense in this case was to be more than a formal academic exercise, and that more than a mere degree was at stake for a man already arrested once for unreliability. The defense took place at the height of the "anti-cosmopolitan campaign," a frenzy of postwar xenophobia whose purpose was to let Soviet intellectuals know that the relative liberalism that had marked the war years had come to an end. On August 14, 1946, the Central Committee issued a resolution condemning ideological laxity in Soviet literature and scholarship. In particular, kowtowing (*nizkopoklonstvo*) to the bourgeois West was attacked, a tendency that was labeled "Veselovskyism." Alexander Veselovsky was one of Russia's greatest scholars, a profound student of romance philology and a founder of the modern study of comparative literature. Although he died in 1906, his example was still an inspiration to many Soviet intellectuals, who were now revealed as stalking horses of Western decadence. One of the major figures who led the attack on Veselovskyism was the theorist of Socialist Realism and quondam Dostoevsky expert, Valery Kirpotin. Not only was Bakhtin's thesis about a French writer, not only was it guilty of the heresy of "formalism," but Kirpotin himself was named as one of the official opponents at the defense.

It all looked very bad. But in the event, Bakhtin defended his work with such rhetorical cunning that the examining committee sought to have him awarded not only the normal degree of *kandidat* but also the more coveted title of Doctor. Conservatives on the panel, led by Kirpotin, managed to block this move, and it was not until 1951 that Bakhtin even received the lower degree. After Bakhtin's "discovery" by a group of young scholars at the Gorky Institute in the early 1960s, a campaign was mounted by Vadim Kozhinov and other admirers to get the Rabelais dissertation published as a book. The tactics were carefully orchestrated: Bakhtin would first reappear on the Soviet scene in 1963 as author of a second edition of the Dostoevsky book originally published in 1929. Bakhtin's friends assumed—correctly—that it would be easier to have this book published and then use the excitement its reissue would create as an argument for bringing out his old dissertation than to battle for the latter's immediate publication. There were nevertheless many adventures between 1963 and 1965 when *Rabelais and His World* (or, as it is called in Russian, *François Rabelais and the Folk Culture of the Middle Ages and Renaissance*) finally saw the light of day.

Although widely appropriated in the West by folklorists, literary critics, and intellectual historians, Bakhtin's vision of carnival has an importance greater than any of its particular applications in any of these disciplines, for the book is finally about freedom, the courage needed to establish it, the cunning required to maintain it, and—above all—the horrific ease with which it can be lost. What saves this celebration of liberty from bathos is the immediate plausibility of the new relations between body, language, and political practice it reveals. The decline of freedom in the Renaissance becomes apparent when it is charted as a proportionate rise of new practices for repressing certain aspects not only of the body, but of language. Rabelais is Bakhtin's chosen subject because in him is manifest for the last time the possibility of expressing in literature the popular, chthonian impulse to carnival. Since then, "the grotesque tradition peculiar to the marketplace and the academic literary tradition have parted ways and can no longer be brought together. . . . The link with the essential aspects of being, with the organic system of popular-festive images, has been broken. Obscenity has become narrowly sexual, isolated, individual, and has no place in the new official system of philosophy and imagery" (p. 109). This decline is, above all, political: the conflict of official versus unofficial forces is fought out not merely at the level of symbols. Bakhtin leaves no doubt that the give-and-take between the medieval church/state nexus on the one hand and the carnival on the other was a very real power struggle. The state had its temporal and spatial borders as did carnival. Bakhtin's book describes the border clashes between these two hostile countries. Carnival laughter "builds its own world in opposition to the official world, its own church versus the official church, its own state versus the official state" (p. 88). And it is clear what forms of governance are typical of each. As Bakhtin says in his opening chapter, he "must stress" a striking peculiarity of carnival laughter, "its indissoluble and essential relation to freedom" (p. 89).

The significance of Rabelais in this view is not only the unique place he occupies in the history of literature but also the lessons he provides for political history: "Rabelais' basic goal was to destroy the official picture of events. . . . He summoned all the resources of sober popular imagery in order to break up official lies and the narrow seriousness dictated by the ruling classes. Rabelais did not implicitly believe in what his time 'said and imagined about itself'; he strove to disclose its true meaning for the people" (p. 439).

Bakhtin concludes his book by quoting from Pushkin's *Boris Godunov*, the section in which Dmitry, the false pretender to Russia's ancient throne, has a nightmare in which:

> The people swarmed on the public square
> And pointed laughingly at me,
> And I was filled with shame and fear.

Bakhtin stresses that the relation between the fate of the pretender and Rabelais's attempts to laugh repression off the stage of history is "not merely metaphoric." By so doing, he makes it clear that his own book is not just a scholarly exercise in poetics of the novel, although it is, of course, quite brilliantly that as well. But it is also an attempt to show the ways in which the Russian revolution had lost touch with its roots in the people and a valiant effort to bring the folk with its corrosive laughter back into the work of politics. World history, says Bakhtin, is the kind of drama in which "every act was accompanied by a laughing chorus." But, he adds, not every age was fortunate enough to have a Rabelais to focus the power of this laughter. It is this role of Coryphaeus to his own age that Bakhtin himself enacts when he reminds us that Rabelais "so fully and clearly revealed the peculiar and difficult language of the laughing people that his work sheds its light on the folk culture of humor belonging to other ages" (p. 474).

Bakhtin's book, then, carnivalizes the present because it is a hope for the future: carnival forms "present the victory of this future over the past. . . . The birth of the new . . . is as indispensable and as inevitable as the death of the old. . . . In the whole of the world and of the people there is no room for fear. For fear can only enter a part that has been separated from the whole, the dying link torn from the link that is being born" (p. 256). In these words, written during the great terror of the Stalinist night, we may not hear a chorus of the people, but surely we can discern at least a single voice that is still there to remind others how necessary to the pursuit of liberty is the courage to laugh.

Michael Holquist

NOTES

An earlier version of this introduction appeared in *boundary 2*, vol. 11, nos. 1–2 (fall/winter 1982/83), pp. 5–19.

1. *Ideology and Utopia*, trans. Louis Wirth and Edward Shils (New York: Harvest Books, 1964), p. 10.

2. *Problemy tvorchestva Dostoevskogo* (Leningrad, 1929); *Problemy poetiki Dostoevskogo*, 2nd rev. and enl. ed. (Moscow, 1963); *Problems of Dostoevsky's Poetics*, edited and translated by Caryl Emerson (Minneapolis: University of Minnesota Press, 1984).

Rabelais and His World

Of all great writers of world literature, Rabelais is the least popular, the least understood and appreciated.

And yet, of all the great creators of European literature Rabelais occupies one of the first places. Belinski called Rabelais a genius, the sixteenth-century Voltaire, and his novel one of the best of times past. Because of his literary power and historical importance, Western literary critics and writers place him immediately after Shakespeare or even next to him. The French Romanticists, especially Chateaubriand and Hugo, included him among the greatest "geniuses of humanity" of all times and nations. He was and is still considered not only a great writer in the usual sense of the word but also a sage and prophet. Here is a typical opinion expressed by the historian Michelet:

Rabelais collected wisdom from the popular elemental forces of the ancient Provençal idioms, sayings, proverbs, school farces, from the mouth of fools and clowns. But refracted by this foolery, the genius of the age and its prophetic power are revealed in all their majesty. If he does not discover, he foresees, he promises, he directs. Under each tiny leaf of this forest of dreams, the fruit which the future will harvest lies hidden. This entire book is a golden bough.[1]

All such judgments and appreciations are, of course, relative. We do not intend to answer the question whether Rabelais can be placed next to Shakespeare or whether he is superior or inferior to Cervantes. But his place in history among the creators of modern European writing, such as Dante, Boccaccio, Shakespeare, and Cervantes, is not subject to doubt. Rabelais not only determined the fate of French literature and of the French literary tongue, but influenced the fate of world literature as well (probably no less than Cervantes). There is also no doubt that he is the most democratic among these initiators of new literatures. He is more closely and essentially linked to popular sources and, moreover, to specific ones. (Michelet enumerates them with considerable accuracy.) These sources determined the entire system of his images and his artistic outlook on the world.

It is precisely this specific and radical popular character of Rabelais' images which explains their exceptional saturation with the future so correctly stressed by Michelet in the appreciation quoted. It also explains Rabelais' "nonliterary" nature, that is the nonconformity of his images to the literary norms and canons predominating in the sixteenth century and still prevailing in our times, whatever the changes undergone by their contents. Rabelais' nonconformity was carried to a much greater extent

---

[1] Jules Michelet. *Histoire de France*, Vol. 10, p. 355. Paris, L. Hachette, 1852–1867. The golden bough was plucked by Aeneas at the bidding of the Cumean sibyl. It was the passkey to the underworld.

than that of Shakespeare or Cervantes, who merely disobeyed the narrow classical canons. Rabelais' images have a certain undestroyable nonofficial nature. No dogma, no authoritarianism, no narrow-minded seriousness can coexist with Rabelaisian images; these images are opposed to all that is finished and polished, to all pomposity, to every ready-made solution in the sphere of thought and world outlook. This accounts for Rabelais' peculiar isolation in the successive centuries. He cannot be approached along the wide beaten roads followed by bourgeois Europe's literary creation and ideology during the four hundred years separating him from us.

Although during these four hundred years there have been many enthusiastic admirers of Rabelais, we can find nowhere a fully expressed understanding of him. The Romantics who discovered him, as they discovered Shakespeare and Cervantes, were incapable of revealing his essence and did not go beyond enraptured surprise. Many were repulsed and still are repulsed by him. The vast majority, however, simply do not understand him. In fact, many of his images remain an enigma.

This enigma can be solved only by means of a deep study of Rabelais' popular sources. If he appears so isolated, so unlike any other representative of "great literature" of these last four centuries of history, we should reflect that this period of literary development may in turn seem unusual when viewed against the background of folk tradition. Rabelais' images are completely at home within the thousand-year-old development of popular culture.

Rabelais is the most difficult classical author of world literature. To be understood he requires an essential reconstruction of our entire artistic and ideological perception, the renunciation of many deeply rooted demands of literary taste, and the revision of many concepts. Above all, he requires an exploration in depth of a sphere as yet little and superficially studied, the tradition of folk humor.

Rabelais is difficult. But his work, correctly understood, casts a retrospective light on this thousand-year-old development of the folk culture of humor, which has found in his works its greatest literary expression. Rabelais' illuminative role in this respect is of the greatest importance. His novel must serve as a key to the immense treasury of folk humor which as yet has been scarcely understood or analyzed. But first of all it is necessary to take possession of this key.

The aim of the present introduction is to pose the problem presented by the culture of folk humor in the Middle Ages and the Renaissance and to offer a description of its original traits.

Laughter and its forms represent, as we have said, the least scrutinized sphere of the people's creation. The narrow concept of popular character and of folklore was born in the pre-Romantic period and was basically completed by von Herder and the Romantics. There was no room in this concept for the peculiar culture of the marketplace and of folk laughter with all its wealth of manifestations. Nor did the generations that succeeded each other in that marketplace become the object of historic, literary, or folkloristic scrutiny as the study of early cultures continued. The element of laughter was accorded the least place of all in the vast literature devoted to myth, to folk lyrics, and to epics. Even more unfortunate was the fact that the peculiar nature of the people's laughter was completely distorted; entirely alien notions and concepts of humor, formed within the framework of bourgeois modern culture and aesthetics, were applied to this interpretation. We may therefore say without exaggeration that the profound originality expressed by the culture of folk humor in the past has remained unexplored until now.

And yet, the scope and the importance of this culture were immense in the Renaissance and the Middle Ages. A boundless world of humorous forms and manifestations opposed the official and serious tone of medieval ecclesiastical and feudal culture. In spite of their variety, folk festivities of the carnival type, the comic rites and cults, the clowns and fools, giants, dwarfs, and jugglers, the vast and manifold literature of parody—all these forms have one style in common: they belong to one culture of folk carnival humor.

The manifestations of this folk culture can be divided into three distinct forms.

1. *Ritual spectacles:* carnival pageants, comic shows of the marketplace.
2. *Comic verbal compositions:* parodies both oral and written, in Latin and in the vernacular.
3. *Various genres of billingsgate:* curses, oaths, popular blazons.

These three forms of folk humor, reflecting in spite of their variety a single humorous aspect of the world, are closely linked and interwoven in many ways.

Let us begin by describing each of these forms.

Carnival festivities and the comic spectacles and ritual connected with them had an important place in the life of medieval man. Besides carnivals proper, with their long and complex pageants and processions, there was the "feast of fools" *(festa stultorum)* and the "feast of the ass"; there was a special free "Easter laughter" *(risus paschalis)*, consecrated by tradition. Moreover, nearly every Church feast had its comic folk aspect, which was also traditionally recognized. Such, for instance, were the parish feasts, usually marked by fairs and varied open-air amusements, with the participation of giants, dwarfs, monsters, and trained animals. A carnival atmosphere reigned on days when mysteries and *soties* were produced. This atmosphere also pervaded such agricultural feasts as the harvesting of grapes *(vendange)* which was celebrated also in the city. Civil and social ceremonies and rituals took on a comic aspect as clowns and fools, constant participants in these festivals, mimicked serious rituals such as the tribute rendered to the victors at tournaments, the transfer of feudal rights, or the initiation of a knight. Minor occasions were also marked by comic protocol, as for instance the election of a king and queen to preside at a banquet "for laughter's sake" *(roi pour rire)*.

All these forms of protocol and ritual based on laughter and consecrated by tradition existed in all the countries of medieval Europe; they were sharply distinct from the serious official, ecclesiastical, feudal, and political cult forms and ceremonials. They offered a completely different, nonofficial, extraecclesiastical and extrapolitical aspect of the world, of man, and of human relations; they built a second world and a second life outside officialdom, a world in which all medieval people participated more or less, in which they lived during a given time of the year. If we fail to take into consideration this two-world condition, neither medieval cultural consciousness nor the culture of the Renaissance can be understood. To ignore or to underestimate the laughing people of the Middle Ages also distorts the picture of European culture's historic development.

This double aspect of the world and of human life existed even at the earliest stages of cultural development. In the folklore of primitive peoples, coupled with the cults which were serious in tone and organization were other, comic cults which laughed and scoffed at the deity ("ritual laughter"); coupled with serious myths were comic and abusive ones; coupled with heroes were their parodies and doublets. These comic rituals and myths have attracted the attention of folklorists.[2]

But at the early stages of preclass and prepolitical social order it seems that the serious and the comic aspects of the world and of the deity were equally sacred, equally "official." This similarity was preserved in rituals of a later period of history. For instance, in the early period of the Roman state the ceremonial of the triumphal procession included on almost equal terms the glorifying and the deriding of the victor. The funeral ritual was also composed of lamenting (glorifying) and deriding the deceased. But in the definitely consolidated state and class structure such an equality of the two aspects became impossible. All the comic forms were transferred, some earlier and others later, to a nonofficial level. There they acquired a new meaning, were deepened and rendered more complex, until they became the expression of folk consciousness, of folk culture. Such were the carnival festivities of the ancient world, especially the Roman Saturnalias, and such were

[2] See an interesting analysis of comic doublets in *Proiskhozhdenie geroicheskogo eposa* "Origin of Heroic Epics" by E. M. Meletinskii, Moscow, 1963, pp. 55–58. The book also contains a bibliography.

medieval carnivals. They were, of course, far removed from the primitive community's ritual laughter.

What are the peculiar traits of the comic rituals and spectacles of the Middle Ages? Of course, these are not religious rituals like, for instance, the Christian liturgy to which they are linked by distant genetic ties. The basis of laughter which gives form to carnival rituals frees them completely from all religious and ecclesiatic dogmatism, from all mysticism and piety. They are also completely deprived of the character of magic and prayer; they do not command nor do they ask for anything. Even more, certain carnival forms parody the Church's cult. All these forms are systematically placed outside the Church and religiosity. They belong to an entirely different sphere.

Because of their obvious sensuous character and their strong element of play, carnival images closely resemble certain artistic forms, namely the spectacle. In turn, medieval spectacles often tended toward carnival folk culture, the culture of the marketplace, and to a certain extent became one of its components. But the basic carnival nucleus of this culture is by no means a purely artistic form nor a spectacle and does not, generally speaking, belong to the sphere of art. It belongs to the borderline between art and life. In reality, it is life itself, but shaped according to a certain pattern of play.

In fact, carnival does not know footlights, in the sense that it does not acknowledge any distinction between actors and spectators. Footlights would destroy a carnival, as the absence of footlights would destroy a theatrical performance. Carnival is not a spectacle seen by the people; they live in it, and everyone participates because its very idea embraces all the people. While carnival lasts, there is no other life outside it. During carnival time life is subject only to its laws, that is, the laws of its own freedom. It has a universal spirit; it is a special condition of the entire world, of the world's revival and renewal, in which all take part. Such is the essence of carnival, vividly felt by all its participants. It was most clearly expressed and experienced in the Roman Saturnalias, perceived as a true and full, though temporary, return of Saturn's golden age upon earth. The tradition of the Saturnalias remained unbroken and alive in the medieval carnival, which expressed this universal renewal and was vividly felt as an escape from the usual official way of life.

Clowns and fools, which often figure in Rabelais' novel, are characteristic of the medieval culture of humor. They were the constant, accredited representatives of the carnival spirit in everyday life out of carnival season. Like Triboulet[3] at the time of Francis I, they were not actors playing their parts on a stage, as did the comic actors of a later period, impersonating Harlequin, Hanswurst, etc., but remained fools and clowns always and wherever they made their appearance. As such they represented a certain form of life, which was real and ideal at the same time. They stood on the borderline between life and art, in a peculiar mid-zone as it were; they were neither eccentrics nor dolts, neither were they comic actors.

Thus carnival is the people's second life, organized on the basis of laughter. It is a festive life. Festivity is a peculiar quality of all comic rituals and spectacles of the Middle Ages.

All these forms of carnival were also linked externally to the feasts of the Church. (One carnival did not coincide with any commemoration of sacred history or of a saint but marked the last days before Lent, and for this reason was called *Mardi gras* or *carême-prenant* in France and *Fastnacht* in Germany.) Even more significant is the genetic link of these carnivals with ancient pagan festivities, agrarian in nature, which included the comic element in their rituals.

The feast (every feast) is an important primary form of human culture. It cannot be explained merely by the practical conditions of the community's work, and it would be even more superficial to attribute it to the physiological demand for periodic rest. The feast had always an essential, meaningful philosophical content. No rest period or breathing spell can be rendered festive per se;

[3] Fevrial, or Le Feurial, was the court fool of Francis I and of Louis XII. He appears repeatedly in Rabelais under the name of Triboulet. (Translator's note.)

something must be added from the spiritual and ideological dimension. They must be sanctioned not by the world of practical conditions but by the highest aims of human existence, that is, by the world of ideals. Without this sanction there can be no festivity.

The feast is always essentially related to time, either to the recurrence of an event in the natural (cosmic) cycle, or to biological or historic timeliness. Moreover, through all the stages of historic development feasts were linked to moments of crisis, of breaking points in the cycle of nature or in the life of society and man. Moments of death and revival, of change and renewal always led to a festive perception of the world. These moments, expressed in concrete form, created the peculiar character of the feasts.

In the framework of class and feudal political structure this specific character could be realized without distortion only in the carnival and in similar marketplace festivals. They were the second life of the people, who for a time entered the utopian realm of community, freedom, equality, and abundance.

On the other hand, the official feasts of the Middle Ages, whether ecclesiastic, feudal, or sponsored by the state, did not lead the people out of the existing world order and created no second life. On the contrary, they sanctioned the existing pattern of things and reinforced it. The link with time became formal; changes and moments of crisis were relegated to the past. Actually, the official feast looked back at the past and used the past to consecrate the present. Unlike the earlier and purer feast, the official feast asserted all that was stable, unchanging, perennial: the existing hierarchy, the existing religious, political, and moral values, norms, and prohibitions. It was the triumph of a truth already established, the predominant truth that was put forward as eternal and indisputable. This is why the tone of the official feast was monolithically serious and why the element of laughter was alien to it. The true nature of human festivity was betrayed and distorted. But this true festive character was indestructible; it had to be tolerated and even legalized outside the official sphere and had to be turned over to the popular sphere of the marketplace.

As opposed to the official feast, one might say that carnival celebrated temporary liberation from the prevailing truth and from the established order; it marked the suspension of all hierarchical rank, privileges, norms, and prohibitions. Carnival was the true feast of time, the feast of becoming, change, and renewal. It was hostile to all that was immortalized and completed.

The suspension of all hierarchical precedence during carnival time was of particular significance. Rank was especially evident during official feasts; everyone was expected to appear in the full regalia of his calling, rank, and merits and to take the place corresponding to his position. It was a consecration of inequality. On the contrary, all were considered equal during carnival. Here, in the town square, a special form of free and familiar contact reigned among people who were usually divided by the barriers of caste, property, profession, and age. The hierarchical background and the extreme corporative and caste divisions of the medieval social order were exceptionally strong. Therefore such free, familiar contacts were deeply felt and formed an essential element of the carnival spirit. People were, so to speak, reborn for new, purely human relations. These truly human relations were not only a fruit of imagination or abstract thought; they were experienced. The utopian ideal and the realistic merged in this carnival experience, unique of its kind.

This temporary suspension, both ideal and real, of hierarchical rank created during carnival time a special type of communication impossible in everyday life. This led to the creation of special forms of marketplace speech and gesture, frank and free, permitting no distance between those who came in contact with each other and liberating from norms of etiquette and decency imposed at other times. A special carnivalesque, marketplace style of expression was formed which we find abundantly represented in Rabelais' novel.

During the century-long development of the medieval carnival, prepared by thousands of years of ancient comic ritual, including the primitive Saturnalias, a special idiom of forms and symbols was evolved—an extremely rich idiom that expressed the unique yet complex carnival experience of the people. This experience, opposed to all that was ready-made and completed, to all pretense at immutability, sought a dynamic expression; it demanded ever changing, playful, undefined forms. All the symbols of the carnival idiom are filled with this pathos of change and renewal, with the sense of the gay relativity of prevailing truths and authorities. We find here a characteristic logic, the peculiar logic of the "inside out" (à *l'envers*), of the "turnabout," of a continual shifting from top to bottom, from front to rear, of numerous parodies and travesties, humiliations, profanations, comic crownings and un-crownings. A second life, a second world of folk culture is thus constructed; it is to a certain extent a parody of the extracarnival life, a "world inside out." We must stress, however, that the carnival is far distant from the negative and formal parody of modern times. Folk humor denies, but it revives and renews at the same time. Bare negation is completely alien to folk culture.

Our introduction has merely touched upon the exceptionally rich and original idiom of carnival forms and symbols. The principal aim of the present work is to understand this half-forgotten idiom, in so many ways obscure to us. For it is precisely this idiom which was used by Rabelais, and without it we would fail to understand Rabelais' system of images. This carnival imagery was also used, although differently and to a different degree, by Erasmus, Shakespeare, Lope de Vega, Guevara, and Quevedo, by the German "literature of fools" (*Narren-literatur*), and by Hans Sachs, Fischart, Grimmelshausen, and others. Without an understanding of it, therefore, a full appreciation of Renaissance and grotesque literature is impossible. Not only belles lettres but the utopias of the Renaissance and its conception of the universe itself were deeply penetrated by the carnival spirit and often adopted its forms and symbols.

Let us say a few initial words about the complex nature of carnival laughter. It is, first of all, a festive laughter. Therefore it is not an individual reaction to some isolated "comic" event. Carni-val laughter is the laughter of all the people. Second, it is universal in scope; it is directed at all and everyone, including the carnival's participants. The entire world is seen in its droll aspect, in its gay relativity. Third, this laughter is ambivalent: it is gay, triumphant, and at the same time mocking, deriding. It asserts and denies, it buries and revives. Such is the laughter of carnival.

Let us enlarge upon the second important trait of the people's festive laughter: that it is also directed at those who laugh. The people do not exclude themselves from the wholeness of the world. They, too, are incomplete, they also die and are revived and renewed. This is one of the essential differences of the people's festive laughter from the pure satire of modern times. The satirist whose laughter is negative places himself above the object of his mockery, he is opposed to it. The wholeness of the world's comic aspect is destroyed, and that which appears comic becames a private reaction. The people's ambivalent laughter, on the other hand, expresses the point of view of the whole world; he who is laughing also belongs to it.

Let us here stress the special philosophical and utopian character of festive laughter and its orientation toward the highest spheres. The most ancient rituals of mocking at the deity have here survived, acquiring a new essential meaning. All that was purely cultic and limited has faded away, but the all-human, universal, and utopian element has been retained.

The greatest writer to complete the cycle of the people's carnival laughter and bring it into world literature was Rabelais. His work will permit us to enter into the complex and deep nature of this phenomenon.

The problem of folk humor must be correctly posed. Current literature concerning this subject presents merely gross modernizations. The present-day analysis of laughter explains it either as purely negative satire (and Rabelais is described as a pure satirist), or else as gay, fanciful, recreational drollery deprived of philosophic content. The important point made previously, that folk humor is ambivalent, is usually ignored.

We shall now turn to the second form of the culture of folk humor in the Middle Ages: the comic verbal compositions, in Latin or in the vernacular.

This, of course, is not folklore proper although some of these compositions in the vernacular could be placed in that category.

But comic literature was infused with the carnival spirit and made wide use of carnival forms and images. It developed in the disguise of legalized carnival licentiousness and in most cases was systematically linked with such celebrations.[4] Its laughter was both ambivalent and festive. It was the entire recreational literature of the Middle Ages.

Celebrations of a carnival type represented a considerable part of the life of medieval men, even in the time given over to them. Large medieval cities devoted an average of three months a year to these festivities. The influence of the carnival spirit was irresistible: it made a man renounce his official state as monk, cleric, scholar, and perceive the world in its laughing aspect. Not only schoolmen and minor clerics but hierarchs and learned theologians indulged in gay recreation as relaxation from pious seriousness. "Monkish pranks" (*Joca monacorum*) was the title of one of the most popular medieval comic pieces. Confined to their cells, monks produced parodies or semiparodies of learned treatises and other droll Latin compositions.

The comic literature of the Middle Ages developed throughout a thousand years or even more, since its origin goes back to Christian antiquity. During this long life it underwent, of course, considerable transformation, the Latin compositions being altered least. A variety of genres and styles were elaborated. But in spite of all these variations this literature remained more or less the expression of the popular carnival spirit, using the latter's forms and symbols.

The Latin parody or semiparody was widespread. The number of manuscripts belonging to this category is immense. The entire official ideology and ritual are here shown in their comic aspect. Laughter penetrates the highest forms of religious cult and thought.

One of the oldest and most popular examples of this literature, "Cyprian's supper" (*coena Cypriani*) offers a peculiar festive and carnivalesque travesty of the entire Scriptures. This work was con-

---

[4] A similar situation existed in ancient Rome where comic literature reflected the licentiousness of the Saturnalias, to which it was closely linked.

secrated by the tradition of "Paschal laughter" (risus paschalis); the faraway echoes of the Roman Saturnalia can be heard in it. Another ancient parody is the "Grammatical Virgil Maro" (Vergilius Maro Grammaticus), a semiparodical learned treatise on Latin grammar which is at the same time a parody of the scholarly wisdom and of the scientific methods of the early Middle Ages. Both works, composed at the very borderline between the antique world and the Middle Ages, inaugurated this humorous genre and had a decisive influence on its later forms. Their vogue lasted almost up to the Renaissance.

In the further development of humorous Latin literature, parodical doublets of every ecclesiastical cult and teaching were created—the so-called parodia sacra, "sacred parody," one of the most peculiar and least understood manifestations of medieval literature. There is a considerable number of parodical liturgies ("The Liturgy of the Drunkards," "The Liturgy of the Gamblers"), parodies of Gospel readings, of the most sacred prayers (the Lord's Prayer, the Ave Maria), of litanies, hymns, psalms, and even Gospel sayings. There were parodies of wills ("The Pig's Will," "The Will of the Ass"), parodies of epitaphs, council decrees, etc. The scope of this literature is almost limitless. All of it was consecrated by tradition and, to a certain extent, tolerated by the Church. It was created and preserved under the auspices of the "Paschal laughter," or of the "Christmas laughter"; it was in part directly linked, as in the parodies of liturgies and prayers, with the "feast of fools" and may have been performed during this celebration.

There were other parodies in Latin: parodies of debates, dialogues, chronicles, and so forth. All these forms demanded from their authors a certain degree of learning, sometimes at a high level. All of them brought the echoes of carnival laughter within the walls of monasteries, universities, and schools.

Medieval Latin humor found its final and complete expression at the highest level of the Renaissance in Erasmus' "In Praise of Folly," one of the greatest creations of carnival laughter in world literature, and in von Hutten's "Letters of Obscure People."

No less rich and even more varied is medieval humorous literature composed in the vernacular. Here, too, we find forms similar to the *parodia sacra:* parodies of prayers, of sermons (the *sermons joyeux* in France), of Christmas carols, and legends of the saints. But the prevailing forms are the secular parody and travesty, which present the droll aspect of the feudal system and of feudal heroics. The medieval epic parodies are animal, jesting, roguish, foolish; they deal with heroic deeds, epic heroes (the comic Roland), and knightly tales ("The Mule without a Bridle," "Aucassin and Nicolette"). There are various genres of mock rhetoric: carnivalesque debates, comic dialogues, and *euloges*. Carnivalesque humor is also reflected in the *fabliaux* and in the peculiar comic lyrics of vagrant scholars.

All these genres are linked to carnivalesque forms and symbols more closely than the Latin parodies. But it is the medieval comic theater which is most intimately related to carnival. The first medieval comic play that has been preserved, *The Play in the Bower* by Adam de la Halle, is a remarkable example of a purely carnivalesque vision and conception of the world. De la Halle's play contains in embryonic form many aspects of Rabelais' own world. The miracle and morality plays acquired to a certain extent a carnivalesque nature. Laughter penetrated the mystery plays; the diableries which are part of these performances have an obvious carnivalesque character, as do also the *soties* produced during the late Middle Ages.

We have here described only a few better known manifestations of humorous literature, which will suffice for the posing of our problem. As we advance in our analysis of Rabelais' work we shall examine in detail these genres, as well as many less known examples of medieval humorous writings.

Let us now look at the third form of the culture of folk humor: certain specific manifestations and genres of medieval and Renaissance familiar speech in the marketplace.

We have already said that during carnival there is a temporary suspension of all hierarchic distinctions and barriers among men and of certain norms and prohibitions of usual life. We added that an ideal and at the same time real type of communication, impossible in ordinary life, is established.

A new type of communication always creates new forms of speech or a new meaning given to the old forms. For instance, when two persons establish friendly relations, the form of their verbal intercourse also changes abruptly; they address each other informally, abusive words are used affectionately, and mutual mockery is permitted. (In formal intercourse only a third person can be mocked.) The two friends may pat each other on the shoulder and even on the belly (a typical carnivalesque gesture). Verbal etiquette and discipline are relaxed and indecent words and expressions may be used. But obviously such familiar intercourse in our days is far from the free familiar communication of the people in carnival time. It lacks the essentials: the all-human character, the festivity, utopian meaning, and philosophical depth. Let us point out that elements of the old ritual of fraternization were preserved in the carnival and were given a deeper meaning. Some of these elements have entered modern life but have entirely lost their primitive connotation.

The new type of carnival familiarity was reflected in a series of speech patterns. Let us examine some of them.

It is characteristic for the familiar speech of the marketplace to use abusive language, insulting words or expressions, some of them quite lengthy and complex. The abuse is grammatically and semantically isolated from context and is regarded as a complete unit, something like a proverb. This is why we can speak of abusive language as of a special genre of billingsgate. Abusive expressions are not homogeneous in origin; they had various functions in primitive communication and had in most cases the character of magic and incantations. But we are especially interested in the language which mocks and insults the deity and which was part of the ancient comic cults. These abuses were ambivalent: while humiliating and mortifying they at the same time revived and renewed. It was precisely this ambivalent abuse which determined the genre of speech in carnival intercourse. But its meaning underwent essential transformation; it lost its magic and its specific practical direction and acquired an intrinsic, universal character and depth. In this new form abuse contributed to the creation of the free carnival atmosphere, to the second, droll aspect of the world. Profanities and oaths (*jurons*) are in many ways similar to abusive language. They too invaded billingsgate speech. Profanities must also be considered a special genre with the same attributes as abuse—isolation from context and intrinsic character. Profanities and oaths were not initially related to laughter, but they were excluded from the sphere of official speech because they broke its norms; they were therefore transferred to the familiar sphere of the marketplace. Here in the carnival atmosphere they acquired the nature of laughter and became ambivalent.

The fate of other patterns of speech, for instance of various indecent expressions, was similar to that of the genres previously discussed. The familiar language of the marketplace became a reservoir in which various speech patterns excluded from official intercourse could freely accumulate. In spite of their genetic differences, all these genres were filled with the carnival spirit, transformed their primitive verbal functions, acquired a general tone of laughter, and became, as it were, so many sparks of the carnival bonfire which renews the world.

We shall later discuss the peculiar verbal forms of the marketplace. Let us here merely stress in conclusion that all these genres and patterns of speech exercised a powerful influence on Rabelais' literary style.

Such are the three basic forms of the culture of folk humor as expressed in the Middle Ages. All the influences we have analyzed have been known to scholars and have been studied by them, especially humorous literature in the vernacular. But these influences have been examined separately, completely severed from their maternal womb—from the carnival, ritual, and spectacle. This means that the studies have been pursued outside the unity of folk culture, the problem of which was not posed. This is why, dealing with the variety and heterogeneous character of these phenomena, the scholars did not see the one deeply original humorous aspect of the world, presented in isolated fragments. The influences were interpreted in the light of cultural, aesthetic, and literary norms of modern times; they were measured not within their own dimensions but according to measurements completely alien to them. They were modernized, which means that they were subject to a false evaluation. The peculiarity of comic imagery, which is one in spite of its variety and is inherent to medieval folk culture and generally foreign to modern times (especially to the nineteenth century), was also not understood. We must now undertake the characterization of this comic imagery.

It is usually pointed out that in Rabelais' work the material bodily principle, that is, images of the human body with its food, drink, defecation, and sexual life, plays a predominant role. Images of the body are offered, moreover, in an extremely exaggerated form. Rabelais was proclaimed by Victor Hugo the greatest poet of the "flesh" and "belly," while others accused him of "gross physiologism," of "biologism," or "naturalism." Similar traits were also found to a lesser degree in other representatives of Renaissance literature, in Boccaccio, Shakespeare, and Cervantes, and were interpreted as a "rehabilitation of the flesh" characteristic of the Renaissance in reaction against the ascetic Middle Ages. Sometimes they were seen as a typical manifestation of the Renaissance bourgeois character, that is, of its material interest in "economic man."

All these and similar explanations are nothing but interpretations according to the narrow and modified meaning which modern ideology, especially that of the nineteenth century, attributed to "materiality" and to the "body."

Actually, the images of the material bodily principle in the work of Rabelais (and of the other writers of the Renaissance) are the heritage, only somewhat modified by the Renaissance, of the culture of folk humor. They are the heritage of that peculiar type of imagery and, more broadly speaking, of that peculiar aesthetic concept which is characteristic of this folk culture and which differs sharply from the aesthetic concept of the following ages. We shall call it conditionally the concept of grotesque realism.

The material bodily principle in grotesque realism is offered in its all-popular festive and utopian aspect. The cosmic, social, and bodily elements are given here as an indivisible whole. And this whole is gay and gracious.

In grotesque realism, therefore, the bodily element is deeply positive. It is presented not in a private, egotistic form, severed from the other spheres of life, but as something universal, representing all the people. As such it is opposed to severance from the material and bodily roots of the world; it makes no pretense to renunciation of the earthy, or independence of the earth and the body. We repeat: the body and bodily life have here a cosmic and at the same time an all-people's character; this is not the body and its physiology in the modern sense of these words, because it is not individualized. The material bodily principle is contained not in the biological individual, not in the bourgeois ego, but in the people, a people who are continually growing and renewed. This is why all that is bodily becomes grandiose, exaggerated, immeasurable.

This exaggeration has a positive, assertive character. The leading themes of these images of bodily life are fertility, growth, and a brimming-over abundance. Manifestations of this life refer not to the isolated biological individual, not to the private, egotistic "economic man," but to the collective ancestral body of all the people. Abundance and the all-people's element also determine the gay and festive character of all images of bodily life; they do not reflect the drabness of everyday existence. The material bodily principle is a triumphant, festive principle, it is a "banquet for all the world."[5] This character is preserved to a considerable degree in Renaissance literature, and most fully, of course, in Rabelais.

The essential principle of grotesque realism is degradation, that is, the lowering of all that is high, spiritual, ideal, abstract; it is a transfer to the material level, to the sphere of earth and body in

[5] A popular Russian expression in old tales and epics to describe a great banquet, usually the happy ending of the story. (Translator's note.)

their indissoluble unity. Thus "Cyprian's supper" and many other Latin parodies of the Middle Ages are nothing but a selection of all the degrading, earthy details taken from the Bible, the Gospels, and other sacred texts. In the comic dialogues of Solomon with Morolf which were popular in the Middle Ages, Solomon's sententious pronouncements are contrasted to the flippant and debasing dictums of the clown Morolf, who brings the conversation down to a strongly emphasized bodily level of food, drink, digestion, and sexual life.[6] One of the main attributes of the medieval clown was precisely the transfer of every high ceremonial gesture or ritual to the material sphere; such was the clown's role during tournaments, the knight's initiation, and so forth. It is in this tradition of grotesque realism that we find the source of the scenes in which Don Quixote degrades chivalry and ceremonial.

In the learned scholastic milieu of the Middle Ages lighthearted grammatical parody was popular. The tradition went back to the previously mentioned "Grammatical Virgil Maro," was maintained throughout the Middle Ages and Renaissance and has survived in oral form in religious schools, colleges, and seminaries of Western Europe. This flippant grammar contains a transposed version of all grammatical categories brought down to the bodily level, especially to the erotic sphere.

Not only parody in its narrow sense but all the other forms of grotesque realism degrade, bring down to earth, turn their subject into flesh. This is the peculiar trait of this genre which differentiates it from all the forms of medieval high art and literature. The people's laughter which characterized all the forms of grotesque realism from immemorial times was linked with the bodily lower stratum. Laughter degrades and materializes.

What is the character of this process of degradation? We shall here answer this question briefly. Rabelais' work will permit us further to define, broaden, and deepen our analysis in the following chapters.

---

[6] These dialogues of Solomon and Morolf are similar in their earthiness to many dialogues of Don Quixote and Sancho.

Degradation and debasement of the higher do not have a formal and relative character in grotesque realism. "Upward" and "downward" have here an absolute and strictly topographical meaning. "Downward" is earth, "upward" is heaven. Earth is an element that devours, swallows up (the grave, the womb) and at the same time an element of birth, of renascence (the maternal breasts). Such is the meaning of "upward" and "downward" in their cosmic aspect, while in their purely bodily aspect, which is not clearly distinct from the cosmic, the upper part is the face or the head and the lower part is the genital organs, the belly, and the buttocks. These absolute topographical connotations are used by grotesque realism, including medieval parody. Degradation here means coming down to earth, the contact with earth as an element that swallows up and gives birth at the same time. To degrade is to bury, to sow, and to kill simultaneously, in order to bring forth something more and better. To degrade also means to concern oneself with the lower stratum of the body, the life of the belly and the reproductive organs; it therefore relates to acts of defecation and copulation, conception, pregnancy, and birth. Degradation digs a bodily grave for a new birth; it has not only a destructive, negative aspect, but also a regenerating one. To degrade an object does not imply merely hurling it into the void of nonexistence, into absolute destruction, but to hurl it down to the reproductive lower stratum, the zone in which conception and a new birth take place. Grotesque realism knows no other lower level; it is the fruitful earth and the womb. It is always conceiving.

This is the reason why medieval parody is unique, quite unlike the purely formalist literary parody of modern times, which has a solely negative character and is deprived of regenerating ambivalence. This genre and all the other modern forms of degradation could not, of course, preserve their former immensely important meaning.

Degradation, whether parodical or of some other type, is characteristic of Renaissance literature, which in that sense perpetuated the best tradition of the culture of folk humor (fully and deeply expressed by Rabelais). But even at this point the material bodily principle was subject to a certain alteration and narrowing. Its universal and festive character was somewhat weakened. True, this process was still at its initial stage as can be observed, for instance, in Don Quixote.

The fundamental trend of Cervantes' parodies is a "coming down to earth," a contact with the reproductive and generating power of the earth and of the body. This is a continuation of the grotesque tradition. But at the same time the material bodily principle has already been reduced. It is undergoing a peculiar crisis of splitting; Cervantes' images of bodily life have begun to lead a double existence.

Sancho's fat belly (*panza*), his appetite and thirst still convey a powerful carnivalesque spirit. His love of abundance and wealth have not, as yet, a basically private, egotistic and alienating character. Sancho is the direct heir of the antique potbellied demons which decorate the famous Corinthian vases. In Cervantes' images of food and drink there is still the spirit of popular banquets. Sancho's materialism, his potbelly, appetite, his abundant defecation, are on the absolute lower level of grotesque realism of the gay bodily grave (belly, bowels, earth) which has been dug for Don Quixote's abstract and deadened idealism. One could say that the knight of the sad countenance must die in order to be reborn a better and a greater man. This is a bodily and popular corrective to individual idealistic and spiritual pretense. Moreover, it is the popular corrective of laughter applied to the narrow-minded seriousness of the spiritual pretense (the absolute lower stratum is always laughing); it is a regenerating and laughing death. Sancho's role in relation to Don Quixote can be compared to the role of medieval parodies versus high ideology and cult, to the role of the clown versus serious ceremonial, to *charnage* versus *carême*. The gay principle of regeneration can also be seen, to a lesser extent, in the windmills (giants), inns (castles), flocks of rams and sheep (armies of knights), innkeepers (lords of the castle), prostitutes (noble ladies), and so forth. All these images form a typical grotesque carnival, which turns a kitchen and banquet into a battle, kitchen utensils and shaving bowls into arms and helmets, and wine into blood. Such is the first, carnival aspect of the material bodily images of *Don Quixote*. But it is precisely this aspect which creates the grand style of Cervantes' realism, his universal nature, and his deep popular utopianism.

A second aspect appears, under Cervantes' pen, as bodies and objects begin to acquire a private, individual nature; they are rendered petty and homely and become immovable parts of private life, the goal of egotistic lust and possession. This is no longer the positive, regenerating and renewing lower stratum, but a blunt and deathly obstacle to ideal aspirations. In the private sphere of isolated individuals the images of the bodily lower stratum preserve the element of negation while losing almost entirely their positive regenerating force. Their link with life and with the cosmos is broken, they are narrowed down to naturalistic erotic images. In *Don Quixote*, however, this process is only in its initial stage.

This second aspect of the material bodily image mingles with the first to form a complex and contradictory combination. Precisely in this double, tense, and contradictory life lies the power and the realism of these images. Such is the peculiar drama of the material bodily principle in Renaissance literature—the drama that leads to the breaking away of the body from the single procreating earth, the breaking away from the collective, growing, and continually renewed body of the people with which it had been linked in folk culture. But this process had not yet been fully completed for the artistic and ideological consciousness of the Renaissance. The bodily lower stratum of grotesque realism still fulfilled its unifying, degrading, uncrowning, and simultaneously regenerating functions. However divided, atomized, individualized were the "private" bodies, Renaissance realism did not cut off the umbilical cord which tied them to the fruitful womb of earth. Bodies could not be considered for themselves; they represented a material bodily whole and therefore transgressed the limits of their isolation. The private and the universal were still blended in a contradictory unity. The carnival spirit still reigned in the depths of Renaissance literature.

The complex nature of Renaissance realism has not as yet been sufficiently disclosed. Two types of imagery reflecting the conception of the world here meet at crossroads; one of them ascends to the folk culture of humor, while the other is the bourgeois conception of the completed atomized being. The conflict of these two contradictory trends in the interpretation of the bodily principle is typical of Renaissance realism. The ever-growing, inexhaustible, ever-laughing principle which uncrowns and renews is combined with its opposite: the petty, inert "material principle" of class society.

To ignore grotesque realism prevents us from understanding correctly not only its development during the Renaissance but also a series of important phenomena belonging to its later manifestations. The entire field of realistic literature of the last three centuries is strewn with the fragments of grotesque realism, which at times are not mere remnants of the past but manifest a renewed vitality. In most cases these are grotesque images which have either weakened or entirely lost their positive pole, their link with the universal and one world. To understand the meaning of these fragments of half dead forms is possible only if we retain the background of grotesque realism.

The grotesque image reflects a phenomenon in transformation, an as yet unfinished metamorphosis, of death and birth, growth and becoming. The relation to time is one determining trait of the grotesque image. The other indispensable trait is ambivalence. For in this image we find both poles of transformation, the old and the new, the dying and the procreating, the beginning and the end of the metamorphosis.

The relation to time, its perception and experience, which is at the basis of these forms was bound to change during their development over thousands of years. At the early stage of the archaic grotesque, time is given as two parallel (actually simultaneous) phases of development, the initial and the terminal, winter and spring, death and birth. These primitive images move within the biocosmic circle of cyclic changes, the phases of nature's and man's reproductive life. The components of these images are the changing seasons: sowing, conception, growth, death. The concept which was contained implicitly in these ancient images was that of cyclical time, of natural and biological life. But grotesque images did not, of course, remain at that primitive level of development. The sense of time and of change was broadened and deepened, drawing into its cycle social and historic phenomena. The cyclical character is superseded by the sense of historic time. The grotesque images with their relation to changing time and their ambivalence become the means for the artistic and ideological expression of a mighty awareness of history and of historic change which appeared during the Renaissance.

But even at this stage of their development, especially in Rabelais, the grotesque images preserve their peculiar nature, entirely different from ready-made, completed being. They remain ambivalent and contradictory; they are ugly, monstrous, hideous from the point of view of "classic" aesthetics, that is, the aesthetics of the ready-made and the completed. The new historic sense that penetrates them gives these images a new meaning but keeps intact their traditional contents: copulation, pregnancy, birth, growth, old age, disintegration, dismemberment. All these in their direct material aspect are the main element in the system of grotesque images. They are contrary to the classic images of the finished, completed man, cleansed, as it were, of all the scoriae of birth and development.

In the famous Kerch terracotta collection we find figurines of senile pregnant hags. Moreover, the old hags are laughing.[7] This is a typical and very strongly expressed grotesque. It is ambivalent. It is pregnant death, a death that gives birth. There is nothing completed, nothing calm and stable in the bodies of these old hags. They combine a senile, decaying and deformed flesh with the flesh

[7] See H. Reich, *Der Mimus, ein literarentwicklungsgeschichtlicher Versuch*, Berlin, 1903, pp. 507–598. Reich interpreted the hag figurines superficially in the naturalistic spirit.

of new life, conceived but as yet unformed. Life is shown in its two-fold contradictory process; it is the epitome of incompleteness. And such is precisely the grotesque concept of the body.

Contrary to modern canons, the grotesque body is not separated from the rest of the world. It is not a closed, completed unit; it is unfinished, outgrows itself, transgresses its own limits. The stress is laid on those parts of the body that are open to the outside world, that is, the parts through which the world enters the body or emerges from it, or through which the body itself goes out to meet the world. This means that the emphasis is on the apertures or the convexities, or on various ramifications and offshoots: the open mouth, the genital organs, the breasts, the phallus, the potbelly, the nose. The body discloses its essence as a principle of growth which exceeds its own limits only in copulation, pregnancy, child-birth, the throes of death, eating, drinking, or defecation. This is the ever unfinished, ever creating body, the link in the chain of genetic development, or more correctly speaking, two links shown at the point where they enter into each other. This especially strikes the eye in archaic grotesque.

One of the fundamental tendencies of the grotesque image of the body is to show two bodies in one: the one giving birth and dying, the other conceived, generated, and born. This is the preg-nant and begetting body, or at least a body ready for conception and fertilization, the stress being laid on the phallus or the genital organs. From one body a new body always emerges in some form or other.

In contrast to modern canons, the age of the body is most fre-quently represented in immediate proximity to birth or death, to infancy or old age, to the womb or the grave, to the bosom that gives life or swallows it up. But at their extreme limit the two bodies unite to form one. The individual is shown at the stage when it is recast into a new mold. It is dying and as yet unfinished; the body stands on the threshold of the grave and the crib. No longer is there one body, nor are there as yet two. Two heartbeats are heard: one is the mother's, which is slowed down.

The unfinished and open body (dying, bringing forth and being

born) is not separated from the world by clearly defined boundaries; it is blended with the world, with animals, with objects. It is
cosmic, it represents the entire material bodily world in all its elements. It is an incarnation of this world at the absolute lower stratum, as the swallowing up and generating principle, as the bodily
grave and bosom, as a field which has been sown and in which new
shoots are preparing to sprout.

Such are the rough outlines of this concept of the body. In Rabelais' novel this concept has been most fully and masterfully expressed, whereas in other works of Renaissance literature it was
watered down. It is represented in painting by Hieronymus Bosch
and the elder Breughel; some of its elements can be found in the
frescoes and bas-reliefs which adorned the cathedrals and even village churches of the twelfth and thirteenth centuries.[8]

This image of the body acquired a considerable and substantial
development in the popular, festive, and spectacle forms of the
Middle Ages: in the feast of the fool, in charivari and carnival, in
the popular side show of Corpus Christi, in the diableries of the
mystery plays, the *soties,* and farces.

In the literary sphere the entire medieval parody is based on the
grotesque concept of the body. It is this concept that also forms the
body images in the immense mass of legends and literary works
connected with the "Indian Wonders," as well as with the Western
miracles of the Celtic sea. It also forms the body images of ghostly
visions and of the legends of giants. We also discover some of these
elements in animal epics, *fabliaux,* and *Schwänke.*

Finally the grotesque concept of the body forms the basis of
abuses, oaths, and curses. The importance of abusive language is
essential to the understanding of the literature of the grotesque.
Abuse exercises a direct influence on the language and the images
of this literature and is closely related to all other forms of "degradation" and "down to earth" in grotesque and Renaissance

---

[8] Emile Mâle offers considerable and valuable material concerning
the grotesque themes in medieval art in his extensive book: *L'Art Re-*
ligieux du XIIème siecle, du XIIIème et de la fin du Moyen Age en
France. Vol. 1, 1902, Vol. 2, 1908, Vol. 3, 1922.

literature. Modern indecent abuse and cursing have retained dead and purely negative remnants of the grotesque concept of the body. Our "three-storied" oaths[9] or other unprintable expressions degrade the object according to the grotesque method; they send it down to the absolute bodily lower stratum, to the zone of the genital organs, the bodily grave, in order to be destroyed. But almost nothing has remained of the ambivalent meaning whereby they would also be revived; only the bare cynicism and insult have survived. Thus these expressions are completely isolated in the system of meaning and values of modern languages and in the modern picture of the world; they are fragments of an alien language in which certain things could be said in the past but which at present conveys nothing but senseless abuse.

However it would be absurd and hypocritical to deny the attraction which these expressions still exercise even when they are without erotic connotation. A vague memory of past carnival liberties and carnival truth still slumbers in these modern forms of abuse. The problem of their irrepressible linguistic vitality has as yet not been seriously posed. In the age of Rabelais abuses and curses still retained their full meaning in the popular language from which his novel sprang, and above all they retained their positive, regenerating pole. They were closely related to all the forms of degradation inherited from grotesque realism; they belonged to the popular-festive travesties of carnival, to the images of the diableries, of the underworld, of the *soties*. This is why abusive language played an important part in Rabelais' novel.

The concept of the body in grotesque realism as discussed in this introduction is of course in flagrant contradiction with the literary and artistic canon of antiquity,[10] which formed the basis of Renais-

---

[9] A colloquial Russian expression for strong and coarse abuse. (Translator's note.)

[10] But not of all antiquity. In the ancient Doric comedy, in "satyric" drama, in Sicilian comic forms, in the works of Aristophanes, in mimes and *Atellanae* we find similar grotesque conceptions; we also find them in Hippocrates, Galen, Pliny, in the symposia, in Athenaeus, Macrobius, Plutarch, and other writings of nonclassical antiquity.

sance aesthetics and was connected to the further development of art. The Renaissance saw the body in quite a different light than the Middle Ages, in a different aspect of its life, and a different relation to the exterior nonbodily world. As conceived by these canons, the body was first of all a strictly completed, finished product. Furthermore, it was isolated, alone, fenced off from all other bodies. All signs of its unfinished character, of its growth and proliferation were eliminated; its protuberances and offshoots were removed, its convexities (signs of new sprouts and buds) smoothed out, its apertures closed. The ever unfinished nature of the body was hidden, kept secret; conception, pregnancy, childbirth, death throes, were almost never shown. The age represented was as far removed from the mother's womb as from the grave, the age most distant from either threshold of individual life. The accent was placed on the completed, self-sufficient individuality of the given body. Corporal acts were shown only when the borderlines dividing the body from the outside world were sharply defined. The inner processes of absorbing and ejecting were not revealed. The individual body was presented apart from its relation to the ancestral body of the people.

Such were the fundamental tendencies of the classic canons. It is quite obvious that from the point of view of these canons the body of grotesque realism was hideous and formless. It did not fit the framework of the "aesthetics of the beautiful" as conceived by the Renaissance.

In this introduction as in the following chapters of our work (especially in Chapter 5), while contrasting the grotesque and the classic canon we will not assert the superiority of the one over the other. We will merely establish their basic differences. But the grotesque concept will, of course, be foremost in our study, since it determined the images of the culture of folk humor and of Rabelais. The classic canon is clear to us, artistically speaking; to a certain degree we still live according to it. But we have ceased long ago to understand the grotesque canon, or else we grasp it only in its distorted form. The role of historians and theorists of literature and art is to reconstruct this canon in its true sense. It should not be interpreted according to the norms of modern times; nor should it be seen as deviation from present-day concepts. The grotesque canon must be appraised according to its own measurements.

Here we must offer more clarification. We understand the word canon not in the narrow sense of a specific group of consciously established rules, norms, and proportions in the representation of the human body. (It is still possible to speak of the classic canon in such a narrow sense at certain phases of its development.) The grotesque image never had such a canon. It is noncanonical by its very nature. We here use the word canon in the wider sense of a manner of representing the human body and bodily life. In the art and literature of past ages we observe two such manners, which we will conditionally call grotesque and classic. We have defined these two canons in their pure, one might say extreme, form. But in history's living reality these canons were never fixed and immutable. Moreover, usually the two canons experience various forms of interaction: struggle, mutual influence, crossing, and fusion. This is especially true during the Renaissance. Even in Rabelais, who was the purest and the most consistent representative of the grotesque concept of the body, we find some classic elements, especially in the episode of Gargantua's education by Ponocrates and the Thélème episode. But for the sake of our research the fundamental differences between the two canons are important. We shall center our attention on these differences.

The specific type of imagery inherent to the culture of folk humor in all its forms and manifestations has been defined by us conditionally as grotesque realism. We shall now have to defend the choice of our terminology.

Let us first examine the term grotesque, giving its history as related to the development of the grotesque itself and of its theory.

Grotesque imagery (that is, the method of construction of its images) is an extremely ancient type; we find it in the mythology and in the archaic art of all peoples, among them, of course, the Greeks and Romans of the preclassic period. During the classic period the grotesque did not die but was expelled from the sphere of official art to live and develop in certain "low" nonclassic areas: plastic comic art, mostly on a small scale, as the previously mentioned Kerch terracottas, comic masks, Sileni, figurines of the demons of fertility, and the popular statuettes of the little monster Tersitus. Humorous vase decorations present the images of grotesque "doublets" (the comic Heracles and Odysseus), scenes from comedies, and symbols of fertility. Finally, in the wider range of humorous literature, related in one form or the other to festivals of carnival type, we have the "satyric" drama, the ancient Attic comedy, the mimes, and others. During the period of late antiquity grotesque imagery attained its flowering and renewal; it embraced nearly all areas of art and literature. Under the influence of the art of Eastern peoples a new kind of grotesque was formed, but aesthetic and artistic thought developed along the lines of classic tradition; therefore, grotesque imagery was not given a consistent definition nor was its meaning recognized in theory.

During its three stages of development—archaic, classic, and late—the essential element of realism was gradually shaped. It would be incorrect to see in grotesque merely "gross naturalism," as has sometimes been done. But this antique imagery is outside the scope of our work.[11] In the following chapters we shall discuss only the manifestations of antique grotesque which influenced Rabelais' novel.

The flowering of grotesque realism is a system of images created by the medieval culture of folk humor, and its summit is the literature of the Renaissance. At that time the term grotesque first appears on the scene but in a narrow sense occasioned by the finding at the end of the fifteenth century of a certain type of Roman ornament, previously unknown. These ornaments were brought to light during the excavation of Titus' baths and were called *grot-*

[11] Interesting material and valuable observations concerning antique and to some extent medieval and Renaissance grotesque are contained in A. Dieterich: "Pulcinella. Pompeian Mural Paintings and Roman Satyric Drama," Leipzig, 1897. (*Pulcinella. Pompeyanische Wandbilder und Romische Satyrspiele.*) The author, however, does not use the word "grotesque." In many respects Dieterich's book is not outdated.

tesca from the Italian word *grotta*. Somewhat later similar ornaments were discovered in other areas of Italy.

What is the character of these ornaments? They impressed the connoisseurs by the extremely fanciful, free, and playful treatment of plant, animal, and human forms. These forms seemed to be interwoven as if giving birth to each other. The borderlines that divide the kingdoms of nature in the usual picture of the world were boldly infringed. Neither was there the usual static presentation of reality. There was no longer the movement of finished forms, vegetable or animal, in a finished and stable world; instead the inner movement of being itself was expressed in the passing of one form into the other, in the ever incompleted character of being. This ornamental interplay revealed an extreme lightness and freedom of artistic fantasy, a gay, almost laughing, libertinage. The gay tone of the new ornament was grasped and brilliantly rendered by Raphael and his pupils in their grotesque decoration of the Vatican loggias.[12]

Such is the fundamental trait of the Roman ornament to which the term grotesque was first applied, a new word for an apparently new manifestation. The initial meaning of the term was in the beginning extremely narrow, describing the rediscovered form of Roman ornament. But in reality this form was but a fragment of the immense world of grotesque imagery which existed throughout all the stages of antiquity and continued to exist in the Middle Ages and the Renaissance. The fragment reflected the characteristic features of this immense world, and thus a further productive

[12] Let us here quote another, excellent definition of the grotesque by L. E. Pinsky; "In the grotesque, life passes through all the degrees, from the lowest, inert and primitive, to the highest, most mobile and spiritualized; this garland of various forms bears witness to their oneness, brings together that which is removed, combines elements which exclude each other, contradicts all current conceptions. Grotesque in art is related to the paradox in logic. At first glance, the grotesque is merely witty and amusing, but it contains great potentialities." (See L. E. Pinsky, *Realism Epochy Vozrozhedenya*, ("Realism of the Renaissance") Goslitizdat. Moscow, 1961, pp. 119–120.

life was ensured for the new term, with gradual extension to the almost immeasurable sphere of grotesque imagery.

But this extension of the term took place very slowly and without a clear theoretical interpretation of the peculiar character and the oneness of the grotesque world. The first attempt at theoretical analysis, or more correctly speaking at description and appraisal of this genre, was made by Vasari; relying on the opinion of Vetruvius, the Roman architect and art expert in the time of Augustus, Vasari pronounced a negative judgment. Vetruvius, whom Vasari quotes approvingly, condemned the new "barbarian" fashion of covering walls with monsters instead of the "bright reflection of the world of objects." In other words, Vetruvius condemned the grotesque from the classic standpoint as a gross violation of natural forms and proportions. Vasari expressed a similar point of view which prevailed for a long time. Only in the second part of the eighteenth century did a deeper and broader understanding of the grotesque make its appearance.

During the domination of the classical canon in all the areas of art and literature of the seventeenth and early eighteenth centuries, the grotesque related to the culture of folk humor was excluded from great literature; it descended to the low comic level or was subject to the epithet "gross naturalism," as we have seen. During this period (actually starting in the seventeenth century) we observe a process of gradual narrowing down of the ritual, spectacle, and carnival forms of folk culture, which became small and trivial. On the one hand the state encroached upon festive life and turned it into a parade; on the other hand these festivities were brought into the home and became part of the family's private life. The privileges which were formerly allowed the marketplace were more and more restricted. The carnival spirit with its freedom, its utopian character oriented toward the future, was gradually transformed into a mere holiday mood. The feast ceased almost entirely to be the people's second life, their temporary renascence and renewal. We have stressed the word almost because the popular-festive carnival principle is indestructible. Though narrowed and weakened, it still continues to fertilize various areas of life and culture.

A special aspect of this process seems important. The literature of these later centuries was not directly subject to the popular-festive culture and remained almost impervious to its influence. The carnival spirit and grotesque imagery continued to live and was transmitted as a now purely literary tradition, especially as a tradition of the Renaissance.

Having lost its living tie with folk culture and having become a literary genre, the grotesque underwent certain changes. There was a formalization of carnival-grotesque images, which permitted them to be used in many different ways and for various purposes. This formalization was not only exterior; the contents of the carnival-grotesque element, its artistic, heuristic, and unifying forces were preserved in all essential manifestations during the seventeenth and eighteenth centuries: in the *commedia dell'arte* (which kept a close link with its carnival origin), in Molière's comedies (related to the *commedia dell'arte*), in the comic novel and travesty of the seventeenth century, in the tales of Voltaire and Diderot (*Les bijoux indiscrets, Jacques le fataliste*), in the work of Swift, and a few others. In all these writings, in spite of their differences in character and tendency, the carnival-grotesque form exercises the same function: to consecrate inventive freedom, to permit the combination of a variety of different elements and their rapprochement, to liberate from the prevailing point of view of the world, from conventions and established truths, from clichés, from all that is humdrum and universally accepted. This carnival spirit offers the chance to have a new outlook on the world, to realize the relative nature of all that exists, and to enter a completely new order of things.

But a clear and precise theoretical understanding of the oneness of these manifestations known as the grotesque, as well as their artistic specificity, developed slowly. The term itself was often replaced by the words arabesque (mostly applied to ornament) and burlesque (literature). Due to the prevailing classic point of view in aesthetics, theoretical interpretation was as yet not possible.

In the second half of the eighteenth century an essential change took place in literature, as well as in the field of aesthetic thought. A literary controversy broke out in Germany around the character of Harlequin, a constant participant in all dramatic performances of that time, even the serious ones. Gottsched and the other classicists demanded this character's expulsion from "the serious and respectable stage" and succeeded for a while. Lessing himself took part in the controversy in Harlequin's defense. Beyond the narrow scope of this dispute there was a wider problem of principle: could manifestations such as the grotesque, which did not respond to the demands of the sublime, be considered art? This problem was discussed in a short essay published in 1761 by Justus Möser, entitled "Harlequin, or the Defense of the Grotesque-Comic" (*Harlekin, oder die Verteidigung des Grotesk-Komischen*). This defense was placed in Harlequin's own mouth. Möser stressed that this grotesque character was a part of a peculiar world or microcosm to which Colombine, the Captain, the Doctor, and other characters also belong—the world of the *commedia dell'arte*. It constitutes a whole; it has its own legitimate order, its own criterion of perfection which does not obey the aesthetics of the beautiful and the sublime. But at the same time Möser considers this world as opposed to the "low" spectacle of the marketplace; he thus narrows the very concept of the grotesque. He further explores certain distinct traits of this peculiar world: he calls it "chimerical," that is, combining heterogeneous elements, and points out that it violates natural proportions, thus presenting elements of caricature and parody. Finally, Möser stresses the principle of humor in the grotesque and traces the origin of laughter to the human soul's need of joy and gaiety. Such is the first and rather limited defense of the grotesque genre.

In 1788 a "History of the Comic Grotesque"[13] was published.

[13] Flögel's book was reprinted in 1862 in a somewhat revised and broadened form by Fr. W. Ebeling, *Flögel's Geschichte des Grotesk-Komischen, Leipzig*, 1862. This revised edition had five printings. In the text that follows we take all quotations from Ebeling's first edition. A new edition, revised by Max Brauer, was published in 1914.

The author, Carl Friedrich Flögel, also wrote a history of comic literature and a "History of Court Jesters." Discussing grotesque, Flögel does not define or limit the grotesque concept either from the historic or from the systematic point of view. He attributes to this genre all that which deviates from the usual aesthetic forms and which sharply emphasizes the exaggeration of the material bodily element. A considerable part of Flögel's book is devoted to the medieval grotesque. He studies the forms of medieval folk festivals (the "feast of fools," the "feast of the ass," the comic side shows of Corpus Christi celebrations), the buffoon literary societies of the late Middle Ages ("Queen Basoche," "Carefree Lads"), *soties,* farces, Shrovetide games, and various types of popular comic performances. Generally speaking, Flögel's survey is somewhat limited; he does not examine the purely literary manifestations of grotesque—for instance, the medieval Latin parody. The lack of a systematic historic point of view has caused a somewhat haphazard choice of material and superficial understanding of the grotesque. Actually, there is no true understanding; the author merely collects his examples as curiosities. Nevertheless, Flögel's book has retained its interest because of the material it presents.

Both Möser and Flögel are aware only of the grotesque comic form based on the humorous principle, and this principle is conceived by them as gay and joyful. Such was also the material analyzed in their works: the *commedia dell'arte* by Möser and medieval grotesque by Flögel.

At precisely the time when Möser and Flögel published their works, oriented toward already-covered ground, the grotesque was entering a new phase of development. Pre-Romanticism and Romanticism witnessed a revival of the grotesque genre but with a radically transformed meaning. It became the expression of subjective, individualistic world outlook very different from the carnival folk concept of previous ages, although still containing some carnival elements. The first important example of the new subjective grotesque was Sterne's *Tristram Shandy,* a peculiar transposition of Rabelais' and Cervantes' world concept into the subjective language of the new age. Another variety of the new grotesque was the Gothic or black novel. In Germany this subjective form had perhaps the most powerful and original development: the *Sturm und Drang* dramatics and early Romanticism (Lenz, Klinger, the young Tieck), the novels of Hippel and Jean Paul, and finally the works of Hoffmann, who strongly influenced the development of the new grotesque in the next period of world literature. Friedrich Schlegel and Jean Paul became its theorists.

Romantic grotesque was an important manifestation of world literature. To a certain degree it was a reaction against the elements of classicism which characterized the self-importance of the Enlightenment. It was a reaction against the cold rationalism, against official, formalistic, and logical authoritarianism; it was a rejection of that which is finished and completed, of the didactic and utilitarian spirit of the Enlighteners with their narrow and artificial optimism. In rejecting this spirit the Romantic grotesque relied first of all on the tradition of the Renaissance, especially on the rediscovered Shakespeare and Cervantes. It was in their light that the medieval grotesque was also interpreted. An important influence was exercised in this field by Sterne, who in a certain sense is even considered the founder of the new genre. As to the direct influence of folk spectacles and carnival forms, which were still alive though degenerate, it was apparently not considerable. The purely literary tradition was predominant. We should however point out the influence of the folk theater, especially the puppet show and the performances given at fairs.

Unlike the medieval and Renaissance grotesque, which was directly related to folk culture and thus belonged to all the people, the Romantic genre acquired a private "chamber" character. It became, as it were, an individual carnival, marked by a vivid sense of isolation. The carnival spirit was transposed into a subjective, idealistic philosophy. It ceased to be the concrete (one might say bodily) experience of the one, inexhaustible being, as it was in the Middle Ages and the Renaissance.

However, the most important transformation of Romantic grotesque was that of the principle of laughter. This element of course remained, since no grotesque, even the most timid, is conceivable in the atmosphere of absolute seriousness. But laughter was cut down to cold humor, irony, sarcasm. It ceased to be a joyful and triumphant hilarity. Its positive regenerating power was reduced to a minimum.

We find a characteristic discussion of laughter in one of the most remarkable works of Romantic grotesque, "The Night Watches" of Bonaventura (the pen name of an unknown author, perhaps Wetzel).[14] These are the tales and thoughts of a night watchman. The narrator describes as follows the meaning of laughter: "Is there upon earth a more potent means than laughter to resist the mockeries of the world and of fate? The most powerful enemy experiences terror at the sight of this satirical mask, and misfortune itself retreats before me, if I dare laugh at it. What else indeed except laughter does this earth deserve, may the devil take it! together with its sensitive companion, the moon."

These lines proclaim the philosophy and universal character of laughter, the characteristic trait of every expression of the grotesque. They praise its liberating power, but there is no hint of its power of regeneration. Laughter loses its gay and joyful tone.

Speaking through the medium of his narrator, the night watchman, the author offers a curious explanation of laughter and of its mythical origin. Laughter was sent to earth by the devil, but it appeared to men under the mask of joy, and so they readily accepted it. Then laughter cast away its mask and looked at man and at the world with the eyes of angry satire.

The transformation of the principle of laughter which permeates the grotesque, that is the loss of its regenerating power, leads to a series of other essential differences between Romantic grotesque and medieval and Renaissance grotesque. These differences appear most distinctly in relation to terror. The world of Romantic grotesque is to a certain extent a terrifying world, alien to man.

14 *Nachtwachen*, 1804. (see R. Steinert's *Nachtwachen des Bonawentura*, Leipzig, 1917.

All that is ordinary, commonplace, belonging to everyday life, and recognized by all suddenly becomes meaningless, dubious and hostile. Our own world becomes an alien world. Something frightening is revealed in that which was habitual and secure. Such are the tendencies of Romantic grotesque in its extreme expression. If a reconciliation with the world occurs, it takes place in a subjective, lyric, or even mystic sphere. On the other hand, the medieval and Renaissance folk culture was familiar with the element of terror only as represented by comic monsters, who were defeated by laughter. Terror was turned into something gay and comic. Folk culture brought the world close to man, gave it a bodily form, and established a link through the body and bodily life, in contrast to the abstract and spiritual mastery sought by Romanticism. Images of bodily life, such as eating, drinking, copulation, defecation, almost entirely lost their regenerating power and were turned into "vulgarities."

The images of Romantic grotesque usually express fear of the world and seek to inspire their reader with this fear. On the contrary, the images of folk culture are absolutely fearless and communicate this fearlessness to all. This is also true of Renaissance literature. The high point of this spirit is reached in Rabelais' novel; here fear is destroyed at its very origin and everything is turned into gaiety. It is the most fearless book in world literature.

Other specific traits are linked with the disappearance of laughter's regenerating power in Romantic grotesque. For instance, the theme of madness is inherent to all grotesque forms, because madness makes men look at the world with different eyes, not dimmed by "normal," that is by commonplace ideas and judgments. In folk grotesque, madness is a gay parody of official reason, of the narrow seriousness of official "truth." It is a "festive" madness. In Romantic grotesque, on the other hand, madness acquires a somber, tragic aspect of individual isolation.

Even more important is the theme of the mask, the most complex theme of folk culture. The mask is connected with the joy of change and reincarnation, with gay relativity and with the merry negation of uniformity and similarity; it rejects conformity to oneself. The mask is related to transition, metamorphoses, the violation of natural boundaries, to mockery and familiar nicknames. It contains the playful element of life; it is based on a peculiar interrelation of reality and image, characteristic of the most ancient rituals and spectacles. Of course it would be impossible to exhaust the intricate multiform symbolism of the mask. Let us point out that such manifestations as parodies, caricatures, grimaces, eccentric postures, and comic gestures are per se derived from the mask. It reveals the essence of the grotesque.[15]

In its Romantic form the mask is torn away from the oneness of the folk carnival concept. It is stripped of its original richness and acquires other meanings alien to its primitive nature; now the mask hides something, keeps a secret, deceives. Such a meaning would not be possible as long as the mask functioned within folk culture's organic whole. The Romantic mask loses almost entirely its regenerating and renewing element and acquires a somber hue. A terrible vacuum, a nothingness lurks behind it. (This theme is strikingly presented in Bonaventura's "Night Watches".) But an inexhaustible and many-colored life can always be descried behind the mask of folk grotesque.

However, the Romantic mask still retains something of its popular carnival nature. Even in modern life it is enveloped in a peculiar atmosphere and is seen as a particle of some other world. The mask never becomes just an object among other objects.

The theme of the marionette plays an important part in Romanticism. This theme is of course also found in folk culture, but in romanticism the accent is placed on the puppet as the victim of alien inhuman force, which rules over men by turning them into marionettes. This image is completely unknown in folk culture. Moreover, only in Romanticism do we find the peculiar grotesque theme of the tragic doll.

The Romantic treatment of the devil is also completely different from that of popular grotesque. In the diableries of the medi-

---

[15] We have in mind the mask and its meaning at the time of the people's festive culture of antiquity and the Middle Ages, and are not concerned with its ancient cultic meaning.

eval mysteries, in the parodical legends and the *fabliaux* the devil is the gay ambivalent figure expressing the unofficial point of view, the material bodily stratum. There is nothing terrifying or alien in him. In Rabelais' description of Epistemon's ghostly vision the devils are excellent and jovial fellows. At times the devils and hell itself appear as comic monsters, whereas the Romanticists present the devil as terrifying, melancholy, and tragic, and infernal laughter as somber and sarcastic.

We must point out that in Romantic grotesque ambivalence offers a sharp, static contrast. Thus the storyteller of the "Night Watches" is the son of the devil, while his mother is a canonized saint. The night watchman himself laughs in church and weeps in the bordello. Thus the ancient popular derision of divinity and medieval humor become in the early nineteenth century the sardonic laughter in church of a lonely eccentric.

Let us finally stress another peculiarity of Romantic grotesque. It is in most cases nocturnal (Bonaventura's "Night Watches," "Hoffman's "Night Tales"). Darkness, not light, is typical of this genre. On the contrary, light characterizes folk grotesque. It is a festival of spring, of sunrise, of morning.[16]

Friedrich Schlegel mentions the grotesque in his "Discourse on Poetry" (*Gespräch über die Poesie*, 1800) without giving any clear terminological definition. He usually calls it "arabesque" and considers it "the most ancient form of human fantasy" and the "natural form of poetry." He finds the grotesque in Shakespeare and Cervantes, in Sterne and Jean Paul. He sees its essence in the fantastic combination of heterogeneous elements of reality, in the breaking up of the established world order, in the free fancy of its images and in the "alternate succession of enthusiasm and irony."

Jean Paul defines the Romantic grotesque even more sharply in his "Introduction to Aesthetics," (*Vorschule der Äesthetik*). He does not use the term grotesque and he conceives it as "destructive humor." Jean Paul interprets it quite broadly, not limiting it to

---

[16] More precisely, folk grotesque reflects the very moment when light replaces darkness, night-morning, winter-spring.

literature and art but including in this category the "feast of fools" and the "feast of the ass," that is, the comic rituals and pageants of the Middle Ages. Among the literary manifestations of grotesque in the Renaissance, Jean Paul quite often refers to Rabelais and Shakespeare. He mentions in particular the "deriding of the entire world" (*Weltverlachung*) in Shakespeare, meaning the "melancholy clowns" and Hamlet.

Jean Paul understands perfectly well the universal character of laughter. "Destructive humor" is not directed against isolated negative aspects of reality but against all reality, against the finite world as a whole. All that is finite is per se destroyed by humor. Jean Paul stresses the radicalism of humor. Through it, the entire world is turned into something alien, something terrifying and unjustified. The ground slips from under our feet, and we are dizzy because we find nothing stable around us. Jean Paul sees a similar universalism and radicalism of destruction of all moral and social stability in the comic ritual and spectacles of the Middle Ages.

He does not separate the grotesque from laughter. He understands that without the principle of laughter this genre would be impossible. But his theory concerns itself only with a reduced form of laughter, a cold humor deprived of positive regenerating power. Jean Paul emphasizes the melancholy character of destructive laughter, saying that the greatest humorist of all would be the devil (of course, in the Romantic meaning of this word).

Jean Paul is attracted by the manifestations of medieval and Renaissance grotesque, and especially by Rabelais and Shakespeare. However, he merely offers the theory of the Romantic; through this prism alone can he observe the past stages of development. He "romanticizes" these stages (mostly through Sterne's interpretation).

The positive element of the grotesque, its last word, is conceived by Jean Paul (as it is by Schlegel) as outside the laughter principle, as an escape from all that is finite and destroyed by humor, as a transfer to the spiritual sphere.[17]

[17] Jean Paul himself used many images typical of the Romantic gro-

In the early 1820's, there was also a revival of grotesque imagery in French Romanticism. We find an interesting presentation of the problem, and one typical of the French Romantic spirit, by Victor Hugo, first in his preface to *Cromwell* and then in his book on Shakespeare.

Hugo gives a broad interpretation of grotesque imagery. He finds it in preclassical antiquity (the hydra, the harpies, the cyclopes, and other archaic images); he further places in this category all postantique literature, starting with medieval forms. "The grotesque," says Victor Hugo, "is everywhere: on one hand, it creates the formless and the terrifying, on the other hand the comic, the buffoon-like." The essential aspect of this form is the monstrous; the aesthetics of the grotesque are to a certain extent the aesthetics of the monstrous. But at the same time Hugo reduces the intrinsic value of the grotesque by declaring that it is a means of contrasting the sublime. The two complete each other, and their unity, most fully achieved in Shakespeare, produces the truly beautiful, which classicism could not attain.

In his book on Shakespeare Hugo gives his most interesting analysis of this imagery and of the comic and material bodily principle, in particular. We shall discuss this work later, for Hugo also expresses in it his appreciation of Rabelais.

Interest in the grotesque and in its early phases of development was shared by other French Romanticists who conceived it as a national tradition. In 1853 Théophile Gautier published an anthology entitled *Les Grotesques*. He collected for this anthology a number of French authors, interpreting the grotesque rather broadly; we find Villon and certain libertine poets of the seventeenth century (Théophile Viau, Saint-Amant, Scarron, Cyrano de Bergerac, and even Scudéry).

Such is the Romantic phase in the development of the grotesque. Two positive elements must be stressed in conclusion:

---

tesque, especially in his "Dreams" and "Visions" (see the P. Bentz edition of works belonging to this genre: *Jean Paul, Träume und Visionen,* Munich, 1954). This edition offers many striking examples of nocturnal and ghostly grotesque.

first, the Romanticists searched for popular roots; second, they never attributed to the grotesque a purely satirical function.

Our analysis of this Romantic phase is, of course, far from complete. Moreover it bears a rather one-sided and even polemical character, since all we are looking for here is the difference between the Romantic aspect of the grotesque and the imagery of the culture of folk humor. But Romanticism made its own important discovery—that of the interior subjective man with his depth, complexity, and inexhaustible resources.

This *interior infinite* of the individual was unknown to the medieval and the Renaissance grotesque; the discovery made by the Romanticists was made possible by their use of the grotesque method and of its power to liberate from dogmatism, completeness, and limitation. The *interior infinite* could not have been found in the closed and finished world, with its distinct fixed boundaries dividing all phenomena and values. Suffice it to compare the rationalized and exhaustive analysis of interior experience by classicism and the images of inner life offered by Sterne and the Romanticists. Here the artistic and heuristic force of the grotesque method is clearly shown. But this aspect is outside the scope of our work.

Let us say a few words on the concept of the grotesque of Hegel and Fischer.

Hegel is concerned only with archaic grotesque, which he defines as the expression of the preclassic and prephilosophic condition of the spirit. Relying mostly on archaic Indian forms, Hegel defines grotesque by three traits: the fusion of different natural spheres, immeasurable and exaggerated dimensions, and the multiplication of different members and organs of the human body (hands, feet, and eyes of Indian gods). Hegel completely ignores the role of the comic in the structure of the grotesque and indeed examines grotesque quite independently of the comic.

E. K. Fischer differs from Hegel. He sees the burlesque, the comic as the essence and the driving force of this genre: "The grotesque . . . is the comic in the form of the miraculous, it is the mythological comic." Fischer's definition has a certain profundity.

It must be added that in the further development of philosophical aesthetics up to our times the grotesque has not been duly understood and evaluated; there was no room for it in the system of aesthetics.

After the decline of Romanticism, in the second half of the nineteenth century, the interest in the grotesque was considerably reduced both in literature and in literary thought and studies. If mentioned at all, it is either listed among the vulgar comic genres or interpreted as a peculiar form of satire, directed against isolated, purely negative objects. Because of such interpretation the deep and universal nature of grotesque images was completely obscured.

The most extensive work devoted to the subject was published in 1894 by the German scientist G. Schneegans, entitled "The History of Grotesque Satire" (*Geschichte der Grotesken Satyre*). This book is largely devoted to Rabelais whom Schneegans considers the greatest representative of this genre. The author also gives a brief description of similar medieval types of imagery. He is the most consistent interpreter of the purely satirical grotesque. In his mind the latter is always negative, it is the exaggeration of the abnormal, an exaggeration that is incredible and therefore becomes fantastic. Through the medium of exaggeration of the abnormal a moral and social blow is dealt to the aberration. Such is the gist of Schneegans' analysis.

Schneegans fails completely to see the positive hyperbolism of the material bodily principle of the Middle Ages and of Rabelais. He fails to grasp the positive regenerating power of laughter. He sees merely the negative, rhetorical satire of the nineteenth century, a laughter that does not laugh. This is the extreme expression of the modernization of laughter in literary analysis. Neither does Schneegans see the universal character of these images. His shortsightedness is typical of the literary approach of the second part of the nineteenth century and of the first decades of the twentieth century. Even in our days the purely satirical interpretation of the grotesque, and of Rabelais' work in particular, is far from outmoded.

Since Schneegans founded his work mostly on Rabelais, we shall return to a further discussion of his book (Chapter Five).

A new and powerful revival of the grotesque took place in the twentieth century, although the word revival is not exactly suited to the most recent forms.

The latest development of this genre is considerably complex and contradictory. Generally speaking, two main lines of development can be traced. The first line is the modernist form (Alfred Jarry), connected in various degrees with the Romantic tradition and evolved under the influence of existentialism. The second line is the realist grotesque (Thomas Mann, Bertold Brecht, Pablo Neruda, and others). It is related to the tradition of realism and folk culture and reflects at times the direct influence of carnival forms, as in the work of Neruda.

The analysis of these developments does not enter our picture. We shall merely discuss the most recent theory of the grotesque according to modernist trends. We have in mind the work of the distinguished German literary critic Wolfgang Kayser: "The Grotesque in Painting and Poetry."[18]

Kayser's book is the first and at the present writing the only serious work on the theory of the grotesque. It contains many valuable observations and subtle analysis. But it offers the theory of the Romantic and modernist forms only, or, more strictly speaking, of exclusively modernist forms, since the author sees the Romantic age through the prism of his own time and therefore offers a somewhat distorted interpretation. Kayser's theory cannot be applied to the thousand-year-long development of the pre-Romantic era: that is, the archaic and antique grotesque (for instance, the satyric drama or the comedy of Attica) and the medieval and Renaissance grotesque, linked to the culture of folk humor. In his book Kayser does not even discuss these manifestations. Instead he bases his deductions and generalizations on the

[18] W. Kayser, *Das Grotesk in Malerei und Dichtung*, 1957. This book was reprinted posthumously in *Rowöhlts deutsche Enzyclopädie* series, 1961.

analysis of Romantic and modernist forms, and it is the latter which, as we have said, determines his concepts. The true nature of the grotesque, which cannot be separated from the culture of folk humor and the carnival spirit, remains unexplained. In the Romantic form this link is loosened and reduced; it has to a certain extent acquired a new meaning. But even at that stage all the basic elements, which have a clearly carnival origin, retain a certain memory of that mighty whole to which they belonged in the distant past. This memory is awakened in the best works of Romantic grotesque—most forcefully in Sterne and Hoffmann, although each expressed it differently. These works are more powerful, deep, and joyful than the objectively philosophical idea which they express. Kayser is unaware of this reawakened tradition nor is he looking for it. The modernist grotesque that inspires his own concept has almost entirely lost its past memories. It formalizes the heritage of carnival themes and symbols.

What are, according to Kayser, the basic characteristics of grotesque imagery?

Kayser's definitions first of all strike us by the gloomy, terrifying tone of the grotesque world that alone the author sees. In reality gloom is completely alien to the entire development of this world up to the romantic period. We have already shown that the medieval and Renaissance grotesque, filled with the spirit of carnival, liberates the world from all that is dark and terrifying; it takes away all fears and is therefore completely gay and bright. All that was frightening in ordinary life is turned into amusing or ludicrous monstrosities.

Fear is the extreme expression of narrow-minded and stupid seriousness, which is defeated by laughter. (We shall find an excellent elaboration of this theme in Rabelais' novel, especially in the Malbrough theme). Complete liberty is possible only in the completely fearless world.

For Kayser the essential trait of grotesque is "something hostile, alien, and inhuman" (*das Unheimliche, das Verfremdete und Unmenschliche*).

He particularly stresses the element of alienation: "The grotesque is the alienated world." Kayser explains this definition by drawing a comparison to the world of the fairy tale. The fairy tale world can be defined as strange and unusual, but it is not a world that has *become* alienated. In the grotesque, on the contrary, all that was for us familiar and friendly suddenly becomes hostile. It is our own world that undergoes this change.

Kayser's definition can be applied only to certain manifestations of modernist form of the grotesque; it is no longer completely adequate for the Romantic period and entirely inapplicable to the preceding stage of development.

Actually the grotesque, including the Romantic form, discloses the potentiality of an entirely different world, of another order, another way of life. It leads men out of the confines of the apparent (false) unity, of the indisputable and stable. Born of folk humor, it always represents in one form or another, through these or other means, the return of Saturn's golden age to earth—the living possibility of its return. The Romantic grotesque does this too, but in its own subjective form. The existing world suddenly becomes alien (to use Kayser's terminology) precisely because there is the potentiality of a friendly world, of the golden age, of carnival truth. Man returns unto himself. The world is destroyed so that it may be regenerated and renewed. While dying it gives birth. The relative nature of all that exists is always gay; it is the joy of change, even if in Romanticism gaiety and joy are reduced to their minimum.

Let us stress once more that the utopian element, the "golden age," was disclosed in the pre-Romantic period not for the sake of abstract thought or of inner experience; it is lived by the whole man, in thought and body. This bodily participation in the potentiality of another world, the bodily awareness of another world has an immense importance for the grotesque.

In Kayser's concept there is no room for the material bodily principle with its inexhaustible wealth and perpetual renewal. Neither do we find in his theory any notion of time, of change and crisis, that is, of all that happens to the sun, to the earth, to man, to human society, of all that true grotesque actually lives by.

Another of Kayser's definitions is characteristic of the modernist interpretation: "the grotesque is a form expressing the *id*."

The *id* is understood by the author not so much in the Freudian as in the existentialist sense of this word. *Id* is an alien, inhuman power, governing the world, men, their life and behavior. Kayser reduces many of the basic grotesque themes to the realization of this power, for instance the puppet theme. He also reduces to this power the theme of madness. According to the author we are always aware of something alien in the madman, as if some inhuman spirit of irony had entered his soul. We have already said that the theme of madness is used in the grotesque in quite a different manner—to escape the false "truth of this world" in order to look at the world with eyes free from this "truth."

Kayser himself often speaks of the freedom of fantasy characteristic of the grotesque. But how is such freedom possible in relation to a world ruled by the alien power of the *id?* Here lies the contradiction of Kayser's concept.

Actually the grotesque liberates man from all the forms of inhuman necessity that direct the prevailing concept of the world. This concept is uncrowned by the grotesque and reduced to the relative and the limited. Necessity, in every concept which prevails at any time, is always one-piece, serious, unconditional, and indisputable. But historically the idea of necessity is relative and variable. The principle of laughter and the carnival spirit on which grotesque is based destroys this limited seriousness and all pretense of an extratemporal meaning and unconditional value of necessity. It frees human consciousness, thought, and imagination for new potentialities. For this reason great changes, even in the field of science, are always preceded by a certain carnival consciousness that prepares the way.

In the grotesque world the *id* is uncrowned and transformed into a "funny monster." When entering this new dimension, even if it is Romantic, we always experience a peculiar gay freedom of thought and imagination.

Let us examine two more points of Kayser's theory.

Summing up his analysis, he asserts that "the grotesque expresses not the fear of death but the fear of life." This assertion, expressed in the spirit of existentialism, presents first an opposition of life to death. Such an opposition is completely contrary to the system of grotesque imagery, in which death is not a negation of life seen as the great body of all the people but part of life as a whole—its indispensable component, the condition of its constant renewal and rejuvenation. Death is here always related to birth; the grave is related to the earth's life-giving womb. Birth-death, death-birth, such are the components of life itself as in the famous words of the Spirit of the Earth in Goethe's *Faust*.[19] Death is included in life, and together with birth determines its eternal movement. Even the struggle of life and death in the individual body is conceived by grotesque imagery as the struggle of the old life stubbornly resisting the new life about to be born, as the crisis of change.

Leonardo da Vinci said: "When man awaits the new spring, the new year, with joyful impatience, he does not suspect that he is eagerly awaiting his own death." Although da Vinci's aphorism is not expressed in grotesque form, it is based on the carnival spirit.

Thus, in the system of grotesque imagery death and renewal are inseparable in life as a whole, and life as a whole can inspire fear least of all.

It must be recalled that the image of death in medieval and Renaissance grotesque (and in painting, also, as in Holbein's or

[19] Geburt und Grab,
    Ein ewiges meer
    Ein wechselnd Weben,
    Ein glühend Leben.

Here we see no opposition between life and death, there is a confrontation of life and the grave, both linked to the devouring womb of the earth and of the body. Both enter as indispensable elements into the living whole of ever changing and renewed life. This is also characteristic of Goethe's concept of the universe. The world in which life and death are opposed and the world in which birth and the grave confront each other are completely different. The latter is the world of folk culture and of Goethe as well.

Dürer's "dance of death") is a more or less funny monstrosity. In the ages that followed, especially in the nineteenth century, the public at large almost completely forgot the principle of laughter presented in macabre images. They were interpreted in an unrelieved, serious aspect and became flat and distorted. The bourgeois nineteenth century respected only satirical laughter, which was actually not laughter but rhetoric. (No wonder it was compared to a whip or scourge.) Merely amusing, meaningless, and harmless laughter was also tolerated, but the serious had to remain serious, that is, dull and monotonous.

The theme of death as renewal, the combination of death and birth, and the pictures of gay death play an important part in the system of grotesque imagery in Rabelais' novel. We shall submit them to a detailed analysis in later parts of our book.

The last point of Kayser's theory to be discussed is his treatment of grotesque laughter. He formulates it as follows: "Laughter combined with bitterness which takes the grotesque form acquires the traits of mockery and cynicism, and finally becomes satanic."

We see that Kayser interprets laughter in the spirit of Bonaventura's night watchman and of Jean Paul's theory of "destructive humor," that is, in the spirit of Romanticism. The gay, liberating and regenerating element of laughter, which is precisely the creative element, is completely absent. However, Kayser is aware of the complexity of this problem and abstains from offering an arbitrary solution.[20]

As we have said, the grotesque became the prevailing form of various modernist movements whose theoretical basis can be found in Kayser's concept. With a few reservations this theory may clarify certain aspects of the Romantic grotesque. But it cannot be extended to the other periods of this imagery's development.

The problem of the grotesque and of its aesthetic nature can be correctly posed and solved only in relation to medieval folk culture and Renaissance literature. The depth, variety, and power

[20] *Op. cit.* ftn. 18, p. 139.

of separate grotesque themes can be understood only within the unity of folk and carnival spirit. If examined outside of this unity, they become one-sided, flat, and stripped of their rich content.

The correctness of the term grotesque as applied to the imagery of medieval folk culture and of the Renaissance which is linked to it can raise no doubts whatever. But how can our term grotesque realism be justified?

We can offer only a preliminary answer to this question here.

The characteristic traits which mark the sharp difference of medieval and Renaissance grotesque from the Romantic and modernist types, are first of all its materialistic concept of being, most adequately defined as realistic. A further concrete analysis of grotesque images will confirm this proposition.

Renaissance grotesque imagery, directly related to folk carnival culture, as we find it in Rabelais, Cervantes, and Shakespeare, influenced the entire realistic literature of the following centuries. Realism of grand style, in Stendhal, Balzac, Hugo, and Dickens, for instance, was always linked directly or indirectly with the Renaissance tradition. Breaking away from this tradition diminished the scope of realism and transformed it into naturalist empiricism.

Even in the seventeenth century some forms of the grotesque began to degenerate into static "character" presentation and narrow "genrism." This degeneration was linked with the specific limitations of the bourgeois world outlook. The last thing one can say of the real grotesque is that it is static; on the contrary it seeks to grasp in its imagery the very act of becoming and growth, the eternal incomplete unfinished nature of being. Its images present simultaneously the two poles of becoming: that which is receding and dying, and that which is being born; they show two bodies in one, the budding and the division of the living cell. At the summit of grotesque and folklore realism, as in the death of one-cell organisms, no dead body remains. (That is, when the single cell divides into two other organisms, it dies in a sense but also reproduces; there is no departure from life into death.) Old age is pregnant, death is gestation, all that is limited, narrowly characterized, and completed is thrust into the lower stratum of the body for recasting and a new birth.

On the other hand, in the process of degeneration and disintegration the positive pole of grotesque realism (the second link of becoming) drops out and is replaced by moral sententiousness and abstract concepts. What remains is nothing but a corpse, old age deprived of pregnancy, equal to itself alone; it is alienated and torn away from the whole in which it had been linked to that other, younger link in the chain of growth and development. The result is a broken grotesque figure, the demon of fertility with phallus cut off and belly crushed. Hence all these sterile images representing "character," all these professional lawyers, merchants, matchmakers, old men and women, all these masks offered by degenerate, petty realism. These types also existed in grotesque realism, but they were not expected to build the picture of life as a whole; they were but the dying part of the life which gave birth. The fact is that the new concept of realism has a different way of drawing the boundaries between bodies and objects. It cuts the double body in two and separates the objects of grotesque and folklore realism that were merged within the body. The new concept seeks to complete each individual outside the link with the ultimate whole—the whole that has lost the old image and has as yet not found the new one. The notion of time has also been transformed.

The literature known as "realism of manners" was already presenting, together with authentic carnival themes, the images of a static grotesque entirely removed from the main flux of time and from the flux of becoming. This is a form either frozen in its duality or split in two. Certain scholars (for instance, Régnier) are inclined to define this genre as the first step of realism. In reality these are but the lifeless and at times meaningless fragments of the mighty and deep stream of grotesque realism.

The manifestations of medieval folk culture as well as grotesque realism have been exhaustively studied, but they were regarded only from the point of view of the historical and literary methods prevailing in the nineteenth century and in the first decades of the twentieth century. These studies were concerned not only with literary works but with specific phenomena such as the "feasts of fools" (F. Bourquelot, Drevs, P. Villetard), the "Paschal laughter" (J. Schmidt, S. Reinach), the "sacred parody" (F. Novati, E. Ilvonen, P. Lehmann), and others which are outside the sphere of art and literature. The antique culture of humor was also examined (A. Dieterich, H. Reich, F. Cornford). Folklorists performed a considerable task in the study of the origin and character of various themes and symbols pertaining to the culture of folk humor. (It is sufficient to recall Frazer's monumental work *The Golden Bough.*) Generally speaking, the number of scholarly works devoted to this subject is almost unlimited.[21] As we pursue the present study we shall refer to the specialized works which deal with this matter.

But all this enormous bulk of literature, with only a few exceptions, is devoid of theoretical pathos. It does not seek to make any broad and firmly established generalizations. The almost immeasurable, carefully selected, and scrupulously analyzed material is neither unified nor properly understood. That which we have called the one world of folk culture of humor appears in these works as a collection of curiosities, not to be included, in spite of its wide scope, in a serious history of European culture and literature. This accumulation of curiosities and indecencies remains outside the circle of creative problems. With such an approach the mighty impact of folk humor on belles lettres and on the very images created by human thought remains almost unexplored.

We shall briefly discuss only two works that pose the theoretical

---

[21] Among Soviet works, O. Freidenberg's book: "Poetics of Subject and Genre" (*Poetica Sujeta i Zhanra*), Goslitizdat, 1936, is very valuable. This work contains an immense body of folklore material directly related to folk culture of humor, especially the antique specimens. But this material is mainly interpreted in the spirit of prelogical thought. The problem of culture of folk humor is not posed.

problem and do so in such a way as to touch upon the two aspects of the culture of folk humor.

In 1903, H. Reich published his voluminous work entitled "The Mime," a work devoted to the historical study of literary development (see footnote 7). The object of Reich's research is essentially the antique and medieval forms of the culture of humor. The author offers an immense, most interesting, and valuable body of material. He correctly shows the unity of the tradition of humor, developed throughout antiquity and the Middle Ages. He grasps the essential, many-centuries-old link of laughter with the images of the body's lower stratum. All this permits Reich to make a correct and practical approach to the problem.

And yet, he does not state his problem per se. Two restrictions seem to have prevented him from doing so.

First, Reich attempts to reduce the entire history of the culture of humor to the history of the mime, that is, to a single genre. True, it is a characteristic one, especially for the later period of antiquity. In Reich's mind, the mime is the center and even the almost unique representative of this tradition. The author goes on to reduce all medieval festive forms and comic literature to the influence of the antique world. He pursues his research beyond the sphere of European culture, which causes him to give forced interpretations and to ignore all that does not fit the mime's Procrustean bed. We must add that Reich himself does not always cope with his concept. His abundant material overflows and carries him beyond the narrow limits reserved for the mime.

Second, Reich modernizes and diminishes the value of laughter as well as of the material bodily principle that is closely linked to it. His conception of laughter's positive elements, of their liberating and regenerating power has a muffled tone, even though he is perfectly acquainted with the antique philosophy of laughter. Neither are laughter's universal character and its philosophical and utopian nature properly understood and evaluated. But the narrowest aspect of his theory is his presentation of the material bodily principle. Reich sees it through the prism of the abstract, differentiating thought of modern times and therefore offers an almost naturalistic interpretation.

Such are the two points which in our mind weaken Reich's theory. However, he has made a considerable contribution to the correct approach to the problem relative to the culture of folk humor. It is to be regretted that his work, containing so much new material and so bold and original, did not exercise in his time the influence it deserved.

The second work that remains to be examined is a small volume published by Konrad Burdach, entitled "Reformation, Renaissance, Humanism."[22] This book also studies the problem of folk culture, but from a different angle. Burdach makes no mention whatever of laughter or of the material bodily principle. His only protagonist is the "idea-image" of "regeneration," "renewal," and "reformation."

Burdach seeks to prove that this idea-image of regeneration in its many variations, although born from the most ancient mythological thought of the Eastern peoples and of antiquity, continued to live and develop during the Middle Ages. It was also preserved in the cult of the Church, (in the liturgy and in baptism, for instance) but remained there in a state of dogmatic petrification. From the time of the religious revival of the twelfth century (Joachim of Floris, Francis of Assisi, and the *Spirituals*) the idea-image was revived; it penetrated wide popular circles, acquired the hue of purely human emotions, and awakened the poetic and artistic imagination. It expressed the growing thirst for regeneration and renewal in the purely earthly sphere.

Burdach retraces the slow and gradual process of secularization that took place in Dante, Petrarch, Boccaccio, and in the ideas and activity of Rienzo.

He correctly surmises that such a historic phenomenon as the Renaissance could not arise merely as a result of the scientific search or of the intellectual efforts of individuals. He writes:

[22] Konrad Burdach, *Reformation, Renaissance, Humanismus*, Berlin, 1918.

Humanism and Renaissance are not the product of knowledge. They do not arise because scholars discover the lost monuments of antique literature and art, and strive to bring them back to life. Humanism and the Renaissance were born from the passionate and boundless expectation and striving of an aging epoch; its soul, shattered to its very depths was thirsting for a new youth.

Burdach is of course completely right in refusing to trace and explain the Renaissance merely through scholarly and bookish sources, through an individual ideological search and "intellectual effort." He is right in stating that the Renaissance was prepared by the Middle Ages, and especially by the twelfth century. And finally, he correctly points out that the word *renaissance* did not mean a revival of the ancient arts and sciences. It was an immensely important and significant word, rooted in the very depths of the ritualistic, ideological, and visual imagery of mankind. However, Burdach did not see and did not grasp the main sphere of being of the Renaissance idea-image, the medieval culture of folk humor. The striving toward renewal and a new birth, "the thirst for a new youth" pervaded the carnival spirit of the Middle Ages and found a multiform expression in concrete sensual elements of folk culture, both in ritual and spectacle. This was the second, festive life of the Middle Ages.

Many figures described by Burdach as preparing the Renaissance reflected the influence of the culture of folk humor and were the forerunners of the new epoch. Such were, for instance, Joachim of Floris, and especially Francis of Assisi and the movement he initiated. Francis called himself and his companions "God's jugglers" (*ioculatores Domini*). Francis' peculiar world outlook, his "spiritual joy" (*laetitia spiritualis*), his blessing of the material bodily principle, and its typically Franciscan degradations and profanation can be defined, with some exaggeration, as a carnivalized Catholicism. Carnival elements were also strong in Rienzo's entire activity. All these movements, which according to Burdach prepared the Renaissance, expressed the liberating and renewing principle of laughter, even though at times in an extremely reduced form. But the author completely ignores this principle. All he is aware of is the serious tone.

Nevertheless, in his attempt to attain a more correct understanding of the relation of the Renaissance to the Middle Ages Burdach contributed to the posing of the problem of the culture of folk humor.

So our problem is posed. However, the immediate object of our study is not the culture of folk humor but the work of Rabelais. The sphere of folk humor is boundless and, as we have said, presents a great variety of manifestations. As far as this culture is concerned, our problem is purely theoretical: to show the oneness and meaning of folk humor, its general ideological, philosophical, and aesthetic essence. The problem can be solved best of all with the help of concrete material in which folk tradition is collected, concentrated, and artistically rendered at its highest level; this is to be found in Rabelais' work. To help us penetrate the very depth of this matter, Rabelais is unique. In his creative world the inner oneness of all the heterogeneous elements emerges with extraordinary clarity. His work is an encyclopedia of folk culture.

However, while using Rabelais' work for the understanding of this culture, we do not wish to transform him merely into a means for attaining a goal outside the sphere of his writings. On the contrary, we are convinced that only thanks to this method of research can we discover the true Rabelais, to show, as it were, Rabelais within Rabelais. Up to now he has been merely modernized: he has been read through the eyes of the new age, and mostly through the eyes of the nineteenth century which were the most shortsighted in this respect. Only that part of his work was read which was the least important for him and for his contemporaries and which, objectively speaking, was the least essential. Rabelais' exceptional charm, which we all feel, remains unexplained to date. To explain it, it is first of all necessary to understand his peculiar language, that is, the language of the culture of folk humor.

CHAPTER ONE

Rabelais in the History of Laughter

*It would be extremely interesting
to write the history of laughter.*
(A. I. HERZEN)

The four-hundred-year history of the understanding, influence, and interpretation of Rabelais is closely linked with the history of laughter itself.

Rabelais' contemporaries, and indeed the entire sixteenth century, somehow understood our author and were able to appreciate him. We know this from the opinions of contemporaries and their immediate successors whose testimony has survived, as well as by the frequent reprints of Rabelais' work in the sixteenth century and in the first third of the seventeenth century. This work was appreciated not only in humanist circles, at court, and by the high bourgeoisie. I shall quote the comment of one of Rabelais' younger contemporaries, the eminent historian Etienne Pasquier. In a letter to Ronsard Pasquier wrote: "Among us there is no one who does not know how much Rabelais, clowning wisely (*en folastrant sagement*) in his *Gargantua* and *Pantagruel* gained the love of the people (*gaigna de grace parmy le peuple*)".[1]

The fact that Rabelais was understood and loved by the men of his time is proved most clearly by the numerous and deep marks of his influence and by the number of imitations inspired by his work.[2] Nearly all the sixteenth-century prose writers after Rabelais (or more correctly speaking, after the publication of the first two volumes of his novels), Bonaventure Des Périers, Noël du Fail, Guillaume Boucher, Jacques Tahureau, were more or less Rabelaisians. Neither was his influence ignored by the historians of his time, Pasquier, Brantôme; nor by the Protestant polemists and pamphletists, Pierre Viret, Henri Estienne, and others. Sixteenth-century literature ended, so to speak, under the sign of Rabelais: in the field of political satire, it was closed by the remarkable "Menippus Satire on the Virtues of the Spanish Catholikon" (1594) directed against the Inquisition, one of the best political satires of world literature,[3] and in the field of belles lettres by "How to Succeed" of Béroalde de Verville,[4] 1612. Both

[1] Étienne Pasquier, *Lettres*, Vol. 2, as quoted in Lazare Sainéan, *L'Influence et la Réputation de Rabelais (Interprètes, lecteurs et imitateurs)*, Paris, J. Gamber, 1930, p. 100.

[2] The history of the appreciation, interpretation, and influence of Rabelais' work has been, for four hundred years, fairly well studied from the factual point of view. Besides a long series of valuable articles in the *Revue Rabelaisienne* (from 1903 to 1913) and in the *Revue du Seizième Siècle* (from 1913 to 1932), two special books have been devoted to this history: Jacques Boulenger, *Rabelais à travers les ages*, Paris, le Divan, 1923; Lazare Sainéan, *L'Influence et la Réputation de Rabelais (Interprètes, lecteurs et imitateurs)*, Paris, J. Gamber, 1930. These books also contain the comments of Rabelais' contemporaries.

[3] *Satyre Menippée de la Vertue du Catholikon d'Espagne*, Ed., Frank, Oppeln, 1884, reprinted from first edition of 1594.

[4] Béroalde de Verville, *Le moyen de parvenir, oeuvres contenants la raison de ce qui a été, est et sera*, with comments, variants and vocabulary by Charles Royer, Paris, 1876.

these works, which mark the end of the century, bear the seal of Rabelais' influence; in spite of their differences their imagery is filled with an almost Rabelaisian grotesque life. Besides the important writers who were able to transpose Rabelais' influence while retaining their independence, we find a great number of minor imitators who left no independent record in the annals of their time.

It must also be stressed that success and recognition came at once to Rabelais during the very first months following the publication of *Pantagruel.*

What is the meaning of this recognition, of these enthusiastic (but by no means surprised) comments of the contemporaries and of the tremendous influence of this novel on the great serious literature of that time—on learned humanists, historians, political and religious pamphletists, and finally on so many imitators?

Rabelais' contemporaries saw his work against the background of a living and still powerful tradition. They could be impressed by the mighty character and success of this work but not by his style and images. They could perceive the oneness of Rabelais' world. They could realize the essential relationship and the links holding together its elements, which in the seventeenth century were to appear heterogeneous and in the eighteenth completely incompatible. They could be interested in the high level of the problems and ideas expressed in the novel's prandial talks, as well as in the trivia, abuses, indecencies, pedantry, and farce, for they knew that one logic pervaded all these elements which in our eyes appear so different. They also vividly felt the link of Rabelais' imagery with the forms of folk spectacle, the festivity of these images, the carnival atmosphere which deeply penetrated their sphere.[5] In other words, the men of Rabelais' time grasped the wholeness and order of the Rabelaisian aesthetic and ideological

[5] We have, for instance, a curious description of a grotesque celebration of the carnival type held in Rouen in 1541. A procession representing a mock funeral carried a banner with the anagram of Rabelais' name; after the feast that followed a guest, wearing a monk's habit, read the "Chronicle of Gargantua," instead of the Bible. (See *op. cit.* ftn. 2, J. Boulenger, p. 17 and L. Sainéan, p. 20.)

world, the unity of his style, and the harmony of all the elements that composed it, for they were informed by the same world outlook, by a single grand style. This is the essential difference in the appreciation of Rabelais' writings in the sixteenth century and in the years that followed. Contemporaries understood this one grand style, while men of the next two centuries began to consider it as some strange individual idiosyncrasy, or as some kind of secret code, a cryptogram containing a system of allusions to events and living persons of the author's time.

The reaction of Rabelais' contemporaries was, however, naïve and impulsive. That which to later generations remained an open question appeared self-evident to the men of the sixteenth century. They could not have answered our own questions, because for them these questions did not as yet exist.

At the same time, we find early in the writings of Rabelais' imitators the first signs of the disintegration of the Rabelaisian style. For instance, in the works of Des Périers and especially of Noël du Fail the Rabelaisian images become petty; they are mitigated and begin to acquire the character of genre and manners. Their universalism is considerably watered down. Another aspect of this process of disintegration appeared when these images began to serve the purpose of satire. In this case a weakening of the ambivalent image's positive pole takes place. When the grotesque is used to illustrate an abstract idea, its nature is inevitably distorted. The essence of the grotesque is precisely to present a contradictory and double-faced fullness of life. Negation and destruction (death of the old) are included as an essential phase, inseparable from affirmation, from the birth of something new and better. The very material bodily lower stratum of the grotesque image (food, wine, the genital force, the organs of the body) bears a deeply positive character. This principle is victorious, for the final result is always abundance, increase.

The abstract idea distorts this nature of the grotesque image. It transforms the center of gravity to a "moral" meaning. Moreover it submits the substratum of the image to the negative element. Exaggeration becomes a caricature. The beginning of this process is found even in early Protestant satire, and later in the previously mentioned "Menippus Satire." But here disintegration is still at its early stage. The grotesque images selected to serve an abstract idea are still too powerful; they preserve their nature and pursue their own logic, independently from the author's intentions, and sometimes contrary to them.

An interesting document revealing this disintegration is the free translation of *Gargantua* into German by Fischart, which bears the grotesque title: *Affenteurliche und Ungeheurliche Geschichtsklitterung* (1575).

Fischart was a Protestant and a moralist; his literary works were connected with "grobianism." At its sources German grobianism was related to Rabelais. The representatives of this school inherited the images of the material bodily life from grotesque realism. They were under the direct influence of folk festival and carnival forms, hence a pronounced hyperbolism of bodily images, especially those of eating and drinking. Exaggeration characterized both grotesque realism and folk festival forms: for instance, gigantic sausages were carried by dozens of men during the Nuremberg carnivals of the sixteenth and seventeenth centuries. But the moral and political ideas of the grobianists (Dedekind, Scheidt, Fischart) lent these images a negative connotation of indecency. In the introduction to his *Grobianus* Dedekind[6] refers to the Lacedemonians who showed their drunken slaves to their children in order to inspire them with an aversion for drunkenness. This goal of inspiring disgust or fear was also pursued by Fischart in his images of Saint Grobianus and the grobianists. The positive nature of the image was thus submitted to the negative purpose of satiric mockery and moral condemnation. This satire was written from the point of view of the *bürger* and the Protestant and was directed against feudal nobility (the *junker*), sunk into the mire of sloth, gluttony, drunkenness, and immorality. Precisely this grobianist point of view (influenced by Scheidt)

---

[6] Dedekind: *Grobianus et Grobiana Libri tres* (first ed. 1549, second ed. 1552). Dedekind's book was translated into German by Fischart's teacher Kaspar Scheidt.

formed in part the basis of Fischart's free translation of Rabe-lais.[7]

But the Rabelaisian images continued to live their century-old life, independently of Fischart's rather primitive ideas. The hy-perbolism of material bodily images (especially those of eating and drinking) was even increased in his translation. The interior symbolism of all these exaggerations, as in the original text, was that of growth, fertility, of a brimming-over abundance. These images reveal the devouring and generating lower stratum. The peculiar festive character of the material bodily principle is also retained. The abstract idea does not penetrate the depths of the image and does not become its organizing principle. Neither is laughter fully transformed as yet into mockery; it still has a rela-tively whole character and is related to the entire living process, to both of its poles. The triumphal tones of birth and renewal can still be heard. Thus the abstract has as yet not mastered all the images in Fischart's translation, but it has to a certain extent transformed its images into an amusing supplement to a moral sermon. This process, which changes the meaning of laughter, could only be completed later and was closely linked to the estab-lishment of the hierarchy of genres and to the place of laughter in this hierarchy.

Ronsard and the Pléiade were already convinced of the exis-tence of the hierarchy of genres. This theory, borrowed from antiquity but revised on French soil, could not of course take root immediately. The Pléiade was still liberal and democratic in relation to these questions. Its members treated Rabelais with great respect and knew how to appreciate him at his true value, especially Du Bellay and Baïf. However, this high appreciation of our author, and the strong influence of his language on that of

[7] We say "in part" because in his translation of Rabelais' novel Fis-chart was not a strict grobianist. Karl Marx wrote a sharp but just criti-cism of sixteenth-century grobian literature. See K. Marx: "Moralizing Criticism and Critical Morals," K. Marx and F. Engels. Works, Vol. 4, pp. 291–295.

the Pléiade, was in flagrant contradiction to his place in the hierarchy of genres, which was the lowest of all, almost outside literary bounds. But this hierarchy was as yet only an abstract and confused idea. Certain social, political, and ideological transformations had still to take place; the circle of readers and literary connoisseurs had to be differentiated and narrowed before the hierarchy could express the interrelation of genres and become a regulating force.

We know that this process was completed in the seventeenth century, but it began to be felt as early as the sixteenth. At that time the appraisal of Rabelais as a merely amusing and gay author was already beginning to take shape. Such was also, as we know, the fate of Cervantes, whose *Don Quixote* was listed for a long time among the amusing books of light literature. At the end of the sixteenth century Rabelais descended lower and lower, to the very confines of great literature and was finally driven out of bounds.

Montaigne, who was forty years younger than Rabelais, wrote in his essays: "As to simply amusing works (*simplement plaisants*), I consider among the new books Boccaccio's *Decameron*, Rabelais, and *Basia* by Jean Second, if they can be referred to this category, worthy to divert us (*dignes qu'en s'amuse*)."[8]

However, Montaigne's "simply amusing" definition is still on the dividing line between the old and the new understanding of "amusing" (*plaisant*), "gay" (*joyeux*), "recreational" (*recréatif*), and similar epithets applied to literary works and so often added to the sixteenth- and seventeenth-century titles of these works.[9] The concept of amusing and gay was not yet narrowed down for Montaigne and had not as yet acquired the tone of something low and irrelevant. Montaigne himself writes in another chapter of his "Essays," "Personally, I like best only books that are amusing

[8] Montaigne, *Essays*, Book II, Chapter 10. This passage was written about 1580.

[9] For instance, the title of one of the remarkable books of the sixteenth century: Bonaventure Des Périers, *Nouvelles recréations et joyeux Devis*, "New Recreations and Gay Conversation."

and light, which amuse me, or those which comfort me and advise me how to order my life and my death (*à regler ma vie et ma mort*)." (Book I, Chapter 38)

From these lines it is clear that among all the works of belles lettres, in the true sense of the word, Montaigne prefers precisely those which are amusing and gay, since by books of comfort and advice he means not belles lettres but works of philosophy, theology, and above all works resembling his own "Essays" (Marcus Aurelius, Seneca, Plutarch). He considers belles lettres as a basically amusing, gay, recreative literary genre.[10] In this sense he is still a man of the sixteenth century, but characteristically enough the question of ordering life and death is already definitely taken out of the realm of gay laughter. Like Boccaccio, Rabelais is "worthy of being amusing," but he does not belong to the number of comforters and advisers who order life and death. And yet Rabelais was precisely such a comforter and adviser in the eyes of his contemporaries. They could still consider these questions on the gay level, the level of laughter.

Rabelais, Cervantes, and Shakespeare represent an important turning point in the history of laughter. Nowhere else do we see so clearly marked the lines dividing the Renaissance from the seventeenth century and the period that followed.

The Renaissance conception of laughter can be roughly described as follows: Laughter has a deep philosophical meaning, it is one of the essential forms of the truth concerning the world as a whole, concerning history and man; it is a peculiar point of view relative to the world; the world is seen anew, no less (and perhaps more) profoundly than when seen from the serious standpoint. Therefore, laughter is just as admissible in great literature, posing universal problems, as seriousness. Certain essential aspects of the world are accessible only to laughter.

---

[10] The epithet *plaisant* was applied in the sixteenth century to all belles lettres in general, independently of their genres. The most venerable work of past ages was in the eyes of the Renaissance the *Roman de la Rose*. In 1527 Clément Marot published a somewhat modernized version of this great monument of world literature, recommending it as follows: "C'est le plaisant livre du "Rommant de la Rose."

The attitude toward laughter of the seventeenth century and of the years that followed can be characterized thus. Laughter is not a universal, philosophical form. It can refer only to individual and individually typical phenomena of social life. That which is important and essential cannot be comical. Neither can history and persons representing it—kings, generals, heroes—be shown in a comic aspect. The sphere of the comic is narrow and specific (private and social vices); the essential truth about the world and about man cannot be told in the language of laughter. Therefore, the place of laughter in literature belongs only to the low genres, showing the life of private individuals and the inferior social levels. Laughter is a light amusement or a form of salutary social punishment of corrupt and low persons.

The Renaissance expressed its attitude toward laughter in the very practice of literary creation and appreciation. Neither was there any lack of theoretical opinion that justified laughter as a universal, philosophical form. This theory of laughter was built almost exclusively on antique sources. Rabelais himself developed it in the old and new prologue of the fourth book of his novel, based mostly on Hippocrates, whose role as the theorist of laughter was at that time important. Not only was his prestige founded on the comments contained in his medical treatise concerning the importance of a gay and cheerful mood on the part of the physician and patient fighting disease,[11] but was also due to the "Hippocratic novel." This was an addendum to "Hippocrates' Aphorisms" (of course apocryphal) concerning the "madness" of Democritus as expressed in his laughter. In the "Hippocratic novel" the laughter of Democritus had a philosophical character, being directed at the life of man and at all the vain fears and hopes related to the gods and to life after death. Democritus here made of his laughter a whole philosophy, a certain spiritual premise of the awakened man who has attained virility. Hippocrates finally agreed with him.

The teaching concerning the therapeutic power of laughter in

11 Especially in the sixth volume of "Epidemics" to which Rabelais alludes in the prologues mentioned.

the "Hippocratic novel" received special recognition and notoriety at the Montpellier Medical School where Rabelais studied and later taught. A member of this school, the famous physician Laurent Joubert, published in 1560 a special work under the characteristic title: *Traité du Ris, contenant son essence, ses causes et ses mervelheus effeis, curieusement recherchés, raisonnés et observés par M. Laur. Joubert* ("a treatise on laughter, containing its essence, causes and wondrous effects curiously studied, discussed and observed by M. Laur. Joubert"). In 1579 Joubert published another treatise in Paris, entitled *La cause morale de Ris, de l'excellent et tres renommé Démocrite, expliquée et temoignée par ce divin Hippocrate en ses Epitres* ("The moral cause of laughter of the eminent and very famous Democritus explained and witnessed by the divine Hippocrates in his epistles"). This work was actually a French version of the last part of the "Hippocratic novel."

Although this treatise on the philosophy of laughter was published after Rabelais' death, it was a belated echo of the thoughts and discussions that were current in Montpellier at the time when Rabelais attended this school and that determined his concept of the therapeutic power of laughter and of the "gay physician."

The second source of the philosophy of laughter at the time of Rabelais was Aristotle's famous formula:[12] "Of all living creatures only man is endowed with laughter." This formula enjoyed immense popularity and was given a broader interpretation: laughter was seen as man's highest spiritual privilege, inaccessible to other creatures. As we know, it concludes Rabelais' introductory poem to *Gargantua*.

Mieux est de ris que de larmes escrire.
Par ce que rire est le propre de l'homme.[13]

Even Ronsard still uses this saying in its broader form; in his poem dedicated to Belleau we find these lines:

---

[12] *De Anima*, Book 3, Chapter 10.
[13] Better to write about laughter than tears,
    For laughter is inherent to man.

Dieu qui soubz l'homme a le monde soumis,
A l'homme seul, le seul rire a permis
Pour s'esgayer et non pas a la beste,
Qui n'a raison ny esprit en la teste.[14]

According to Aristotle, a child does not begin to laugh before
the fortieth day after his birth; only from that moment does it become a human being. Rabelais and his contemporaries were also
familiar with the saying of Pliny that only one man, Zoroaster, began to laugh at the time of his birth; this was interpreted as an
omen of his divine wisdom.

Finally, the third source of the Renaissance philosophy of laughter is Lucian, especially his image of Menippus laughing in the
kingdom of the dead. Lucian's work "Menippus, or the Descent
into Hades" had an essential influence on Rabelais, more precisely
on the episode of Epistemon's journey to hell in *Pantagruel.*
Another important influence was Lucian's "Dialogues."

Here are a few characteristic excerpts from the "Dialogues":

"Menippus, Diogenes advises you, if mortal subjects for laughter begin to pall, come down below, and find much richer material;
where you are now, there is always a dash of uncertainty in it; the
question will always intrude, who can be quite sure about the
hereafter? Here you can have your laugh out in security, like me."
(Diogenes and Pollux)[15]

"Oh, all right, Menippus; suppose you leave your independence
behind you, and your plain-speaking and your indifference, and
your high spirits and your jests. No one else here has a jest . . ."
(Charon, Hermes, and various shades)[16]

Charon: Where did you pick up this Cynic, Hermes? The noise he

[14] God who subjected the world to man,
  To man alone permitted laughter
  To be merry, not to the beast
  Who has neither reason nor spirit.
[15] Lucian, *Works.* translated by H. W. Fowler and F. G. Fowler. 4
vols. Oxford Univ. Press, 1905. Vol. 1, p. 107. By permission of the
Clarendon Press, Oxford.
[16] *Ibid.,* p. 122.

made on the crossing, too! laughing and jeering at all the rest, and singing, when everyone else was at his lamentations.
Hermes: Ah, Charon, you little know your passenger! Independence, every inch of him: he cares for no one. 'Tis Menippus.
(Charon and Menippus)[17]

Let us stress in this Lucianic image of the laughing Menippus the relation of laughter to the underworld and to death, to the freedom of the spirit, and to the freedom of speech.

Such are the three most popular antique sources of the Rabelaisian philosophy of laughter. They influenced not only Joubert's treatise but also the opinions current in literary and humanist circles concerning the meaning and virtue of laughter. All three sources define laughter as a universal philosophical principle that heals and regenerates; it is essentially linked to the ultimate philosophical questions concerning the "regulation of life" which Montaigne interprets in strictly serious tones.

Rabelais and his contemporaries were also familiar, of course, with the antique conception of laughter from other sources—from Athenaeus, Macrobius, and others. They knew Homer's famous words about the undestroyable, that is, eternal laughter of the gods, and they were familiar with the Roman tradition of the freedom of laughter during the Saturnalia and the role of laughter during the triumphal marches and the funeral rites of notables.[18] Rabelais in particular makes frequent allusion to these sources.

[17] *Ibid.*, p. 144.
[18] H. Reich offers considerable material concerning the antique tradition of freedom and mockery, especially in the mimes. He quotes corresponding lines from Ovid's *Tristia*. Ovid justifies his frivolous verses by alluding to the tradition of mimic freedom and the permissible mimic improprieties; he quotes Martial who in his epigrams justifies his license by recalling the traditional deriding of emperors and generals during the triumphal marches. Reich analyzes the interesting apology of the mime by the rhetor of the sixth century Choricius, which parallels the Renaissance apology of laughter. While defending the mime, Choricius had first of all to take up the defense of laughter. He discusses the Christians' accusations that laughter provoked by the mime is from the devil and declares that man differs from the beast by his ability to speak and laugh. The gods laugh in Homer, and Aphrodite "smiled sweetly." The

Let us stress once more that for the Renaissance (as for the antique sources described above) the characteristic trait of laughter was precisely the recognition of its positive, regenerating, creative meaning. This clearly distinguishes it from the later theories of the philosophy of laughter, including Bergson's conception, which bring out mostly its negative functions.[19]

The antique tradition has an essential meaning for the Renaissance, which offered an apology of the literary tradition of laughter and brought it into the sphere of humanist ideas. As to the aesthetic practice of Renaissance laughter, it is first of all determined by the traditions of the medieval culture of folk humor. However, in the conditions of the Renaissance we do not see the direct continuation of these traditions; they enter a completely new and superior phase of existence. In the Middle Ages folk humor existed and developed outside the official sphere of high ideology and literature, but precisely because of its unofficial existence, it was marked by exceptional radicalism, freedom, and ruthlessness. Having on the one hand forbidden laughter in every official sphere of life and ideology, the Middle Ages on the other hand bestowed exceptional privileges of license and lawlessness outside these spheres: in the marketplace, on feast days, in festive

austere Lycurgus erected a statute to laughter, calling it the gift of the gods. Choricius cites an example: the treatment of an invalid with the help of a mime and the laughter he provoked. Choricius' apology resembles in many ways the defense of laughter in the sixteenth century, especially the Rabelaisian version. Choricius says: Let us stress the universal character of the conception of laughter; it distinguishes man from the beast, it is of divine origin, and finally it is linked to medical treatment, to healing. (See H. Reich, *Der Mimus, ein literarentwicklungsgeschichtlicher Versuch,* Berlin, 1903, pp. 52–55, 185 ff., and 207.

[19] The conception of the creative power of laughter was known also by other ancient civilizations. In an Egyptian alchemist's papyrus of the third century, preserved in Leiden, the creation of the world is attributed to divine laughter: ". . . when God laughed seven gods were born to rule the world . . . when he burst out laughing there was light . . . he burst out laughing for the second time, the waters were born, at the seventh burst of laughter the soul appeared." (See S. Reinach, "Le Rire rituel," in *Cultes, Mythes et Religions,* Paris, 1908, Vol. 4, pp. 112–113.)

recreational literature. And medieval laughter knew how to use these privileges widely.

In the Renaissance, laughter in its most radical, universal, and at the same time gay form emerged from the depths of folk culture; it emerged but once in the course of history, over a period of some fifty or sixty years (in various countries and at various times) and entered with its popular (vulgar) language the sphere of great literature and high ideology. It appeared to play an essential role in the creation of such masterpieces of world literature as Boccaccio's *Decameron,* the novels of Rabelais and Cervantes, Shakespeare's dramas and comedies, and others. The walls between official and nonofficial literature were inevitably to crumble, especially because in the most important ideological sectors these walls also served to separate languages—Latin from the vernacular. The adoption of the vernacular by literature and by certain ideological spheres was to sweep away or at least weaken these boundaries.

A number of other factors concerned with the disintegration of the feudal and theocratic order of the Middle Ages also contributed to the fusion of the official and nonofficial. The culture of folk humor that had been shaped during many centuries and that had defended the people's creativity in nonofficial forms, in verbal expression or spectacle, could now rise to the high level of literature and ideology and fertilize it. Later, in times of absolute monarchy and the formation of a new official order, folk humor descended to the lower level of the genre hierarchy. There it settled and broke away from its popular roots, becoming petty, narrow, and degenerate.

A millenium of folk humor broke into Renaissance literature. This thousand-year-old laughter not only fertilized literature but was itself fertilized by humanist knowledge and advanced literary techniques. In Rabelais we see the speech and mask of the medieval clown, folk and carnival gaiety, the defiance of the democratic cleric, the talk and gestures of the mountebank—all combined with humanist scholarship, with the physician's science and practice, and with political experience. (The author, as a confidant of the brothers DuBellay, was initiated in the secrets of world affairs.) In this new combination medieval laughter was destined to change. Its wide popular character, its radicalism and freedom, soberness and materiality were transferred from an almost elemental condition to a state of artistic awareness and purposefulness. In other words, medieval laughter became at the Renaissance stage of its development the expression of a new free and critical *historical* consciousness. It could acquire this character only because the buds and shoots of new potentialities had been prepared in the medieval period. How were the forms of this medieval culture of humor developed?

As we have said, laughter in the Middle Ages remained outside all official spheres of ideology and outside all official strict forms of social relations. Laughter was eliminated from religious cult, from feudal and state ceremonials, etiquette, and from all the genres of high speculation. An intolerant, one-sided tone of seriousness is characteristic of official medieval culture. The very contents of medieval ideology—asceticism, somber providentialism, sin, atonement, suffering, as well as the character of the feudal regime, with its oppression and intimidation—all these elements determined this tone of icy petrified seriousness. It was supposedly the only tone fit to express the true, the good, and all that was essential and meaningful. Fear, religious awe, humility, these were the overtones of this seriousness.

Early Christianity had already condemned laughter. Tertullian, Cyprian, and John Chrysostom preached against ancient spectacles, especially against the mime and the mime's jests and laughter. John Chrysostom declared that jests and laughter are not from God but from the devil. Only permanent seriousness, remorse, and sorrow for his sins befit the Christian.[20] During the struggle against the Aryans, Christians were accused of introducing elements of the mime—song, gesticulation, laughter—into religious services.

[20] See Reich, *op. cit.* ftn. 18, p. 116 ff.

But this intolerant seriousness of the official church ideology made it necessary to legalize the gaiety, laughter, and jests which had been eliminated from the canonized ritual and etiquette. Thus forms of pure laughter were created parallel to the official forms.

At the same time certain religious cults inherited from antiquity were influenced by the East and in some cases by local pagan rites, especially by the rites of fertility. Rudiments of gaiety and laughter are present in these forms. They can be found in the liturgy and in funeral rites, as well as in the rites of baptism, of marriage, and in other religious services. But these rudiments are sublimated and toned down.[21] If performed in a zone near a church, they had to be authorized. These rites of pure laughter were even permitted as a parallel to the official cults.

Such were first of all the "feasts of fools" (*festa stultorum, fatuorum, follorum*) which were celebrated by schoolmen and lower clerics on the feast of St. Stephen, on New Year's Day, on the feast of the Holy Innocents, of the Epiphany, and of St. John. These celebrations were originally held in the churches and bore a fully legitimate character. Later they became only semilegal, and at the end of the Middle Ages were completely banned from the churches but continued to exist in the streets and in taverns, where they were absorbed into carnival merriment and amusements. The feast of fools showed a particular obstinacy and force of survival in France (*fête des fous*). This feast was actually a parody and travesty of the official cult, with masquerades and improper dances. These celebrations held by the lower clergy were especially boisterous on New Year's Day and on Epiphany.

Nearly all the rituals of the feast of fools are a grotesque degradation of various church rituals and symbols and their transfer to the material bodily level: gluttony and drunken orgies on the altar

---

[21] The history of tropes presents in this respect considerable interest. The gay, joyful tone of the tropes led to the development of certain elements of church drama (see Léon Gautier, *Histoire de la Poésie Liturgique, I (Les Tropes)*, Paris, 1886) Also J. P. Jacobsen, *Essai sur les origines de la comédie en France au Moyen age*, Champion, Paris, 1910.

table, indecent gestures, disrobing. We shall later analyze some of these rituals.[22]

This celebration, as we have said, was preserved in France with particular stubborness. A peculiar apology for the feast appeared in a circular letter of the Paris School of Theology in 1444. The defenders refer to the fact that the feast was established in the earliest age of Christianity by our ancestors who knew best what they were doing. The apology further stresses that the feast has not a serious but a purely jesting character. Such a gay diversion is necessary "so that foolishness, which is our second nature and seems to be inherent in man might freely spend itself at least once a year. Wine barrels burst if from time to time we do not open them and let in some air. All of us men are barrels poorly put together, which would burst from the wine of wisdom, if this wine remains in a state of constant fermentation of piousness and fear of God. We must give it air in order not to let it spoil. This is why we permit folly on certain days so that we may later return with greater zeal to the service of God."

In this remarkable apology, foolishness and folly, that is, laughter, are directly described as "man's second nature" and are opposed to the monolith of the Christian cult and ideology.

It was precisely the one-sided character of official seriousness which led to the necessity of creating a vent for the second nature of man, for laughter. "The feast of fools" at least once a year became a vent for laughter; the material bodily principle linked with it then enjoyed complete freedom. Here we have an unambiguous recognition of the second festive life of medieval man.

Laughter at the feast of fools was not, of course, an abstract and purely negative mockery of the Christian ritual and the Church's hierarchy. The negative derisive element was deeply immersed in the triumphant theme of bodily regeneration and renewal. It was "man's second nature" that was laughing, the lower bodily stratum which could not express itself in official cult and ideology.

[22] Concerning the feast of fools see F. Bourquelot, *l'Office de la Fête des fous*, Sens, 1859; H. Villetard, *Office de Pierre de Corbeil*, Paris, 1907, and *Remarques sur la fête des fous, Paris, 1911.*

The curious apology quoted above belongs to the fifteenth century. But we find similar opinions expressed in earlier times. Rabanus Maurus, abbot of Fulda, an austere churchman of the ninth century, composed an abridged version of the *coena Cypriani*. He dedicated it to King Lothar II *ad jocunditatem*, that is, for amusement's sake. In his letter of dedication Maurus seeks to justify the gay and degrading tone of the *coena* by the following arguments: "Just as the Church contains good and bad men, so does this poem contain the latter's speeches." These "bad men" of the austere churchman correspond to men's "second foolish nature." Later Pope Leo XIII proposed a similar formula: "Since the church is composed of the divine and the human element, the latter must be disclosed with complete sincerity, as it is said in the Book of Job."

In the early Middle Ages folk laughter penetrated not only into the middle classes but even into the highest circles of the church. Rabanus Maurus was no exception. The attraction of folk humor was strong at all the levels of the young feudal hierarchy, both lay and ecclesiastical. This can be explained as follows:

1. The official ecclesiastical and feudal culture of the seventh, eighth, and ninth centuries was still weak and not completely formed.

2. Folk culture was strong and impossible to ignore; some of its elements had to be used for propaganda.

3. The tradition of the Roman Saturnalia and other forms of Roman legalized folk humor was still alive.

4. The Church adapted the time of Christian feasts to local pagan celebrations (in view of their christianization), and these celebrations were linked to cults of laughter.

5. The young feudal system was still relatively progressive and therefore of a relatively popular nature.

For these reasons a tradition of a relatively tolerant attitude toward folk humor could be formed during that early period. This tradition continued to live, although suffering more and more restrictions. In the following periods (up to the seventeenth century) it became customary to found the defense of laughter on the authority of former churchmen and theologians.

Authors and collectors of *facéties,* anecdotes, and jokes of the
seventeenth and eighteenth centuries usually quoted medieval
scholars and theologians. Thus Melander, who edited one of the
most complete anthologies of comic literature, *Jocorum et seri-
orum libri duo* (first edition in 1600, the last in 1643) presents his
work by listing several scores of names of eminent scholars and
theologians who had written *facéties* before him. The best collection of German *Schwänke* was made by the monk Johannes Pauli,
a famous preacher, under the title "Laughter and Seriousness"
(*Schimpf und Ernst*), and its first edition was published in 1522.
Describing the aim of this work in his preface, Pauli expressed an
opinion similar to that quoted earlier in the apology of the feast
of fools. He wrote that he had composed his book "in order that
the spiritual children cloistered in monasteries might have something to read to amuse their minds and for relaxation's sake: it is
not possible to always abide in a serious mood."

The purpose of such comments (and we could quote many
others) was to explain and somehow justify laughter near the precincts of the church and to justify the "sacred parody" (*parodia
sacra*), that is, the parody of sacred texts and rites. Neither was condemnation lacking. Conciliar judicial prohibitions of the feast of
fools were many times proclaimed. The oldest prohibition of the
Council of Toledo was issued in the first half of the seventh century. The last judicial prohibition of the feast of fools in France was
the decision of the Parliament of Dijon in 1552—more than nine
centuries after the first condemnation. During all these nine centuries the feast continued to be celebrated in semilegal conditions.
The latest French variant was a procession of a carnival type which
was organized in Rouen by the *Societas cornardorum.* (It was during one of these processions, in 1540, that the name of Rabelais was
recalled and during the banquet the "Chronicale of Gargantua"
was read instead of the gospel.)[23] Thus Rabelaisian laughter
seemed to return to the mother's womb, the tradition of the ancient ritual and spectacle.

[23] Two anthologies of this society's materials were published in the
sixteenth century.

The feast of fools is one of the most colorful and genuine expressions of medieval festive laughter near the precincts of the church. Another of its expressions is the "feast of the ass" commemorating Mary's flight to Egypt with the infant Jesus. The center of this feast is neither Mary nor Jesus, although a young girl with an infant takes part in it. The central protagonist is the ass and its braying. Special "asinine masses" were celebrated. An *officium* of this mass composed by the austere churchman Pierre Corbeille has been preserved. Each part of the mass was accompanied by the comic braying, "hinham!" At the end of the service, instead of the usual blessing, the priest repeated the braying three times, and the final Amen was replaced by the same cry. The ass is one of the most ancient and lasting symbols of the material bodily lower stratum, which at the same time degrades and regenerates. It is sufficient to recall Apuleius' "Golden Ass," the widespread ass-mimes of antiquity, and finally the image of the ass as the symbol of the bodily lower stratum in the legends of Francis of Assisi.[24] The "feast of the ass" is one of the oldest variants of this theme.

The "feast of fools" and the "feast of the ass" are specific celebrations in which laughter plays the leading role. In this sense they are similar to their close relatives: carnival and charivari. But in all the other Church feasts of the Middle Ages, as we pointed out in our introduction, laughter also played a more or less important part, ordering the popular, marketplace aspect of the religious occasion. As a material bodily principle laughter had a fixed relation to the feast; it was preeminently a festive laughter. Let us first of all recall the *risus paschalis*. During the Easter season laughter and jokes were permitted even in church. The priest could tell amusing stories and jokes from the pulpit. Following the days of lenten sadness he could incite his congregation's gay laughter as a joyous regeneration. This is why it was called "Easter

[24] The lasting character of the ass image and its specific meaning is shown in Russian literature: the "braying of an ass" in Switzerland awakened Prince Myshkin and reconciled him with a foreign land and with life (Dostoevsky: "The Idiot"). The ass and its braying is one of the leading images in Blok's poem: "The Night Garden."

laughter." The jokes and stories concerned especially material bodily life, and were of a carnival type. Permission to laugh was granted simultaneously with the permission to eat meat and to resume sexual intercourse (forbidden during Lent). The tradition of *risus paschalis* was still alive in the sixteenth century, at the time of Rabelais.[25]

Besides "Easter laughter" there was also "Christmas laughter." While paschal gaiety mostly featured amusing tales and anecdotes, Christmas laughter was expressed in gay songs. These songs of an extremely worldly content were heard in churches; some religious hymns were sung to worldly, even street tunes. For instance, a score of the *Magnificat* which has been preserved proves that this religious chant was sung to the tune of clownish street rigmaroles. This tradition was especially maintained in France. The spiritual content was combined with worldly tunes and with elements of material bodily degradation. The theme of birth of the new was organically linked with the theme of death of the old on a gay and degrading level, with the images of a clownish carnivalesque uncrowning. This is why the French *Noël* could later develop into one of the most popular genres of the revolutionary street song.

Laughter and the material bodily element, as a degrading and regenerating principle, played an essential role in other festivities held outside or near to the church, especially those which bore a local character. The latter absorbed elements of ancient pagan celebrations and represented a Christian substitute for them. Such were the rejoicings marking the consecration of a church (the first masses) and the feast of the patron saint. Local fairs were usually held at that time with their entire repertory of folk recreations, accompanied by unbridled gluttony and drunken orgies.[26] Eating

[25] See J. P. Schmidt: *De risu paschalis*, Rostock, 1847, and S. Reinach, *Le Rire rituel*, *op. cit.* ftn. 19, Vol. 4, pp. 127–129. Both Easter and Christmas laughter are linked with the tradition of the Roman popular Saturnalia.

[26] The interest lies not in the *mores* which patronized gluttony and drunkenness, but in the fact that they acquired a symbolic utopian meaning of a "feast for all the world," the triumph of material abundance, growth, and renewal.

and drinking were also the main features of the commemoration of the dead. When honoring patrons and benefactors buried in the church, the clergy organized banquets and drank to their memory the so-called *"poculum charitatis"* or *"charitas vini."* A record of the Kvedlinburg Abbey openly states that the clergy's banquet feeds and pleases the dead: *plenius inde recreantur mortui.* The Spanish Dominicans drank to the memory of their deceased patrons, toasting them with the typical ambivalent words *viva el muerto.*[27] In these examples the gaiety and laughter have the character of a banquet and are combined with the images of death and birth (renewal of life) in the complex unity of the material bodily lower stratum.

Certain feasts acquired a specific tinge depending on the season when they were celebrated. The autumn feasts of Saint Martin and of Saint Michael had a bacchanalian overtone and these saints were the patrons of winemaking. Sometimes the individual traits of the saint would serve the development of degrading rituals and spectacles. Thus on the feast of Saint Lazarus in Marseilles there were processions with horses, mules, asses, bulls, and cows. The people masqueraded and danced in the streets and squares performing the "great dance" (*magnum tripudum*). Probably this arose from the fact that Lazarus belonged to a cycle of legends of hell which had a material bodily topographical connotation, hell representing the lower stratum.[28] He was also linked with the theme of death and regeneration. This is why this feast could absorb some elements of ancient local pagan celebrations.

Laughter and the bodily principle were legalized in many other drinking parties, as well as in other private celebrations or public entertainments.

We shall return to the subject of carnival and Shrovetide laughter[29] in good time. But we must here stress once more the essential

[27] See Fr. W. Ebeling, *Flögel's Geschichte des Grotesk-Komischen,* 1st ed., Leipzig, 1862, p. 254.

[28] We shall further describe this cycle of legends. Let us recall that "hell" was an indispensable feature of carnival.

[29] Carnival, with its complex system of images was the fullest and purest expression of the culture of folk humor.

relation of festive laughter to time and to the change of seasons. The calendar aspect of the feast of kings was revived and experienced in its popular form of laughter outside of the church. Here appeared the relation to the change of seasons, to the phases of the sun and moon, to the death and renewal of vegetation, and to the succession of agricultural seasons. In this succession all that is new or renews, all that is about to draw nearer is emphasized as a positive element. And this element acquires a wider and deeper meaning: it expresses the people's hopes of a happier future, of a more just social and economic order, of a new truth. The gay aspect of the feast presented this happier future of a general material affluence, equality, and freedom, just as the Roman Saturnalia announced the return of the Golden Age. Thus, the medieval feast had, as it were, the two faces of Janus. Its official, ecclesiastical face was turned to the past and sanctioned the existing order, but the face of the people of the marketplace looked into the future and laughed, attending the funeral of the past and present. The marketplace feast opposed the protective, timeless stability, the unchanging established order and ideology, and stressed the element of change and renewal.

The material bodily lower stratum and the entire system of degradation, turnovers, and travesties presented this essential relation to time and to social and historical transformation. One of the indispensable elements of the folk festival was travesty, that is, the renewal of clothes and of the social image. Another essential element was a reversal of the hierarchic levels: the jester was proclaimed king, a clownish abbot, bishop, or archbishop was elected at the "feast of fools," and in the churches directly under the pope's jurisdiction a mock pontiff was even chosen. The members of this hierarchy of fools sang solemn mass. At many of these feasts kings and queens were elected for a day, as on Epiphany and on St. Valentine's day. The custom of electing such ephemeral kings and queens (rois pour rire) was especially widespread in France, where nearly every popular banquet was presided over by them. From the wearing of clothes turned inside out and trousers slipped over the head to the election of mock kings and popes the same topographical logic is put to work: shifting from top to bottom, casting the high and the old, the finished and completed into the material bodily lower stratum for death and rebirth. These changes were placed into an essential relation with time and with social and historical change. The element of relativity and of becoming was emphasized, in opposition to the immovable and extratemporal stability of the medieval hierarchy.

Indeed, the ritual of the feast tended to project the play of time itself, which kills and gives birth at the same time, recasting the old into the new, allowing nothing to perpetuate itself. Time plays and laughs! It is the playing boy of Heraclitus who possesses the supreme power in the universe ("domination belongs to the child"). The accent is placed on the future; utopian traits are always present in the rituals and images of the people's festive gaiety. Thus were developed the rudiments that were to flower later in the sense of history as conceived by the Renaissance.

Summing up, we can say that laughter, which had been eliminated in the Middle Ages from official cult and ideology, made its unofficial but almost legal nest under the shelter of almost every feast. Therefore, every feast in addition to its official, ecclesiastical part had yet another folk carnival part whose organizing principles were laughter and the material bodily lower stratum. This part of the feast had its own pattern, its own theme and imagery, its own ritual. The origin of the various elements of this theme is varied. Doubtless, the Roman Saturnalia continued to live during the entire Middle Ages. The tradition of the antique mime also remained alive. But the main source was local folklore. It was this folklore which inspired both the imagery and the ritual of the popular, humorous part of the feast.

Lower- and middle-class clerics, schoolmen, students, and members of corporations were the main participants in these folk merriments. People of various other unorganized elements which belonged to none of these social groups and which were numerous at that time also participated in the celebrations. But the medieval culture of folk humor actually belonged to all the people. The truth of laughter embraced and carried away everyone; nobody could resist it.

The enormous bulk of medieval parodical literature is also linked directly or indirectly to the forms of festive folk humor. It is possible, as certain scholars assert (for instance, Novati), that various parodies of the scriptures and of religious rites were directly intended for the celebration of the feast of fools and were closely related to them. But this cannot be said about most of these sacred parodies. What is important is not the direct relation but the more general link of medieval parodies with legalized festive humor and freedom. All medieval parodical literature is recreative; it was composed for festive leisure and was to be read on feast days. It is, therefore, filled with the atmosphere of freedom and license. These gay parodies of the sacred were permitted on feast days, as was the *risus paschalis,* meat, and sexual intercourse. The parodies were filled with the same popular sense of the changing time and of renewal on the material bodily level. Here, too, is the prevailing logic of the ambivalent lower stratum.

School and university recreation had great importance in the history of medieval parody. These recreations usually coincided with feast days. All feast day privileges granted by tradition to laughter and jokes were fully accorded to recreation. Not only could the students relax from the official ideological system, from scholarly wisdom and academic rules, but they were allowed to transform these disciplines into gay, degrading games, and jokes. They were first of all freed from the heavy chains of devout seriousness, from the "continual ferment of piety and the fear of God." They were freed from the oppression of such gloomy categories as "eternal," "immovable," "absolute," "unchangeable" and instead were exposed to the gay and free laughing aspect of the world, with its unfinished and open character, with the joy of change and renewal. This is why the medieval parodies were not formal literary and negative satires of sacred texts or of scholarly wisdom; they merely transposed these elements into the key of gay laughter, into the positive material bodily sphere. Everything they touched was transformed into flesh and matter and at the same time was given a lighter tone.

We shall not discuss at length the basic elements of medieval parodies, some of which will be described later. We shall merely define the place of sacred parody within the culture of medieval folk humor as a whole.[30]

Medieval parody, especially before the twelfth century, was not concerned with the negative, the imperfections of specific cults, ecclesiastic orders, or scholars which could be the object of derision and destruction. For the medieval parodist everything without exception was comic. Laughter was as universal as seriousness; it was directed at the whole world, at history, at all societies, at ideology. It was the world's second truth extended to everything and from which nothing is taken away. It was, as it were, the festive aspect of the whole world in all its elements, the second revelation of the world in play and laughter.

This is why medieval parody played a completely unbridled game with all that is most sacred and important from the point of view of official ideology. The oldest grotesque parody, "Cyprian's supper" (composed in about the fifth or sixth century) transformed all sacred history from Adam to Christ into a fantastic clownish banquet using in grotesque fashion its most important events and symbols.[31]

[30] Other than separate sections in works devoted to the general history of medieval literature (for example, Ebert, Curtius) there are three special works describing sacred parody: (1) F. Novati, *La parodia sacra nelle letterature moderne*, (see Novati's, *Studi critici e letterari*, Turin, 1889. (2) Eero Ilvonen, *Parodies de thèmes pieux dans la poésie française du moyen age*, Helsingfors, 1914. (3) Paul Lehmann, *Die Parodie im Mittelalter*, Munich, 1922. The three works complement each other. Novati embraces the widest field of sacred parody (his work is not outdated and remains basic). Ilvonen offers a series of critical texts of French parody only (the combination of French and Latin languages, a frequent feature of parodical literature). The texts are preceded by a general introduction concerning medieval parody and contain the author's own commentaries. Lehmann gives an excellent introduction to the literature of sacred parody but limits himself exclusively to the Latin. All three authors conceive medieval parody as something isolated and specific; they do not, therefore, disclose the organic link of this parody with the larger world of the culture of folk humor.

[31] See the analysis of Cyprian's supper in Novati, *op. cit.* ftn. 30, p.

Another ancient work of recreational character, *Joca monaco-rum,* was more restrained. It dates from the sixth to seventh centuries and is of Byzantine origin; it was very popular in France from the seventh century on. In Russia, it had its own history, which was studied by A. N. Veselovsky and I. N. Zhdanov). It was a frivolous catechism with a number of comic questions on Biblical themes—an amusing game but more restrained than the "supper."

During the following centuries, especially in the eleventh, parody drew into its game all the themes of the official teaching and cult of the Church and, in general, all the forms of the serious attitude toward the world. Many parodies of the most important prayers—"Our Father," "Hail Mary," the creed—have been preserved, as well as parodical hymns, for instance, the *Laetebundus* and the litanies. Neither did the parodists hesitate to approach the liturgy. We have the "Liturgy of the Drunkards," the "Liturgy of the Gamblers," and the "Money Liturgy." There are parodies of the gospels: "The Money Gospel of the Mark of Silver," "The Money Gospel of the Paris Student," "The Gambler's Gospel," and "The Drunkard's Gospel." There were parodies of monastic rule, of ecclesiastical decrees and the constitutions of the Councils, of papal bulls and encyclicals, as well as of sermons. As early as the seventh and eighth centuries we find parodies of wills (for instance "The Pig's Will," The Will of the Ass") and of epitaphs.[32] We have already mentioned the parody of the grammar, which was very

---

266, and further in Lehmann, *op. cit.* ftn. 30, pp. 25 ff. The critical edition of the text of the "Supper" can be found in *Monumenta Germaniae storica: Poetae latini* IV, Ed. G.H. Pertz, p. 856.

[32] There is a great number of these parodies; besides the use of various elements of cult and *ordo* there is a wide range of comic animal epics. For instance, the *Speculum stultorum* by Nigel Wireker. This is the story of the ass Brunellus, who goes to Salerno in order to get rid of his meager tail, studies theology and law in Paris, then becomes a monk and founds his own order. On his way to Rome he falls into the hands of his master. Many parodies of epitaphs, medical prescriptions, blessings, prayers, and monastic rules are scattered through this work.

popular in the Middle Ages. Finally, there were parodies of legal texts and laws.

Besides parodical literature in the strict sense of the word, the jargon of clerics, monks, schoolmen, judges, as well as popular speech were filled with travesties of religious texts, prayers, proverbs, and sayings of common wisdom—all studded with the names of saints and martyrs. Not a single saying of the Old and New Testaments was left unchallenged as long as it could provide some hint of equivocal suggestion that could be travestied and transposed into the language of the material bodily lower stratum.

In Rabelais Friar John is the incarnation of the mighty realm of travesty of the low clergy. He is a connoisseur of "all that concerns the breviary" (*en matière de brevière*); this means that he can reinterpret any sacred text in the sense of eating, drinking, and eroticism, and transpose it from the Lenten to the carnival "obscene" level. Generally speaking, we can find in Rabelais' novel a sufficiently abundant material of travestied sacred texts and sayings which are scattered throughout his work. For instance, Christ's last words on the cross, *sitio* ("I thirst") and *consummatum est* (it is consummated) are travestied into terms of eating and overindulgence.[33] *Venite, apotemus* (come and have a drink) replaced *venite adoremus*. In another part of the novel Friar John utters a Latin sentence characteristic of medieval grotesque: *Ad formam nasi cognoscitur ad te levavi,* "by the shape of my nose you will know (how) I lift up." The first part of this sentence is related to the supposition prevalent in those days even among physicians that the size of the phallus could be surmised by the size of the nose. The second part of the sentence, "I will lift up," is the beginning of Psalm 121; thus a sacred text receives an indecent interpretation. The debasing transposition is strengthened by the last

[33] For the 1524 edition Rabelais made certain expurgations from his novel from considerations of prudence: he eliminated all allusions to the Sorbonne (the theology school of the University of Paris) but he did not even think of eliminating the *sitio* and similar travesties of sacred texts, so secure were the rights of carnival and the freedom of laughter.

syllable of the quotation *vi,* which in French has a connotation related to the phallus.

In both antique and medieval grotesque the nose had usually this link with the phallus. In France there existed an entire mock litany composed of texts from sacred scriptures and prayers beginning with the Latin negation *ne,* as *ne advertas* (do not avert), *ne revoces* (do not call upon), which was known as *"noms de tous les nez."* All these are characteristic examples of how even distant analogies and connotations were sought in order to travesty the serious and make it ring with laughter. In everything, in meaning and image, in the sound of sacred words, parody discovered the Achilles' heel that was open to derision, some trait which permitted linkage to the bodily lower stratum. The unofficial legend of many saints was constructed on the name alone: for instance, St. Vitus' name was connected with the lower stratum (the phallus), and the current expression "to honor St. Mamik" meant to visit a mistress.

It can be said that all the nonofficial speech of medieval clerics (and of all the medieval intelligentsia) as well as the speech of simple folk was deeply infused with images of the lower stratum —with obscenities and curses, profanities and swearing, with travestied sacred texts turned inside out; everything that was absorbed by that speech was to submit to the degrading and renewing power of the mighty lower stratum. And such did familiar speech remain at the time of Rabelais. Friar John's and Panurge's talk is typical.[84]

Laughter's universal character is obvious in the parodies de-

[84] In the sixteenth century Protestant circles deplored the joking and degrading use of sacred text in familiar verbal intercourse. Henri Estienne, Rabelais' contemporary, complained in his "Apology of Herodotus" of the continual profaning use of sacred words during drinking bouts. He quoted many examples of this usage; thus while a goblet of wine was turned upside down, the words of the penitential psalm: "Create a clean heart in me, O God, and renew a right spirit within my bowels" was usually recited. Even the sick afflicted with venereal disease used sacred texts to describe their ailment and their sweat (see H. Estienne, *Apologie pour Hérodote,* 1, 16, 1566.

scribed above. Medieval laughter is directed at the same object as medieval seriousness. Not only does laughter make no exception for the upper stratum, but indeed it is usually directed toward it. Furthermore, it is directed not at one part only, but at the whole. One might say that it builds its own world versus the official world, its own church versus the official church, its own state versus the official state. Laughter celebrates its masses, professes its faith, celebrates marriages and funerals, writes its epitaphs, elects kings and bishops. Even the smallest medieval parody is always built as part of a whole comic world.

This universal character of laughter was most clearly and consistently brought out in the carnival rituals and spectacles and in the parodies they presented. But universality appears as well in all the other forms of medieval culture of humor: in the comic elements of church dramas, in the comic *dits* (fairy tales) and *débats* (debates), in animal epics, *fabliaux* and *Schwänke*.[35] The main traits of laughter and of the lower stratum remain identical in all these genres.

It can be said that medieval culture of humor which accompanied the feasts was a "satyric" drama, a fourth drama, after the "tragic trilogy" of official Christian cult and theology to which it corresponded but was at the same time in opposition. Like the antique "satyric" drama, so also the medieval culture of laughter was the drama of bodily life (copulation, birth, growth, eating, drinking, defecation). But of course it was not the drama of an individual body or of a private material way of life; it was the drama of the great generic body of the people, and for this generic body birth and death are not an absolute beginning and end but merely elements of continuous growth and renewal. The great body of satyric drama cannot be separated from the world; it is perfused with cosmic elements and with the earth which swallows up and gives birth.

Next to the universality of medieval laughter we must stress

[35] True, such manifestations already express at times the specific limitations of early bourgeois culture; in those cases the material bodily principle becomes petty and degenerate to a certain extent.

another striking peculiarity: its indissoluble and essential relation to freedom. We have seen that this laughter was absolutely unofficial but nevertheless legalized. The rights of the fool's cap were as inviolable as those of the *pileus* (the clown's headgear of the Roman Saturnalias).

This freedom of laughter was, of course, relative; its sphere was at times wider and at times narrower, but it was never entirely suspended. As we have seen, free laughter was related to feasts and was to a certain extent limited by the time allotted to feast days. It coincided with the permission for meat, fat, and sexual intercourse. This festive liberation of laughter and body was in sharp contrast with the stringencies of Lent which had preceded or were to follow.

The feast was a temporary suspension of the entire official system with all its prohibitions and hierarchic barriers. For a short time life came out of its usual, legalized and consecrated furrows and entered the sphere of utopian freedom. The very brevity of this freedom increased its fantastic nature and utopian radicalism, born in the festive atmosphere of images.

The atmosphere of ephemeral freedom reigned in the public square as well as at the intimate feast in the home. The antique tradition of free, often improper, but at the same time philosophical table talk had been revived at the time of the Renaissance; it converged with the local tradition of festive meals which had common roots in folklore.[36] This tradition of table talk was continued

[36] Up to the second part of the sixteenth century, the literature of free talk (with prevailing material bodily themes) was characteristic. The following were table, recreational, or promenading talks: Noël du Fail, "Rustic and Facetious Talks" (*Propos rustiques et facétieux*), 1547, and Entrapel's "Tales and New Discourses" (*Contes et nouveaux discours d'Entrapel*), 1585; Jacques Tahureau, *Dialogues*, 1562; Nicolas de Chaulières, "Morning Talks" (Matinées), 1585, and "Postprandial Talks" (Les Après-diners); Guillaume Boucher, "After Supper Talks" (Soirées), 1584–1597. "How To Succeed in Life" by Béroalde de Verville, already mentioned, also belongs to this category. All these works represent the special type of carnivalized dialogue and reflect to a greater or lesser extent Rabelais' influence.

during the following centuries. We find similar traditions of bacchic prandial songs which combine universalism (problems of life and death) with the material bodily element (wine, food, carnal love), with awareness of the time element (youth, old age, the ephemeral nature of life, the changes of fortune); they express a peculiar utopian strain, the brotherhood of fellow-drinkers and of all men, the triumph of affluence, and the victory of reason.

The comic rituals of the feast of fools, the feast of the ass, and the various comic processions and ceremonies of other feasts enjoyed a certain legality. The diableries were legalized and the devils were allowed to run about freely in the streets and in the suburbs a few days before the show and to create a demonic and unbridled atmosphere. Entertainments in the marketplace were also legalized as well as carnival. Of course, this legalization was forced, incomplete, led to struggles and new prohibitions. During the entire medieval period the Church and state were obliged to make concessions, large or small, to satisfy the marketplace. Throughout the year there were small scattered islands of time, strictly limited by the dates of feasts, when the world was permitted to emerge from the official routine but exclusively under the camouflage of laughter. Barriers were raised, provided there was nothing but laughter.

Besides universalism and freedom, the third important trait of laughter was its relation to the people's unofficial truth.

The serious aspects of class culture are official and authoritarian; they are combined with violence, prohibitions, limitations and always contain an element of fear and of intimidation. These elements prevailed in the Middle Ages. Laughter, on the contrary, overcomes fear, for it knows no inhibitions, no limitations. Its idiom is never used by violence and authority.

It was the victory of laughter over fear that most impressed medieval man. It was not only a victory over mystic terror of God, but also a victory over the awe inspired by the forces of nature, and most of all over the oppression and guilt related to all that was consecrated and forbidden ("mana" and "taboo"). It was the defeat of divine and human power, of authoritarian commandments and prohibitions, of death and punishment after death, hell and all that is more terrifying than the earth itself. Through this victory laughter clarified man's consciousness and gave him a new outlook on life. This truth was ephemeral; it was followed by the fears and oppressions of everyday life, but from these brief moments another unofficial truth emerged, truth about the world and man which prepared the new Renaissance consciousness.

The acute awareness of victory over fear is an essential element of medieval laughter. This feeling is expressed in a number of characteristic medieval comic images. We always find in them the defeat of fear presented in a droll and monstrous form, the symbols of power and violence turned inside out, the comic images of death and bodies gaily rent asunder. All that was terrifying becomes grotesque. We have already mentioned that one of the indispensable accessories of carnival was the set called "hell." This "hell" was solemnly burned at the peak of the festivities. This grotesque image cannot be understood without appreciating the defeat of fear. The people play with terror and laugh at it; the awesome becomes a "comic monster."

Neither can this grotesque image be understood if oversimplified and interpreted in the spirit of abstract rationalism. It is impossible to determine where the defeat of fear will end and where joyous recreation will begin. Carnival's hell represents the earth which swallows up and gives birth, it is often transformed into a cornucopia; the monster, death, becomes pregnant. Various deformities, such as protruding bellies, enormous noses, or humps, are symptoms of pregnancy or of procreative power. Victory over fear is not its abstract elimination; it is a simultaneous uncrowning and renewal, a gay transformation. Hell has burst and has poured forth abundance.

We have said that medieval laughter defeated something which was more terrifying than the earth itself. All unearthly objects were transformed into earth, the mother which swallows up in order to give birth to something larger that has been improved. There can be nothing terrifying on earth, just as there can be nothing frightening in a mother's body, with the nipples that are made to suckle, with the genital organ and the warm blood. The earthly element of terror is the womb, the bodily grave, but it flowers with delight and a new life.

However, medieval laughter is not a subjective, individual and biological consciousness of the uninterrupted flow of time. It is the social consciousness of all the people. Man experiences this flow of time in the festive marketplace, in the carnival crowd, as he comes into contact with other bodies of varying age and social caste. He is aware of being a member of a continually growing and renewed people. This is why festive folk laughter presents an element of victory not only over supernatural awe, over the sacred, over death; it also means the defeat of power, of earthly kings, of the earthly upper classes, of all that oppresses and restricts.[37]

Medieval laughter, when it triumphed over the fear inspired by the mystery of the world and by power, boldly unveiled the truth about both. It resisted praise, flattery, hypocrisy. This laughing

[37] Profound thoughts concerning the functions of laughter in the history of culture were expressed by Herzen (though he was not acquainted with the laughing Middle Ages): "laughter contains something revolutionary . . . Voltaire's laughter was more destructive than Rousseau's weeping." (Works in nine volumes, Goslitizdat, Moscow, 1956. Vol. 3, p. 92.) And elsewhere: "Laughter is no matter for joking, and we shall not give up our right to it. In the antique world, the public roared with laughter on Olympus and upon earth while listening to Aristophanes and his comedies, and roared with laughter up to Lucian. Humanity ceased to laugh from the fourth century on; it did nothing but weep, and heavy chains fell on the mind amidst moans and pangs of remorse. As soon as the fever of fanaticism subsided, men began to laugh once more. It would be extremely interesting to write the history of laughter. In church, in the palace, on parade, facing the department head, the police officer, the German administrator, nobody laughs. The serfs are deprived of the right to smile in the presence of the landowners. *Only equals may laugh.* If inferiors are permitted to laugh in front of their superiors, and if they cannot suppress their hilarity, this would mean farewell to respect. To make men smile at the god Apis is to deprive him of his sacred rank and to transform him into a common bull." (A. I. Herzen, *On Art,* published by "Art," Goslitizdat, Moscow, 1954, p. 223.)

truth, expressed in curses and abusive words, degraded power. The medieval clown was also the herald of this truth.

In his article devoted to Rabelais, Veselovsky characterized as follows the clown's social meaning:

In the Middle Ages, the clown is the lawless herald of the objectively abstract truth. At a time when all life was built within the conventional frameworks of caste, prerogative, scholastic science and hierarchy, truth was localized according to these frameworks; it was relatively feudal, scholastic, etc., drawing its strength from its given milieu; thus truth was a mere result of the rights it could practically exercise. Feudal truth was the right to oppress the slave, to despise his work, to go to war, to hunt in the peasants' fields. . . . Scholastic truth was the right to possess exclusive knowledge outside of which nothing made sense; therefore knowledge had to be defended against everything that could obscure it. . . . All general human truth, not adapted to the caste, to an established profession, i.e., to determined rights, was excluded. It was not taken into consideration, it was despised, dragged to the stake on the slightest suspicion. It was only tolerated in a harmless form, arousing laughter, without any pretense at any serious role. Thus was the clown's social meaning determined.[38]

Veselovsky gives a correct definition of feudal truth. He is also right to assert that the clown was the herald of another, nonfeudal, nonofficial truth. But this nonofficial truth can hardly be determined as "objectively abstract." Furthermore, Veselovsky sees the clown as isolated from all the mighty culture of medieval humor. He, therefore, considers laughter an external defensive form of this "objective abstract truth," a defense of human value in general, which the clown proclaimed using this external form. If there had been no repressions, no stake, truth would have cast off the clown's attire; it could have spoken in serious tones. Such an interpretation of medieval laughter appears incorrect in our mind.

No doubt laughter was in part an external defensive form of truth. It was legalized, it enjoyed privileges, it liberated, to a cer-

[38] See A. N. Veselovsky. "Collected Articles," Goslitizdat, Leningrad, 1939, pp. 441–442.

tain extent, from censorship, oppression, and from the stake. This element should not be underestimated. But it would be inadmissible to reduce the entire meaning of laughter to this aspect alone. Laughter is essentially not an external but an interior form of truth; it cannot be transformed into seriousness without destroying and distorting the very contents of the truth which it unveils. Laughter liberates not only from external censorship but first of all from the great interior censor; it liberates from the fear that developed in man during thousands of years: fear of the sacred, of prohibitions, of the past, of power. It unveils the material bodily principle in its true meaning. Laughter opened men's eyes on that which is new, on the future. This is why it not only permitted the expression of an antifeudal, popular truth; it helped to uncover this truth and to give it an internal form. And this form was achieved and defended during thousands of years in its very depths and in its popular-festive images. Laughter showed the world anew in its gayest and most sober aspects. Its external privileges are intimately linked with interior forces; they are a recognition of the rights of those forces. This is why laughter could never become an instrument to oppress and blind the people. It always remained a free weapon in their hands.

As opposed to laughter, medieval seriousness was infused with elements of fear, weakness, humility, submission, falsehood, hypocrisy, or on the other hand with violence, intimidation, threats, prohibitions. As a spokesman of power, seriousness terrorized, demanded, and forbade. It therefore inspired the people with distrust. Seriousness had an official tone and was treated like all that is official. It oppressed, frightened, bound, lied, and wore the mask of hypocrisy. Seriousness was avaricious, committed to fasts. When its mask was dropped in the festive square and at the banquet table, another truth was heard in the form of laughter, foolishness, improprieties, curses, parodies, and travesties. All fears and lies were dispersed in the face of the material bodily festive principle.

It would be wrong, however, to presume that medieval seriousness did not impress the people. As long as there was room for fear, medieval man was as yet too weak before the forces of nature and society to resist it. The seriousness of fear and suffering in their religious, social, political, and ideological forms could not but be impressive. The consciousness of freedom, on the other hand, could be only limited and utopian. It would therefore be a mistake to presume that popular distrust of seriousness and popular love of laughter, as of another truth, could always reach full awareness, expressing a critical and clearly defined opposition. We know that men who composed the most unbridled parodies of sacred texts and of cults often sincerely accepted and served religion. We have evidence that some of these men ascribed a didactic and educational quality to these parodies. For instance, a monk of St. Gallen's monastery declared that the many parodies featuring drunkards and gamblers were composed to inspire disgust of drinking and gambling; these parodies, he said, brought many students to repentance.[39] In medieval man's soul attendance at official mass could coexist with a gay parody of truth in which a world is "turned inside out." The joyous truth, based on confidence in the material-spiritual forces proclaimed by the Renaissance, was elementally asserted in the Middle Ages through the images of laughter; however, the consciousness of each individual could not free itself from fear and weakness. Freedom granted by laughter often enough was mere festive luxury.

Thus, distrust of the serious tone and confidence in the truth of laughter had a spontaneous, elemental character. It was understood that fear never lurks behind laughter (which does not build stakes) and that hypocrisy and lies never laugh but wear a serious mask. Laughter created no dogmas and could not become authoritarian; it did not convey fear but a feeling of strength. It was linked with the procreating act, with birth, renewal, fertility, abundance. Laughter was also related to food and drink and the people's earthly immortality, and finally it was related to the future of things to come and was to clear the way for them. Seriousness was therefore elementally distrusted, while trust was placed in festive laughter.

[39] This opinion reflects the moralizing tendency expressed later by grobianism, and at the same time the desire to render parody harmless.

The men of the Middle Ages participated in two lives: the official and the carnival life. Two aspects of the world, the serious and the laughing aspect, coexisted in their consciousness. This coexistence was strikingly reflected in thirteenth- and fourteenth-century illuminated manuscripts, for instance, in the legendaries, that is, the handwritten collections of the lives of the saints. Here we find on the same page strictly pious illustrations of the hagiographical text as well as free designs not connected with the story. The free designs represent chimeras (fantastic forms combining human, animal, and vegetable elements), comic devils, jugglers performing acrobatic tricks, masquerade figures, and parodical scenes—that is, purely grotesque, carnivalesque themes. All these pictures are shown on the same page, which like medieval man's consciousness contains both aspects of life and the world.[40] Not only miniatures but the decorations of medieval churches, as well as religious sculpture, present a similar coexistence of the pious and the grotesque. Most characteristic is the role of the chimera, this quintessence of the grotesque, which invades every sphere of painting. However, in medieval art a strict dividing line is drawn between the pious and the grotesque; they exist side by side but never merge.

And so medieval culture of folk humor was fundamentally limited to these small islands of feasts and recreations. Official serious culture existed beside them but strictly divided from the marketplace. The shoots of a new world outlook were sprouting, but they could not grow and flower as long as they were enclosed in the popular gaiety of recreation and banqueting or in the fluid realm of familiar speech. In order to achieve this growth and flowering, laughter had to enter the world of great literature.

[40] See an extremely interesting book: *An Unknown Monument of Book-Art*, Goslitizdat, Moscow and Leningrad, 1963. This is an attempt to reconstruct a French collection of legends of the thirteenth century. The book is edited by V. S. Liublinsky, and offers a striking illustration of the coexistence of the serious and laughing worlds. (See V. S. Liublinsky's excellent analysis on pp. 63–73).

By the end of the Middle Ages a gradual disappearance of the dividing line between humor and great literature can be observed. The lower genres begin to penetrate the higher levels of literature. Popular laughter appears in epics, and its intrinsic value is increased in mysteries. Various genres, such as moralities, *soties,* farces, are developed. Buffoon societies, such as the "Kingdom of Basoche" and "Carefree Lads"[41] are founded in the fourteenth and fifteenth centuries. The culture of laughter begins to break through the narrow walls of festivities and to enter into all spheres of ideological life. Official seriousness and fear could be abandoned even in everyday life.

This process was completed during the Renaissance. Medieval laughter found its highest expression in Rabelais' novel. It became the form of a new free and critical historical consciousness. And this supreme form of laughter had been prepared in the Middle Ages.

As to antique tradition, it played a considerable part only in the growing awareness and theoretical clarification of the medieval heritage. We have seen that the Renaissance was based on antique sources. However, in the French Renaissance of the sixteenth century the leading role did not belong to the "classical" tradition of antiquity, such as epics and tragedy, nor to the strict genre of lyrics, that is, to the tradition which determined the classicism of the seventeenth century. The Renaissance in France was dominated by Lucian, Athenaeus, Helius, Plutarch, Macrobius, and other erudites, rhetors, and satirists of the later period of antiq-

---

[41] The "Kingdom of Basoche" was a society for the production of morality plays. It was composed of the secretaries of parliamentary attorneys. The first privilege was bestowed on the society in the days of Philippe le Bel. Later the *basochiens* organized a special game, the "parades" which widely used the privileges of libertinism and impropriety. The *basochiens* composed also parodies of sacred texts and *sermons joyeux,* comic sermons. The "Kingdom of Basoche" was often the object of prohibitions and repressions. In 1547 this society was finally suspended. The society of *Enfants sans soucis* produced the *soties.* The head of this society was called *prince des sots.*

uity.[42] Using Reich's terminology, the sixteenth century presented in the first place the "mimic" tradition of antiquity, the antique "biological" and "ethological" image, the dialogue, the symposium, the brief scene, the anecdote and proverb. But all these elements are related to the medieval tradition of laughter and are in tune with it.[43] This is a carnivalized antiquity.

Renaissance philosophy, based on antique sources, was not completely adequate to the true practice of laughter of that period. This philosophy did not reflect that which was essential, the historical orientation of this laughter.

Literary as well as other documents of that period prove a clear and carefully defined awareness of a great turning point, of a radical change of historical epochs. This awareness was particularly strong in France in the twenties and the early thirties of the sixteenth century and was more than once expressed in thoughtful statements. The men of that time bade farewell to the "darkness of the Gothic age" and welcomed the rising sun of the new epoch. It is sufficient to recall Rabelais' letter of dedication to André Tiraqueau and Gargantua's famous letter to Pantagruel.

[42] The authors of comedy, Aristophanes, Plautus, Terence, did not exercise any considerable influence. It has become commonplace to compare Rabelais to Aristophanes, but their resemblance cannot be explained by Aristophanes' influence on Rabelais. Although Rabelais was familiar with Aristophanes (among the eleven books preserved in his *ex libris* is a volume of Aristophanes in Latin translation), there are but few traces of his influence in Rabelais' novel. A certain similarity in the methods of treating the comic element can be explained by the resemblance of folkloric and carnival sources but should not be exaggerated. Euripedes' only satirical drama which has been preserved, "Cyclops," was well known by Rabelais: he quotes it twice in his novel.

[43] The nature of Rabelais' own erudition and that of the men of his time, their tastes and preferences in the choice of antique sources, have been well analyzed by J. Plattard in *L'Invention et la composition dans l'Oeuvre de Rabelais, Sources, invention et composition*, 1910. P. Villey's work on Montaigne's sources, *Sources et evolution des Essais de Montaigne*, Paris, 1910, can be a useful complement to Plattard. Already the Pléiade was introducing certain changes in the choice of the antique heritage in preparation for the seventeenth century with its definite and clear stand in favor of "classic antiquity."

The medieval culture of humor had long prepared the forms which could express this historic awareness. These forms were precisely related to time, to the future. They uncrowned and renewed the established power and official truth. They celebrated the return of happier times, abundance, and justice for all the people. Thus had the new awareness been initiated and had found its most radical expression in laughter.

B. A. Krzhevsky most excellently described this development in his article on Cervantes:

> The deafening peals of laughter which progressive Europe burst into while pushing century-old feudalism into the grave was a gay and obvious proof of her sensing a change of atmosphere. These peals of laughter with "historic" overtones shook not only Italy, Germany, or France (I have especially Rabelais' *Gargantua* and *Pantagruel* in mind), but found a mighty echo beyond the Pyrenees.[44]

All popular-festive images were made to serve this new historical awareness, from common masquerades and mystifications (whose role in Renaissance literature is immense, especially in Cervantes) to more complex carnival forms. This was a mobilization of all the century-old celebrations: the gay farewell to winter, to Lent, to the old year, to death; and the gay welcome to spring, to Shrovetide, to the slaughtering of cattle, to weddings, and to the new year. In a word, it was the mustering of all the long-matured images of change and renewal, of growth and abundance.

These images saturated with time and the utopian future, reflecting the people's hopes and strivings, now became the expression of the general gay funeral of a dying era, of the old power and old truth.

Humor prevailed not only in belles lettres. In order to gain popularity, to become accessible to all and to win their confidence, Protestant leaders began to use these comic forms in their satire and even in their theoretical works. The use of the French vernac-

[44] "Early bourgeois realism" (*Ranniy burshuazny realism*) edited by N. Y. Berkovsky. Leningrad, 1936, p. 162.

ular also played an important part. Henri Estienne published his Protestant satirical pamphlet, "The Apology of Herodotus" (*L'Apologie pour Hérodote*, 1566) and was thereafter called the "Pantagruel of Geneva." Calvin said of him that "he turned religion into Rabelaisian style" (*tournoita la Rabelaiserie*). Estienne's satire is truly written in Rabelaisian form and is filled with popular humor. In 1544 the famous Protestant leader Pierre Viret offered an interesting and typical defense of the comic element in theological writings:

> If it seems to them [to serious theologians] that such themes can only be treated with the greatest seriousness and modesty, I do not deny that the word of God demands a respectful approach. But it should also be understood that the word of God is not so harsh and austere as to prevent its importance and majesty from being combined with elements of irony, farce, proper playfulness, sharp sallies and jokes.

A similar opinion is expressed by the unknown author of the "Christian Satires on the Papal Kitchen" (*Satires chrestiennes de la Cuisine Papale*, 1560) in his address to his reader:

> I recall Horace's lines: "What prevents him who says the truth from laughing?" And indeed, truth must be taught according to various methods, so that it may be grasped not only with the help of demonstration of strong authority, but also when it is adorned with some gay stories (*quelques facéties*).

At that time the people could be approached only if armed with the nonofficial instrument of laughter; for men, as we have seen, were suspicious of seriousness and were accustomed to relate sincere and free truth to laughter.

Even the first French translation of the Bible, done by Olivétan, reflects the influence of Rabelais' language and style. Olivétan's library contained Rabelais' work. In his research on Calvin, Doumergue gives a good analysis of Olivétan's translation: "The Bible of 1535 reveals that naïve popular humor which made Olivétan one of the founders of the French language, placing him between Rabelais and Calvin; nearer in style to Rabelais, to Calvin in thought."[45]

The sixteenth century represents the summit in the history of laughter and the high point of this summit is Rabelais' novel. After this work a rather sharp descent starts with the Pléiade. We have already described the fate of laughter in the eighteenth century: it loses its essential link with a universal outlook, it is combined with negation, and with a negation that is dogmatic. Limited to the area of the private, eighteenth-century humor is deprived of its historical color; true, its relation to the material bodily principle is preserved, but this very principle acquires the nature of a trivial private way of life.

How did this process of laughter's degradation start?

The seventeenth century was marked by the stabilization of the new order of the absolute monarchy. A relatively progressive "universally historic form" was created and was expressed in Descartes' rationalist philosophy and in the aesthetics of classicism. Rationalism and classicism clearly reflect the fundamental traits of the new official culture; it differed from the ecclesiastic feudal culture but was also authoritarian and serious, though less dogmatic. New prevailing concepts were established which, according to Marx, the new ruling class inevitably presented as eternal truths.[46]

In the new official culture there prevails a tendency toward the stability and completion of being, toward one single meaning, one single tone of seriousness. The ambivalence of the grotesque can no longer be admitted. The exalted genres of classicism are freed from the influence of the grotesque tradition of laughter.

However, the tradition of the grotesque is not entirely extinct; it continues to live and to struggle for its existence in the lower canonical genres (comedy, satire, fable) and especially in non-

[45] Doumergue, Jean, *Calvin*. Lausanne (Bridel) 7 vols., 1899–1927. Vol. 1, p. 121.

[46] See K. Marx and F. Engels, "Works," Vol. 3, pp. 45–48.

canonical genres (in the novel, in a special form of popular dialogue, in burlesque). Humor also goes on living on the popular stage (Tabarins, Turlupins, and others). All these genres had a more or less oppositional character that permitted the grotesque to enter their sphere, while still remaining within the limits of official culture; therefore the nature of laughter and of the grotesque was transformed and degraded.

This bourgeois line of development of Rabelaisian grotesque laughter will be further discussed in greater detail. Here we shall merely point out another form acquired by carnival and Rabelaisian imagery in the seventeenth century—a form that was obviously linked to the mood of the rebellious aristocracy of that time but had a more general meaning. Rabelais' characters became the protagonists of court festivals, masquerades, and ballets. In 1622 a masquerade held in Blois was entitled "The Birth of Pantagruel." Panurge, Friar John, and the Sibyl of Panzoult appeared in this performance together with the giant-infant and his wet nurse. In 1628 a ballet was produced at the Louvre under the title of "Sausages" (on the theme of the "Sausage war"); a few years later there was another ballet called "The Pantagruellists," and in 1638 a Rabelaisian "Bouffonnade" (based on the Third Book). Similar performances were also given later.[47]

These performances prove that the spectacular nature of Rabelais' images was still well understood. Neither was the popular-festive and carnivalesque origin of Rabelaisian phantasmagoria forgotten.[48] But at the same time these images had moved from the marketplace to court masquerades, and their style and meaning had, of course, undergone certain changes.

Such was one of the lines of popular-festive tradition during the new era. The court festivals with their masquerades, processions,

[47] See J. Boulenger, *Rabelais à travers les ages*, p. 34. See also the special article of H. Clouzot, *Ballets de Rabelais au XVII siècle* in *Revue des Études Rabelaisiennes*, Vol. 5, p. 90

[48] Modern France created comic opera on Rabelaisian material: Massenet's *Panurge* (produced in 1913) and Mariotti's *Gargantua* (produced in 1935 at the Opéra-comique).

allegories, and fireworks owed their existence in part to the carnival tradition. Court poets, especially in Italy, produced these festivities and were connoisseurs of their field. They understood its philosophical and utopian contents. Such a connoisseur was Goethe at the court of Weimar, where he was in charge of these performances and where he studied the traditional forms with great attention, seeking to discover the meaning of the different masks and symbols.[49] He was able to adapt these images to the historic process in his own work and to disclose the "philosophy of history" which they contained. The profound influence of popular festive imagery on Goethe's writings has not as yet been sufficiently appreciated and studied.

Having followed the line of court masquerades combined with other traditions, the style of popular festive forms began, as we have said, to degenerate. It acquired alien elements of ornate and abstract allegory. The ambivalent improprieties related to the material bodily lower stratum, were turned into erotic frivolity. The popular utopian spirit and the new historic awareness began to fade.

Another typical line of bourgeois development of the popular festive heritage was the seventeenth-century "comic novel" of Sorel, Scarron, and others. Sorel's spirit was already in many respects bourgeois and limited, as clearly expressed in his theoretical views on literature. He sets himself against artistic invention and fantasy and adopts the stand of narrow common sense, of the sober bourgeois practical spirit. He writes a novel in order to divert the public from reading useless novels. He sees in *Don Quixote* a mere parody of the *roman de chevalerie,* of fancy, daydreams, and idealism, a parody offered from the point of view of common sense and the practical mind. This is a typical narrowly bourgeois interpretation of Cervantes' novel.

But Sorel's own creative work does not correspond to this theory. His writings are complex and contradictory, abounding in

---

[49] These studies found their expression (in part) in the masquerade scene in the second part of Goethe's *Faust*.

traditional images, presented at a stage of transition in which their change of meaning is far from completed.

Nearest of all to Sorel's theoretic views is his novel "The Extravagant Shepherd" (*Le Berger Extravagant*). This is a pastoral *Don Quixote* simplified and reduced to a bare literary parody of the shepherd theme, popular in those days. But in spite of this superficially rational and narrow tendency, the novel contains a number of traditional images and overtones. Their meaning goes far beyond the author's initial intentions. Such is, for instance, the theme of the madness or stupidity of the hero, Lysis. As in *Don Quixote*, the hero's madness permits a whole series of carnival crownings and uncrownings, of travesties and mystifications. This theme (madness) permits the world to abandon its official routine and to join the hero's carnivalesque fancies. Though these overtones are weakened in Sorel's novel, they still preserve the smouldering fires of popular festive laughter, its regenerating bodily lower stratum. However, these deeper elements of the traditional carnival themes and images seem almost to contradict the author's own intentions.

Let us, for instance, mention the scene in which the small village of Saint Cloud, expecting the end of the world, universal deluge, and conflagration, indulges in a huge rustic orgy. We see here certain points of resemblance to Rabelais' system of images. We must also point out the famous "banquet of the gods" (*banquet des dieux*) in the third book of the novel.

Sorel's best novel, *Francion,* presents in its traditional themes and images a more substantial and productive character. We must first of all point out the role of scholastic *facéties* in this novel (and the great importance of scholastic recreation in the history of medieval literature). The picture of Bohemia with its mystification, travesties, and parodies is extensively treated in Sorel's novel. Let us next look at Raymond's mystification and at one of the best episodes of the novel, the orgy in his castle. Finally, we must stress the episode of the mock election of the pedantic scholar Hortensius as king of Poland. This is a completely carnivalesque and saturnalian game (the arena being Rome). However, the historic awareness disclosed in these images is considerably weakened and narrowed.

The traditions of grotesque realism are even more feeble and narrow in seventeenth-century literature, with its dialogue. We have here in mind the "Cackle of the Confined Woman" (*Caquet de l'accouchée*), a short piece which was published in several installments in 1622 and in a separate volume in 1663. This work seems to have been composed by several authors. It presents the usual female gathering at the bedside of a woman recovering from childbirth. The tradition of such gatherings is very old.[50] They were marked by abundant food and frank conversation, at which social conventions were dropped. The acts of procreation and eating predetermined the role of the material bodily lower stratum and the theme of these conversations. In this particular piece the author eavesdrops on the women's chatter while hiding behind a curtain. However in the conversation that follows, the theme of the bodily lower stratum (for instance, the Rabelaisian topic of swabs) is transferred to private manners. This female cackle is nothing but gossip and tittle-tattle. The popular frankness of the marketplace with its grotesque ambivalent lower stratum is replaced by chamber intimacies of private life, heard from behind a curtain.

Caquets were fashionable in those days. Female chatter is presented in the "Cackle of Fisherwomen" (*Caquets des Poissonnières*), 1621–1622, and in the "Cackle of the Women of the Faubourg Montmartre" (*Caquets des Femmes du Faubourg Montmartre*), 1622. Another characteristic example of this genre is "The Loves, Intrigues and Cabals of the House Servants in the Mansions of our Time" (*Amours, intrigues et cabales des domestiques des grandes maisons de notre temps*), 1625. This piece is concerned with the chitchat and gossip of the footmen and maids of a wealthy household; it has to do not so much with the masters as with the top members of the servant staff. The entire work is

---

[50] Étienne Pasquier and Henri Estienne mention them in the sixteenth century.

based on eavesdropping and voyeurism and frank discussion of what was heard and seen. Compared to the dialogue-containing literature of the sixteenth century, this work shows the complete degeneracy of marketplace frankness: it is nothing but the washing of personal unclean underwear. Seventeenth-century literature with its dialogue was a preparation to the "alcove realism" of private life, a realism of eavesdropping and peeping which reached its climax in the nineteenth century. The seventeenth-century dialogues are interesting historical documents reflecting this degeneracy; the frank talk of marketplace and banquet hall were transformed into the novel of private manners of modern times. And yet a tiny spark of the carnival flame was still alive in these writings.

The tradition of popular-festive theme and images can be found in a somewhat different aspect in the works of the libertine poets: Saint-Amant, Théophile Viau, d'Assouci. These works preserve the philosophical meaning of the images but acquire an epicurian individualistic coloring. The libertine poets were directly and strongly influenced by Rabelais. The epicurean individualistic interpretation of the images of the material bodily lower stratum was current during the following centuries; it paralleled their private, naturalistic interpretation.

Other aspects of popular-festive images appeared in Scarron's "comic novel." The company of itinerant actors is not merely a tiny professional world; it is contrasted to all the well-ordered and established world. It is an almost unreal microcosm removed from the sphere of conventions and binding rules and enjoying certain rights and freedoms of carnival. To some degree it has been granted popular-festive privileges. The itinerant actors' bandwagon spreads the festive carnival atmosphere that pervades the life and manners of the performers themselves. Such was also Wilhelm Meister's conception of the theater (Goethe). The utopian fascination of the world of the theater is still felt in our time.

Besides the "comic novel," Scarron's writings contain other aspects of the broader complex of popular, festive, grotesque, and parodical forms and images. Such are his burlesque poems, his grotesque comedies, and especially his "Virgil in Travesty," (*Virgile travesti*), a description in verse of the fair of Saint Germain and its carnival.[51] Finally, his famous "Boutades of Captain Matamore" presents quasi-Rabelaisian images of grotesque. Thus Matamore declares in one of his *boutades* that hell is his wine cellar and heaven his larder; the dome of heaven is his bed, the backs of the bed are the poles, and the watery abyss his night-pot (*et mon pot à pisser les abîmes de l'onde*). It must be added that Scarron's parodies, especially his "Virgil in Travesty," are already far removed from the universal and positive parodies of popular culture and are nearer to the narrow and purely literary forms of the modern age.

All the writings just discussed belong to the preclassic times of the seventeenth century, that is, to the period preceding the reign of Louis XIV. Rabelais' influence is here combined with the still living, direct tradition of the people's festive laughter. This is why Rabelais did not as yet appear exceptional, unlike anything else. Later the atmosphere in which Rabelais was understood vanished almost entirely, and he became a strange and solitary author who needed special interpretation and commentary. This is eloquently expressed in La Bruyère's famous comments on Rabelais. This part of his book "Characters and Mores of this Age" (*Les Caractères et les Moeurs de ce siècle*, 1688) appeared only in the fifth edition, in 1690. We quote this comment in the original and follow it with a detailed analysis:

Marot et Rabelais sont inexcusables d'avoir semé l'ordure dans leurs écrits; tous deux avaient assez de génie et de naturel pour pouvoir s'en passer, même à l'égard de ceux qui cherchent moins à admirer qu'à rire dans un auteur. Rabelais surtout est incompréhensible: son livre est une énigme, quoiqu'on en veuille dire, inexplicable; c'est une chimère, c'est le visage d'une belle femme avec les pieds et une queue de serpent ou de quelque autre bête plus

[51] In the *Foire Saint Germain* and the *Recueil de quelques vers burlesques*, 1648. The description of the Saint Germain Fair with its carnivalesque entertainment is also given in Sorel's unfinished novel *Polyandre, histoire comique*, 1648.

difforme: c'est un monstrueux assemblage d'une morale fine et ingénieuse et d'une sale corruption. Où il est mauvais, il passe bien loin au delà du pire, c'est le charme de la canaille: où il est bon il va jusques à l'exquis et à l'excellent, il peut être le mets des plus délicats.[52]

This commentary clearly formulates the "problem of Rabelais" as it was presented at the time of mature classicism. The point of view of this era, the aesthetics of that time, found correct and adequate expression in La Bruyère's words. It is not a rationalized and narrow aesthetic canon or literary manifesto that is proclaimed by La Bruyère but a wider, more organic aesthetic conception of the era of stabilization. For this reason it is important to analyze his opinion.

First of all, Rabelais' work appears two-faced to La Bruyère, but he has lost the key that could have locked together its two heterogeneous aspects. He considers the combination of the two aspects in a single novel by a single author as "incomprehensible." One of these aspects is described by La Bruyère as "filth" (l'ordure), and "delight for the rabble" (charme pour la canaille). Moreover, in this negative aspect of his work, Rabelais "excels by far the worst" (il passe bien loin au delà du pire). The other, positive, aspect of Rabelais' work is described by La Bruyère as "genius and originality" (génie, naturel) as "exquisite and excellent," fit to entertain the most delicate (le mets des plus délicats).

---

[52] "Marot and Rabelais are inexcusable for scattering so much filth in their writings: they both had genius and originality enough to be able to do without it, even for those who seek rather what is comical than what is admirable in the author. Rabelais above all is incomprehensible: his book is a mystery, a mere chimera; it has a lovely woman's face with the feet and tail of a serpent or of some more hideous animal. It is a monstrous jumble of delicate and ingenious morality and of filthy depravation. Where it is bad, it excels by far the worst, and is fit only to delight the rabble; and when it is good, it is exquisite and excellent, and may entertain the most delicate."

From *Characters of Jean de la Bruyère*, translated by Henri van Laun, p. 23. Routledge & Kegan Paul Ltd., 1926. First edition 1885. Reproduced by permission.

Rabelais' negative aspect as seen by La Bruyère consists first of all in his sexual and scatological obscenity, his curses and oaths, *double entendres* and vulgar quips—in other words, the tradition of folk culture in Rabelais' work, laughter and the material bodily lower stratum. The positive aspect is the purely literary, humanist element. The grotesque tradition peculiar to the marketplace and the academic literary tradition have parted ways and can no longer be brought together. All that recalls the grotesque and festive marketplace is the *charme de la canaille*. The indecencies, which have such a large place in Rabelais' work, are perceived in quite different tones by La Bruyère and his contemporaries. The link with the essential aspects of being, with the organic system of popular-festive images, has been broken. Obscenity has become narrowly sexual, isolated, individual, and has no place in the new official system of philosophy and imagery. Such transformation also took place in relation to the other elements of folk humor. All its genres were torn away from the original stem, the ambivalent material bodily lower stratum that supported them; thus they lost their true meaning. The words of wisdom, the subtle remarks, the broad social and political ideas were broken off this original stem; they became literary, academic, and assumed a completely different tone at the time of La Bruyère. They could now be defined by such words as *exquis* and *mets des plus délicats*. The combination of these heterogeneous elements (heterogeneous from the new point of view) in Rabelais appears to La Bruyère as a *monstrueux assemblage* ("a monstrous jumble"). To characterize this strange combination La Bruyère uses the image of the chimera—a significant symbol. The chimera is grotesque; in classic aesthetics there was no place for it. The combination of human and animal forms is one of the most ancient images, but it is completely alien to La Bruyère, the faithful spokesman of his time. He is used to conceive being as something finished, stable, completed, clear, and firm. He draws a dividing line between all bodies and objects. Even the moderate grotesque image of Melusine in popular legends appears to him a monstrous mixture.

La Bruyère, as we have seen, appreciated Rabelais' *morale*

fine. By this he means first of all "manners," character, that which generalizes and typifies an author's observation of human nature and life. In fact, this is the sphere of antique *moraliae* which La Bruyère could appreciate in Rabelais. But he accepts this sphere in a more narrow sense than did antiquity. He ignores the link between the *moraliae* and the antique feasts, banquets, laughter, which can still be traced in his predecessor Theophrastus.

Such is La Bruyère's opinion. His double-edged interpretation of Rabelais continued valid during the period that followed. Popular laughter, the material bodily lower stratum, extreme grotesque exaggeration and clowning, the comic folk elements— all these he rejected in Rabelais as the "heritage of the crude sixteenth century." Yet he retained Rabelais' "psychology," the "types" he presented, as well as his craftsmanship and social satire. The first attempt to understand Rabelais' work *as a whole* and to see all its elements as indispensable was made by Stapfer in his book published in the second part of the nineteenth century.[53] However, the historic and allegoric method of interpreting Rabelais was made as early as the seventeenth century.

Rabelais' work is extremely difficult. It contains a great number of allusions, which were often understood only by his contemporaries and sometimes by his closest friends alone. The work is encyclopedic; it contains many special terms referring to different branches of knowledge and technology. Finally, it contains a great number of new and difficult words which Rabelais was the first to introduce into the French language. It is obvious that he needs commentaries and interpretations. Rabelais, himself, laid a foundation for this approach by adding to the fourth book of his novel a "Brief Declaration." (Rabelais' authorship of *Brève déclaration* is almost certain.)

Rabelais' declaration offered the basis for the philological commentary on his work. It was in 1711 that Le Duchat's famous commentary appeared, but it has retained its importance up to our times. Le Duchat's work remained unique. Before and after

[53] Paul Stapfer, *Rabelais,* A. Colin, Paris, 1889.

this author's attempt, and even in our days comments and interpretations in this field followed a completely different line, neither philological nor strictly historical.

In the prologue to the first book of his novel, *Gargantua,* Rabelais points out the hidden meaning of his work: "Here you will find a novel savor, a most obstruse doctrine; here you will learn the deepest mysteries, the most agonizing problems of our religion, our body politic, our economic life."

We shall return to explain this passage. It could hardly be understood as a simple conventional means to awaken the reader's interest, although such means were used in the literature of the fifteenth and sixteenth centuries. Berni, for instance, makes a similar declaration in his burlesque "Roland in Love." What is important now is the attempt to decipher Rabelais which led in the seventeenth century to the historic-allegorical interpretation— an interpretation which was to prevail for almost three centuries of Rabelaisiana.

The first historic-allegorical interpretation of Rabelais' images was made in the sixteenth century. The well-known historian Jacques Auguste de Thou expressed in his biography the following opinion concerning Rabelais:

He wrote a remarkable book in which, with a quasi-Democritean freedom and with an almost clownish biting irony and under imaginary names he recreated as in a theater all the conditions of human and political existence and exposed them to the laughter of the entire people.

The characteristics perceived in this commentary are indeed typical of Rabelais: the universal, popular, and festive nature of laughter, in the manner of Democritus, directed at all the conditions of human and political existence, the theatrical character of the images, and, finally real historical characters appearing under imaginary names. This is the opinion of a man who as early as the sixteenth century correctly grasped the essential traits of Rabelais' novel. However, this opinion was expressed in the second part of the century when Rabelais' laughter already sounded far too clownish. The historian is seeking under these imaginary names definite persons and definite events; in other words, he is beginning to reevaluate the allegorical element in Rabelais' writings. Doubtless the tradition of replacing Rabelais' characters and the various episodes of his novel by real historic figures and events of political and court life was started as early as the sixteenth century, was transmitted to the seventeenth century, and was adopted by the historic-allegorical method.

In the seventeenth century there appeared keys to Rabelais' writings. Such a key was used for the first time in 1659 in relation to the Amsterdam edition of Rabelais' work and was modified for various later editions up to that of M. A. L. Sardou in 1874–1876, which gave a summary of all the keys. Various decipherings were added to the 1663 Amsterdam edition. It offers, for instance, a characteristic historic-allegorical interpretation of the episode of Gargantua's gigantic mare, which to rid herself of the gadflies pursuing her destroys with her tail the entire Beauce forest: "Everyone knows that this mare is Madame d'Étampes, the king's mistress, who had ordered the Beauce forest to be cut down. . . ." The commentator here refers to a legend dating from the sixteenth century.

But the true initiator of the historic-allegorical method was Pierre Antoine Le Motteux. He published in England (where he emigrated after the revocation of the edict of Nantes in 1693) an English translation of Rabelais by Urquhart, adding to it a biography, a preface, and a commentary. He analyzed the various keys previously suggested and then presented his own interpretation. This commentary became the main source of the later development of the historic-allegorical method.

The Abbé Marsy who published in Amsterdam a "Modernized Rabelais" (1752) with commentaries[54] was a prominent representative of this method. Finally, the most important monument of the historic-allegorical method is the *Variorum,* an edition of

---

[54] The full title of this work is *Le Rabelais moderne ou ses oeuvres mises a la portée de la plupart des lecteurs"* (8 small volumes).

Rabelais' works in nine volumes.[55] The editors used the research of all the other preceding commentators and offer an entire system of interpretation.

Such are the basic elements of the external development of this method. What does it essentially consist of? It is extremely simple: a specific character or event can be found behind each of Rabelais' images. The entire novel is a system of historical allusions. The method of deciphering is based on tradition, dating from the sixteenth century; it consists of comparing Rabelais' images to the historic events of his time, using various techniques of checking and confrontation. Tradition being contradictory and checking arbitrary, it is obvious that the same image can be deciphered differently by various representatives of this method. Let us give some examples:

Gargantua is usually considered an impersonation of Francis the First, but Le Motteux sees in him Henri d'Albret. Panurge is believed by some to be Cardinal d'Amboise, by others, Cardinal Charles de Lorraine, and by still others Jean de Montluc, while certain commentators consider that he is Rabelais himself. Picrochole is believed to be Lodovico Sforza or Ferdinand of Aragon, while Voltaire saw him as Charles V. The representatives of the historic-allegorical method try to decipher every detail as an allusion to an authentic occurrence. Thus the swabs in the famous episode of the First Book are not only interpreted as a whole but individually—and there are a number of them. In one instance Gargantua used a March cat as a swab and suffered lacerations. Some commentators interpret this episode as an event in the life of Francis I, who at eighteen caught a venereal disease from a Gascon mistress. In the novel Gargantua was cured only when he applied his mother's gloves to the scratches, and this is seen as an allusion to the sympathy shown Francis by his mother during his

[55] *François Rabelais: Les Oeuvres de Rabelais, édition Variorum:* critical edition edited by Johanneau and Esmangart, Dalibon, Paris, 1823–1826.

sickness. Thus the entire episode is transformed into a complex system of specific allusions.

The historic-allegorical method is at present completely rejected by Rabelais scholars.[56] The novel doubtless contains many allusions to historical personages and events, but it is quite impossible to apply them rigidly throughout the entire story. It would be vain to look for a definite, unique key to every image. Even if a specific allusion can be presumed, the historic-allegorical method cannot in most cases provide a precise deciphering; as we have said, tradition contradicts itself, and all confrontations and checkings are arbitrary.

Finally, and this clinches the matter, even an unveiled and substantiated allusion does not offer any essential element for the artistic and ideological understanding of the image. The image is always deeper and wider, it is linked to tradition, it has its own aesthetic logic independent of the allusion. For example, even if the episode of Gargantua's swabs is correctly interpreted, it offers us nothing for the understanding of the symbol itself. The swab is one of the widespread images of scatological literature, of anecdotes, familiar colloquial genres, curses, billingsgate metaphors, and analogies. Neither is this image new in literature. After Rabelais we find it in the "Cackle of the Confined Woman" described earlier. The swab is widely used in epigrams on writers and their works. Even if one single allusion involving the swab could be positively identified (if such an allusion exists in Rabelais' novel), it would not help us understand the traditional meaning of this image—symbol of the material bodily lower stratum— nor its specific artistic function in the novel.[57]

How can we explain why the historic-allegorical method enjoyed such exclusive prestige for almost three centuries? Why did such exceptional minds as Voltaire in the eighteenth century and

[56] But of course, even in modern times, attempts are made to decipher Rabelais' novel as a kind of cryptogram.

[57] We shall analyze in Chapter 6 the special function and artistic meaning of this episode.

Michelet in the nineteenth pay tribute to this method? And finally, what was the *raison d'être* of the method?

The fact is that the tradition of popular-festive laughter that informed Rabelais' work began to decline. It ceased to be a living and common interpretation of Rabelaisian images. The authentic aesthetic and ideological key to these images was lost, together with the tradition that had produced them. And so the commentators began to look for false keys.

The historic-allegorical method illustrates the disintegration of laughter that took place in the seventeenth century. The sphere of laughter became more and more narrowed and lost its universal character. On the one hand it became linked to all that was typical and common in everyday life. On the other hand it was related to personal invective; that is, it was directed at one single, private person. The historical universal individuality ceased to be the object of laughter. This quality of carnival humor gradually ceased to be understood. When there was no typical character, commentators began to look for a specific individual.

Of course popular-festive laughter admits allusions to distinct personages. But these allusions are only an overtone of the grotesque images, whereas the historic-allegorical method transforms these allusions into the prevailing note. The authentic grotesque image does not lose its force even when the allusions have been forgotten and replaced by new ones.

In the seventeenth century an important process was started in all ideological spheres. Generalization, empirical abstraction, and typification acquired a leading role in the world picture.

This process was completed in the eighteenth century. The very pattern of the world was changed. Next to the general the singular remains, acquiring its meaning only as a specimen of the general, only so far as it is typical, average, and can be generalized. On the other hand, singularity became something indisputable; it acquired the importance of a fact which can raise no objections. Hence the tendency to primitive documentation. A single fact, documentarily established, accompanied by the general and typical, begins to play the leading role in the conception of the world. This pattern was most strikingly shown in artistic creation (especially in the eighteenth century) and led to the specific limitations of realism in the age of the Enlightenment.

If the documentary novel belongs to the eighteenth century, the *roman à clef* was written throughout the seventeenth century. Such was the Latin novel *Satyricon* (London, 1603) of the English writer John Barclay, which enjoyed a great success in the first part of that century and was also reprinted several times in French. Though the novel is set in the antique world, it is a biographical *roman à clef*, and indeed a key deciphering the characters' names was added to the publication. This peculiar masquerade travesty of well-known contemporary figures lent the novel a special interest. The historic-allegorical method at the early stage of its development interpreted Rabelais' work, too, in the spirit of the "masquerade" novel with a key.

Such were the fundamental lines in the development of laughter in the Rabelaisian tradition of the seventeenth century. True, there still existed certain rather important phenomena related to the popular-festive tradition. We have Molière in mind. But these phenomena have a special character and are outside our field of observation.

Let us now examine the eighteenth century. In no other time was Rabelais so little understood and appreciated as during that era. The interpretation of his work reveals the weak rather than the strong points of the Enlightenment. The Enlighteners had a lack of historical sense, an abstract and rationalist utopianism, a mechanistic conception of matter, a tendency to abstract generalization and typification on one hand, and to documentation on the other hand. They were quite incapable of understanding and appreciating Rabelais; to them he was a typical representative of "the wild and barbaric sixteenth century." This point of view was clearly expressed by Voltaire:

Rabelais in his extravagant and unintelligible book let loose an extreme jollity and an extreme impertinence; he poured out erudition, filth and boredom; you will get a good story two pages long, at the price of two volumes of nonsense. Only a few eccentric persons pride themselves on understanding and esteeming this work as a whole; the rest of the nation laughs at the jokes of Rabelais and holds his book in contempt. He is regarded as chief among buffoons; we are annoyed that a man who had so much wit should have made such wretched use of it; he is a drunken philosopher who wrote only when he was drunk.[58]

Voltaire's commentary is characteristic. To him Rabelais' world appears extravagant, impossible to understand. He sees in it a mixture of erudition, dirt, and boredom. The gulf between the two heterogeneous incompatible elements appears to him far wider than it did to La Bruyère. He believed that only a few readers endowed with an eccentric taste could accept the novel as a whole. His opinion concerning the attitude of the "rest of the nation" is characteristic: it seems that they all laugh at the novel, as they did previously, but now they also despise it. The concept of laughter has been radically transformed. In the sixteenth century everybody laughed at Rabelais' novel but nobody despised him for it. Now, in the eighteenth century, the gay, century-old laughter becomes something despicable; despicable also is the fact that Rabelais was called the "chief among buffoons." Finally, Rabelais' own declaration (in the prologues) that he writes only while eating and drinking is understood by Voltaire in its literal and trivial sense. The substantial traditional link of wise and free speech with food and wine, the specific "truth" of table talk is no longer understood by Voltaire (though this tradition was still alive). The entire aspect of the popular banquet in Rabelais' novel lost its meaning.[59]

Voltaire sees in Rabelais' work merely a naked and straight satire, the rest is nothing but a dead weight. In his "Temple of Taste" (*Temple du goût*, 1732), Voltaire presents "God's library"

[58] Voltaire, "Philosophical Letters," translated by Ernest Dilworth, p. 106. Copyright © 1961 by The Bobbs-Merrill Co., Inc., reprinted by permission of the publishers.

[59] After 1758, when Voltaire reread *Gargantua* his attitude became more benevolent, though essentially it varied but little; he appreciates Rabelais almost exclusively for his anticlericalism.

in which nearly all books are abridged and revised by the muses. Voltaire places Rabelais' novel in this library, it is "abridged to one-eighth." Such treatment of former writers is typical of the Enlighteners.

An attempt to abridge and expurgate Rabelais was actually made in the eighteenth century. In his *Modernized Rabelais* the Abbé Marsy not only stripped the novel's language of its dialect and archaic forms but also mitigated the book's indecencies. The Abbé Perraud went even further when he published in 1752 in Geneva the *Ouevres choisies*. All that was coarse and indecent was removed from this selection. Finally, in 1776 an expurgated text was published "especially for the ladies" in the famous *Bibliothèque universelle des romans* (1775–1778).[60] All three editions are characteristic of the time and of its attitude toward Rabelais.

Thus, generally speaking, the Enlighteners failed to understand and to appreciate Rabelais, at least within the sphere of their theoretical knowledge. In the age of Enlightenment, according to Engels, "cogitative reason became the yardstick of all that existed."[61] This abstract rationalism and antihistoricism, this tendency to generalization and nondialectic thought (the break between negation and affirmation) prevented the Encyclopedists from grasping theoretically the nature of ambivalent festive laughter. The image of the contradictory, perpetually becoming and unfinished being could not be reduced to the dimensions of the Enlighteners' reason. It must be added, however, that Voltaire in his *Contes philosophiques* and in his "Maid of Orleans," as well as Diderot in *Jacques le fataliste* and especially in *Les bijoux indiscrets,* were not far removed from Rabelaisian imagery, though in a somewhat limited and rationalized aspect.

The influence of carnival forms, themes, and symbols on eighteenth-century literature is considerable. But this influence is

---

[60] In the nineteenth century, an expurgated edition of Rabelais was planned by George Sand (in 1847), but her project did not materialize. Rabelais' novel revised for young readers was first published, as far as we know, in 1888.

[61] Karl Marx and F. Engels, *Works:* Vol. 5, p. 16.

formalized; carnival is merely an artistic means made to serve aesthetic aims, mostly for subject and composition. Voltaire uses carnival forms for satire which still preserves its universality and its philosophy, but laughter is reduced to bare mockery. Such is precisely the famous "laughter of Voltaire"; its force is almost entirely deprived of the regenerating and renewing element. All that is positive is placed beyond the sphere of laughter and represents an abstract idea.

Carnival forms serve a different role in rococo literature. Here the gay positive tone of laughter is preserved. But everything is reduced to "chamber" lightness and intimacy. The frankness of the marketplace is turned into privacy, the indecency of the lower stratum is transformed into erotic frivolity, and gay relativity becomes skepticism and wantonness. And yet, in the hedonistic "boudoir" atmosphere a few sparks of the carnival fires which burn up "hell" have been preserved. In the setting of gloomy seriousness so widespread in the eighteenth century, rococo perpetuated after a fashion the traditional carnivalesque spirit.

At the time of the French Revolution Rabelais enjoyed a tremendous prestige in the eyes of its leaders. He was even made out to be a prophet of the revolution. His hometown, Chinon, was renamed Chinon-Rabelais. The men of that time well understood Rabelais' deeply revolutionary spirit, but they could not offer a new and true interpretation of that spirit. The most important document related to this subject is Ginguené's book published in 1791, entitled: "Of the Influence of Rabelais on the Revolution of our Time and on the Decree Concerning the Clergy." Ginguené basically adopts the historic-allegorical method, but he uses it with greater circumspection. He seeks to discover Rabelais' social and political concepts, but using a historicism which is obvious and typical of a man of the eighteenth century. He presents Rabelais as a systematic foe of royal power. In reality, however, Rabelais was never an enemy of this power but on the contrary perfectly understood its progressive meaning in his time.[62]

---

[62] True, Rabelais understood fairly well the relative nature of this progressiveness.

This is Ginguené's basic mistake. He also misunderstood grotesque exaggeration, seeing in it purely negative satire. For instance, the enormous amounts of food, drink, and clothes spent on Gargantua prove, according to Ginguené, how heavy were the king's expenses imposed upon the people. He does not see the theme of abundance conveyed in these expenditures, nor does he understand the ambivalent logic of the material bodily lower stratum. It would be naïve indeed to interpret Rabelaisian abundance as excessive spending inscribed in the king's budget. In this sense Ginguené's book remains on the level of the usual interpretations of his time.

The disintegration of popular laughter, after its flowering in Renaissance literature and culture, was practically completed, and marked at the same time the end of the formative phase of the satirical or merely amusing comic literary genres that were to prevail in the nineteenth century. The genres of reduced laughter—humor, irony, sarcasm—which were to develop as stylistic components of serious literature (especially the novel) were also definitely formed. We are not concerned with the study of these phenomena.[63] We are merely interested in tracing the major tradition of popular-festive laughter which prepared Rabelais' novel, and the Renaissance in general, and gradually declined during the next two centuries.

Our work has basically a historic and literary character, though it is more or less closely linked with the problems of historic poetics. But we will not raise any wider, more general aesthetic problems, especially those concerning the aesthetics of laughter.

[63] The most extensive form of reduced laughter in modern times (especially starting with Romanticism) is irony. This problem is treated in the interesting book of the Swiss scholar, Beda Allemann: *Ironie und Dichtung*, 1956. This book analyzes the interpretation and forms of irony as presented by Schlegel, Kierkegaard, Nietzsche, Thomas Mann, and Musil. This analysis is fine and deep, but it considers irony a purely literary phenomenon, and does not show its link with the culture of folk humor.

We shall discuss only one historically determined aspect of laughter pertaining to folk culture in the Middle Ages and in the Renaissance. Moreover, we shall examine it not in its entirety but only within the limits permitted by the analysis of Rabelais' work. In this respect our study can offer only a certain amount of material for the philosophy and aesthetics of laughter. Nothing more.

The historically determined culture of folk humor which is the object of our study was not opposed to all seriousness in general. It was opposed to the intolerant, dogmatic seriousness of the Middle Ages which also presented a historically determined form. But the history of culture and literature knew other forms of seriousness. Thus, antique culture developed tragic seriousness, which found its greatest expression in the genre of Greek tragedy. Tragic seriousness is universal (this is why it is possible to speak of a "tragic philosophy"); it is infused with the spirit of creative destruction. Tragic seriousness is absolutely free of dogmatism. A dogmatic tragedy is as impossible as dogmatic laughter, and the classical tragedies rise above it. Both authentic tragedy and authentic ambivalent laughter are killed by dogmatism in all its forms and manifestations. In antique culture tragedy did not exclude the laughing aspect of life and coexisted with it. The tragic trilogy was followed by the satyric drama which complemented it on the comic level. Antique tragedy did not fear laughter and parody and even demanded it as a corrective and a complement.[64] Therefore, in the antique world there could be no sharp distinction between official and folk culture, as later appeared in the Middle Ages.

Another form of seriousness was created in the antique world, which was also devoid of narrow dogmatism (in principle) and was capable of being tested in the crucible of laughter. This was critical philosophy. Its founder, Socrates, was directly linked with the carnival forms of antiquity that fertilized the Socratic dialogue and freed it from one-sided rhetorical seriousness.

[64] See the analysis by A. Dieterich in *Pulcinella. Pompeyanische Wandbilder und Romische Satyrspiele.* Leipzig, 1897.

In the culture of modern times a specific form of seriousness, strict and scientific, has acquired considerable importance. In principle, this form is exempt from all intolerant dogmatism and presents, by its very nature, the form of a problem, is self-critical and uncompleted. Starting with the Renaissance, this new seriousness exercised a powerful influence on literature also, of course undergoing certain transformations in this field.

The sphere of belles lettres itself and its various stages of development—epics, lyrics, and drama—presented many forms of deep and pure, but open seriousness, always ready to submit to death and renewal. True open seriousness fears neither parody, nor irony, nor any other form of reduced laughter, for it is aware of being part of an uncompleted whole.[65]

In world literature there are certain works in which the two aspects, seriousness and laughter, coexist and reflect each other, and are indeed whole aspects, not separate serious and comic images as in the usual modern drama. A striking example is Euripides' *Alcestis* in which tragedy is combined with the satyric drama (which apparently becomes the fourth drama). But the most important works in this category are, of course, Shakespeare's tragedies.

True ambivalent and universal laughter does not deny serious-

[65] Pushkin's Mozart accepts both laughter and parody, while the somber agelast Salieri does not accept them and fears them. Here is the dialogue between Mozart and Salieri after they have listened to the blind violinist:
Salieri:
And you can laugh?
Mozart:
Ah, Salieri,
Cannot you laugh yourself?
Salieri:
No,
I do not laugh when some unworthy painter
Smears Raphael's Madonna,
I do not laugh when a buffoon
Insults in parody the Alighieri.
(Pushkin, "Mozart and Salieri," Scene 1.)

ness but purifies and completes it. Laughter purifies from dogmatism, from the intolerant and the petrified; it liberates from fanaticism and pedantry, from fear and intimidation, from didacticism, naïveté and illusion, from the single meaning, the single level, from sentimentality. Laughter does not permit seriousness to atrophy and to be torn away from the one being, forever incomplete. It restores this ambivalent wholeness. Such is the function of laughter in the historical development of culture and literature.

Our remarks concerning the various forms of seriousness and their relation to laughter are somewhat outside the framework of the present study. It remains for us in this chapter to examine two last questions: first, the appreciation of Rabelais by the French Romanticists, and second, the condition of Rabelaisiana in our time.

In the Introduction we described the attitude of the French Romanticists (especially Victor Hugo) toward the grotesque in general. We shall now look at their attitude toward Rabelais, whom they considered, with Shakespeare, as one of the most important representatives of grotesque imagery.

Let us first turn to Chateaubriand. He expresses an idea typical of the Romanticists when he refers to the "mother-geniuses" (génies mères), who give birth and nourish all the other great writers of a nation. There are only five or six mother-geniuses in the whole world. Rabelais is among them, together with Homer, Shakespeare, and Dante. Rabelais created French literature, just as Homer created Greek and Roman literature, Shakespeare the English, and Dante the Italian. Rabelais could not have received higher praise. How different from the assessment of Voltaire for whom Rabelais was merely the chief of the buffoons, despised by his own nation.

The idea of mother geniuses, shared by nearly all Romanticists, was fruitful in its own time. It induced the Romanticists to seek the seed of the future in the past and to appreciate the past from the point of view of that future which it had fertilized and generated. A similar Romantic concept is that of the "beacon-genius of humanity" (*esprit phare de l'humanité*) which casts its light far into space. This idea reveals in literary masterpieces such as Shakespeare, Dante, Rabelais, not only that which they contain already, as a complete, entirely assimilated product, but also the seeds of that which is to come, in other words, all that is to be disclosed and brought to flower in the generations conceived by the ancestral geniuses. Ancient masterpieces open new vistas, new potentialities. Thus did the Romanticists make new and fruitful discoveries in Shakespeare, Cervantes, and Rabelais.

These theories and their consequences mark the profound difference between the Romanticists and the Enlighteners. The latter saw in literary masterpieces and in their authors less than they contained: from the point of view of nonhistorical rationality there was too much that was superfluous and incomprehensible in these works; they had to be expurgated and abridged. Voltaire's picture of "God's library," where all books are revised, is typical. The Enlighteners tended to impoverish the world. In their minds there is much less of the real world than can be imagined; they exaggerated reality at the expense of archaisms, fantasies, and daydreams. This purely static concept of reality colored their appreciation of literary works and made them want to edit them.

The Romanticists developed a broadened concept of reality and lent a great importance to time and to historic becoming. Thanks to this concept, they strove to see in a masterpiece much more than that which appeared on the surface. They sought to discover the signs of the future, the embryo, the shoots, the seeds, the prophecies and revelations. Let us recall the appreciation of the historian Michelet quoted on the first page of this book.

The broad concept of the Romanticist commentators has its positive and its negative aspects. The positive aspect is historicity, the awareness of time and of becoming. Reality loses its static, naturalistic, and uncertain character (restrained only by abstract rationalist thought); the living future enters reality in the form of new tendencies, potentialities, and foresights. The historical aspect of reality is in an essential relation to freedom, thus overcoming the determinist and mechanistic approach. In the domain of creative literature the Romanticist concept justifies deviations from all that is static and humdrum, from documentation and typification. Finally, it justifies the grotesque and grotesque fantasy as an artistic presentation of time and of things to come. These are the indubitable merits of the Romanticist appreciation.

The negative aspect of this appreciation is its idealism, its false concept of the role and limitations of subjective consciousness. The Romanticists often added invention to reality, depicting things which never existed. Fantasy degenerated into mysticism, human freedom broke away from necessity and became a super-material force.[66]

The most profound and full appreciation of Rabelais was expressed by Victor Hugo. Even though he did not devote a book or even an article to this subject, his comments are scattered throughout his works. His most detailed and systematic analysis is contained in his book on Shakespeare.

Hugo's analysis is based on an idea concerning human genius, similar to Chateaubriand's theory of mother-geniuses. Each of these geniuses is completely original and incarnates a definite aspect of being: his own invention and discovery (*tout génie a son invention et sa découverte*). Hugo lists fourteen of these initiators. His choice is rather unusual: Homer, Job, Aeschylus, Isaiah, Ezekiel,. Lucretius, Juvenal, Tacitus, the apostle Paul, the apostle John, Dante, Rabelais, Cervantes, Shakespeare. In chronological order Rabelais is listed after Dante and before Cervantes and Shakespeare. Hugo gives a characterization of each genius, including Rabelais.

Hugo does not construct his analysis as a historic-literary definition. He offers instead a series of free Romantic variations on the theme of the absolute material bodily stratum and bodily topography. According to Hugo, the belly is the center of Rabe-

[66] We do not pose the problem of Romanticism in all its complexity. We are merely concerned with the factors that permitted this movement to discover and understand (in part) Rabelais and the grotesque.

lais' topography; it is his artistic discovery. The basic function of the belly is paternity and maternity. In relation to this destroying and generating lower stratum, Hugo offers the grotesque image of a serpent inside man; "these are his bowels." Generally speaking, Hugo understood correctly the role of the lower stratum as the organizing principle of the entire system of Rabelaisian images. But at the same time he conceives this principle on an abstract moral level. Man's bowels "tempt, betray and punish." The destroying force of the topographic lower stratum is interpreted in ethical and philosophical terms.

Victor Hugo's variations on the belly theme develop further along the lines of moral and philosophical pathos. He proves (with examples in hand) that the "bowels" can be tragic and heroic, but that they simultaneously start a process of man's disintegration and degeneration (*Le ventre mange l'homme*). Alcibiades is transformed into Trimalchiones; the orgy is turned into gluttony. Instead of Diogenes his barrel alone remains. In Hugo's variations the ambivalent lower stratum falls apart to form these moral-philosophical images and antitheses.

Hugo correctly understands the essential relation of Rabelaisian laughter to death and to the struggle between life and death (in their historic aspect). He sees a special connection between eating, swallowing, laughter, and death. More than that, he sees the link between Dante's hell and Rabelais' gluttony: "Rabelais has placed in a barrel the world which Dante thrust into hell." The seven circles of the Inferno are the hoops of the Rabelaisian barrel. If, instead of the image of the barrel, Hugo had chosen the image of the open mouth and the swallowing belly, his metaphor would have been even more accurate.

Having correctly pointed out the relation between laughter, death of the old world, hell, and banquet imagery (devouring and swallowing), Hugo falsely interpreted this connection. He tried to lend it, as we have said, a moral-philosophical character. He failed to understand the regenerating and renewing power of the lower stratum. This failure diminishes the value of his observations.

Let us stress that Hugo had a clear understanding of the universal and perceptive aspect of Rabelais' images, and not merely as *mores* such as gluttony and drunkenness. However, he lends them a spirit that is not entirely Rabelaisian.

In regard to Shakespeare and Rabelais, Hugo offers an interesting characterization of genius and of a work of genius. In his mind the grotesque nature of creative work is the sign of genius. A writer who is a genius (Shakespeare and Rabelais being in this category) differs from writers who are merely great by the exaggeration, excessiveness, obscurity (*obscurité*) and monstrosity (*monstruosité*) of images and of the writings as a whole.

In this statement both the positive and the negative aspects of Hugo's concept are revealed. The special traits that he considers the sign of genius, in the Romanticist sense of this word, must be attributed to writers who reflect essentially and deeply the great moments of crisis in world history. These writers deal with an uncompleted, changing world, filled with the disintegrating past and with the as yet unformed future. A peculiar positive and one might say objective incompleteness is inherent in these writings. They are imbued with an only partially expressed future for which they have to leave the way open. Hence their many different meanings, their apparent obscurity. Hence their rich and varied heritage. Hence also the apparent monstrosity, that is, the lack of connection with the canons and norms of all completed, authoritarian, and dogmatic eras.[67]

Victor Hugo has a true awareness of these moments of crisis in history, but his theoretic expression of it is false. To a certain extent it is metaphysical; moreover, he attributes the objective traits of the historical process at the time of crisis to the nature of genius, not dissociating genius from its time and history. In his characterization of men of genius he proceeds by contrasts, enhancing the signs of their genius in order to create a sharp static contrast with other writers.

[67] During those moments of crisis folk culture with its conception of an uncompleted being and gay time had a powerful influence on great literature and was strikingly manifested in the Renaissance.

Rabelaisian themes are often found in the poetic works of Victor Hugo. Here, too, he stresses the universalism of Rabelais' images and the philosophical depth of his laughter. In his later poetry Hugo's attitude toward Rabelaisian laughter changes. Its universal, all-embracing character now appears to him to be uncanny and out of perspective. Rabelais represents neither the low level nor the summit, he does not allow us to pause, he is ephemeral (fleeting, without a future). Such an interpretation proves a deep lack of understanding of the peculiar optimism expressed in Rabelaisian laughter—a lack that was already manifest in Hugo's earlier writings. From the very beginning laughter in his mind was mostly a negation, a degrading and destroying principle. Though he repeated Nodier's definition of Rabelais as the *Homère bouffon,* though he used similar definitions: *Homère du rire, la moquerie épique,* he never fully understood the epic quality of Rabelaisian laughter.

It is interesting to compare Hugo's later commentaries with the distich of Rabelais' contemporary, the historian Etienne Pasquier, who treated a similar theme:

Sic homines, sic et coelestia numina lusit,
Vix homines, vix ut numina laesa putes.

(He so played with men and heavenly gods that neither men nor gods were offended by his game.) Thus Pasquier offered a better definition of the role played by Rabelaisian laughter than did Victor Hugo; he understood its deep optimism, its popular-festive nature, its epic and not iambic style.

In the second part of the nineteenth century Rabelais—his work and his life—became the object of detailed scholarly study. A number of monographs were devoted to him, and a serious historical and philological analysis of his text was initiated. But a wider scope of studies marked the first years of the twentieth century.

The history of these studies will not be discussed in the present book. We shall limit ourselves to a brief outline of the condition of Rabelaisiana in our time.

In 1903 the Society for the Study of Rabelais was founded *(La Société des Etudes Rabelaisiennes).* This is an important landmark. The society was composed of the pupils and friends of the Rabelaisian scholar Abel Lefranc. It became the center of these studies not only for France but also for England and America. A journal, *Revue des Etudes Rabelaisiennes,* was published. In 1913 this periodical was replaced by another publication with a wider program, the *Revue du Seizième siècle,* which was followed in 1934 by the revue *Humanisme et Renaissance* with an even wider range of interests.

All the textual work concerning Rabelais was centered around the Society and its journals and was devoted to problems of language, to the discovery of sources and the establishment of a scholarly biography. Finally, it was concerned with historical interpretation on a strictly scientific basis. A scholarly edition of Rabelais' writings began to be published by Lefranc, the director of the Society, in 1912, and by 1932 five volumes of this publication had appeared. These volumes contained the first three books of the novel.[68] After this date the publication was suspended. This edition with its text and variants, with its broad and solid commentaries represents an exceptional scholarly achievement.

We shall allude to the separate works of the Rabelais Society where appropriate to our text. We must first of all mention the fundamental work devoted to the language of Rabelais by Lazare Sainéan, vice president of the Society: *La langue de Rabelais,* Vol. 1, 1922, and Vol. 2, 1923.

In the field of source analysis and the study of Rabelais' erudition a valuable contribution was made by Jean Plattard: *(L'oeuvre de Rabelais, Sources, invention, et composition),* 1910.

---

[68] *Oeuvres de François Rabelais. Edition critique publiée par Abel Lefranc, Jacques Boulenger, Henri Clouzot, Paul Dorneaux, Jean Plattard et Lazare Sainéan.* The first volume published in 1912, the fifth (Third Book) in 1931.

The author also made a first attempt to synthesize a scientific biography: *Vie de Rabelais,* 1928.[69] Let us mention the valuable work on Rabelaisian texts by Jacques Boulenger, the secretary of the Society, and on Rabelaisian anatomical references by Henri Clouzot. The contribution of the president of the Society, Abel Lefranc, especially in his introductory articles to the first three books of the novel which he edited, presents exceptional interest because of the abundance of material.

We shall deal further with the works just mentioned as well as with other Rabelaisian studies. We shall here mainly add to our list a rather detailed monograph by Georges Lote: *La Vie et l'oeuvre de François Rabelais,* Paris, 1938.

Thanks to the work of the members of the Society and of other contemporary scholars, the understanding and the philological study of Rabelais' text have been considerably facilitated. Important material has been collected toward a deeper realization of Rabelais' place in history and toward establishing the relation of his work to the time in which he lived and to the literature which preceded him. But this material collected with the painstaking care of scholars still awaits a synthesis. We do not find a full-sized portrait of Rabelais in these scholarly writings. In general, Rabelaisians are careful to avoid any extensive synthesis or far-reaching conclusions. The only books that attempt to offer such a synthesis (and a prudent one indeed) are the study by Plattard, 1910, and to some extent, Lote's monograph. But in spite of the important material collected by Plattard and Lote, and in spite of some fine observations especially by Lote, such a synthesis does not satisfy us. In fact, it is even less satisfactory than the previous attempts by Stapfer, 1889, or by the German scholar Schneegans.

Modern Rabelaisiana, based on positivism, is restricted to the collection of material. Such collection is, of course, both necessary and useful. But the absence of a serious method and of a broad

---

[69] The basic biographical works relating to distinct periods in Rabelais' life: Dubouchet: *Rabelais à Montpellier,* 1887. A. Heulhard: *Rabelais ses voyages en Italie et son exil à Metz,* 1891. A. Bertrand: *Rabelais à Lyon,* 1894. J. Plattard: *Adolescence de Rabelais en Poitou,* 1923.

view limits the perspective of even such attentive research to a limited circle of biographical facts, insignificant events of the times, and literary (mostly printed) sources. As to folklore sources, they are studied superficially within the confines of their current narrow interpretation. The folklore of laughter, with all its variety and originality, remains almost entirely outside the sphere of research. All the carefully assembled material does not go beyond the framework of official culture, while Rabelaisiana as a whole can by no means fit such a framework. The Abel Lefranc school considers laughter as a secondary phenomenon which does not concern the serious problems of Rabelais' novel but is rather a means to gain popularity among the masses or a camouflage. The key problem of the culture of folk laughter is not posed.

An important landmark in Rabelaisiana was the publication of Lucien Febvre's book in 1942, *Le Problème de l'incroyance au XVIème siècle: la religion de Rabelais*. This work was directed against Abel Lefranc and his school. Febvre does not discuss the novel's artistic aspect; neither does he touch upon Rabelais' biographical sources, a field in which Lefranc and his followers were especially productive. Lucien Febvre is exclusively concerned with Rabelais' philosophy, particularly with his attitude toward Catholicism.

The author's main goal is to understand Rabelais within his cultural and intellectual milieu and the opportunities offered in his time. According to Febvre, the sixteenth century cannot be grasped if the individual is isolated from the "moral climate" and the "intellectual atmosphere" of that epoch. The historian's main task is to discover how the men of 1532 (the year of publication of the first book, *Pantagruel*) listened to Pantagruel speaking, how these men (not we) could understand him. We must read Rabelais' text with the eyes of his contemporaries, of the people of the sixteenth and not of the twentieth century. The historian's most grievous sin, says Febvre, is the sin of anachronism.

Having made these fully justified methodological demands, Febvre criticizes Abel Lefranc's assertion that Rabelais professed in his work a systematic rationalist atheism. Using a great amount of valuable material from various fields of sixteenth century culture and thought, Febvre seeks to prove that in the world outlook of that time (whether philosophical or scientific) there was no room for systematic rationalist unbelief. It had no ground to stand upon; every negation must be founded in order to have social value or historical meaning. Subjective and capricious negation without support (the plain "I deny") has no historical importance. Neither sixteenth-century philosophy nor science (actually the latter did not exist) could offer such support for the denial of religion. Systematic rationalism was impossible.[70]

Febvre's entire book seeks to prove this proposition. As we have said, the author uses a great amount of material of indubitable value, independently of the work's main thesis. In the light of this research, many long established views concerning sixteenth-century culture must be revised. In order to understand the various aspects of this culture, Febvre offers considerable information. But on the other hand his study gives little help, and only indirectly, for the understanding of Rabelais' novel as an artistic work and of his artistic view and awareness of the world. Rabelais' artistic thought fits neither rationalist atheism nor a religious faith, no matter whether Catholic, Protestant, or the "religion of Christ" of Erasmus. Rabelais' religion is wider and deeper-rooted. It ignores all intolerant seriousness, all dogmatism. His view of the world is neither pure negation nor pure affirmation. Both Lefranc and Febvre fail to make us understand Rabelais' philosophy. They also fail to make us understand correctly the entire sixteenth century.

The fact is that Febvre, like Lefranc, ignores the culture of folk humor of the Middle Ages and the Renaissance. Only the serious level of thought and culture exists in his mind. In his brilliant analysis of the various spheres of sixteenth-century culture, Febvre actually remains within its official framework. Therefore,

[70] Lucien Febvre, *Le Problème de l'incroyance au XVIème siècle, la religion de Rabelais*, Paris, 1942, pp. 380–381.

he sees and appreciates in Rabelais' novel only that which can be understood and interpreted on that serious level. That which is essential, the true Rabelais, remains outside his scope of vision.

As we have said, Febvre considers anachronism, modernization, as the historian's most grievous sin. He rightly accuses Lefranc of this sin, as well as other Rabelaisians. But, alas! he himself commits this sin in relation to laughter. He hears Rabelais' laughter with the ears of the twentieth century, rather than with those of the sixteenth. This is why he could not read *Pantagruel* with their eyes and see that which is essential in this book. He misses the main point of Rabelais' laughter, its universal and philosophic character. He does not understand that a philosophy of laughter, a universal comic aspect of the world are possible. He looks for Rabelais' philosophy when the latter is not laughing, or more correctly, whenever Rabelais seems to *him* to be entirely serious. When Rabelais laughs, he is merely joking in Febvre's eyes, and these jokes seem to him innocent enough. Like all jokes, they say nothing about philosophy, which can only be serious. Thus Febvre endows the sixteenth century with the concept of laughter and of its functions in culture as they appear in modern times, especially in the nineteenth century.

Febvre tells in his book how surprised he was by the analysis of the *Pantagruel* prologue offered by Lefranc in the introductory article. He was especially puzzled by Lefranc's conclusion that Rabelais was a conscientious propagandist of systematic atheism. In order to verify this statement, he picks up "with a certain anxiety" his own volume of Rabelais, opens the book of *Pantagruel,* and laughs! He is no longer concerned with the "crescendo of impiety" described by his opponent. (*On reprend son Rabelais avec quelque inquiétude. On ouvre le "Pantagruel". On rît. On ne songe plus au "crescendo de l'impieté"*). Febvre finds "nothing hidden, nothing frightening, no sacrilege." All he discovers are "clerical jokes" (*de vieilles plaisanteries cléricales*) which existed before Rabelais.[71]

71 *Ibid.,* pp. 160–161.

Here we clearly see Febvre's attitude toward Rabelais' jokes; they merely make him laugh. *On rit.* But it is precisely this *on rit* which needs to be analyzed. Do we of the twentieth century laugh as did Rabelais and his contemporaries? And what of these "old clerical jokes"? If they do not hide the serious, abstract atheist tendencies as seen by Lefranc, they may contain something else, something far more meaningful, profound, artistically concrete— the comic aspect of the world. The author seems to think that laughter is the same in every time and age, that a joke is always nothing more than a joke. And so he centers his fine historic analysis on the serious parts of Rabelais' novel (or those which appear serious to him). He leaves laughter aside, as nonhistorical and unchanging.

Febvre ignores the comic aspect of the world, evolved during hundreds and thousands of years in the infinitely varied culture of folk humor, and first of all, in comic rites and pageants. Analyzing the "clerical jokes" such as *sitio* and *consummatum est,* which impressed Lefranc by their boldness, Febvre merely points to their traditional character and to their harmless nature. He does not see that these jokes are particles of an immense whole, of the popular carnival spirit, of the world that laughs. In order to grasp this whole it would be necessary to discover the historical meaning of these century-old phenomena—the *parodia sacra,* the *risus paschalis,* and the immense medieval comic literature. First of all, of course, all the rites and spectacles of carnival forms should be grasped. But Febvre does not undertake this study. His attention is centered, as we have seen, on the "serious" phenomena of thought and culture (in the spirit of the twentieth century). For instance, discussing Erasmus and his influence on Rabelais, he does not mention "In Praise of Folly," the work which is precisely the most in tune with the Rabelaisian world. All he is interested in is the serious Erasmus. Only a small portion of his book, entitled "some clerical jokes" is devoted to the comic aspect of his subject, five of five hundred pages.[72] The author discusses the

[72] *Ibid.,* pp. 161–165.

principle of laughter in another small portion of his book devoted to the preachers Menot and Maillard who used Rabelaisian *facéties* in their sermons. There are a few other remarks scattered throughout the book concerning the comic elements of sixteenth-century culture, but they are treated in the spirit of nineteenth- and twentieth-century interpretation. It is characteristic that in a book devoted to the most carnivalesque writer of world history the word "carnival" is mentioned only once (in the analysis of Epistemon's ghostly visions).

In one part of his book Febvre seems to be inclined to recognize the historicity of laughter. He writes that "irony is the daughter of time."[73] But he does not further develop this idea. It is only used in order to restrict the element of laughter. The author declares that Rabelais' novel contains many more direct assertions than is generally believed. Irony, he says, is often heard where it does not exist.

We find such a statement radically wrong. Only relative seriousness is possible in Rabelais' world. Even the lines which in a different context or taken separately would be completely serious (Thélème, Gargantua's letter to Pantagruel, the chapter about the hero's death) acquire in their context an overtone of laughter; the reflexes of surrounding comic images react on them. The aspect of laughter is universal and embraces everything. But it is precisely this universalism, the peculiar truth of laughter that Febvre does not see. In his mind, truth can speak only in solemn tones. Neither does he perceive ambivalence.

Febvre's assertion that irony in Rabelais is heard where it should not be heard is no less incorrect on a wider historical level. In the world culture of the past there is much more irony, a form of reduced laughter, than our ear can catch. The literature, including rhetoric, of certain eras like Hellenism and the Middle Ages is flooded with various reduced forms of laughter, though we have ceased to be aware of some of them. We often lose the sense of parody and would doubtless have to reread many a text of

---

[73] *Ibid.*, p. 172.

world literature to hear its tone in another key. But first of all it is necessary to understand the nature of folk humor in bygone years, to grasp its philosophy, its universalism, its ambivalence, and its link with time. All of these have been almost entirely lost in modern humor.

The fact that Febvre ignores this folk culture leads him to a distorted conception of the Renaissance and of the French sixteenth century. He does not see, nor does he want to see, the exceptional freedom and the complete absence of dogmatism of artistic thought that were typical of that epoch. He fails to grasp them because he finds nothing that supports them. He presents a narrow and false picture of that time.

The era of the Renaissance in general and the French Renaissance in particular was marked in the literary sphere first of all by the fact that the highest potentials of folk humor had attained the level of great literature and had fertilized it. Without being aware of this fact it is impossible to understand either the culture or the literature of the sixteenth century. Of course it would be inadmissible to see folk humor alone in all the rich, complex, and contradictory output of that age. But it was precisely the infiltration of folk humor into great literature that has remained unexplored until now. The failure to understand it had a most unfortunate influence on the understanding of Rabelais.

In conclusion we have to agree with the sharp criticism of Febvre's book by P. Dek in his article "Our Failure in the Appreciation of the Work of Rabelais": "Febvre's book is the most subtle attempt of all those made during four hundred years after Rabelais' death to tear his work away from the people."[74]

Let us briefly examine the condition of Rabelaisiana in our country.

[74] See P. Dek, *Siem Viekov Romana* ("Seven centuries of the novel"), *Inostrannaya Literatura*, Goslitizdat, Moscow, 1962, p. 121. See also an extensive criticism of Febvre in L. E. Pinsky, *Realism Epokhi Vozrozhdeniya* (Realism of the Renaissance), Goslitizdat, Leningrad and Moscow, 1961, pp. 106–114.

Prerevolutionary Russian literary criticism was almost entirely unconcerned with Rabelais. We had no Rabelaisians. Not a single book or monograph was published on this subject. The entire Russian scholarly literature in this field is limited to a rather extensive article by A. N. Veselovsky,[75] "Rabelais and His Novel" and a brochure by I. Focht (devoid of all scientific value).[76]

The article by A. N. Veselovsky had an indisputable scholarly interest for its time (1878). This paper appeared long before the development of a strictly scholarly Rabelaisiana in France, and a quarter of a century before the founding of *La Societé des Etudes Rabelaisiennes*. The article contains a number of observations which were valuable and new for that time, concerning the epoch when the novel was written as well as the various aspects of Rabelais' work. Some of these observations were accepted; but from our point of view Veselovsky's interpretation contains many errors.

In his explanation of the novel's fundamental character, its genesis and evolution, Veselovsky brings out first and foremost the narrow and conjectural elements which picture the French royal court and various representatives of the ruling class, the French feudal aristocracy, the officials, and the bourgeoisie. The role of the people and their special condition are not taken into consideration. Thus, Rabelais' optimism of the first period of his life, up to October 1534, is interpreted by Veselovsky as arising from his naïve faith in the triumph of humanism because of the support of the court, and from his friendship with the leaders of the Reformation. The changes in his outlook and tone in the following books are seen by Veselovsky as the result of the defeat of humanism and of his break with the Protestant leaders. But such emotional reactions as naïve faith and disappointment are

[75] A. N. Veselovsky, *Izbranniy Statiy*, Goslitizdat, Leningrad, 1939.

[76] I. Focht, *Rabelais, ego Zhyzn i tvorchestvo*, 1914. In addition, the French lecturer of the former St. Petersburg University, Jean Fleury, published in 1876–1877 in Paris a monograph on Rabelais, not devoid of interest for its time, though this has no connection with Russian Rabelaisiana.

incompatible with Rabelais' powerful laughter. A change in the politics of the court and ruling class was of but little importance for this laughter, filled with a thousand-year-old wisdom. A political crisis was nothing more than a tempest in a teapot, the crowning and uncrowning of a clown of the Roman Saturnalia and European carnivals. Rabelais' optimism is the people's optimism, and all the hopes and disappointments arising from limited potentialities of the age are but the overtones of his novel. Veselovsky turns them into its basic tone. He does not see the popular background of the political theme.

Neither does Veselovsky grasp the peculiar character and the revolutionary nature of folk humor reflected in Rabelais' work. He almost entirely ignores the existence of the gay Middle Ages and underestimates the ancient tradition of folk culture. He conceives Rabelais' laughter as the expression of a primitive, elementary, almost animal joyfulness of a "village boy let loose."[77]

Similarly, in the view of European Rabelaisians Veselovsky knew only the official Rabelais. He analyzed only the novel's periphery, which reflects the trends of the humanist club of Marguerite of Angoulême and the movement of the early Reformation leaders, among others contemporary happenings. But Rabelais' work expressed basically the most radical interests, hopes, and thoughts of the people, which had nothing to do with these relatively progressive movements of the aristocratic and bourgeois Renaissance.

In accordance with European nineteenth-century Rabelaisiana, Veselovsky brings out first of all the Thélème episode which he offers as a key to Rabelais' philosophy and to his entire novel. In reality, Thélème is characteristic neither of Rabelais' philosophy nor of his system of images, nor of his style. Though this episode does present a popular utopian element, it is fundamentally linked with the aristocratic movements of the Renaissance. This is not a popular-festive mood but a court and humanist utopia, which has

[77] See a more detailed criticism of Veselovsky's image in Chapter 2.

rather the flavor of Princess Marguerite's circle than that of the marketplace. In this respect, Thélème is not in line with Rabelais' imagery and style.

Veselovsky's interpretation largely determined the treatment of Rabelais in our university courses almost until our time.

Until World War II Soviet literary critics did not change this situation substantially. Rabelais, one of the greatest realists of world literature, was for a long time almost totally ignored. There was a short article of a mainly informative character by A. A. Smirnov in the Literary Encyclopedia, and a similar article by B. A. Krzhevsky was added to the second edition of the novel's incomplete translation. A chapter in a history of French literature by A. K. Dzhivelegov and two short original articles: "The Story of the Great Gargantua" by V. F. Shishmareff,[78] and "Rabelais and Humanism" by I. E. Verzmen[79]—this is about all that was published here concerning our author. There was not a single monograph, no serious attempt to revise the Rabelaisian heritage in the light of the principles and aims of Soviet literary studies, especially in connection with the theories and history of realism and folk literature.

After World War II the situation changed. In 1948 the first Soviet monograph on Rabelais, by E. M. Evnina,[80] was published. This work has indubitable merits. The complete neglect of the comic principle in Rabelais' novel characteristic of European commentators is not to be found in E. M. Evnina's book. In her eyes Rabelais is essentially a comic writer. True, the author defines Rabelais as a satirist, but she interprets satire very broadly; unlike Schneegans and other critics, she attributes to laughter positive elements: joy, gaiety, exultation. As seen by this author, Rabelais is many-faced and ambivalent (though Evnina does not use this expression). Such an interpretation permits an interesting and detailed analysis of Rabelais' peculiar methods of treating the comic

[78] *Sbornik statey v chest ac, A. I Sobolevskogo*, Leningrad, 1928.
[79] *Uch. zap. MGPI*, Vol. 1, 1935.
[80] E. M. Evnina, "François Rabelais" (Goslitizdat, Moscow, 1948)

element. Evnina's work is a valuable contribution to Soviet Rabelaisiana.

A number of popular works devoted to our subject appeared during the postwar period: the centennial article of I. I. Anissimov on "François Rabelais" (*Znamya,* Vol. 5, 1953); the article by E. M. Gordeev, "The Great Humanist, Rabelais" (*in Sbornik Novye Veka,* 7, ed. Akademiya Nauk Litovskoi SSR Moscow, 1955); the introductory article of S. D. Artamonov to "Gargantua and Pantagruel" (translated by N. M. Ljubimov, Goslitizdat, 1961) and his brochure "François Rabelais" (ed. of *Khudozhestwennaya Literatura,* 1964). The interesting and original brochure, "The Artistic Method of Rabelais" by S. T. Vaĭman appeared in 1964.

But the most important event in Soviet Rabelaisiana was the publication of L. E. Pinsky's essay: "The Laughter of Rabelais" in his book: "Realism of the Renaissance."[81] Unlike most Rabelais scholars, Pinsky considers laughter the basic organizing principle in Rabelais' novel; it is not the external but the inner form of his vision and understanding of the world. Pinsky does not separate laughter from the world outlook nor from the ideological contents of the novel. And it is from this angle that he offers a critical survey of the appreciation and understanding of Rabelais throughout the ages. His conclusion is:

... the interpretation of his work was fruitful only when it did not belittle the meaning of laughter and when the comic principle was not separated from the libertarian and progressive idea, from the contents of "Gargantua and Pantagruel." Only then was a new and vital aspect of this work unfolded. Throughout all these centuries Rabelais remained for his perceptive audience the genius *par excellence* of the comic.[82]

We fully agree with this statement.

Pinsky systematically denies the satirical nature of Rabelais'

---

[81] L. E. Pinsky, *Realism Epochy Vozrozhedenya,* "Realism of the Renaissance," Goslitizdat, Moscow, 1961, pp. 87–223. Pinsky's initial conception was expressed in his article "The Comic Element in Rabelais." (*Voprossy literatury,* 1959, No. 5).

[82] *Op. cit.,* p. 118.

laughter. He is not a satirist in the ordinary sense of the word. His laughter is by no means directed at the distinct, purely negative aspects of reality. Only a few secondary characters and episodes of the novel's last books can be described as satirical. As to the leading characters, Rabelais' laughter lends them a truly positive aspect. Pinsky thus formulates his idea:

> ... this is not a satire in the precise meaning of the word, it does not express indignation about vice or anger at evil in social and cultural life. The Pantagruelesque company, especially Friar John and Panurge, are not satirical figures, they are the very impersonation of laughter. The comic aspect of the spontaneous manifestations of sensuality: Friar John's gluttony, Panurge's concupiscence, the improprieties of young Gargantua, are not supposed to arouse the reader's indignation. The language and the very image of the narrator, Alcofribas Nasier, one of the members of the Pantagruellists' little company, obviously excludes the satiric tone in connection with Panurge. The latter is a close friend, an *alter ego* of the narrator, as well as one of his main characters. Panurge must amuse his audience, he must make it laugh, surprise it, and even teach it in his own way. In no way must he arouse its indignation.[83]

Pinsky discloses convincingly the element of knowledge in Rabelais' laughter and its link with truth. Laughter purifies the consciousness of men from false seriousness, from dogmatism, from all confusing emotions. Let us quote once more from Pinsky's work:

> Laughter in "Pantagruel" is at the same time a theme and an argumentation. The reader must regain the gift that sorrow has deprived him of, the gift of laughter. He must return to the normal condition of human nature, so that truth may be disclosed to him. For Spinoza, a hundred years later, the path of truth was to lead to liberation from emotions. His motto was: not to weep, nor to laugh, but to know. For Rabelais, man of the Renaissance, laughter was precisely a liberation of the emotions that dim the knowledge of life. Laughter proves the existence of clear spiritual vision and bestows it. Awareness of the comic and reason are the two attributes of human' nature. Truth reveals itself with a smile when man abides in a nonanxious, joyful, comic mood.[84]

---

[83] *Ibid.,* p. 174.
[84] *Ibid.,* p. 174.

Pinsky's acknowledgement of the ambivalence of Rabelaisian laughter is important. He writes: "One of the most remarkable traits of Rabelais' laughter is its multiplicity of meaning, its complex relation to the object. Frank mockery and praise, uncrowning and exaltation, irony and dithyramb, are here combined."[85] And elsewhere: "Rabelais' laughter simultaneously denies and asserts, or more correctly speaking it seeks and hopes like the very company of the 'thirsting Pantagruellists.' Boundless enthusiasm concerning knowledge and cautious irony alternate with each other. The very tone of this laughter shows that two opposite principles can be put together even in form."[86]

Pinsky further discloses the basic sources of Rabelais' laughter. He is interested not in the exterior, formal methods of the comic, but in its sources. He sees one such source in "the very movement of life," that is, in becoming, change, gay relativity. He writes:

In Rabelais' comic affect there is the feeling of the general relativity of great and small, exalted and lowly, of the fantastic and the real, the physical and the spiritual; the feeling of rising, growing, flowering and fading, of the transformation of nature eternally alive.

Pinsky sees another source of the comic closely linked to the first one in the persistent *joie de vivre* of human nature:

In the prologue to the fourth book, Pantagruelism is described as a gaiety of spirit before which all that is incidental is powerless. The source of the comic in Rabelais' work is not only the impotence of the incidental which cannot slow down the movement of life (since "everything moves irretrievably toward its end" as says the writing on the Temple of the Holy Bottle); neither is this source merely found in the flow of time and the movement of society in history, the law of succession of kingdoms and empires. A no less important source is, as we have said, this indestructible *joie de vivre*, capable of rising above the incidental, to conceive it precisely as something transient.[87]

[85] *Ibid.*, p. 181.
[86] *Ibid.*, p. 183.
[87] *Ibid.*, p. 147.

These quotations prove that the author thoroughly understands the ancient link of laughter with time, with time's successive changes. He stresses this link in other parts of his book.

We have discussed only the basic elements of the conception of Rabelaisian laughter as developed by Pinsky. This author gives a subtle and deep analysis of the major episodes of the novel and of its leading characters (Gargantua, Pantagruel, Friar John, and Panurge). The analysis of Panurge is particularly profound and interesting. The author correctly states the immense importance of this image (similar to that of Shakespeare's Falstaff) for the understanding of the philosophy of the Renaissance.

Pinsky does not examine the history of laughter and of the culture of folk humor. Neither does he discuss Rabelais' medieval sources. His method is basically to remain within Rabelais' own time. However, he does point out the carnivalesque character of Rabelaisian laughter.

Such is the present state of Soviet Rabelaisiana. It is apparent from our brief survey that, unlike contemporary Western European scholars, our commentators do not separate Rabelais' artistic vision from his laughter but rather strive to interpret correctly its original traits.

In conclusion we wish to say a few words about N. M. Ljubimov's translation.[88] The publication of this work is an important event. We may say that the Russian public has read Rabelais for the first time, has heard for the first time his laughter. Though the novel was translated into Russian as early as the eighteenth century, these earlier versions presented only excerpts; the originality and wealth of Rabelais' language were not even approximately rendered. This is an exceptionally difficult task. It was even said that Rabelais was untranslatable—an opinion shared by A. N. Veselovsky. Therefore, among all the classics of world literature Rabelais alone did not penetrate into the sphere of Russian culture, as did Shakespeare and Cervantes, for example. This was a

---

[88] Ljubimov, N.M., *Gargantjua i Pantagrjuel,* Goslitizdat, Moscow, 1961.

serious gap since it was in him that the great world of comic folk culture was revealed. Now, thanks to Ljubimov's remarkable, almost completely adequate translation, Rabelais has begun to speak in Russian, with his unique familiarity and spontaneity, with his immeasurable depth, with his comic imagery. It would be impossible to overestimate the importance of this event.

CHAPTER TWO

The Language of the Marketplace in Rabelais

I want to understand you,
I study your obscure language.
(A. S. PUSHKIN, *"POEM COMPOSED DURING*
A SLEEPLESS NIGHT")

We shall examine first of all those elements of Rabelais' language that, from the seventeenth century on, were a stumbling block for his admirers and readers, those that La Bruyère considered "filthy depravation" and Voltaire "impertinence." Let us call these components conditionally and metaphorically the marketplace and billingsgate elements of the novel. It was precisely this language that the Abbé Marsy and Abbé Perraud tried to expurgate in the eighteenth century and George Sand in the nineteenth. These elements still prevent public reading of Rabelais, although in other respects no author is better suited for such reading.

Even in our time the billingsgate in Rabelais makes him difficult for his readers and not merely for the average public. It is hard to weave these coarse words into the artistic texture of the novel. The specific meaning that many of these terms have acquired in modern times distorts a correct interpretation of Rabelais' writings; the terms were then universal and far removed from pornography. For this reason, connoisseurs and scholars have adopted an indulgent view concerning this inevitable heritage of the "naïve and coarse sixteenth century," stressing the innocent character of these old-fashioned improprieties. In the eighteenth century Abbé Galiani found a witty expression for this tolerance: "Rabelais' indecency," he wrote, "is naïve; it is like the backside of a poor man."

A similar tolerance concerning Rabelais' "cynicism" was shown by Veselovsky. He used, however, a less Rabelaisian image by saying: "If you like, Rabelais is cynical, but as a healthy village boy who has been let loose from a smoky hut into the spring air; he rushes madly on, across the puddles, besmirching passersby with mud and laughing merrily when lumps of clay cover his legs and face, ruddy with springlike, animal gaiety."[1]

Let us examine Veselovsky's statement; let us, for a brief moment, take seriously his image of the village boy and confront it with the peculiar traits of Rabelais' cynicism.

First of all, the image of the village boy is inadequate. Rabelais' cynicism belongs to the city marketplace, to the town fair and the carnival square of the late Middle Ages and of the Renaissance. Further, this is not the individual gaiety of a boy let loose from a smoky hut but the collective gaiety of the people gathered at the fair, not the naïve gaiety of a boy "rushing madly across puddles" but a popular, festive gaiety that was gradually formed during many centuries. However, the season is correctly chosen in Veselovsky's picture: this is a truly springlike carnivalesque, Paschal laughter. One might say that these forms of gay Shrovetide cynicism are transferred to a historic spring, to the new era.

---

[1] A. N. Veselovsky, "Collected Articles," Goslitizdat, Leningrad, 1939, p. 241.

The very image of the boy must be revised. He is the symbol of youth, of immaturity and incompleteness. Such an image holds good only superficially; Rabelais' youth is the youth of antiquity, the "playing boy" of Heraclitus. From the historic point of view, Rabelais' cynicism belongs to the most ancient stratum of his novel.

Let us pursue our critical remarks. Veselovsky's village boy besmirches the passersby with mud: a far too tame and modernized metaphor. To besmirch means to debase. But grotesque debasement always had in mind the material bodily lower stratum, the zone of the genital organs. Therefore debasement did not besmirch with mud but with excrement and urine. This is a very ancient gesture. The modern euphemism "mudslinging" is derived from it.

We know that defecation played a considerable role in the ritual of the "feast of fools." During the solemn service sung by the bishop-elect, excrement was used instead of incense. After the service the clergy rode in carts loaded with dung; they drove through the streets tossing it at the crowd.

This gesture was also part of the ritual of charivari. We have a description of a sixteenth-century charivari in the *Roman du Fauvel*, from which we learn that tossing of dung at passersby was accompanied by another ritualistic gesture: throwing salt into a well.[2] Scatological liberties (mostly verbal) played an important role during carnivals.[3]

In Rabelais' novel drenching or drowning in urine is commonly described. Let us recall the famous episode in the First Book in which Gargantua drenches in urine the curious Parisians who have thronged around him. Also in the First Book is the episode in which Gargantua's mare drowns part of Picrochole's army in her urine at the Gué de Vède, and the episode in which the pilgrims are immersed in Gargantua's urine. Finally, in the Second Book

---

[2] See *Roman du Fauvel* in *Histoire littéraire de la France*, 32:146. (Académie des inscriptions des belles lettres), Paris, Imprimerie nationale, 1733–1819. L'un getoit le bren au visage . . . L'autre getoit le sel au puis. (One throws dung at the face, the other throws salt into the well.)

[3] In Hans Sachs, for instance, there is a carnivalesque "play of the dung."

Anarchus' camp is flooded in similar fashion. We shall return to these episodes; for the present we are merely concerned with unmasking one of the traditional debasing gestures lurking behind Veselovsky's euphemistic metaphor "besmirching with mud."

Tossing of excrement is also known from ancient literature. The fragments of Aeschylus' satyric drama "The Collector of Bones" contain an episode in which a "vile-smelling vessel," that is, a chamber pot, is thrown at the head of Odysseus. A similar episode is presented in a satyric drama by Sophocles, "The Feast of the Achaeans," which has been preserved. Other such episodes are related to the comic Heracles as pictured on antique vases, drunk and lying at the door of a hetaera while an old procuress empties a chamber pot on his head, or armed with this vessel and pursuing another figure. Finally, we have a fragment from the *Fabulae Atellanae* of Pomponius: "Thou Diomedes, hast drenched me in urine." (This play was probably a revised version of "The Feast of the Achaeans.")

These examples prove that the slinging of excrement and drenching in urine are traditional debasing gestures, familiar not only to grotesque realism but to antiquity as well. Their debasing meaning was generally known and understood. We can find probably in every language such expressions as "I shit on you." (Bowdlerized equivalents are: "I spit on you" or "I sneeze on you.") At the time of Rabelais the usual expression was *bren pour luy* (as used by Rabelais in the first book of his novel). This gesture and the words that accompany it are based on a literal debasement in terms of the topography of the body, that is, a reference to the bodily lower stratum, the zone of the genital organs. This signifies destruction, a grave for the one who is debased. But such debasing gestures and expressions are ambivalent, since the lower stratum is not only a bodily grave but also the area of the genital organs, the fertilizing and generating stratum. Therefore, in the images of urine and excrement is preserved the essential link with birth, fertility, renewal, welfare. This positive element was still fully alive and clearly realized in the time of Rabelais.

In the well-known episode of Panurge's flock in the Fourth Book,

the merchant Dingdong praises his sheep by saying that their urine
is endowed with the magic power to increase the fertility of the
earth, as does the urine of the gods. In the *briefve déclaration*
added to the Fourth Book Rabelais himself (or in any case, a contemporary and a man belonging to the same cultural circle) gives
the following explanation of this passage: "if God had urinated
here" (*si Dieu y eust pissé*). This is a popular expression in Paris
and in all France among the simple folk who consider blessed the
place where Our Lord urinated or performed some other act of
nature, as for instance the one related by Saint John, 9:6, ". . . he
spat on the ground and made clay of the spittle."[4]

This passage is characteristic. It proves that at the time of folk
legends the language of excrement was closely linked with fertility
and that Rabelais himself knew this link and made use of it in
full awareness. Further, we see that Rabelais did not hesitate to
combine the words "our Lord" and "the Lord's blessing" with the
image of excrement. (These images were already combined in the
popular expression he quotes.) He saw no sacrilege in doing so
and did not anticipate the stylistic abyss that was to draw the line
between the two terms for the men of the seventeenth century.

For the correct understanding of these carnivalesque gestures
and images we must take into consideration that all such gesticulations and verbal images are part of the carnival as a whole, infused
with one single logic of imagery. This is the drama of laughter
presenting at the same time the death of the old and the birth of
the new world. Each image is subject to the meaning of the whole;
each reflects a single concept of a contradictory world of becoming,
even though the image may be separately presented. Through its
participation in the whole, each of these images is deeply ambivalent, being intimately related to life-death-birth. This is why such
images are devoid of cynicism and coarseness in our sense of the
words. But these images, such as the tossing of excrement and
drenching in urine, become coarse and cynical if they are seen

[4] See the Rabelais edited by L. Moland, *François Rabelais. Tout ce
qui existe de ses oeuvres*, Paris, 1884, p. 478.

from the point of view of another ideology. If the positive and negative poles of becoming (death-birth) are torn apart and opposed to each other in various diffuse images, they lose their direct relation to the whole and are deprived of their ambivalence. They then retain the merely negative aspect, and that which they represent (defecation, urination) acquires a trivial meaning, our own contemporary meaning of these words. The images, or more correctly speaking, the verbal expressions, continue to live in popular colloquialisms but with a radically transformed aspect. True, they still preserve a distant echo of the old philosophy, a faint memory of billingsgate liberties. Only thus can their vitality and persistence be explained.

Rabelais scholars usually understand and evaluate the novel's billingsgate and marketplace elements in the spirit of modern interpretation, distinct from the carnival action as a whole. The deep ambivalence of these images is no longer understood.

Let us offer a few other examples proving that in the time of Rabelais the principle of regeneration, fertility, and renewal was still fully alive in these images.

Folengo's *Baldus,* a macaronic work, had a certain influence on Rabelais; we find in it an episode in hell in which Zingar resurrects a youth by drenching him in urine.

In the "Extraordinary Chronicle"[5] Gargantua urinates for three months, seven days, thirteen hours and forty-seven minutes, thus giving birth to the river Rhone and to seven hundred ships.

In Rabelais (Second Book) all the warm medicinal springs of France and Italy were generated by the hot urine of the sick Pantagruel.

In the Third Book (Chapter 17) we find an allusion to the antique myth in which the urine of Jupiter, Neptune, and Mercury gave birth to Orion (from the Greek οὐροεῖν, to urinate). Rabelais, drawing on Ovid's *Fasti,* presents this episode thus: Jupiter, Neptune and Mercury . . . *officialement, forgèrent Orion.* The "offi-

---

[5] This is an extended edition of "The Great Chronicles." Some passages are borrowed from *Pantagruel.* The author is François Girault.

cial" was an officer of the Church police, but in the debasing spirit of familiar speech the word meant a chamber pot, and this meaning was already a part of fifteenth-century vocabulary. (We in Russia sometimes call a chamber pot "the general.") Rabelais, making an exceptionally free play on words, created *officialement.* The debasing and generating power of urine is fancifully combined in this image.

Another example can be found in the famous *Manneken-Pis* of the Brussels fountain. This is an ancient figure of a boy urinating with complete openness. The people of Brussels consider him their mascot.

There are many similar examples which we shall discuss later, but for the present we shall limit ourselves to those already described. The images of feces and urine are ambivalent, as are all the images of the material bodily lower stratum; they debase, destroy, regenerate, and renew simultaneously. They are blessing and humiliating at the same time. Death and death throes, labor, and childbirth are intimately interwoven.[6] On the other hand, these images are closely linked to laughter. When death and birth are shown in their comic aspect, scatological images in various forms nearly always accompany the gay monsters created by laughter in order to replace the terror that has been defeated. For this reason, too, these images are indissolubly linked with the underworld. It

---

[6] In world literature and especially in anonymous oral tradition we find many examples of the interweaving of death throes and the act of defecation, or the closeness of defecation to the moment of death. This is one of the widespread forms of degrading death and dying. This type of degradation could be called the "Malbrough theme." From the works of great literature I shall cite only one remarkable satire by Seneca, *Ludus morte Claudii,* in which the emperor dies at the moment of defecation. In Rabelais' novel the Malbrough theme is introduced in several variants; for instance, the inhabitants of the "Isle of Winds" die while emitting gases, and their souls leave the body via the rectum. In another passage Rabelais cites the example of the Roman who died because of emitting a certain sound in the presence of the emperor. These images not only degrade the dying but lend a body to death, transforming it into a gay monster.

can be said that excrement represents bodies and matter that are mostly comic; it is the most suitable substance for the degrading of all that is exalted. For this reason it plays an important part in comic folklore and in the grotesque realism of Rabelais' novel, as well as in current degrading familiar speech. But when Victor Hugo says in connection with Rabelais' world, *totus homo fit excrementum,* he ignores the regenerating and renewing element of the images, already lost in Europe's literary consciousness.

But let us go back to Veselovsky's picture of the village boy. We see that the metaphor of mudslinging is quite inadequate. It is abstract and moral, whereas Rabelais' cynicism is a system of grotesque degrading, similar to the tossing of excrement and drenching in urine. It is a gay funeral. This system of degradation in various forms and expressions permeates the entire novel from beginning to end; it even gives form to the images that are far from cynical in the narrow sense of the word. All these are but elements of one whole laughing aspect of the world.

The entire picture offered by Veselovsky is quite unsatisfactory. That to which he alludes in the metaphor of the naïve boy, indulgently forgiving his mudslinging, is nothing else than the culture of folk humor developed through thousands of years; this culture has a depth of meaning which is far from naïve. Humor and cynicism may least of all be defined as naïve and do not need our indulgence. Instead they demand our careful and attentive analysis.[7]

We have discussed the cynicism, the indecencies, and the billingsgate in Rabelais' novel. But all these terms are conventional

[7] A similar formula for a disdainfully indulgent treatment of Rabelais was given by Voltaire in his *Sottisier:* "Marot, Amyot, and Rabelais are praised, as small children are usually praised if by chance they happen to say something clever. These writers are approved because their time is despised and children are lauded because nothing is expected from their age." This is a characteristic attitude of the Enlighteners toward the past, especially toward the sixteenth century. It is too often repeated in this form or another, in our time. We should discard once for all this completely false conception of the sixteenth century.

and far from adequate. First of all, these elements are not isolated; they are an organic part of the entire system of images and style. They become isolated and specific only for modern literary consciousness. Within the system of grotesque realism and popular festive forms they were an essential part of the imagery representing the material bodily lower stratum. True, they were unofficial in character, but so too was all popular-festive literature of the Middle Ages, so too was laughter. We, therefore, brought out the billingsgate and marketplace images only conventionally. We mean by these terms all that is directly linked with the life of the people, bearing its mark of nonofficial freedom; but at the same time these images cannot be referred to as popular-festive literature in the strict sense of this word.

First of all, we have in mind certain forms of familiar speech—curses, profanities, and oaths—and second the colloquialisms of the marketplace: the *cris de Paris* and the announcements made during fairs by quacks and vendors of drugs. These genres are not "separated by a Chinese wall" from the literature and spectacles of folk festivals; they are part of them and often play in them a leading stylistic role. We continually find them in the *dits* and *débats,* in diableries, *soties,* and farces. The colloquial and artistic forms are sometimes so closely interwoven that it is difficult to trace a dividing line, and no wonder, since the barkers and vendors of drugs were also actors in performances at the fair. The *cris de Paris* were composed in verse and were sung in a peremptory tone. The style of the barker inviting customers to his booth did not differ from that of the hawker of chapbooks, and even the long titles of these books were usually composed in the form of popular advertisements. The marketplace of the Middle Ages and the Renaissance was a world in itself, a world which was one; all "performances" in this area, from loud cursing to the organized show, had something in common and were imbued with the same atmosphere of freedom, frankness, and familiarity. Such elements of familiar speech as profanities, oaths, and curses were fully legalized in the marketplace and were easily adopted by all the festive genres, even by Church drama. The marketplace was the center of all that is unofficial; it enjoyed a certain extraterritoriality in a world of official order and official ideology, it always remained "with the people."

This popular aspect was especially apparent on feast days. The dates of the fairs were usually adapted to the great feasts of the year but were extended over a long period. For instance, the famous fairs of Lyon were held four times a year, and each lasted fifteen days. Thus every year Lyon led for two months a life of fairs and carnivals, for even if there was no carnival, strictly speaking, its atmosphere reigned at every fair.

Thus, the unofficial folk culture of the Middle Ages and even of the Renaissance had its own territory and its own particular time, the time of fairs and feasts. This territory, as we have said, was a peculiar second world within the official medieval order and was ruled by a special type of relationship, a free, familiar, marketplace relationship. Officially the palaces, churches, institutions, and private homes were dominated by hierarchy and etiquette, but in the marketplace a special kind of speech was heard, almost a language of its own, quite unlike the language of Church, palace, courts, and institutions. It was also unlike the tongue of official literature or of the ruling classes—the aristocracy, the nobles, the high-ranking clergy and the top burghers—though the elemental force of the folk idiom penetrated even these circles. On feast days, especially during the carnivals, this force broke through every sphere, and even through the Church, as in "the feast of fools." The festive marketplace combined many genres and forms, all filled with the same unofficial spirit.

In all world literature there is probably no other work reflecting so fully and deeply all aspects of the life of the marketplace as does Rabelais' novel. But before examining these aspects at closer range we must first sketch Rabelais' contact with this sphere as well as the limited biographical material permits.

Rabelais was familiar with the marketplace and fairs of his time. As we shall see, he made good use of his experience and projected it forcefully in his novel.

In Fontenay-le-Comte, where he spent his youth in a monastery of the Cordeliers, he had been taught humanist and Greek culture, but at the same time he had been introduced to the peculiar culture of the marketplace. A fair famous throughout France was at that time held three times a year at Fontenay-le-Comte. A great number of salesmen and customers, not only from France but also from other countries, assembled in the town. According to G. Boucher, many foreigners, especially Germans, came to the fair. Itinerant hawkers, gypsies, and the obscure *déclassés,* so numerous in those days, also came to Fontenay-le-Comte, and from records of the sixteenth century we learn that this town developed its own popular argot. It was here that Rabelais could observe the life of the fair and listen to its voices.

Later Rabelais traveled in the province of Poitou with Bishop Geoffroi d'Estissac. Here he observed the fair of Saint Maixent and the famous fair of Niort; he recalls the hubbub of the latter in his novel. Generally speaking, the fairs of Poitou were known at that time for their elaborateness.

Here Rabelais became acquainted with another important aspect of these gatherings, the marketplace spectacles. He learned about life on the theater scaffoldings *(les échafauds)* which he describes in his novel. These scaffoldings were put up on the square, and the people crowded around them. Lost in the crowd, Rabelais attended mysteries, moralities, and farces. The towns of Poitou, Montmorillon, Saint Maixent, Poitiers, and others, were famous for their theatrical productions.[8] This is the reason why Rabelais chose Saint Maixent and Niort as a setting for Villon's *facéties* described in the Fourth Book. France's dramatic culture was at that time closely related to the marketplace.

During the next period of Rabelais' life, concerning which there is no documentary record (1528–1530), he apparently journeyed to the universities of Bordeaux, Toulouse, Bourges, Orléans, and Paris. Here he was initiated into the students' Bohemian life. This experience was broadened during the following years when Rabelais studied medicine at Montpellier.

We have already pointed out the importance of school festivals

---

[8] See H. Clouzot: *L'ancien théâtre en Poitou,* 1900.

and recreation in medieval culture and literature. The school-men's exuberant compositions had already attained the level of great literature and played in it a substantial role. These recreative writings were also related to the marketplace. School parodies, travesties, *facéties* in Latin and in the vernacular, prove this relation and bear inner resemblance to popular forms. Many school spectacles were organized in the streets. In Montpellier on Epiphany students led carnival processions and danced in the square. The university often produced morality plays and farces outside the campus.[9]

Apparently Rabelais took part in student recreations. J. Plattard believes that during his student years, especially in Montpellier, he wrote a series of anecdotes, *facéties,* and witty debates. He acquired in comic literature the experience that enabled him to create *Pantagruel* so quickly.

In the next period of Rabelais' life, spent in Lyon, his relations with the marketplace became even closer and more intimate. We have mentioned already the famous Lyon fairs, which occupied about two months of each year. Life during that time was extremely animated in that southern city with its large Italian colony. Rabelais himself recalls in the Fourth Book the carnival of Lyon during which the grotesque statue of the glutton "Maschecroûte," a typical gay monster, was carried in procession. The chroniclers of that time described other mass festivals: the feast of printers and the election of the "prince of tradesmen."

Rabelais was linked by even closer ties to the Lyon fairs, since they represented one of the most important markets of publishing and bookselling, second only to Frankfurt. Both these cities were the center of book distribution and literary advertising. Books were published with an eye to the fairs, summer, autumn, and winter being the busy seasons. Lyon determined more or less the

[9] This student recreational literature was part of marketplace culture; its social element was related to folk culture and was sometimes completely fused with it. Among the anonymous authors of these works of grotesque realism (usually in Latin) there were probably many students or graduates.

dates of book publication in France and consequently also fixed the time at which authors submitted their manuscripts to publishers. A. Lefranc successfully established the chronology of Rabelais' works by using the dates of the Lyon fairs. These dates regulated the production of all books, even the scientific ones, but especially popular works and recreational literature.[10]

Rabelais, who had first published three scholarly works, later became the provider of mass literature and therefore entered into a closer relationship with the fairs. He not only had to calculate their dates but also their demands, tastes, and fashions. He published almost simultaneously his *Pantagruel* (which followed directly in the steps of the popular book by an anonymous author "The Great Chronicles of Gargantua") and the *Pantagrueline Prognostication,* an almanac for the year 1533. The *Prognostication* is a gay travesty of the New Year prophecies so popular at that time. This composition, containing only a few small pages, was reprinted during the following years and was followed by others. Indeed, we have certain data and even a few fragments of Rabelais' calendars for the years 1535, 1541, 1546, and 1550. We can surmise, as does L. Moland,[11] that this is not the complete list of calendars published by Rabelais. He probably brought them out every year, beginning in 1533, and was the accredited publisher. Both the "Prognostics" and the calendars are related to time, to the New Year, and finally, to the marketplace.

There is no doubt that during the following years of his life Rabelais preserved a vivid interest in the fairs and maintained relations with their various activities. The meager biographical data in our possession do not offer us, however, any positive facts in this respect.[12] But we have an important document dating from

[10] The combined publishing of erudite scholarly works and literature for fairs and carnivals was typical of those times.

[11] *Op. cit.* ftn. 4.

[12] Rabelais' legendary biography presents him as a popular figure of the marketplace. According to this legend, his life was full of mystifications, travesties, and clownery. L. Moland rightly calls this legendary figure *un Rabelais de carême-prenant* (a carnival Rabelais).

Rabelais' last journey to Italy. On March 14, 1549, Cardinal Jean du Bellay organized a popular festival in Rome on the occasion of the birth of the son of King Henry II. Rabelais attended this festival and described it in detail, using for this account his own letters to Cardinal Guizou. This description was published in Paris and Lyon under the title of "The Sciamachy and Festival Offered in Rome in the Palace of His Eminence Monsignor du Bellay."

In the first part of this festival, performed in a piazza, a battle was fought with dramatic effects, fireworks, and even casualties (later shown to be straw dummies). The festival had a typical carnivalesque character. The traditional hell was presented in the form of a globe ejecting flames. This globe was known as the "jaws of hell" and "Lucifer's head."[13] At the end of the festival a gigantic banquet was offered to the people, with enormous, truly Pantagruelesque quantities of sausages and wine.

Such festivals are characteristic of the Renaissance. Burckhardt has shown how important was their influence on the artistic form and philosophy of that period and on its very spirit. He did not exaggerate the importance of that influence; it was even greater than he thought.[14]

Rabelais was not so much interested in the official aspect of the festivities of his time as in their popular, unofficial elements. These were the elements that influenced his work. He could observe in them the most varied forms of comic folklore, so rich and colorful in his time.

Depicting in the First Book young Gargantua's studies under the guidance of Ponocrates, Rabelais says:

Instead of herborizing, they would inspect the shops of druggists, herbalists and apothecaries, studiously examining the sundry fruits, roots, leaves, gums, seeds and exotic unguents and learning how they could be diluted or adulterated. He viewed jugglers, mountebanks and medicasters . . . carefully observing

[13] L. Moland, *op. cit.* ftn. 4, p. 599.
[14] True, Burckhardt had in mind not so much the popular marketplace festivities as the courtly official feasts.

their tricks and gestures, their agile capers and smooth oratory. His favorites were those from Chauny in Picardy who are born jabberers . . . (Book 1, Chapter 24)

This episode of young Gargantua's education can be legitimately interpreted as autobiographical, since Rabelais himself studied all these aspects of popular life. Let us stress that popular spectacles and popular medicine, herbalists and druggists, hawkers of magic unguents and quacks, could be seen side by side. There was an ancient connection between the forms of medicine and folk art which explains the combination in one person of actor and druggist. This is why the images of the physician and the medical element are organically linked in the novel with the entire traditional system of images. In the previous quotation we see medicine and the theater displayed side by side in the marketplace.

Such is the history of Rabelais' physical connection with the marketplace, as far as we can deduce it from the meager biographical data. But how did the marketplace enter the sphere of his novel and how was it reflected in it?

This question first arises in relation to the atmosphere of the marketplace and the organization of its verbal idiom. We encounter it at the beginning of each book of the novel, in the famous prologues. We started our study with a chapter devoted to these elements, precisely because we enter into the marketplace world from the very first lines of the five books, in the prologue to *Pantagruel*, chronologically the first book to be written and published.

How is the prologue of *Pantagruel* constructed? It begins thus:

O most illustrious and most valorous champions, gentlemen and all others who delight in honest entertainment and wit. I address this book to you. You have read and digested the *Mighty and Inestimable Chronicles of the Huge Giant Gargantua.* Like true believers you have taken them upon faith as you do the texts of the Holy Gospel. Indeed, having run out of gallant speeches, you have often spent hours at a time relating lengthy stories culled from these *Chronicles* to a rapt audience of noble dames and matrons of high degree. On this count, then, you deserve vast praise and sempiternal memory. (Book 2, Prologue)

Here we see combined the praise of the "Chronicles of Gargantua" and of the readers who enjoy this chapbook. The praise and glorification are composed in the advertising spirit of the barker at a show or the hawker of chapbooks, who praise not only their wondrous merchandise but also the "most illustrious" public. This is a typical example of the tone and style of the fair.

But of course these announcements have nothing in common with naïve and direct practical advertisements. They are filled with popular-festive laughter. They toy with the objects that they announce, and they include in this free game all the "sacred" and "exalted" topics that they can fit into their oratory. In the quoted lines the admirers of the "Chronicles" are compared to true believers (*vrais fidèles*) who put their faith in it as in a sacred text, and who therefore deserve honor, praise, and undying memory (*mémoire sempiternelle*). Thus Rabelais recreates that special marketplace atmosphere in which the exalted and the lowly, the sacred and the profane are leveled and are all drawn into the same dance. Such have always been the announcements at the fair. They did not demand conventional forms or official speeches. They enjoyed the privileges of the people's laughter. Popular advertising is always ironic, always makes fun of itself to a certain extent (as does the advertising of our own peddlers and hawkers).[15] At the fair even cupidity and cheating have an ironical, almost candid character. In the medieval street cry there was always laughter, more or less forceful.

In the quoted excerpt from the prologue there are no neutral objective words. All are words of praise: *très illustres, très chevaleureux, gentillesses, honnestetés, grandes, inestimables,* and so forth. (I quote from the original text.) The superlative is the prevailing tone; actually, all the adjectives are used in this mode. But it is, of course, no rhetorical tone; rather it is an ironically

---

[15] Meaning Russian street vendors. (Translator's note.)

and maliciously exaggerated style. It is the superlative of grotesque realism: the wrong side, or rather, the right side of abuse.

In the following paragraphs of the prologue we hear the cry of the quack and druggist at the fair. He praises the "Chronicles" as an excellent remedy for toothache and offers a prescription for its use: to be wrapped in warm linen and applied to the sensitive area. Such mock prescriptions are one of the most widespread genres of grotesque realism.[16] Further, the "Chronicles" is praised as a potent medicine for pain inflicted by gout and venereal disease.

Sufferers from gout and venereal disease are often featured in Rabelais' novel and in comic literature of the fifteenth and sixteenth centuries, especially. Gout and syphilis are "gay diseases," the result of overindulgence in food, drink, and sexual intercourse. They are essentially connected with the material bodily lower stratum. Pox was still a "fashionable disease" in those days.[17] As to gout, it was widespread in grotesque realism; we find it as far back as Lucian.[18]

In this part of the prologue there is the traditional combination of medicine and art, but it is not this overt fusion of physician and artist in one person which is important. Here a literary work (the "Chronicles") is proclaimed as a writing which not only entertains and provokes laughter but also cures. This is announced

[16] A mock prescription of the early Middle Ages recommending a remedy for baldness has been preserved.

[17] Syphilis appeared in Europe during the last years of the fifteenth century. It was known as the *maladie de Naples*. The other vulgar name for it was *gorre* (meaning luxury or pomp), or *grand gorre*, that is, sumptuosity, magnificence. In 1539 a work was published under the title of *Le Triomphe de la très haulte et puissante Dame Vérole* (The triumph of the very noble and powerful Lady Vérole).

[18] Lucian wrote a comic tragedy in verse: *Tragopodagra*. Its heroes are Podagrus and Podagra, the physician, the executioner, and the chorus. Rabelais' junior contemporary Fischart wrote the *Podagrammisch Trostbüchlein* in which he offered comic praise of gout, considered the consequence of overeating and laziness. Ambivalent praise of a malady, especially of syphilis and gout, was common.

with the accent of the quack and the barker of the fair. In the prologue of the Fourth Book Rabelais resumes this theme and bases the curative power of laughter on the teaching of Hippocrates, Galen, Plato, and others.

Having enumerated the "Chronicles" ' merits in the prologue of the Second Book, the author continues:

> Is this nothing? Then find me a book in any language, in any branch of art and science that possesses such virtues, properties and prerogatives. Find it, I say, and I will buy you a pint of tripes! No, gentlemen, no, none such exists. My book is peerless, incomparable, nonpareil, and—I maintain it in the teeth of hellfire—unique! If anyone contradicts me, let him be herewith denounced as a false prophet, a champion of predestination, a poisoner, and a seducer of the people. (Book 2, Prologue)

Besides the enormous accumulation of superlatives, typical of marketplace advertising, we find the characteristic method of testifying to the speaker's honesty: comic pledges and oaths. He promises to pay "a pint of tripes"; he is ready to assert in the teeth of hellfire that no better book exists, it is unique. Such ironic parodies were current in advertisements of the fair.

Let us pay special attention to the "pint of tripes." This word figures more than once in Rabelais as well as in all the literature of grotesque realism (in the Latin versions the word *viscera* corresponds to tripe). In the given context the words refer, of course, to food. The stomach and bowels of cattle, tripe, were carefully cleaned, salted, and cooked. Tripe could not be preserved long; they were therefore consumed in great quantities on slaughtering days and cost nothing. Moreover, it was believed that after cleaning, tripe still contained ten per cent excrement which was therefore eaten with the rest of the meal. We shall find tripe again in one of *Gargantua's* most famous episodes.

But why did this image play such a role in grotesque realism? Tripe, stomach, intestines are the bowels, the belly, the very life of man. But at the same time they represent the swallowing, devouring belly. Grotesque realism played with this double image, we might say with the top and the bottom of the word. We have already quoted Henri Estienne, who showed that in the time of Rabelais it was customary to turn a wineglass upside down, repeating the words of the penitential psalm: "create a clean heart in me, O God: and renew a right spirit in my bowels" Wine cleanses the intestines (*viscera*). But our image is more complex. The bowels are related to defecation and excrement. Further, the belly does not only eat and swallow, it is also eaten, as tripe. In "the palaver of the potulent" (First Book) one guest says to another as he prepares drinks, "Have you anything to send to the river? That's where tripe is washed." Here he had in mind the food he had just eaten as well as his own belly. Further, tripe is linked with death, with slaughter, murder, since to disembowel is to kill. Finally, it is linked with birth, for the belly generates.

Thus, in the image of tripe life and death, birth, excrement, and food are all drawn together and tied in one grotesque knot; this is the center of bodily topography in which the upper and lower stratum penetrate each other. This grotesque image was a favorite expression of the ambivalence of the material bodily lower stratum, which destroys and generates, swallows and is swallowed. The "swing" of grotesque realism, the play of the upper with the lower sphere, is strikingly set into motion; the top and the bottom, heaven and earth, merge in that image. We shall further see the remarkable symphony of laughter derived by Rabelais from the ambivalent and varied meaning of the word tripe in the first chapters of *Gargantua* (the feast of the cattle slaughter, the palaver of the potulent, the birth of Gargantua).

In our example the pint of tripe as the author's pledge does not only mean a cheap variety of food but also life, the bowels, in the sense of "all my tripes." This picture, too, is ambivalent.

The last line of the excerpt is no less typical. After words of praise the author turns to curses (the reverse of marketplace praise). Those who do not share the positive view of the "Chronicles" are branded as poisoners and seducers of the people. These pejoratives were especially applied to persons accused of heresy, doomed to the stake. The play with serious and dangerous subjects continues. The author compares the "Chronicles" to the

Bible and the Gospels. Like the Church, he condemns all dissidents for heresy with all the inevitable consequences. The bold allusion to the Church and Church politics has a realistic note. The abusive words "champions of predestination" obviously had in mind the Protestants who professed this doctrine.

Thus we have on the one hand the author's exaggerated praise of the "Chronicles" as the best, the only book in the world, his praise of those who read it and believe in it and are ready to die for it, of those who defend their belief in the potency of the book and give up their life for it (in the ironic ambivalent form of the "pint of tripe"). On the other hand there is the accusation of heresy for all who disagree. All this is a parody of the Church as the only guardian of salvation and interpreter of the Gospels. But this dangerous parody is offered in the form of laughter and gay advertisements, the language and style of the fair being strictly observed. The barker of a show would not be accused of heresy, no matter what he might say, provided he maintained his clownery. Rabelais maintained it. The comic aspect of the world was legalized. He was not afraid to declare in his prologue that more copies of the "Chronicles" were sold than those of the Bible during nine years.

The prologue ends in a torrent of abuses and curses hurled at the author if there is a single lie in his book, as well as at those who do not believe him:

However, before I conclude this prologue, I hereby deliver myself up body and soul, belly and bowels, to a hundred thousand bastketfuls of raving demons, if I have lied so much as once throughout this book. By the same token, may St. Anthony sear you with his erysipelatous fire . . . may Mahomet's disease whirl you in epileptic jitters . . . may the festers, ulcers and chancres of every purulent pox infect, scathe, mangle and rend you, entering your bumgut as tenuously as mercuralized cow's hair . . . and may you vanish into an abyss of brimstone and fire, like Sodom and Gomorrah, if you do not believe implicitly what I am about to relate in the present *Chronicles* . . . (Book 2, Prologue)

These are typical billingsgate abuses. The passing from excessive praise to excessive invective is characteristic, and the change from the one to the other is perfectly legitimate. Praise and abuse are, so to speak, the two sides of the same coin. If the right side is praise, the wrong side is abuse, and vice versa. The billingsgate idiom is a two-faced Janus. The praise, as we have said, is ironic and ambivalent. It is on the brink of abuse; the one leads to the other, and it is impossible to draw the line between them. Though divided in form they belong to the same body, or to the two bodies in one, which abuses while praising and praises while abusing. This is why in familiar billingsgate talk abusive words, especially indecent ones, are used in the affectionate and complimentary sense. (We shall further analyze many examples from Rabelais.) This grotesque language, particularly in its oldest form, was oriented toward the world and toward all the world's phenomena in their condition of unfinished metamorphosis: the passing from night to morning, from winter to spring, from the old to the new, from death to birth. Therefore, this talk showers both compliments and curses. Perhaps our example does not clearly typify this, but its ambivalence raises no doubt. This ambivalence determines the organic and spontaneous character of the change from praise to abuse and back to praise again, as well as the uncertainty as to whom the talk is addressed.[19]

We shall resume this topic of simultaneous praise and abuse in Chapter 6. This phenomenon is reflected in imagery and is extremely important for the understanding of entire periods of the development of thought. This development has not as yet been analyzed, but in a preliminary and rather simplified way we

[19] At close range, this many-faced person is the crowd which surrounds the barker's booth, and also the many-faced reader. Praise and abuse are showered on this person, for some in the audience may be the representatives of the old, dying world and ideology—agelasts, that is, men who do not know how to laugh, hypocrites, slanderers who live in darkness; others are the representatives of a new world, a world of light, laughter, and truth. Together they form one people, dying and renewed, and this people is abused and praised simultaneously. But this interpretation is at the closest range. In the longer view, beyond the crowd, there is the whole world, unfinished, uncompleted, which generates in dying and is born to die.

can say that it is based on the conception of the world as eternally unfinished: a world dying and being born at the same time, possessing as it were two bodies. The dual image combining praise and abuse seeks to grasp the very moment of this change, the transfer from the old to the new, from death to life. Such an image crowns and uncrowns at the same moment. In the development of class society such a conception of the world can only be expressed in unofficial culture. There is no place for it in the culture of the ruling classes; here praise and abuse are clearly divided and static, for official culture is founded on the principle of an immovable and unchanging hierarchy in which the higher and the lower never merge.

Although the combination of praise and abuse is completely alien to official genres, it is characteristic of folk culture. The distant echoes of this dual form can still be heard in the familiar speech of our days. Since folk culture has not been profoundly studied, the fusion of praise and abuse has not been brought to light.

The content of the billingsgate expressions in the curses of the prologue is typical. Nearly all of them refer to a specific part of the human body. The first, directed at the author himself, rends him apart; the speaker gives himself up to the devil, body, soul, and bowels. We encounter once more the words *tripes* and *boyaulx*.

Of the seven oaths hurled at the reluctant listeners, five call down diseases upon them: (1) Saint Anthony's fire (erysipelas), (2) epilepsy, (*mau de terre vous vire*), (3) and (4) ulcers of the feet and lameness (*le maulubec vous trousque*), (5) bleeding diarrhea (*caque sangue vous vire*) and inflammation of the rectum (*le mau fin feu . . . vous puisse entrer au fondement*).

These curses offer a grotesque view of the body; they burn it, hurl it to the ground, cripple the legs, cause diarrhea, and griping; in other words, they turn the body inside out, causing the anus to protrude. Curses always indicate a downward motion, directed to the ground, the legs, the buttocks.

The two last of the seven curses also denote this downward

movement: fire from heaven and the brimstone abyss—in other words the threat of being hurled into the underworld.

All these curses are uttered in their traditional form. One, in Gascon (*le maulubec vous trousque*), is used more than once in Rabelais' novel. Another, judging from the refrain and assonance in the original French text, contains fragments of some popular street ditty. In many curses the body part is combined with cosmic images: lightning, earth, brimstone, fire, ocean.

The curses at the end of the prologue bring it to a dynamic conclusion in a powerful and rough debasing gesture, the "grotesque swing" which lowers it to earth before it comes to a stop. Rabelais usually concludes his speeches either with an abuse or an invitation to feasting and drinking.

Such is the structure of *Pantagruel's* prologue. It is written from beginning to end in the style and tone of the marketplace. We hear the cry of the barker, the quack, the hawker of miracle drugs, and the bookseller; we hear the curses that alternate with ironic advertisements and ambiguous praise. The prologue is organized according to the popular verbal genres of hawkers. The words are actually a cry, that is, a loud interjection in the midst of a crowd, coming out of the crowd and addressed to it. The man who is speaking is one with the crowd; he does not present himself as its opponent, nor does he teach, accuse, or intimidate it. He *laughs* with it. There is not the slightest tone of morose seriousness in his oration, no fear, piety, or humility. This is an absolutely gay and fearless talk, free and frank, which echoes in the festive square beyond all verbal prohibitions, limitations, and conventions.

At the same time, however, this entire prologue is a parody and travesty of the ecclesiastical method of persuasion. Behind the "Chronicles" stands the Gospel; behind the offer of the "Chronicles" as the only book of salvation stands the exclusiveness of the Church's truth; behind the abuses and curses are the Church's intolerance, intimidation, and *autos-da-fé*. The ecclesiastical policy is translated into the language of ironical hawking. But the prologue is wider and deeper than the usual grotesque parody. It travesties the very foundations of medieval thought, the methods of establishing truth and conviction which are inseparable from fear, violence, morose and narrow-minded seriousness and intolerance. The prologue introduces us into a completely different atmosphere, the atmosphere of fearless, free, and gay truth.

The prologue of *Gargantua* (the second prologue chronologically speaking) has a more complex structure. Billingsgate abuse is here combined with elements of scholarly humanism and with a parody of Plato's *Symposium*. But the language of the marketplace and its intonations of praise-abuse still retain the leading role. They acquire, however, a more subtle and varied tone, applied to richer combinations of themes and topics.

The prologue starts with the characteristic address: "Hail, O most valiant and illustrious drinkers! Your health my precious and pox-ridden comrades . . ." (*Beuveurs très illustres et vous Véroles très précieux . . .*) This address immediately creates the familiar tone of the further conversation with the readers, or more correctly speaking, with the listeners, since the style of the prologue is that of oral speech.

Abuse and praise are mingled in this address. The positive superlative mode is combined with such semi-insulting terms as "drinkers" and "pox-ridden comrades." This is abusive praise and praiseful abuse, typical, as we have seen, of the marketplace.

The entire prologue is built like the announcement of a barker speaking to the crowd gathered in front of his booth. We constantly encounter expressions of the advertising type; the familiar tone intended for an audience is here quite obvious.

We also find, scattered throughout the prologue to *Gargantua,* abuse addressed to third persons: an "empty-headed monk," a "dullard," a "dirty fellow," a "grumbler."

Familiar, friendly abuse and direct cursing make up the verbal dynamics of the prologue and determine its style. The beginning of the discourse presents the image of Socrates as described by Alcibiades in Plato's *Symposium*. Alcibiades' comparison of Socrates with Silenus was popular among the humanists. It was used by Budé and cited by Erasmus in three of his works, one of which,

The Sileni of Alcibiades, was apparently Rabelais' source, although he was familiar with the *Symposium*. Rabelais subordinated this current humanist theme to the style of his prologue, sharply stressing the praise-abuse combination.

Here is how Rabelais retells the description of Socrates by Alcibiades:

> ... judging by his exterior, you would not have given an onion skin for him. He was ill-shaped, ridiculous in carriage, with a nose like a knife, the gaze of a bull and the face of a fool. His ways stamped him a simpleton, his clothes a bumpkin. Poor in fortune, unlucky when it came to women, hopelessly unfit for all office in the Republic, forever laughing, forever drinking neck to neck with his friends, forever hiding his divine knowledge under a mask of mockery ...
>
> Yet had you opened this box, you would have found in it all kinds of priceless, celestial drugs: immortal understanding, wondrous virtue, indomitable courage, unparalleled sobriety, unfailing serenity, perfect assurance and heroic contempt for whatever moves humanity to watch, to bustle, to toil, to sail ships overseas and to engage in warfare. (Book 1, Prologue)

As far as content is concerned, we have no considerable deviations from Plato and Erasmus, but the contrasts of Socrates' exterior and interior image are expressed in more familiar tones. The choice of words and expressions and their very accumulation bring these lines nearer to the abusive style, to Rabelais' usual techniques of piling up curses. We sense behind this verbal arrangement the hidden dynamics of this abuse. Socrates' interior qualities are also brought out more vigorously in the form of a eulogy. Once more, behind the verbal arrangement we detect the secret dynamics of marketplace praise.

Let us now note a characteristic detail. According to Plato (in the *Symposium*) Sileni are sold in sculpturers' shops; if opened, the image of a god is found in them. Rabelais transfers the Sileni to the druggists' stores, which young Gargantua visited when studying life in the Paris streets. The statuettes contained various drugs, among them a popular remedy, a powder of precious stones supposed to have healing power. These drugs are enumerated in the hawking style used by the apothecaries and quacks at the fairs in the time of Rabelais.

All the other images of the prologue are also steeped in the atmosphere of the fair. We find everywhere the abuse-praise combination as the basic moving force which determines the style and the dynamics of the speeches. There are almost no objective words, that is, words which imply neither praise nor abuse. The comparative and superlative are commonly used. For instance: "how much more reconciling, smiling and beguiling wine is than oil," or "these fine, full-flavored volumes." In the first case we hear the rhythmic beat of the vendor. In the second case the word "full-flavored" lauds the supreme quality of venison and meats. The market that young Gargantua visited under Ponocrates' wise guidance cries out in this prologue, with its herbalists and apothecaries, with exotic unguents, with the tricks and oratory of the people from Chauny, "born jabberers" and experts in cheating. All the images of the new humanist culture, and there are many of them in this prologue, are steeped in the atmosphere of the market.

Let us quote from the end of the prologue: "And now, my hearties, be gay, and gayly read the rest, with ease of body and in the best of kidney! And you, donkey-pizzles, hark! May a canker rot you! Remember to drink to me gallantly, and I will counter with a toast at once." (Book 1, Prologue)

As we see, this prologue ends on a note somewhat different from that of the prologue introducing *Pantagruel*. Instead of a string of oaths, we have here an invitation to drink and be merry. Here too we find abuses, but they have an affectionate tone. The same persons are addressed as "my hearties" (*mes amours*) and donkey-pizzles" (*viédazes*). We also find the Gascon expression *le maulubec vous trousque* that we have already encountered in the *Pantagruel* prologue. In these last lines of the *Gargantua* prologue the entire Rabelaisian complex is offered in its most elementary expression: the gaiety, the indecent abuse, and the banquet. But this is also the most simplified festive expression of the ambivalent lower stratum: laughter, food, the procreative force, abuse.

The dominant images of the prologue are those of the banquet. The author eulogizes wine as much more pleasing than oil. (Oil is the symbol of sanctimonious wisdom and piety, while wine is the symbol of gay and free truth.) Most of the epithets and comparisons applied by Rabelais to spiritual things have what one might call an edible character. The author boldly states that he writes only while eating and drinking, and adds: "Is that not the proper time to commit to the page such sublime themes and such profound wisdom? Homer the paragon of all philologists, knew it perfectly well and Ennius also, the father of the Latin poets . . ." (Book 1, Prologue)

Finally, the central theme of the prologue, the invitation to seek the secret meaning of the work, is also expressed in images of eating, gnawing a bone, finding the marrow and eating it. The image of swallowing the secret meaning is extremely typical of Rabelais and of the entire system of popular-festive images. We have merely mentioned a few of them here; we shall devote a chapter to these banquet images.

The marketplace vocabulary also plays a leading role in the prologue to the Third Book. This prologue is outstanding; of all Rabelais' prologues it has the greatest wealth of themes.

The prologue starts with the address: "Good people, most illustrious topers, thrice-precious gouty gentlemen, I wonder whether you ever saw Diogenes, the Cynic philosopher?" Further, the prologue develops in the form of a familiar conversation with the audience, full of images of banquets, comic folk elements, puns, allusions, and verbal travesties. J. Plattard, commenting on the A. Lefranc edition of Rabelais, correctly defines this introduction: "This is the tone of a barker which justifies the coarsest jokes."

The prologue ends with a string of billingsgate abuses that are extraordinarily colorful and dynamic. The author invites his audience to drink glassfuls of wine from his barrel, which is as inexhaustible as a cornucopia. But he invites only good men, lovers of wine and merriment who know how to drink. As to the others, the pompous and haughty hypocrites, he chases them away from his barrel:

Back, curs, to heel! Out of my way, back from the barrel, out of the sunlight, you scum of the devil! Away, hypocrites and sham Abrahams! How dare you come here, arsing and parsing, mumbling for my wine and then bepiddling my barrel? Look out! here is the stuff Diogenes willed to be laid beside him after death so he might exterminate such deadly larvae and gravelice as yourself. To your flock, mastiffs; fly hence, buzzards, by all the devils of hell!

What you are still here? By God, for my part, if I stomach you, let me surrender my share of Paradise—yes, my share of Papimany, the Pope's temporal possessions! Grrrrrrr! Grrrrr! Kssssss! Kssss! Away, away with them! Are they not yet gone?

May you never contrive a shit without first being lambasted with stirrup-straps . . . may you never squeeze out a piddle without being previously strappadoed . . . and may you never know bodily heat save that induced by the cudgel! (Book 3, Prologue)

Abuses and blows have more definite targets here than in the *Pantagruel* prologue; they are aimed at the representatives of the old, gloomy truth of medieval philosophy, of "Gothic darkness," the somberly hypocritical and serious, the messengers of darkness. They are the enemies of the new, free, and gay truth, symbolized by the barrel of Diogenes which has been transformed into a cask of wine. They dare to criticize this wine of gay truth and to urinate into the barrel. This is an allusion to denunciations, slander, persecution inflicted by those whom Rabelais called "agelasts" upon the new truth. These enemies have come in order to *culletans articuler mon vin.* The word *articuler* means to criticize, to condemn, but Rabelais shows that it contains the syllable *cul,* the backside, which lends it a debasing, abusive connotation. (The word *culletans* means swinging the buttocks to and fro.) In the last chapter of *Pantagruel* Rabelais uses this method of abuse in a broader sense. Speaking of the hypocritical monks who spend their time reading "Pantagruelesque books" not for amusement's sake but in order to denounce and slander them, he writes: *scavoir est articulant, monarticulant, torticulant, culletant, couilletant et diabliculant, c'est à dire calumniant.* Ecclesiastical censorship (of the Sorbonne), a calumny directed against the gay truth, is cast down to the bodily *cul*, lower stratum, and the reproductive organs (*couillon*). Further, Rabelais pursues this debasement, comparing the ecclesiastical censors to the ragamuffins who roam the countryside during the cherry season, picking cherrystones from children's excrement and selling them.

Let us turn back to the conclusion of the prologue. Its dynamism is still further increased by reproducing the shouts of the shepherds inciting their dogs to chase the flocks (Grrrrrr! Grrrrr! Kssss!). The last lines of the prologue contain a sharp abusive debasement. In order to express the mediocrity and lack of productivity of these gloomy slanderers of good wine, the author declares that they are unable to urinate, defecate, or be sexually stimulated unless they are beaten. In other words, they can be productive only under the stress of fear and suffering (in the original text *sanglades d'estivières* and *à l'estrapade,* i.e., public torture and whipping). This masochism of gloomy calumniators is here a grotesque degradation of fear and suffering, the two leading motives of medieval ideology. The image of defecation from fear is a traditional debasement not of the coward only but of fear itself; this is one of the important variants of the "Malbrough theme." It is treated in detail by Rabelais in the Fourth Book in the episode that was the last he was to write himself. In the Third and Fourth Books, especially in the Fourth, Panurge has become a pious and cowardly man. Terrorized by mystic fantasies as he sat in the dark storeroom, he mistook the cat for the devil and defecated from fear. Thus a mystical vision caused by fear has been transformed into a bodily image. Rabelais even gives here a medical analysis of this occurrence:

The retentive faculty of the nerve which restrains the muscle called sphincter (arsehole to you!) had slackened before the violence of Panurge's terror during his fantastic visions. Add to this the thunder of the cannonade, always more dreadful between decks than above, and you need not wonder at Panurge's distress.

One of the symptoms and mishaps of fear is that it usually opens the back door of the rotunda where fecal guests await their turn to emerge. (Book 4, Chapter 67)

Further, Rabelais tells the story of Pantolfe de la Cassina of Siena, who suffered from constipation and asked the innkeeper to frighten him with a pitchfork. He tells another story about François Villon, who praised King Edward of England for having painted the French royal arms in his privies; the emblem filled the English sovereign with fear. Edward thought that he was thus debasing France, but actually the terrifying picture helped him to relieve himself. This old tale dating from the thirteenth century has been preserved in several variants referring to different historic personages, but it always shows fear as a remedy for constipation.

This debasement of suffering and fear is an important element in the general system of degradation directed at medieval seriousness. Indeed all Rabelais' prologues are devoted to this theme. We saw that the prologue of *Pantagruel* is a travesty that transposes the medieval conception of the only salutary truth into the flippant language of advertising. The prologue of *Gargantua* debases the "hidden meaning," the "secret," the "terrifying mysteries" of religion, politics, and economics. Degradation is achieved by transforming these mysteries into festive scenes of eating and drinking. Laughter must liberate the gay truth of the world from the veils of gloomy lies spun by the seriousness of fear, suffering, and violence.

The theme of the Third Book's prologue is similar. It is the defense of the gay truth and of the right to laughter. It is the debasement of medieval gloom and slander. The last scene of abuse and the chasing away of the hypocrites from Diogenes' barrel of wine (the symbol of the gay and free truth) brings a dynamic conclusion to all these degradations.

It would be a mistake to think that the Rabelaisian debasement of fear and suffering was prompted by coarse cynicism. We must not forget that the image of defecation, like all the images of the lower stratum, is ambivalent and that the element of reproductive force, birth, and renewal is alive in it. We have already sought to prove this, and we find here further substantiation. Speaking of the masochism of the gloomy slanderers, Rabelais also mentions sexual stimulus together with defecation.

At the end of the Fourth Book Panurge, who defecated from fear and was mocked by his companions, finally rids himself of his terror and regains his cheerfulness. He exclaims:

Oh, ho, ho, ho, ho! What the devil is this? Do you call this ordure, ejection, excrement, evacuation, *dejecta*, fecal matter, *egesta, copros, scatos,* dung, crap, turds? Not at all, not at all: it is but the fruit of the shittim tree, 'Selah! Let us drink.' (Book 4, Chapter 67)

These are the last words of the Fourth Book, and actually the last sentence of the entire book that was written by Rabelais' own hand. Here we find twelve synonyms for excrement, from the most vulgar to the most scientific. At the end it is described as a tree, something rare and pleasant. And the tirade concludes with an invitation to drink, which in Rabelaisian imagery means to be in communion with truth.

Here we find the ambivalent image of excrement, its relation to regeneration and renewal and its special role in overcoming fear. Excrement is gay matter; in the ancient scatological images, as we have said, it is linked to the generating force and to fertility. On the other hand, excrement is conceived as something *intermediate between earth and body,* as something relating the one to the other. It is also an intermediate between the living body and dead disintegrating matter that is being transformed into earth, into manure. The living body returns to the earth its excrement, which fertilizes the earth as does the body of the dead. Rabelais was able to distinguish these nuances clearly. As we shall see further, they were not alien to his medical views. Moreover, as an artist and an heir to grotesque realism, he conceived excrement as both joyous and sobering matter, at the same time debasing and tender; it combined the grave and birth in their lightest, most comic, least terrifying form.

Therefore, there is nothing grossly cynical in Rabelais' scatological images, nor in the other images of grotesque realism: the slinging of dung, the drenching in urine, the volley of scatological abuse hurled at the old, dying, yet generating world. All these images represent the gay funeral of this old world; they are (in the dimension of laughter) like handfuls of sod gently dropped into the open grave, like seeds sown in the earth's bosom. If the image is applied to the gloomy, disincarnated medieval truth, it symbolizes bringing it "down to earth" through laughter.

All this should not be forgotten in the analysis of the scatological images that abound in Rabelais' novel.

Let us return to the prologue of the Third Book. As yet we have looked only at its first and last lines. It begins with the cry of the barker and ends with billingsgate abuse, but these marketplace forms, with which we are already familiar, do not exhaust our subject. There is another, important aspect of this life; in it we hear the voice of the herald announcing mobilization, siege, war, or calling all corporations and guilds to order. This is the historic setting of the marketplace.

The central image of the third prologue is Diogenes and his behavior during the siege of Corinth. Rabelais apparently borrowed this image from Lucian's treatise "How to write history," but he was also familiar with the Latin translation of this episode given by Budé in his dedication to the "Annotations to the Pandects." But this brief scene is completely transformed in the prologue, where it becomes full of allusions to contemporary events: the struggle of France against Charles V and the defensive measures undertaken in Paris. These measures adopted by the citizens are described in every detail. The prologue offers the famous enumeration of defensive engineering works and armaments. This is the largest listing of its kind in world literature. For instance, there are thirteen terms for swords and eight for lances.

This enumeration of war engines and weapons has an oral

character. It is a loud street ordinance. We have many of these ordinances in the literature of the late Middle Ages, especially in the mysteries. They contain, in particular, long listings of weapons. Thus, in the parade of the "Old Testament Mystery Play" (fifteenth century), Nebuchadnezzar's officers name forty different types of arms. In another fifteenth-century mystery, "The Martydom of St. Quentin," the Roman commander, too, names forty different weapons.

These declamations had a popular form. They represented a display of armed forces that had to impress the people. Heralds made similar announcements about types of weapons, regiments, and banners at the time of call to arms and mobilization for campaigns. (See the call to arms of King Picrochole in Rabelais' novel.) There were also listings of soldiers receiving an award or killed in battle. These calls and enumerations were loud and solemn in tone; they were impressive because of the long lists of names and military terms as well as the long orations made on these occasions by the heralds, as featured by Rabelais.

The lengthy strings of names and military terms and the accumulation of epithets, which sometimes covered several pages, were common in the fifteenth and sixteenth centuries. We find a great number of them in Rabelais. For instance, in the third prologue 64 adjectives describe the actions and manipulations applied by Diogenes to his barrel, as a parallel to the citizen's activities. Again, in the Third Book we find 303 epithets describing the male sexual organ in good or bad condition, and 208 epithets depicting the stupidity of the clown Triboulet. In *Pantagruel* there are 144 titles of books in Saint Victor's library and in the same book 79 characters representing hell. In the Fourth Book, we have 140 names of cooks who entered the "pig" in the sausage war. There are also in this book 212 comparisons in the description of *carême-prenant* and 138 dishes offered by the gastrolaters to their god. All these epithets express either praise or abuse in hyperbolic form. But there are, of course, essential differences in these terms and they serve an artistic purpose. We shall return to their aesthetic and stylistic value in our last chapter; here we shall merely point out their specific traits: their monumental character and their parade and marketplace form.

The announcements lend the third prologue a completely new tone. Of course Rabelais brings no herald into his novel. The enumerations are recited by the same author who spoke in the voice of the barker, who "cried out" like a hawker and hurled a volley of abuse at his enemies. But now he speaks in the solemn and pompous tone of the town herald, resounding with the national patriotic enthusiasm of the time when Rabelais was writing his novel. The historic importance of that time is directly expressed in the following words: "I would deem it very disgraceful indeed to stand aside as but an idle spectator whilst so many valiant and eloquent heroes perform soul-stirring roles in the magnificent epic spectacle all Europe watches today."

But even this solemn, pompous, and monumental tone is combined in the prologue with other elements, for instance, with indecent jokes about the Corinthian women who served military defense after their own fashion. We continue to hear the laughter of the marketplace. Rabelais and his contemporaries were not afraid of humor in their rendition of history; they were afraid only of petrified narrow seriousness.

In the prologue Diogenes does not take part in the military activities of his fellow citizens. But in order to manifest his zeal at this important moment of history, he rolls his barrel up to the fortifications and performs a number of senseless and aimless manipulations. To describe these gestures, Rabelais uses sixty-four terms borrowed from technology and various trades. This feverish activity around the barrel is a parody of the citizens' serious preparations. But here again there is no bare negation of this patriotic work; the accent is placed on the fact that Diogenes' flippant parody is also useful, that he also serves in his way the defense of Corinth. No one should be idle, but laughter is not an idle occupation. The right to laughter and gay parody is here opposed not to the heroic citizens of Corinth but to the gloomy calumniators, to the enemies of free humor. Therefore when the author compares his role to that of Diogenes at the siege of Corinth, he transforms his tub into a barrel filled with wine, Rabelais' favorite image of gay and free truth. We have already discussed the scene of the calumniators and agelasts driven away from the barrel.

Thus, the prologue of the Third Book uncrowns intolerant seriousness and defends the rights of laughter which must prevail even in the most serious historic struggle.

The same theme is presented in the two prologues of the Fourth Book (the so-called "old prologue" and the letter of dedication to Cardinal Odet). In these prologues Rabelais develops his doctrine of the gay physician and of the healing virtue of laughter founded on Hippocrates and on other medical authorities. There are also many marketplace laments, especially in the "old prologue." We shall here examine the image of the physician who amuses his patients.

We must stress first of all that this image of the physician in the prologues of the Fourth Book contains substantial popular elements. Rabelais' physician is unlike the caricature of the professional narrow-minded doctor in the literature of a later period. The Rabelaisian image is complex, universal, and ambivalent; this paradoxical figure is a composite of Hippocrates' noble physician "equal to God" and of the *scatophagus* who devours excrement in antique comedies, mimes, and medieval *facéties*. The physician is essentially connected with the struggle of life and death in the human body and has a special relation to childbirth and the throes of death. He participates in death and procreation. He is not concerned with a completed and closed body but with the one that is born, which is in the stage of becoming. The body that interests him is pregnant, delivers, defecates, is sick, dying, and dismembered. In one word, it is the body as it appears in abuses, curses, oaths, and generally in all grotesque images. As a participant and witness of the struggle between life and death in the invalid's body, the physician is specifically linked with elimination, especially with urine, which played an important part in ancient medicine. Old prints usually represent the doctor examining a glass of urine.[20] He reads in it the patient's fate; it answers the question of life and death. In his letter to Cardinal Odet Rabelais cited the case of the severe doctor and quoted from Maître Pathelin (a character in a farce) the patient's typical question.

Doctor, doesn't my urine tell
If I shall perish or get well?
(Book 4, Letter to Cardinal Odet)

Thus urine and other eliminations (excrement, vomit, sweat) had in ancient medicine the connotation of life and death (in addition to their link with the lower stratum of the body and with earth).

Rabelais' image of the physician is still more complex. In his mind the cement which holds all these different elements together, from Hippocrates to the comic doctor, is precisely laughter in its universal, ambivalent sense. In his letter to Cardinal Odet, the author offers a characteristic definition of the medical practice: "Hippocrates fittingly compares the practice of medicine to a struggle, and also to a farce with three characters: the patient, the physician and the disease."

The farcical concept of the physician and of the struggle of life and death (with scatological accessories and a universal meaning) is typical for the time of Rabelais. We find it in the works of certain sixteenth-century authors and in the anonymous literature of *facéties, soties,* and farces. For instance, in one of the farces the gay and carefree "children of folly" enter the service of the "World." But the "World" cannot be pleased and is irritable, it is sick. A physician is called and after examining the "World's" urine diagnoses a disease of the brain. The patient fears a universal catastrophy, a destruction by flood and fire. Finally, the "children of folly" bring back their patient to a cheerful and carefree mood.

Compared to Rabelais' picture, the *facétie* is far more coarse and

[20] One of these engravings, from a book dated 1534, is reproduced in Georges Lote's monograph *La Vie et l'oeuvre de François Rabelais*, Paris, Droz, 1938, pp. 164–165, Table VI.

primitive. But the traditional composition of the images is similar to that in the novel, including the flood and fire in their carnivalesque aspect. The universal and cosmic nature of these images is clearly shown in the *soties*, but they bear a rather abstract character nearer to allegory.

We have examined the role of the marketplace and its voices in Rabelais' work. We said that the popular genres penetrated the literary sphere of that time, and we have seen this exemplified in the prologues. We shall now deal with certain genres of this category individually.

Let us first look at the simplest genre but one that is important for Rabelais—the street cries, especially the cries of Paris. The *cris* were loud advertisements called out by the Paris street vendors[21] and composed according to a certain versified form; each cry had four lines offering and praising a certain merchandise. The first collection of Paris cries was compiled by Guillaume de Villeneuve in the thirteenth century, the last by Clément Jaquain in the sixteenth century. (These are the cries of Rabelais' time). There is considerable material belonging to the period between these two dates, especially to the first half of the fifteenth century. Thus the history of the famous cries can be traced through almost four centuries.[22]

The *cris de Paris* were very popular. A special *Farce* featuring these advertisements was produced in the sixteenth century and was similar to the "Comedy of Proverbs" and the "Comedy of Songs" created a century later. The seventeenth-century painter Abraham Bosse has a picture called the "Cries of Paris," representing the city's street vendors.

This genre is an important document of those times, not only for the historian of language and culture but also for the literary

[21] We still use the expression *le dernier cri.*

[22] See Alfred Franklin, *Vie privée d'autrefois: L'Annonce et la Réclame*, which gives the cries of Paris at different periods. Also J. G. Kastner, *Les Voix de Paris, essai d'une histoire littéraire et musicale des cris populaires*, Paris, 1857.

critic. The cries had no specific character like that of modern advertisements. Neither did literature of that time, even in its higher forms, exclude any type of human speech, though of a practical and "lowly" nature. The national French language of that period was becoming for the first time the language of great literature, science, and ideology. Before this time it had been the language of folklore, of the marketplace, the street, the bazaar or the merchant row—the language of the *cris de Paris*. The intrinsic value of the "lowly" language in creating the literary forms was considerable.

The role of the cries in the marketplace and in the streets was important. The city rang with these many voices. Each food, wine, or other merchandise had its own words and melody and its special intonations, its distinct verbal and musical imagery. We may judge of this immense variety from the 1545 collection by Truque: "One hundred and seven cries which are cried every day in Paris." Even the examples given in this collection do not embrace the entire subject, since many more cries than those listed by Truque could be heard in the Paris streets. We must recall that not only was all advertising oral and loud in those days, actually a cry, but that all announcements, orders, and laws were made in this loud oral form. Sound, the proclaimed word, played an immense role in everyday life as well as in the cultural field. It was even greater than in our days, in the time of the radio. (As for the nineteenth century, compared with the era of Rabelais it was silent.) This fact should not be ignored when studying the style of the sixteenth century and especially the style of Rabelais. The culture of the common folk idiom was to a great extent a culture of the loud word spoken in the open, in the street and marketplace. And the cries of Paris played their own considerable part in this culture.

What did the *cris* mean to Rabelais?

We find direct allusions to this genre in his novel. When King Anarchus was defeated and deposed, Panurge decided to put him to work and made him a vendor of greensauce. He trained the king to cry his merchandise, but the miserable Anarchus could not learn fast enough. Rabelais does not give us the contents of the advertisement, but in the Truque collection of 1545 a "green sauce" is listed among the 107 items.

But the matter is not restricted to Rabelais' direct or indirect allusions to the cries of Paris. Their influence and their parallel meaning should be examined in a far wider and deeper sense.

First of all we must be reminded of the important role of advertising and announcements in Rabelais' novels. True, it is not always possible to distinguish in the novel the images of commercial advertising of the city streets from those of the barker, apothecary, actor, quack, and astrologer making their announcements at the fairs, but the *cris* doubtless made their contribution to Rabelais' work. Their influence is found in certain of the epithets in the novel that reveal a culinary origin and are borrowed from the vocabulary praising the foods and wines offered for sale.

Under Rabelais' pen the names of dishes, venison, vegetables, wines, household objects, and kitchen utensils have an intrinsic value. An object is named for its own sake. The world of food and material objects occupies considerable space in the novel. But this is the very world which was daily offered in all its richness and variety in the cries of the street vendors. We also find food, drink, and houseware in the paintings of the Flemish masters, as well as in the minute descriptions of banquets so often presented in sixteenth-century literature. All that was related to the table and kitchen suited the taste and spirit of the times. But the cries of Paris represented in themselves a noisy kitchen and a loud, abundantly served banquet; every food and dish had its own rhyme and melody. Together, they made a never-ending symphony of feasting, a symphony that obviously influenced literary images, and those of Rabelais in particular.

In writings contemporary to our author banquet and kitchen imagery was not narrowed to the petty details of everyday life but had a more or less universal meaning. One of the best Protestant satires of the second part of the sixteenth century is entitled: "The Satire of the Pope's Kitchen" (*Les Satires chrestiennes de la Cuisine Papale*). The eight satires represent the Catholic church as a gigantic kitchen spread all over the earth: chimneys form the belfry, the bells are cooking pans, the altars dining tables. The various prayers and rituals are pictured as foods, an extremely rich culinary nomenclature being used for this purpose. The Protestant satire is the heir to grotesque realism. It debases the Catholic church and its rituals by bringing them down to the lower bodily stratum symbolized by food and kitchen. A universal meaning is obviously given to these images.

The link with the lower stratum is even more clearly shown in the culinary images of macaronic poetry. It can also be clearly seen in the *moralités,* farces, *soties,* and other genres where symbolically broad kitchen and banquet scenes play a considerable part. We have already mentioned the meaning of food and kitchen utensils in such popular-festive forms as carnivals, charivari, and diableries; the participants of these shows were armed with oven forks, pokers, roasting spits, pots, and pans. We know of the huge sausages and buns specially prepared for carnivals and carried in solemn procession.[23] Indeed, one of the oldest forms of hyperbolic grotesque was the exaggerated size of foodstuffs. In this exaggerated form of valuable matter we see for the first time the positive and absolute meaning of size and quantity in an aesthetic image. Hyperboles of food parallel the most ancient hyperboles of belly, mouth, and phallus.

A distant echo of these material positive hyperboles is heard in literature presenting symbolically enlarged images of the inn, the hearth, and the market. Even in Zola's "The Belly of Paris" we find such a symbolic enlargement, a kind of "mythologization" of a market. Victor Hugo has many Rabelaisian allusions. Describing his voyage down the Rhine, he exclaims in one scene in which he enters an inn with its blazing hearth: *Si j'étais Homère ou Rabelais, je dirais: cette cuisine est un monde dont cette cheminée est le soleil.* (If I were Homer or Rabelais I would say that this kitchen is a world and this chimney its sun). Hugo understood to perfec-

[23] For instance, during the Königsberg carnival of 1583 the butchers made a sausage weighing 440 pounds which had to be carried by 90 butchers. In 1601 the sausage weighed 900 pounds. Even today gigantic artificial sausages or pretzels can be seen in the windows of bakeries and pork stores.

tion the universal, cosmic meaning of the kitchen and hearth in the Rabelaisian system of images.

So we have seen that the *cris* were connected with one of the most important trends of thought in the imagery of the sixteenth century. They were interpreted in the light of the hearth and the kitchen which in its turn reflected the light of the sun. They were part of the great utopia of the banquet. It is in this broad connection that we must recognize the direct influence of the cries of Paris on Rabelais and their importance in helping us to understand his work and the entire literature of the Renaissance.[24]

For Rabelais and his contemporaries the cries of Paris were not a mere document of life in the modern sense of the world. This genre, which later became in literature a mere picture of mores, was filled with philosophic meaning for our author. The cries were not isolated from current events, from history. They were an essential part of the marketplace and street, they merged with the general popular-festive and utopian world. Rabelais heard in them the tones of a banquet for all the people, "for all the world." These utopian tones were immersed in the depths of concrete, practical life, a life that could be touched, that was filled with aroma and sound. This was completely in accord with the specific character of all Rabelaisian images, which combine a broad universalism and utopianism with extraordinarily concrete, obvious, and vivid traits, strictly localized and technically precise.

The declamations of the vendors of various drugs are very similar to the cries of Paris. These tirades are one of the oldest practices of the market. The image of the physician advertising his remedy is also one of the oldest in world literature. Among Rabelais' French predecessors let us recall Rutebeuf, the author of the famous *Diz de l'herberie* ("The Tale of the Herbs"). Rutebeuf presents the

[24] Among Rabelais scholars L. Sainéan stressed the importance of the *cris de Paris* in connection with Rabelais' work in his remarkable and abundantly documented book devoted to Rabelais' language. However, Sainéan does not treat his theme fully and is content to list Rabelais' direct allusions to the cries. See *La Langue de Rabelais*, Vol. 1, 1922, p. 275.

typical cry of a quack praising his medicines in grotesque, satiric form. The doctor has a remarkable herb that increases sexual potency. The connection of the doctor with regeneration as well as with death is, as we have seen, traditional.

In Rutebeuf this theme is subdued; in Rabelais it is usually expressed in all its force and frankness. Medical hawking is scattered throughout the novel, in crude or in disguised form. We have mentioned the prescription of the "Chronicles" as a remedy for toothache, gout, and syphilis. The element of medical hawking also appears in the third prologue, and a somewhat more subtle form in Friar John's praise of the monastic habit as a remedy for sexual impotence and of the breviary as a cure for insomnia.

An interesting example of more complex medical advertisement is the famous praise of "pantagruelion" which concludes the third book. This eulogy of incombustible hemp is borrowed from Pliny's praise of flax in his "Natural History." But as in all cases when Rabelais borrowed from other sources, he completely transformed the writing. In his own context it is marked with his typical seal. Pliny's praise of flax is purely rhetorical. Genetically speaking, rhetoric is related to the marketplace but nothing has remained of the marketplace in Pliny's text; it is the product of refined culture. Rabelais, on the other hand, has a popular tone similar to that of the "Tale of the Herbs," the cry of the collector of medicinal plants and of the vendor of wonder unguents. We also find in Rabelais the echo of local folklore, of legends similar to our own "magic grass."[25] From the marketplace style and folklore Pantagruel's announcement acquires its utopian radicalism and its deep optimism, completely alien to the pessimistic Pliny. But of course the exterior form of the cries is considerably mitigated in the eulogy of pantagruelion.

In post-Rabelaisian literature we must note the brilliant use of medical advertisement borrowed from the Menippus satire. This remarkable work, which has been discussed previously, is saturated

[25] A legendary plant in Russian folklore, listed by Dahl, a nineteenth-century Russian scholar. (Translator's note.)

with marketplace elements. The introductory part of the satire (corresponding to the *cri* of the moralities and *soties*) portrays a Spanish quack. While the members of the League are holding a meeting at the Louvre, the quack is busy outside selling a miraculous universal drug which preserves from all misfortunes and evils and which is called the "Spanish Catholikon." He cries out the praise of this drug and its many virtues. This exaggerated eulogy gaily and bitingly unmasks Catholic politics. The introduction creates the atmosphere of cynical frankness with which the members of the League denounce themselves and their own plans, as shown in the next chapters of the satire. The announcement of the Spanish quack resembles Rabelais' prologues in its structure and parodical spirit.

The cries of Paris and the cries of quacks and druggists operating at the fairs belong to the eulogizing genres of folk humor. They too, of course, are ambivalent; they too are filled with both laughter and irony. They may at any moment show their other side; that is, they may be turned into abuses and oaths. They too exercise the debasing function, they materialize the world, lending it a bodily substance. They are essentially connected with the lower stratum.

The other side of marketplace hawking is represented, as we have said, by abuses, curses, and oaths. They are ambivalent, but it is the negative pole of the lower stratum which here prevails: death, sickness, disintegration, dismemberment of the body, its rending apart and swallowing up.

We have analyzed a series of curses and abuses in our discussion of the prologues. Now we shall have to examine another form of billingsgate speech, the profanities and oaths. They are related to the curses and abuses in origin and also in ideological and artistic function.

Abuses, curses, profanities, and improprieties are the unofficial elements of speech. They were and are still conceived as a breach of the established norms of verbal address; they refuse to conform to conventions, to etiquette, civility, respectability. These elements of freedom, if present in sufficient numbers and with a precise intention, exercise a strong influence on the entire contents of speech, transferring it to another sphere beyond the limits of conventional language. Such speech forms, liberated from norms, hierarchies, and prohibitions of established idiom, become themselves a peculiar argot and create a special collectivity, a group of people initiated in familiar intercourse, who are frank and free in expressing themselves verbally. The marketplace crowd was such a collectivity, especially the festive, carnivalesque crowd at the fair.

The character of the elements capable of transforming a language and of creating a free collectivity of familiar intercourse was subject to certain changes in each successive period. Many improprieties that in the seventeenth century acquired the power of transforming the context of speech did not possess this power in the time of Rabelais. They did not then transgress the limits of the established language. Unofficial (unprintable) argot also varied in force. Every age has its own norms of official speech and propriety.[26] And every age has its own type of words and expressions that are given as a signal to speak freely, to call things by their own names, without any mental restrictions and euphemisms. The use of these colloquialisms created the atmosphere of frankness, inspired certain attitudes, a certain unofficial view of the world. These liberties were fully revealed in the festive square when all hierarchic barriers between men were lifted and a true familiar contact was established. Here all men became conscious participants in that one world of laughter.

In Rabelais' time the so-called *jurons*, that is, profanities and oaths, were just such colloquialisms. They were mostly concerned with sacred themes: "the body of Christ," "the blood of Christ," holy days, saints, and relics. In most cases these expressions were the remnants of ancient sacral formulas. The *jurons* abounded in familiar speech; distinct social groups and even individuals had their own vocabulary of oaths, or a favorite that they used con-

---

[26] Concerning the historic transformations of speech norms in connection with obscenities, see Ferdinand Brunot, *Histoire de la langue française,* Vol. 4, Chapter 5, *L'honnêteté dans le langage.*

tinually. Among Rabelais' heroes Friar John, especially, marks his speech with a flow of oaths; he cannot make a single step without them. When Ponocrates asks him why he uses them, the friar answers that they adorn his speech. They are the flowers of Cicero's rhetoric. Neither does Panurge spare his profane language.

Oaths, as we have seen, were the unofficial element of speech. They were even directly forbidden. The struggle to suppress them was conducted from both sides: by the Church and government on one hand and by the "chamber" humanists on the other. The latter saw oaths as useless, parasitical forms of speech which only polluted it and were the heritage of the barbaric Middle Ages. This is the point of view expressed by Ponocrates in the dialogue with Friar John. The Church and government disapproved of the sacrilegious use of holy names, and under the Church's influence the government often condemned the *jurons* in ordinances proclaimed by the heralds. Such ordinances were issued by Charles VII, Louis XI (May 12, 1478), and by Francis I (March, 1525). These condemnations and prohibitions merely strengthened the oath's unofficial character; they sharpened the feeling that the use of a *juron* meant a breach of the norm of established speech. This in turn intensified the color of speech studded with oaths, rendering it familiar and free. Oaths began to be considered as a certain rejection of official philosophy, a verbal protest.

Forbidden fruit is sweet. Even the kings who issued the ordinances against profane language had their own favorite oaths; they were used by public consensus as the nonofficial nicknames of these sovereigns. The oath sworn by Louis XI was *Pasques Dieu* (the Lord's Easter), *Bonjour Dieu* (good day of the Lord) was that of Charles VII, and Louis XII was partial to *le diable m'emporte* (may the devil take me). Francis I swore by "the word of honor of an honest man" (*foy de gentilhomme*). Rabelais' contemporary, Roger de Collerye, wrote a typical poem on the subject of these oaths:

Quand la "Pasques Dieu" decédá
Le "Bond Jour Dieu" lui succéda
Au "Bond Jour Dieu" defunt et mort,

Succéda la "Diable m'emport",
Luy decédé, nous voyons comme
Nous duist la "Fay de Gentil Homme."[27]

Just as these characteristic oaths attributed to certain high personages became their nicknames, so specific groups and professions were represented by typical *jurons*. Rabelais gives a dynamic picture of the marketplace with its social elements represented by their characteristic *jurons*. When young Gargantua arrives in Paris and, wearied by the crowd's curiosity, drenches it in urine, Rabelais does not describe these people; he merely cites the oaths and curses which broke out at that moment. We can thus identify these various social elements:

"Upon my word, I think these boobies want me to pay my welcome here and give the Bishop an offertory. Quite right, too! I'll treat them! They'll get their drink! I'll recognize my obligations and liquidate I shall!—but only *par ris*, for sport!"

Then smiling, he unfastened his noble codpiece and lugging out his great pleasure-rod, he so fiercely bepissed them that he drowned two hundred and sixty thousand four hundred and eighteen, exclusive of women and children.

By sheer fleetness of foot, a certain number escaped this mighty pissflood, and reaching the top of the Montagne Sainte Geneviève, beyond the University, sweating, coughing, hawking and out of breath, they began to swear and curse, some in anger, others in jest:

"God's plague and pox take it! I'll deny God if ..."
" 'Sblood."
"Christ, look ye, its *Mère de ... merde ...* shit, Mother of God."
"*Pocapedion!* God's head!" roared a Gascon.
"*Das dich Gots leyden Schend!*" bellowed a German trooper.
"God's passion roil you!"
"*Pote de Christo!*" an Italian voice rang out. "Christ's power!"
"*Ventre St. Quenet*" ... By the bellies of all the apostles ... God's

[27] When the "Lord's Easter" died
    The "good day of the Lord" succeeded,
    The "good day of the Lord" defunct and dead,
    "May the Devil take me" followed,
    When it was deceased—we heard
    "The word of honor of an honest man."

virtue . . . by St. Fiacre of the land of Brie."
(Book 1, Chapter 17)

They swore by "God's Easter" and "Christmas," by "Devil take me," by "Word of honor of an honest man," by Saint Sausage and Saint Mamica. And each time they called upon a saint they cried out: *nous sommes baignés pour ris* (we are drenched for fun). Therefore, the city formerly called Leucetia (which in Greek means whiteness) was from that day on called "Par-ris," Paris.

We have here a vivid and dynamic "loud" image of the motley crowd of sixteenth-century Paris. We hear the Gascon swearing "by the head of God," the German *landsknecht* oath, and that of the greengrocer calling upon Saint Fiacre, who was the patron saint of gardeners in the Brie province, while the shoemaker calls upon Saint Thibault, and the drunkard upon Saint Godegran. All the other oaths (there are twenty-one of them) have some specific nuance, some suggestion or association. We find the French kings' oaths, already alluded to, aligned in chronological order, an arrangement that confirms the popularity of these royal nicknames. We probably no longer grasp all these nuances and allusions, but they were clearly understood by Rabelais' contemporaries.

This "loud" talking image of the crowd is, as we have seen, built exclusively on oaths, in other words, outside the norms of official speech. The verbal reaction of the crowd is organically merged with Gargantua's traditional popular gesture, as free as the crowd's response. Both reveal the unofficial aspect of the world.

The gesture and the oaths create the setting for the extremely free parodies of the names of saints. Thus, one of the men in the crowd calls upon Saint Sausage, which here symbolizes the phallus, while the other swears by Saint Godegran,[28] or *Godet grand*, which means a large tumbler. Grand Godet was also the name of a popular tavern on the Place de Grèves (Villon mentions it in his "Testament"). Others invoke Saint Foutin, a parody of Saint Photin, and Saint Vitus, who in this context also suggests the phallus. Finally,

---

[28] Rabelais alludes to a legend in which the martydom of this saint is related to baked apples (a debasing carnivalesque image).

the people call upon Saint Mamica, which was the nickname for a mistress. Thus, all the saints invoked are travesties in the sense that they have connotations either of indecencies or of feasting.

In this carnivalesque atmosphere we grasp the meaning of Rabelais' story of Gargantua's drowning 260,418 people in his urine "exclusive of women and children." This scriptural formula is taken directly from the Gospel story of the crowd fed with 5 loaves of bread. (Rabelais quite often uses these formulas.) Thus the entire episode of the drenching in urine and the crowd's reaction is a travestied allusion.[29] We shall see that this is not the only travesty of that kind in Rabelais' novel.

Before performing his carnivalesque gesture, Gargantua declares that he will do this only *par ris,* for sport or laughter's sake. And the crowd concludes its volley of oaths by using the same expression, which, as the author tells us, is the origin of the word *Paris.* Thus, the entire episode is a gay carnivalesque travesty of the city's name. At the same time it is a parody of the local legends about the origin of names in general (serious and poetic forms of these legends were popular in France and were created by Jean Lemaire and the other poets of the school of rhetoricians). The name of Paris, the names of saints and martyrs, as well as the Gospel miracle, were all drawn into the game for laughter's sake. This was a game in which "exalted" and "sacred" things were combined with images of the lower stratum (urine, erotic images, and banquet travesties). Oaths, as the unofficial elements of speech and the profanation of the sacred, were organically woven into the game and were in tune with it.

What is the thematic content of the oaths? It is mainly the rending of the human body. Swearing was mostly done in the name of the members and the organs of the divine body: the Lord's body, his head, blood, wounds, bowels; or in the name of the relics of saints and martyrs—feet, hands, fingers—which were preserved in churches. The most improper and sinful oaths were those invok-

[29] This is an incomplete travesty, merely a travestied allusion. Such risqué hints are frequent in the recreational parodies of Shrovetide, that is, in grotesque realism.

ing the body of the Lord and its various parts, and these were precisely the oaths most frequently used. The preacher Menot (one of Rabelais' senior contemporaries) condemned in his sermons the excessive use of these oaths, saying: "the one seizes God by his beard, the other by his throat, the third by his head. . . There are some who speak of Christ the Saviour's humanity with less respect than does a butcher about meat."

The moralist Eloi d'Amervalle condemned the oaths in his diablerie (1507); he clearly showed the carnivalesque aspect of a body rent to pieces which is the origin of most swearing.

Ils jurent Dieu, ses dents, sa teste,
Son corps, son ventre, barbe et yeuix,
Et le prennent par tant de lieux,
Qu'il est haché de tous costez
Comme chair a petits pastez.[30]

D'Amervalle was certainly unaware that he was giving an accurate historical and cultural analysis of the oath. But as a man who lived between the fifteenth and sixteenth centuries, he was familiar with the carnival role of butchers and cooks, of the carving knife, and of the minced meat for dressings and sausages.

The dismembered body and its anatomization play a considerable part in Rabelais' novel. This is why the theme of oaths and curses is organically woven into the pattern of Rabelaisian images. Friar John, a great lover of oaths, is nicknamed "d'Entommeure," chopped meat. Sainéan sees here a double allegory: the friar's bellicose spirit and his love of the culinary arts.[31] The important fact is that the fighting temperament (war, battles) and the kitchen cross each other at a certain point, and this point is the dismembered, minced flesh. Culinary images accompanying battle scenes were widely used in the fifteenth and sixteenth centuries; they were frequent precisely in the sphere where literature was con-

[30] They swear by God, by his teeth and head,
   His body, his stomach, beard and eyes,
   So that he is entirely chopped up
   Like minced meat for pies.
[31] Sainéan, *op. cit.* ftn. 24, Vol. 2, 1923, p. 472.

nected with folk tradition of humor. Pulci compared the battle-field of Ronceveaux to "a kettle filled with blood-stew of heads, legs and other members of the human body."[32] These images can already be found in the epics of the minstrels.

Friar John is truly the *d'Entommeure* in both senses of this word; the essential link between the two meanings is clearly shown in Rabelais' work. In the episode of the "sausage war" Friar John develops the idea of the military importance of cooks, basing his idea on historic examples of marshals and others who were cooks. The friar becomes the commander of 154 cooks armed with spits, forks, and frying pans, and leads them into the "pig," which plays the role of the Trojan horse. During the battle Friar John behaves as a systematic "anatomizer," transforming human bodies into "minced meat."[33] His anatomizer function is also pictured in the battle in the vineyard (in which, incidentally, he uses the staff of a cross). This episode contains a long and detailed anatomic list of wounded members and organs, broken bones, and joints. Here is an excerpt from this chapter:

He brained some, smashed the legs and arms of others, broke a neck here, cracked a rib there. He flattened a nose or knocked an eye out, crushed a jaw or sent thirty-two teeth rattling down a bloody gullet. Some had their shoulderblades dislocated, others their thighs lammed to pulp, others their hips wrenched, others their arms battered beyond recognition.
(Book 1, Chapter 27)

This long enumeration is typical of Rabelais' anatomization and dismemberment of the human body. The anatomic and culinary treatment is based on the grotesque image of the dissected body which we have already seen in the discussion of abuses, curses, and oaths.

[32] In the high epic style, too, we find battles symbolized by a banquet, as in our "Song of the Campaign of Igor" [a Russian epic poem of the twelfth century].

[33] These words are connected by Rabelais himself (Book Four, Chapter 16) in the oath: *A tous les millions de diables qui te puissent anatomiser la cervelle et en faire des entommeures.*

And thus, the oaths with their profane culinary dismemberment of the sacred body have brought us back to the culinary theme of the *cris de Paris;* they have returned us to the grotesque bodily billingsgate themes: diseases, monstrosities, organs of the lower stratum. All the elements examined in the present chapter are related to each other both in form and theme. All of them, independently of their literal content, refer to the unofficial aspect of the world, unofficial in tone (laughter) and in contents (the lower stratum). All of them relate to the world's gay matter, which is born, dies and gives birth, is devoured and devours; this is the world which continually grows and multiplies, becomes ever greater and better, ever more abundant. Gay matter is ambivalent, it is the grave and the generating womb, the receding past and the advancing future, the becoming.

In spite of their variety, the images analyzed in the present chapter are marked by the inner unity of medieval folk culture; but in Rabelais' novel this unity is organically related to the new Renaissance principle. In this respect the prologues are especially typical; all five (there are two in the Fourth Book), are excellent examples of Renaissance journalism based on popular genres. We have seen in them the uncrowning of the old medieval philosophy relegated to the past; on the other hand, the prologues are filled with allusions and echoes of the ideological and political highlights of the day.

The genres we have examined are relatively primitive; some are even archaic. They have, however, great power of travesty, of debasement, and materialization which render the world more carnal. They are deeply traditional and popular, bringing an atmosphere of freedom, frankness, and familiarity. Therefore Rabelais needed them for stylistic purposes. We have seen their role in the prologues, they helped to create an absolutely gay, frank, and fearless speech that was necessary for the attack undertaken by Rabelais against "Gothic darkness." These primitive marketplace genres prepared the setting for the popular-festive forms and images of the language in which Rabelais expressed his own new truth about the world. Our next chapter is devoted to this language.

CHAPTER THREE

Popular-Festive Forms and Images in Rabelais

Time is a playing boy who moves the draughts.
Domination belongs to the child.
(HERACLITUS).

At the end of the preceding chapter we spoke of the "anatomiz-ing" presentation of beatings and blows and of Rabelais' peculiar "carnival and culinary" anatomy. These scenes are frequent in his novel, but they do not describe commonplace events. Let us analyze some of them.

In the Fourth Book, Pantagruel and his companions visit the island of the Catchpoles. Its inhabitants earn their living by letting themselves be thrashed. Friar John selects a "red-snouted" catch-pole (*Rouge museau*) and pays him twenty gold crowns: "Friar John swung his staff manfully, thwacking and cracking Redsnout so lustily on belly and back, on head and legs that, as he fell to earth, a battered pulp, I feared for the Catchpole's death." (Book 4, Chapter 16.) We see that the anatomic enumeration of the parts of the body has not been neglected. Rabelais goes on to relate: "Then he gave him his twenty crowns. But the churl rose, happy as a king—or a pair of kings, for that matter." (*Et mon villain debout, aisé comme un roy ou deux.*)

This image of a "king" and "two kings" is here directly introduced in order to describe the highest degree of happiness reached by the Catchpole who has received his reward. But the image is essentially related to the gay thrashings and abuse as well as to the red snout of the Catchpole, to his apparent death, sudden return to life, and jumping up like a clown who has received a beating.

Here is a dimension in which thrashing and abuse are not a personal chastisement but are symbolic actions directed at something on a higher level, at the king. This is the popular-festive system of images, which is most clearly expressed in carnival (but, of course, not in carnival alone). In this dimension, as previously pointed out, the kitchen and the battle meet and cross each other in the image of the rent body. At the time of Rabelais these images were still alive and full of meaning in various forms of folk entertainments as well as in literature.

In such a system the king is the clown. He is elected by all the people and is mocked by all the people. He is abused and beaten when the time of his reign is over, just as the carnival dummy of winter or of the dying year is mocked, beaten, torn to pieces, burned, or drowned even in our time. They are "gay monsters." The clown was first disguised as a king, but once his reign had come to an end his costume was changed, "travestied," to turn him once more into a clown. The abuse and thrashing are equivalent to a change of costume, to a metamorphosis. Abuse reveals the other, true face of the abused, it tears off his disguise and mask. It is the king's uncrowning.

Abuse is death, it is former youth transformed into old age, the living body turned into a corpse. It is the "mirror of comedy" reflecting that which must die a historic death. But in this system death is followed by regeneration, by the new year, new youth, and a new spring. Therefore, abuse is followed by praise; they are two aspects of one world, each with its own body.

Abuse with uncrowning, as truth about the old authority, about the dying world, is an organic part of Rabelais' system of images. It is combined with carnivalesque thrashings, with change of costume and travesty. Rabelais drew these images from the living popular-festive tradition of his time, but he was also well versed in the antique scholarly tradition of the Saturnalia, with its own rituals of travesties, uncrownings, and thrashings. (These are the sources with which we too are familiar, especially through Macrobius' *Saturnalia*.) Concerning the clown Triboulet, Rabelais recalls Seneca's words (without naming him and apparently quoting from Erasmus) that kings and clowns have the same horoscope.[1] It is obvious that he also knew the Gospel story of the mock crowning, uncrowning, and scourging of "the king of the Jews."

In his novel Rabelais describes the uncrowning of two kings: Picrochole in the First Book (*Gargantua*) and Anarchus in the Second Book (*Pantagruel*). He presents these degradations in a purely carnivalesque spirit but is also influenced by antique and Gospel traditions.

King Picrochole fled after his defeat; on his way he killed his horse in anger because it had slipped and fallen. In order to continue his journey, Picrochole tried to steal the ass of a nearby mill, but the miller thrashed him, removed his royal robes, and clothed him in a smock. Later the deposed king worked in Lyon as a common laborer.

Here we see the elements of the traditional system of images: uncrowning, travesty, thrashing. But we also find some echoes of

---

[1] Seneca speaks of this in his remarkable saturnalian satire, which we have already mentioned, as presenting the uncrowning of the king at the moment of his death (and defecation) and after death in the kingdom of the Underworld, where he is transformed into a "comic monster," a miserable slave and gambler who has lost his fortune.

the Saturnalia, in that the uncrowned king becomes a slave. Moreover, antique slaves were sent to the mill for punishment, where they were beaten and made to tread the millstone. Finally, the ass is the Gospel-symbol of debasement and humility (as well as concomitant regeneration).[2]

King Anarchus' uncrowning is pictured in a similar carnivalesque spirit. After having defeated Anarchus, Pantagruel turns him over to Panurge; the latter first of all dresses the former king in a strange clownish costume and then sends him out as a vendor of greensauce, the lowest step in the social hierarchy. Nor are thrashings omitted. True, Panurge does not beat him but weds him to a grumpy old hag who abuses and thrashes him. Here once more the traditional carnivalesque tradition is strictly observed.[3]

As we have said, Rabelais' own legendary life story offers us his carnival image. There are many tales about his travesties and mystifications. One story concerns his masquerade before death; during his last illness Rabelais asked to be dressed in a domino and quoted the Holy Scripture from Revelation: *beati qui in Domini moriuntur* ("blessed are those who die in the Lord"). The carnivalesque character of this episode is obvious. The disguise is here implemented by the travesty of the scriptural text.

But let us return to the red-snouted Catchpole thrashed and rewarded at the same time "like two kings." The image of thrashing along with anatomizing has conjured up characteristic carnival elements, for instance, the comparison to the old king who is 'dead and to the new one who is resurrected. All believe the Catchpole to have been beaten to death (the old king), but he

[2] The ass was also one of the images of the popular-festive system of the Middle Ages, for instance in the "feast of the ass."

[3] As a parallel image on a higher level we may recall the ancient Russian custom of the uncrowning of the dying czars who received the tonsure and were clothed in the monastic habit, which they wore till their last moment. All are familiar with Pushkin's dramatic scene of this ceremony in the death of Boris Godunov. The parallelism of the images is almost complete. (This is also shown in the no less famous opera of Mussorgsky. Translator's note.)

jumps up alive and gay (the new king). His red snout is the clown's rouged mask. All the other scenes of fighting and beating have a similar carnivalesque character in Rabelais' novel.[4]

The episode of the Catchpole's thrashing is preceded by four chapters devoted to a similar thrashing in the house of the Lord of Basché and to the "tragic farce" enacted by François Villon at Saint Maixent.

The noble Lord of Basché invented an ingenious method of thrashing some Catchpoles, slanderers who came to his castle with a summons to court. In Touraine, where the episode took place, as well as in Poitiers and other French provinces, there existed the custom of the so-called *nopces à mitaines* ("gauntlet weddings"). During the wedding feast the guests cuffed each other jokingly. The person who was subjected to these light blows could not complain; they were consecrated and legalized by custom. And so each time a slanderer came to Basché's castle, a mock wedding was celebrated, and the plaintiff inevitably had to join the guests.

First, an old fat red-faced Catchpole arrived at the castle. During the wedding feast the guests, as usual, began to cuff each other and then it was the visitor's turn:

... they whacked with lusty gauntlet, knocking their enemy dizzy ... bruising his whole frame ... making one eye like nothing so much as a poached egg with black-butter sauce ... smashing eight ribs, staving in his chest, and cleaving his shoulder-blades in four ... breaking his jaw into three separate parts ... and accomplishing the whole amid good-natured laughter (... *et le tout en riant*).
(Book 4, Chapter 12)

The carnivalesque character of this chastisement is obvious. We even see here a carnival within a carnival but with realistic consequences for the beaten slanderer. The very custom of the gauntlets is a carnival rite, linked with fertility, with procreative force, with time. Custom grants the right of a certain freedom and

---

[4] We find the echo of these episodes in later literary works, especially in those of authors who follow the Rabelaisian line, for instance, Scarron.

familiarity, the right to break the usual norms of social relations. In our episode the wedding is fictional; it is a farce, a mystification, but it is also a scene of dual meaning in which the slanderer receives real blows dealt with "armed fists." Let us also stress the culinary and medical description of the thrashing.

The carnivalesque style is brought out even more sharply in the punishment of the second Catchpole who arrived four days later. In contrast to the first visitor, this man is young, tall, and thin. The first and second visitors, though not appearing at the same time, form a typical comic pair based on contrasts: fat and thin, old and young, tall and short.[5] Such contrasting pairs still appear in comic plays and circus shows. Don Quixote and Sancho belonged to this category.[6]

A mock wedding is also arranged for the second visitor; the participants are directly described by Rabelais as *les personnaiges de la farce*. As the slanderer, a protagonist of the coming beating, enters the hall, all the persons present (the chorus) begin to laugh, and so does their guest (*à son entrée chacun comença soubrire, chiquanous rioit par compaignie*). Thus the farce opens. At the given signal the wedding ritual begins. Then, when the food and wine are brought in, the traditional cuffing is started:

They laid on so heartily that blood spurted from his mouth, nose, ears and eyes. Catchpole was beaten to a pulp; his shoulders dislocated; his head, neck, back and breast pounded into mincemeat. You may take my word for it that Avignon, in carnival time, never produced youngsters that played more melodiously at thump-socket than these vassals of My Lord of Basché upon the

[5] We find such a comic pair on the "Isle of Catchpoles." Besides Redsnout, selected by Friar John, there was also a tall thin individual who complained of not being chosen.

[6] Comic pairs are a very ancient phenomenon. Dieterich reproduces in *Pulcinella* the comic figure of the boastful soldier and his arms-bearer on an antique vase of southern Italy (Hamilton collection). The resemblance of the soldier and his escort to Don Quixote and Sancho is striking, except that the two figures on the vase have an enormous phallus. (Dieterich: *Pulcinella*, p. 239.)

person of Catchpole. The poor fellow fell, in a faint, to the ground.

They poured several gallons of wine into his snout; they tied yellow and green ribbons, for favors, to his doublet; and they set him on his snotty horse.

(Book 4, Chapter 14)

We see once more the anatomizing dismemberment and the culinary and medical terms which accompany it: mouth, eyes, head, neck, back, chest, arms are listed. This is a carnival dismemberment of the protagonist of the comic play. It offers Rabelais the occasion to mention the carnival of Avignon and the game known as Rafa played by the students; their cuffing was not administered more "melodiously" than the one inflicted on the Catchpole.

The end of the scene is characteristic; the beaten visitor is actually travestied as a king of clowns. His face is drenched in wine, probably red wine, since he is "red-faced" like Friar John's Catchpole. And finally, he is decorated with yellow and green ribbons as a carnival victim.[7]

In the famous enumeration of the 216 games played by Gargantua (Book One, Chapter 22) there is one called *au boeuf violles*. In certain French cities a custom was preserved almost to our time to lead a fatted ox through the streets during carnival season. This was the time when the slaughter of cattle and the eating of meat were still permitted (as well as weddings and sexual intercourse, forbidden during Lent). The ox was led in solemn procession accompanied by the playing of violas, hence its name *boeuf violles*. Its head was decorated with multicolored ribbons. Unfortunately, we do not know in what the game of *boeuf violles* consisted, but most likely it implied some cuffing. The ox was to be slaughtered, it was to be a carnivalesque victim. It was a king, a procreator, symbolizing the city's fertility; at the same time, it was the sacrificial meat, to be chopped up for sausages and patés.

We can now see why the beaten Catchpole was decorated with

---

[7] Probably the colors of Lord Basché's livery.

ribbons. Thrashing is as ambivalent as abuse changed into praise. There is no pure abstract negation in the popular-festive system of images; it tends to embrace both poles of becoming in their contradiction and unity. The one who is thrashed or slaughtered is decorated. The beating itself has a gay character; it is introduced and concluded with laughter.

The picture of the thrashing of the third Catchpole at Lord Basché's house is the most interesting and most elaborately described. This time the slanderer arrives with two witnesses. Once more the fictional wedding is arranged. During the feast the visitor himself suggests that the good old tradition of *nopces à mitaines* be resumed and is the first to start the cuffing:

At once the gauntlets rained down upon him to good purpose. Catchpole's head was split in nine different places. The first bailiff's right arm was broken. The second bailiff's upper jaw was dislocated, so that it fell halfway over his chin, baring his uvula, with great prejudice to his molar, masticatory and canine teeth.

Trudon changed the rhythm of his drumming; at once gauntlets vanished miraculously, and refreshments were served, ever more plentiful. The general merriment increased: friend drank to friend, and the whole company to Catchpole and his bailiffs.

"God damn this wedding!" cried Oudart. "That cursed bailiff there dislocatocrushosnuggered my shoulder."

But for all his wrath, he drank the fellow's health, punctuating his toasts with the old-fashioned refrain and the old-fashioned thump. The unjawed bailiff joined his hands, as though in prayer, in a pantomime of apology. (He could not speak!)

Loire complained bitterly that the bailiff with dislocated shoulders had, with his leg-of-mutton fist, fetched his elbow such a thwack that he was bruisedblackandcontusedblue down to his very heels.

(Book 4, Chapter 15)

The injuries inflicted upon the Catchpole and his bailiffs are, as usual, described with the anatomizing enumeration of injured organs. The thrashing itself has a special solemn and festive character; it is administered at a banquet to the accompaniment of the bridal drum, and it changes its rhythm when the punishment is over and when a new outburst of merriment marks the feast.

The change of the drum's rhythm and the new spirit of the feast bring us to a new comic phase: the mocking of the victim who was beaten. Those who did the thrashing pretend to have been thrashed. Each plays the role of a crippled person and accuses the visitors. This unbridled scene grows in impact; each actor gives an exaggerated description of his injury in incredibly long and complex orations. Rabelais chose the words they use not without calculation; they illustrate by various sounds the nature of the injury. The length and variety of the syllables render the number and the violence of the blows. When spoken, they cripple the organs of speech, like tongue twisters. Their very length and difficulty of pronunciation grow constantly with every participant in the game; if Oudart's word has eight syllables (in the French text), the one uttered by Loire has thirteen. Thanks to this method, the unrestrained character of carnival penetrates the language of this scene, which is further developed thus:

Trudon protested, as he put his handkerchief over his left eye; and pointed to his drum, stove in on one side:

What harm had I done them? They were not content to maim-anglescotchblemishdisfigurepunch my poor eye, they had to bash in my drum. God knows, tabors are usually beaten and drumskins pierced at weddings, but taborers, far from being struck, are royally entertained. Let the devil use my drum for a nightcap! (Book 4, Chapter 15)

The scene of the beaten slanderers grows in impetus: the handkerchief over the black eye, the broken drum. The word describing the degree of injuries also continues growing, it now contains more syllables, and the syllables present a greater variety.

The image of the drum is also characteristic. For the correct understanding of the entire episode and the peculiar nature of the injuries, it is necessary to hold in mind the fact that the wedding drum had an erotic connotation. To beat this drum or any similar instrument meant to perform the sexual act; the "drummer" (*tabourineur* or *taboureur*) was the lover. In Rabelais' days this meaning was generally known. Rabelais himself, in the First Book, Chapter 3, speaks of the *taboureurs* of emperor Octavian's daughter, that is, her lovers. He also uses the word drum in the erotic sense in the Second Book, Chapter 25, and in the Third Book, Chapter 28. Words like "stroke," "to strike," to "beat," and "stick" (baston) were also used in this sense. The phallus was called baston de mariage or baston à un bout; we find this expression in the Third Book, Chapter 18.[8] Of course, the bridal cuffing also had the meaning of the sexual act. It was used in describing the beating of the Catchpoles, which occurred during a bridal cuffing accompanied by the sound of a drum.

This is why the entire episode described above presents no ordinary fight, no commonplace blows administered in everyday life. The blows have here a broadened, symbolic, ambivalent meaning; they at once kill and regenerate, put an end to the old life and start the new. The entire episode is filled with a bacchic atmosphere.

At the same time, the thrashing of the Catchpoles has also a fully realistic meaning, as far as the seriousness of the injuries and their final aim are concerned. They are thrashed in order to free the Lord of Basché once for all from his enemies' intrigues, and this is successfully achieved. The Catchpoles are also the representatives of the old law, of the rights of a world that is dying and receding, but they are inseparable from the new world. Born from the old, they participate in its ambivalence, dying and being reborn, yet tending toward the mortal, negative pole. The beating is a feast of death and regeneration in the comic aspect. Ambivalent volleys of blows are showered on the Catchpoles; they are bridal creative blows accompanied by the sound of drums and the tinkling of festive goblets. The Catchpoles are beaten like kings.

And such are all the thrashings in Rabelais' novel. These feudal kings (Picrochole and Anarchus), these aged masters of the Sor-

---

[8] The words for "ninepins" (quilles) and "to play at ninepins" were also used in the erotic sense. All these expressions, lending this interpretation to words like "stick," "pin," "drum," can often be found in the works of Rabelais' contemporaries, for instance in the Triomphe de la dame Vérole, previously mentioned.

bonne (Janotus de Bragmardo), these sacristans (Ticklepecker), hypocritical monks, morose slanderers, gloomy agelasts, are killed, rent, beaten, chased, abused, cursed, derided; they are representatives of the old world but also of that two-bodied world that gives birth in death. By cutting off and discarding the old dying body, the umbilical cord of the new youthful world is simultaneously broken. The Rabelaisian images fix the very moment of this transfer which contains the two poles. Every blow dealt to the old helps the new to be born. The caesarian operation kills the mother but delivers the child. The representatives of the old but generating world are beaten and abused. Therefore, the punishment is transformed into festive laughter.

Let us quote another excerpt from the end of this episode:

The bride, weeping for laughter and laughing for tears, complained hysterically. Catchpole had not stopped smiting her, without choice or distinction of members; worse, he had rumpled her hair, and, worst of all, he had grasspressqueezedrubbangropricknockneadedandcrumpled her privipudendapeehole . . . . The steward appeared and with his arm in a sling, as though it had been utterly bashbangdislocodecimated.

"It was Satan himself made me attend this wedding," he grumbled. "As a result, by God's power, my arms are crackcrumblecrusharrowed. Do you call this a wedding? . . . Yes, by God, I call it the marriage described by Lucian in his *Symposium*. You remember: the philosopher of Samosata tells how the king of the Lapithae celebrated a marriage that ended in war between Lapithae and Centaurs."
(Book 4, Chapter 15)

The ambivalence inherent in all the images of this episode acquires here the form of an oxymoronic combination, characteristic of Rabelais' writings: the bride "weeping for laughter and laughing for tears." The bride's receiving of blows, which were, it is true, erotic rather than simply harsh (bridal beating), is also typical. In the steward's words concluding the scene we must bring out two points: first, a debasing *jeu de mot* or pun in the original French text, which reduces the word engagement (*fiançailles*) to defecation (*fiantailles*), a device typical of grotesque realism; and second, the allusion to Lucian's "feast of the Lapithae." Of all antique banquets this particular "symposium" is nearest to Rabelaisian scenes, especially to the one just described. Lucian's banquet also ends in a fight, but there is a marked difference. The fight featured in his "symposium" is a symbolical broadening of the traditional material of his images and seems not to be his intention. He retains an abstract rationalist, somewhat nihilist character. Lucian's traditional images always defy his intentions; they are incomparably richer than his own. He uses a tradition, but its value and quality are almost forgotten by him.

Let us sum up the episode we have been analyzing—the thrashing in the house of Basché. All the events shown in this episode present the character of a popular-festive comic performance: it is a gay and free play, but it is also full of deep meaning. Its hero and author is time itself, which uncrowns, covers with ridicule, kills the old world (the old authority and truth), and at the same time gives birth to the new. In this game there is a protagonist and a laughing chorus. The protagonist is the representative of a world which is aging, yet pregnant and generating. He is beaten and mocked, but the blows are gay, melodious, and festive. The abuses also follow this merry and creative pattern. The protagonist is adorned as a comic victim with bright ribbons. The images of the bodies rent apart are also important. As each Catchpole is beaten, a detailed anatomizing description is added to the scene. The thrashing of the third Catchpole and of his bailiffs offers a particularly large amount of torn flesh. Beside the direct injuries inflicted upon them, there is a long list of indirectly hurt organs and members: sprained shoulders, black eyes, crippled legs and arms, injured genital parts. It is a bodily sowing, or more correctly speaking, a bodily harvest, something like a fragment from Empidocles. There is a combination of the battlefield with the kitchen or butcher shop. But such is also, as we know, the theme of billingsgate oaths and curses. For the present, we merely outline the image of the grotesque body. We shall devote a special chapter to the analysis of its meaning and sources.

Thus, everything in this episode is styled in the popular-festive comic spirit. But these forms, developed during thousands of years, serve the new historic aims of the epoch; they are filled with powerful historic awareness and lead to a deeper understanding of reality.

The episode of Master Villon's trick at Saint Maixent is related to the thrashing at the house of Basché and is described by Lord Basché in his instructions to the participants in the comic game. We shall discuss this story at the end of the chapter.

All the scenes of thrashing in Rabelais' novel bear, as we have said, a similar character. They are all profoundly ambivalent; everything in them is done with laughter and for laughter's sake, *et le tout en riant.*

Let us briefly look at two more of these scenes. In one of them blood is transformed into wine; in the other the fight is changed into a feast.

The first scene is the famous episode of the beating by Friar John of 13,622 men in the abbey close. This is a most cruel massacre:

> . . . he felled them like so many hogs. He brained some, smashed the legs and arms of others, broke a neck here, cracked a rib there. He flattened a nose or knocked an eye out, crushed a jaw or sent thirty-two teeth rattling down a bloody gullet. Some had their shoulderblades dislocated, others their thighs lammed to pulp, others their hips wrenched, others their arms battered beyond recognition. Let a wretched fellow seek hiding amid the densest vines and Friar John ripped him up the back, gutting him like a cur. Let another take to his heels and Friar John split his head at the lamboid suture. Let a third scramble up a tree and Friar John impaled him by the fundament . . . . Where a man had the temerity to offer resistance, Friar John gave an exhibition of muscular competence as he bashed in the rashling's chest, exposing heart and lungs. Thumping others under the ribs, he mauled their stomachs so severely that they died at once. A whack on the navel and what enemy tripe came spurting forth! . . . Undoubtedly, this was the most horrible spectacle ever seen upon earth.
> (Book 1, Chapter 27)

We have here the very image of a bodily harvest.

When the novices came running up to the friar (in the same

chapter), he ordered them to cut the throats of the survivors: "The little monkeys throttled and dispatched all those Friar John had struck down. Can you guess what instruments they used? Those fine little edge-tools children use hereabouts to scoop the kernel out of ripe walnuts."

This terrible slaughter was undertaken by Friar John in order to save the wine of the monastery's new crop. And this entire episode is filled not only with gay tones but with triumphant ones. This is the "Vineyard of Dionysus," the *vendange,* the feast of the grape harvest. For it was precisely at this time that the fight in the abbey close took place. Beyond the blood-saturated mass of torn bodies, the childish little edge-tools of the novices give us a glimpse of the vats of that *purée septembrale* (September-pulp) so often mentioned by Rabelais. Blood is changed into wine.[9]

Let us now have a look at the other episode. We find it in the Second Book, Chapter 26. Pantagruel and his two companions defeat the 660 knights of King Anarchus. By an ingenious use of gunpowder they burn their enemies, and immediately afterward sit down to a gay feast, Carpalim having brought back from his hunt an enormous amount of venison:

> Invoking the nine Muses, Epistemon fashioned nine splendid antique wooden spits; Eusthenes helped skin the game; Panurge laid two cuirassier saddles down to serve as andirons. Promoting their prisoner to the rank of cook, they had their venison roasted by the fire in which the enemy burned. Then they doused their food with vinegar and fell to with a vengeance, guzzling like so many famished devils. To see them wolf down their food was a triumphant spectacle.
> (Book 2, Chapter 26)

[9] The theme of transformation of blood into wine is found in Don Quixote in the episode of the hero's fight against the giants. This theme was developed even more strikingly in the "Golden Ass" of Apuleius. Lucius kills on his doorstep the men whom he mistakes for robbers. He beholds the blood which he has shed. Next morning he is summoned to court and accused of murder. He is threatened with capital punishment, but it turns out that he was the victim of a mystification. The corpses were merely wineskins. The gloomy court proceedings are turned into a scene of general laughter.

Thus the fire on which the knights were burned was changed into a gay kitchen hearth on which a pile of venison was roasted. The popular-festive nature of this bonfire and of the burning of the knights (the effigies of winter, death, the old year), immediately followed by the banquet, becomes even clearer from the story's further development. Pantagruel and his companions decide to put up a triumphal monument on the site of the battle and feast. Pantagruel plants a post on which he hangs up the archaic attributes of the defunct knights: armor, spurs, a coat of mail, a steel gauntlet, leggings. The rhymed inscription on the trophy lauds the victory of the sane human mind over heavy armor (the knights were burned through the new device of gunpowder). Meanwhile, Panurge erects another post to which he attaches the remaining trophies of the feast: a pair of horns, the hide and legs of a roebuck, a hare's ears, and bustards' wings. To these he adds a cruet of vinegar, a horn with salt, a spit, a larding stick, a saltcellar, and a glass. The inscription on the post praises the feast and gives a recipe.[10]

The two trophies clearly express the ambivalent character of the entire system of popular-festive images. The historic theme of the victory of gunpowder over the knight's heavy armor and castle walls (as in Pushkin's "Scenes of Knightly Times") marks the victory of the inventive mind over uncouth, primitive force. This theme is here offered in a carnivalesque form, and in keeping with this mood the second trophy presents comic kitchen paraphernalia. The death of the old world and the merriment of the new world are combined in this system of images. The bonfire which has consumed the old is transformed into the kitchen hearth. The phoenix is reborn from its ashes.

Let us recall in this connection Panurge's Turkish episode in which he almost suffers martyrdom at the stake for his faith but

[10] In the Italian work of Folengo (nonmacaronic) entitled *Orlandino*, there is a purely carnivalesque description of a tournament of Charlemagne. The knights gallop astride asses, mules, and cows; they carry baskets instead of shields and kitchen utensils, pails, pots and pans, on their heads instead of helmets.

is miraculously saved. The episode is presented as a parody of martyrs and miracles in which the stake is replaced by a hearth. Panurge is being roasted on a spit and wrapped in lard, for he is not considered sufficiently fattened. He escapes miraculously and roasts his tormentor. The episode ends in praise of the roast on the spit.

Thus blood is transformed into wine; ruthless slaughter and the martyr's death are transformed into a merry banquet; the stake becomes a hearth. Bloodshed, dismemberment, burning, death, beatings, blows, curses, and abuses—all these elements are steeped in "merry time," time which kills and gives birth, which allows nothing old to be perpetuated and never ceases to generate the new and the youthful. This interpretation is not Rabelais' abstract conception; it is, so to speak, immanent in the traditional popular-festive system of images which he inherited. He did not create this system, but it rose in him to a higher level of historical development.

But perhaps all these images are nothing but a dead and crippling tradition? Perhaps these little ribbons tied to the arms of the victimized Catchpole, these endless blows and abuses, these dismembered bodies and kitchen utensils, are nothing but the meaningless remnants of ancient philosophies, nothing but an empty form, a dead weight, which prevents the author from seeing and representing the true reality of modern times?

This would be a most absurd supposition. True, the system of popular-festive images was developed and went on living over thousands of years. This long development had its own scoria, its own dead deposits in manners, beliefs, prejudices. But in its basic line this system grew and was enriched; it acquired a new meaning, absorbed the new hopes and thoughts of the people. It was transformed in the crucible of the people's new experience. The language of images developed new and more refined nuances.

Thanks to this process, popular-festive images became a powerful means of grasping reality; they served as a basis for an authentic and deep realism. Popular imagery did not reflect the naturalistic, fleeting, meaningless, and scattered aspect of reality but the very process of becoming, its meaning and direction. Hence the universality and sober optimism of this system.

It is this imagery that lives in Rabelais' work as a realistic and entirely conscious life; it lives fully and up to the minutest detail: the ribbons on the sleeve of one Catchpole, the red face of another, the staff and cross and faded lilies brandished by Friar John, and his nickname: *D'entommeure*. There is not a single dead or useless remnant in these images; instead they are saturated with actuality, with one consistent meaningfulness. Rabelais' clear, thoughtful (yet not narrowly rationalist) artistic consciousness is present in every one of these details.

This does not mean, of course, that each detail was invented, carefully thought out, and weighed in the author's abstract mind. Rabelais was consciously and artistically in possession of his style, the great style of popular-festive forms. The logic of this carnivalesque genre suggested to him the Catchpole's red snout, his merry resurrection after his chastisement, and the two kings to whom he was compared. But he scarcely selected these images separately. He still lived, as did his contemporaries, in the world of these forms; he breathed their atmosphere, used their idiom with assurance, and had no need of constant abstract self-control.

We have shown the essential link of blows and abuses with uncrowning. In Rabelais abuse never assumes the character merely of personal invective; it is universal, and when all is said and done it always aims at the higher level. Behind each victim of abuse and blows Rabelais sees the king, the former king, the pretender. But at the same time the images of all these uncrowned personages are real and very much alive. And so are all these Catchpoles, intriguers, sombre hypocrites and slanderers, whom he beats, chases, and abuses. They are all subject to mockery and punishment as individual incarnations of the dying truth and authority of prevailing thought, law, and virtues.

This old authority and truth pretend to be absolute, to have an extratemporal importance. Therefore, their representatives (the agelasts) are gloomily serious. They cannot and do not wish to laugh; they strut majestically, consider their foes the enemies of eternal truth, and threaten them with eternal punishment. They do not see themselves in the mirror of time, do not perceive their own origin, limitations and end; they do not recognize their own ridiculous faces or the comic nature of their pretentions to eternity and immutability. And thus these personages come to the end of their role still serious, although their spectators have been laughing for a long time. They continue to talk with the majestic tone of kings and heralds announcing eternal truths, unaware that time has turned their speeches into ridicule. Time has transformed old truth and authority into a Mardi Gras dummy, a comic monster that the laughing crowd rends to pieces in the marketplace.[11]

Kind master Rabelais deals with these dummies pitilessly, cruelly, but merrily. Actually, it is gay time itself in whose name and with whose voice the master speaks. Rabelais does not torture living persons. Let them go, but first of all let them remove their royal robes and pompous academic gowns of the Sorbonne in which they masquerade as heralds of divine truths. Rabelais is even disposed to grant them a little hut in the backyard and a mortar to crush onions for "greensauce," as he did King Anarchus. Or he may give them some cloth for a new pair of trousers, or a soup tureen, a sausage, or firewood such as he offered Master Janotus de Bragmardo.

Let us now turn to the episode of Master Janotus. It is related to the stealing of the bells from Notre Dame cathedral by young Gargantua. (Book One, Chapters 17–20.)

The theme of the stealing of the bells was borrowed by Rabelais from the "Great Chronicles," but he broadened and transposed it for the novel. Gargantua steals the historic bells in order to hang them on the harness of his giant mare, which he intends to send

[11] All these representatives of old authority and truth are, in the words of Marx "mere comedians of the world order whose real heroes have already died" (see K. Marx and F. Engels, "Works", Vol. 1, p. 118). The culture of folk humor conceives all these false pretenses of immovable stability and eternity in the perspective of ever-changing and renewed time.

back to his father with a load of fish and cheese. Uncrowning the cathedral bells and hanging them on a horse is a typical carnivalesque gesture of debasement. It combines a destructive theme with that of renewal on another, material bodily level.

The image of a small tinkling bell (usually a cowbell) appears even in the most ancient carnivals as an indispensable accessory. Small bells are usually found in the mythical images of the "wild army," the "wild hunt," and of "Erl-King's retinue," which in the most distant period of antiquity were combined with carnival processions. Cowbells figure in the descriptions of fourteenth-century charivari in the *Roman de Fauvel.* The role of bells on the clown's costume and staff is well known. We still hear the jingling of carnival bells on bridal vehicles.[12] In his description of the diableries produced by Villon, Rabelais writes that the performers wore belts with cowbells and mulebells which made an abominable noise.[13] And we find once more in this episode the image of the stolen bells of Notre Dame.

In the story of the burning of the 660 knights and of the transformation of the funeral pyre into a kitchen hearth, Pantagruel declared in the middle of the feast when all were busily chewing: "Would to God you all had two pairs of church bells hanging on your chins . . . and I the great bells of Rennes, Poitiers, Tours and Cambrai. By heaven! we would boom out a fine carillon to the wagging of our chops." (Book Two, Chapter 26).

Church bells, cowbells, and mulebells are to be attached not only to animals but to the beards of the feasting guests. The ringing and jingling of bells is to mark the movement of the munching jaws. It is hard to find an image picturing more strikingly, though coarsely, the logic of abusive uncrowning, destruction and regeneration. The bells have been uncrowned at their highest level; they are to be removed from the belfries of Poitiers, Rennes, Tours, and Cambrai and are to be suddenly used again in the context of festive food. They will revive their sound by marking the rhythm of masticating jaws. Let us add that this strange use of

[12] The Russian troika. (Translator's note.)
[13] Book 4, Chapter 13.

bells, suddenly introduced into the picture, leads to the rebirth of their image. They arise before us as something completely new, in a setting that is unusual and alien to bells as they commonly appear. The sphere in which the new birth of an image takes place is a material bodily sphere, in this case a banquet. Let us also stress the literal, topographically exact nature of the debasement: the bells are brought down from the high belfries and made to accompany chewing jaws.

The banquet atmosphere that is to regenerate the bells is, of course, far removed from the animal act of eating as well as from a private, intimate entertainment. This is a feast "for all the world," the feast of a popular giant and his companions around a historic hearth; a feast that has consumed the old feudal culture.

Let us return once more to our episode of the stolen bells of Notre Dame. It is now obvious why Gargantua wants to transform them into harness bells for his horse. As the story goes on they are continually linked with carnivalesque images. The commander of the monastic order of Saint Anthony would also like to steal those bells in order to ring them and make the bacon tremble in the pantries (he collects his dues from the people in pork). The main reason for the return of the bells, as Janotus de Bragmardo declares, is the beneficial influence of their sound on the fertility of vines in the Paris region. The other decisive reason is the promise made him of a gift of sausage and hose if he brings back the bells. Thus throughout the episode the bells are continuously ringing in joyous, carnivalesque tones.

Who is Janotus de Bragmardo? In Rabelais' conception, he is the senior member of the Sorbonne. This school was the defender of orthodoxy and of invulnerable divine truth. It controlled the fate of every religious opinion or book. The Sorbonne, as we know, condemned and prohibited all the books of Rabelais' novel as they appeared in succession, but fortunately the school was no longer powerful at that time. Janotus de Bragmardo was the representative of this honorable faculty. But for precaution (for it would still be imprudent to joke about the Sorbonne), Rabelais removed all apparent signs of Janotus de Bragmardo's connection with this institution.[14] The scholar was to persuade Gargantua by means of a wise and eloquent oration to return the bells. He was promised, as we have seen, a handsome "carnivalesque" reward of hose and sausage and wine.

When Janotus, wearing the formal academic gown and accompanied by his assistants, made his appearance with comic solemnity at Gargantua's apartment, this strange company was at first mistaken for a carnival procession:

Master Janotus, with a haircut like that affected by Julius Caesar, settled the traditional doctoral hood over his coot-like head. Next he antidoted his stomach against possible contamination, with cakes baked in the most secular ovens and holy water from his excellently stocked cellar. Then, he proceeded to Gargantua's. Before him crawled three black beadles; behind him he dragged five or six servile and artless Masters of Arts, all of them mildewed and rotten as cheeses.

Ponocrates met them as they entered and was terrified at their motley: he was convinced they must be crazed mummers. He therefore asked one of the artless magisters what this masquerade meant. For answer, he was told they wished to recover the missing bells.

(Book 1, Chapter 18)

The entire carnival setting is brought out in the persons of the Sorbonne faculty members. They are transformed into clowns, into a gay, grotesque procession. "Holy water" from the cellar was a current parody of wine.

Learning what has happened, Gargantua and his companions decide to play a trick on Janotus. He is made to drink "theologically"[15] while they return the bells to the city officials whom they have meanwhile summoned. Thus Janotus has to deliver his oration to a hilarious audience and merely for their amusement. This mystification brings out even more forcefully the comic aspect of

[14] In the canonical edition of the first two books of his novel (1542) Rabelais deleted all direct allusions to the Sorbonne, replacing the word "Sorbonnites" by the word "Sophist."

[15] "Theological drinking" and "theological wine" mean a good drinking bout (a debasing travesty).

the master of the Sorbonne; he has dropped out of real life, he is a dummy, continuing to play his part seriously, unaware of the audience's laughter.

Janotus' oration itself is an excellent parody of the Sorbonnites' eloquence, of their method of argumentation, and their Latin speech. This parody almost deserves to be placed next to the "Letters of Obscure People." But the Janotus oration displays from beginning to end and with utmost artistry the image of senility. A tape recording of his speech would show how full it is of sounds imitating all forms and degrees of coughing, spitting, short breath, and wheezing. It is marked by omissions, lapses, interruptions of thought, and the desperate search for the right word. Janotus frankly complains of his age. This biological image of man's senility is subtly combined with the social, ideological, and linguistic decrepitude of the Sorbonnites. It is the old year, the old winter, the old king, turned into a clown.

The Sorbonnite dummy is mocked. As to the old man, he is given what he needs, and according to his own words he needs very little—to be near his fireplace, his table, and a full soup tureen. This is all that remains of Janotus' pretentious demands. Gargantua generously compensates him, but the Sorbonnite is ridiculed and completely destroyed.

All the episodes we have discussed in this chapter, as well as the individual scenes of battles, fights, beatings, the uncrowning of people and objects (for instance, the bells) are presented by Rabelais in the popular-festive carnival spirit. Therefore, all the episodes are ambivalent: destruction and uncrowning are related to birth and renewal. The death of the old is linked with regeneration; all the images are connected with the contradictory oneness of the dying and reborn world. Not only the episodes discussed but the entire novel is filled with that carnivalesque atmosphere. More than that, a number of important scenes are directly related to feasting and festivity.

We give here a broadened meaning to the word "carnivalesque." As a special phenomenon, carnival has survived up to our time. Other manifestations of popular-festive life, related to it in style and character (as well as origin) have died out long ago or have degenerated so far as to become undistinguishable. Carnival is a well-known festivity that has been often described throughout many centuries. Even during its later development in the eighteenth and nineteenth centuries it still preserved certain fundamental traits in a quite clear, though reduced, form. Carnival discloses these traits as the best preserved fragments of an immense, infinitely rich world. This permits us to use precisely the epithet "carnivalesque" in that broad sense of the word. We interpret it not only as carnival per se in its limited form but also as the varied popular-festive life of the Middle Ages and the Renaissance; all the peculiarities of this life have been preserved in carnival, while the other forms have deteriorated and vanished.

But even in its narrow sense carnival is far from being a simple phenomenon with only one meaning. This word combined in a single concept a number of local feasts of different origin and scheduled at different dates but bearing the common traits of popular merriment. This process of unification in a single concept corresponded to the development of life itself; the forms of folk merriment that were dying or degenerating transmitted some of their traits to the carnival celebrations: rituals, paraphernalia, images, masques. These celebrations became a reservoir into which obsolete genres were emptied.

Obviously, this consolidation took place in its own way, not only in various countries and at various seasons but even in different cities. The clearest, classic carnival forms were preserved in Italy, especially in Rome. The next most typical carnivals were those of Paris. Next came Nuremberg and Cologne, which adopted a more or less classic form at a somewhat later period. In Russia this process did not develop at all; the various aspects of folk merriment of a national or local character (shrove days, Christmas, fairs) remained unchanged. They offered none of the traits typical of Western European amusements. Peter the Great, as we know, tried to bring to Russia the later European style of the "feast of fools" (for example, the election of the all-clowns' pope) and the pranks of the April fool, but these customs did not take root and did not mix with local traditions.

Even in the cities where the process of development acquired a more or less classic character (as in Rome, Paris, Nuremberg, and Cologne), local festivities formed the basis of carnival. Its ritual was enriched by these local traits, which otherwise were doomed to vanish.

Many of these popular-festive forms that had lent some of their essential elements to carnival continued to lead contemporaneously their own pallid existence. This was, for instance, the case of the French charivari; its main traits had been transferred to carnival, but it still retained a feeble resemblance to bridal mockery (if the marriage for some reason or other was not considered normal). It is still presented in our days, as a cat-concert under the windows of newlyweds. Furthermore, all the elements of folk merriment which constituted the second, unofficial part of holy days and legal feasts continued to exist independently; however, they had many traits in common with the carnival rituals: the election of kings and queens for a day on the feast of the Epiphany ("the feast of beans") and on St. Valentine's day. These common elements are determined by the fact that they are all related to time, which is the true hero of every feast, uncrowning the old and crowning the new.[16] These popular unofficial forms of merriment continued, of course, to surround the feasts of the Church. Every fair, usually scheduled for the dedication of a church or a first mass, preserved carnivalesque traits. Finally, the carnivalesque character appeared on private family occasions, christenings and memorial services, as well as on agricultural feasts, the harvest of grapes (*vendange*) and the slaughter of cattle, as described by Rabelais. We also saw the carnivalesque character of the *nopces à mitaines,* a typical bridal ritual. The common denominator of the carnivalesque genres is the essential link of these feasts with "gay time." Whenever the free popular aspect of the feast is preserved,

[16] Actually, every feast day crowns and uncrowns, and has therefore its own king and queen. See this theme in the *Decameron,* where a king and queen are elected for every day of the festive discourses.

the relation with time is maintained, and this means the persistence of its carnivalesque flavor.

But when carnival developed in the narrow sense of the word and became the center of all popular forms of amusement, it diminished all the other feasts and deprived them of almost every free and utopian folk element. The other feasts faded away; their popular character was reduced, especially because of their connection with ecclesiastic or political rituals. Carnival became the symbol and incarnation of the true folk festival, completely independent of Church and State but tolerated by them. This was true of the Roman carnival described by Goethe in his famous sketch in 1788; and true also of the 1895 carnival in that city, pictured by Dieterich for his *Pulcinella* (and dedicated to his Roman friends and to the similar 1897 celebration). In Dieterich's time this festival was the only surviving vivid and colorful testimony of true popular life as it existed in bygone centuries.

In the time of Rabelais folk merriment had not as yet been concentrated in carnival season, in any of the towns of France. Shrove Tuesday (*Mardi Gras*) was but one of many occasions for folk merriment, although an important one. A considerable role in the festive life of the marketplace was played, as we have said, by the fairs held three or four times a year in several towns. The amusements offered at the fairs usually bore a carnivalesque character. Let us recall the numerous popular celebrations of the city of Lyon. At the time of Rabelais the later forms of "the feast of fools" were still preserved, as in the amusements organized in Rouen and Eure by the *Societas Cornadorum* which elected a mock abbot (*Abbas Cornadorum* or *Abbé des Conards*) and organized processions.

Rabelais was of course quite familiar with the motley carnival life that existed in his time both in the cities and in the country. How are the feasts directly reflected in his novel?

In the very beginning of the novel (Book One, Chapters 4, 5, and 6), we find the description of the "feast of cattle slaughter" with a merry banquet during which Gargantua's miraculous birth takes place. This is one of the most remarkable episodes of the

novel and the most characteristic of Rabelais' manner of presentation. We must carefully analyze this passage.

Here is the beginning of the episode:

> The occasion and manner of Gargamelle's delivery were as I
> am about to relate; if you don't believe me, may your vent-peg
> slip, may your stopper fail your (rectal) organ, your fundament
> fall and your flue pipe collapse.
>
> This is exactly what happened to Gargamelle, on February
> third, after dinner. And why? Because she had eaten too abun-
> dantly of tripe . . . of that tripe which comes from beeves which
> are fattened in their stalls and put to graze in meadows . . . in
> meadows which bear two crops of grass each year . . .
>
> Three hundred and sixty-seven thousand and fourteen of these
> fat beeves had been slaughtered. They were to be salted on Shrove
> Tuesday so that there would be pressed beef aplenty that spring
> for the invocation of thirst and its subsequent exorcization by
> wine.
>
> (Book 1, Chapter 4)

The leading theme of this excerpt is the material bodily affluence, a generating and growing superabundance. All the images
are subjected to this theme. First, all the events are related to
Gargamelle's delivery. This is the setting and the background for
the act of birth. A curse hurled at those who will not believe the
author appears in the very first lines; it interrupts the story and
at the same time prepares us for the next picture. Gargamelle's
labor began precisely at the moment when her right intestine fell
out due to the overeating of tripe, the intestines of fattened oxen.
Bowels, intestines, with their wealth of meaning and connotation
are the leading images of the entire episode. In our excerpt these
images are introduced as food: *gaudebillaux,* an equivalent of
grasses tripes, the ox's fatty intestines. But Gargamelle's labor and
the falling out of the right intestine link the devoured tripe with
those who devour them. The limits between animal flesh and the
consuming human flesh are dimmed, very nearly erased. The
bodies are interwoven and begin to be fused in one grotesque
image of a devoured and devouring world. One dense bodily
atmosphere is created, the atmosphere of the great belly. The

esssential events of our episode take place within its walls: eating, the falling-out of intestines, childbirth.

The theme of productivity and growth introduced at the very beginning of the novel by Gargamelle's labor is developed in the images of abundance and fullness of material goods: fat-rich intestines of the oxen elaborately fattened on choice meadows yielding grass twice a year. A grandiose number, 367,014 of these oxen have been slaughtered. The word "fattened" and its derivatives (*grosses, engressez, gras*) are repeated four times in three lines. The slaughter is performed in order to have an abundant supply (*tas*) of meat.

This theme of abundance of material goods is here directly linked with Mardi Gras, when the salting of the slaughtered oxen is to be done. Mardi Gras is Shrove Tuesday. A carnivalesque atmosphere permeates the entire episode; it ties into one grotesque knot the slaughter, the dismemberment and disemboweling, bodily life, abundance, fat, the banquet, merry improprieties, and finally childbirth.

At the end of the excerpt there is a typical debasement: the *commemoration des saleurs*. Salted hors d'oeuvres as an extraordinary addition to dinner are defined by the liturgical term of "commemoration," which meant a short prayer to the saint whose feast was celebrated on that day, in other words, an extraordinary addendum to prayer. Thus an allusion to the liturgy is inserted in the story.

Finally, let us point out the stylistic peculiarities of this excerpt. The first part is constructed like a chain. The word that ends one sentence starts the next (in the French text), and thus each link is joined to the succeeding one. Such a construction increases the density, the unbroken wholeness of this world made of abundant fat, meat, bowels, and childbirth.

Let us follow the episode's further development. Since the intestines of the slaughtered oxen cannot be preserved a long time, Grangousier invites the inhabitants of all the neighboring villages to his feast:

. . . they summoned all the citizenry of Sinais, Seuilly, La Roche Clermault and Vaugaudry, without forgetting their friends from Coudray-Montpensier, and Gué de Vède and other neighbors, all accomplished tosspots, debonair fellows and hal fine cuedrivers, skilled tailpushers alll
(Book 1, Chapter 4)

Thus, the feast for which thousands of oxen were slaughtered has a widely popular character. It is "a feast for all the world." And such was the essence of every carnivalesque celebration.

The description of the neighbors invited by Grangousier is colorful too. They are presented in the last sentence as *beaux joueurs de quilles*. We already know that *quille* in Rabelais' time had an erotic connotation; thus the account of the guests as offered here is on the material bodily level of the entire episode.

Grangousier warns his wife about the danger of eating too much tripe, saying that there are no intestines without dung. In spite of this warning, Gargamelle consumes sixteen quarters, two bushels, and six pecks of tripe; her bowels are inflated by these all-too-generous portions.

Here the author introduces the theme of dung, closely related to the concept of bowels in general and to intestines in particular, since even after thorough washing some excrement is retained in them. In this image, once more the limits between the devouring and the devoured body are erased; the contents of the animal intestines contribute to the formation of fecal matter in the human bowels. Animal and human organs are interwoven into one indissoluble grotesque whole. The author's concluding exclamation in this paragraph, *O belle matière fécale,* is characteristic of the entire atmosphere of this episode. Let us recall that in grotesque realism this image represented in most cases gay matter.

Immediately after this scene all the guests betook themselves to the meadow of La Saussaie, made merry, and danced to the tune of flutes and bagpipes. This carnivalesque interlude is organically related to all the other images of this episode. We repeat, in the atmosphere of Mardi Gras, reveling, dancing, music were all closely combined with slaughter, dismemberment, bowels, excrement, and other images of the material bodily lower stratum.

For the correct understanding of the entire novel, as well as the present episode, it is necessary to turn away from the limited and reduced aesthetic stereotypes of modern times; they are far from adequate to the main lines of development in world literature and art of past ages. It would be especially inadmissible to modernize Rabelais' images by attempting to fit them to the differentiated, narrowed, one-sided concepts that dominate the modern system of thought. In grotesque realism and in Rabelais' work the image of excrement, for instance, did not have the trivial, narrowly physiological connotation of today. Excrement was conceived as an essential element in the life of the body and of the earth in the struggle against death. It was part of man's vivid awareness of his materiality, of his bodily nature, closely related to the life of the earth.

Therefore, Rabelais does not and cannot display any "gross naturalism" or "physiologism." In order to understand him we must read him with the eyes of his contemporaries; we must see him against the background of the thousand-year-old tradition which he represents. Then the episode of Gargamelle's labor will appear to us as a high and at the same time gay drama of the body and of the earth.

The fifth chapter (Book One) is devoted to the famous "Palaver of the Potulent." This is a carnivalesque symposium. It has no external logical continuity, no unifying abstract idea or problem (as in a classic symposium). But the "Palaver of the Potulent" has a deep internal unity. It is one grotesque play of debasement carefully organized up to the minutest detail. Nearly every replica contains a formula from the higher level—ecclesiastical, liturgical, philosophical, or juridical—or some words of the scriptures applied to eating and drinking. The conversation is actually concerned with two topics: the ox tripes that are being consumed and the wine that washes down the food. But this material bodily lower stratum is travestied as images and formulas of the holy spiritual upper level.

We must stress the play of words in the images of bowels. One of the guests says: *Je laverois volonttiers les tripes de ce veau que j'ay ce matin habillé*. The word *habiller* means to "dress" or "clothe," but it can also mean to "dress" the meat of a slaughtered animal. Thus, when the guest speaks of "the calf I dressed this very morning," he means in the first place himself, dressed for the occasion, but also the calf that was dismembered, dressed, and consumed. Similarly, the tripe means at the same time the guest's own intestines, which he intends to wash with wine, and the consumed bowels which he wants to wash down.

Here is another *double entendre* constructed on the same pattern: *Voulez-vous rien mandez a la rivière? Cestuy cy* [the glass of wine] *vas laver les tripes*. Here again the word *tripes* has a double meaning: that of the guest's own bowels and the consumed bowels of the ox. The dividing line between man's consuming body and the consumed animal's body is once more erased.

The hero of the next chapter is Gargamelle's birth-giving womb. Here is the beginning of her labor:

A few moments later, she began to groan, lament and cry out. Suddenly crowds of midwives came rushing up from all directions. Feeling and groping her below, they found certain loose shreds of skin, of a rather unsavory odor, which they took to be the child. It was, on the contrary, her fundament which had escaped with the mollification of her right intestine (you call it the bumgut) because she had eaten too much tripe, as I explained above. (Book 1 Chapter 6)

Here is the anatomy of the lower parts (*le bas*) in a literal sense. The grotesque knot of the womb is tied even more tightly: the right intestine that fell out, the consumed ox tripe, the womb that is giving birth (the mother's intestine is mistaken for the baby)— all these elements are indissolubly interwoven.

The midwife who rushes to the rescue uses too potent an astringent:

As a result of Gargamelle's discomfort, the cotyledons of the placenta of her matrix were enlarged. The child, leaping through the breach and entering the hollow vein, ascended through her diaphragm to a point above her shoulders. Here the vein divides into two; the child accordingly worked his way in a sinistral direction, to issue, finally, through the left ear.

No sooner born, he did not like other babes cry: "Whaay! Whaay!" but in a full, loud voice bawled: "Drink, drink, drink!" as though inviting the company to fall to. What is more, he shouted so lustily, that he was heard throughout the regions of Beuxe (pronounced "booze") and Bibarois (which in sound evokes bibbers and is how the Gascons pronounce "Vivarais").
(Book 1, Chapter 6)

The anatomical analysis ends with the unexpected and completely carnivalesque birth of Gargantua through his mother's ear. The child does not go down, but up. This is a typical grotesque turnover. A similar comic note is heard in Gargantua's first cry, calling for a drink.

Let us sum up our analysis of this episode.

All the images develop the theme of the feast: slaughter of cattle, disemboweling, dismemberment. The images continue to unfold along the lines of a banquet: devouring of the dismembered body. They are later transferred to the anatomic description of the generating womb. These images create with great artistry an extremely dense atmosphere of the body as a whole in which all the dividing lines between man and beast, between the consuming and consumed bowels are intentionally erased. On the other hand, these consuming and consumed organs are fused with the generating womb. We thus obtain a truly grotesque image of one single, superindividual bodily life, of the great bowels that devour and are devoured, generate and are generated. But this, of course, is not an "animal" or "biological" bodily life. We see looming beyond Gargamelle's womb the devoured and devouring womb of the earth and the ever-regenerated body of the people. The child that is born is the people's mighty hero, the French Heracles.

In this episode, as in all others told by Rabelais, the merry, abundant and victorious bodily element opposes the serious medieval world of fear and oppression with all its intimidating and intimidated ideology. As in the prologue of *Pantagruel*, these

chapters end in a gay and free travesty of the medieval methods of
faith and persuasion:

> Now I suspect that you do not thoroughly believe this strange
> nativity. If you do not, I care but little, though an honest and
> sensible man believes what he is told and what he finds written.
> Does not Solomon say in *Proverbs* (XIII, 15): "*Innocens credit
> omni verbo*, the innocent believeth every word," and does not St.
> Paul (I Corinthians, 13) declare: "*Charitas omnia credit*, Charity
> believeth all."
> Why should you not believe what I tell you? Because, you reply,
> there is no evidence. And I reply in turn that for this very reason
> you should believe with perfect faith. For the gentlemen of the
> Sorbonne say that faith is the argument of non-evident truths.
> Is anything I have related beyond our law or faith, contrary to
> our reason, or opposed to Divine Scriptures? For my part, I find
> nothing in the Holy Bible that stands against it. And if such had
> been the will of God, would you affirm that He could not accom-
> plish it? Ha, I pray you, do not ambiguembrangle your minds with
> such vain conceits. I tell you that nothing is impossible to God
> and, if He but pleased, women would henceforth give birth to
> their children through the left ear.
> (Book 1, Chapter 6)

Further, the author recalls a number of strange births from antique mythology and legends.

This entire passage is a brilliant parody of the medieval doctrine of faith, as well as of the methods of defending and teaching
it: through quotations from the Scriptures, intimidation, threats,
and accusations of heresy. The concentrated atmosphere of the
merry bodily elements prepares the uncrowning of the doctrine of
faith as "the argument of nonevident truths."

The most important episode of *Gargantua*, Picrochole's war,
develops in the atmosphere of another feast, the harvest of grapes
(*vendange*).

The *vendange* played an important role in the life of France.
During this season even state institutions and the courts were
closed, since all were busy in the vineyards. All the events and
images of the Picrochole war are shown in this setting of harvest
time.

The pretext for the war was the conflict between the peasants of Seuilly who guarded the ripened vineyards and the bakers of Lerne who had brought a load of cakes for sale. The peasants wanted to eat some cakes with their grapes (a combination which, incidentally, has the effect of a purge). The bakers refused to sell their goods and insulted the peasants. A fight broke out. Wine and bread, grapes and cakes form a liturgical complex, subjected here to a debasing parody (the fact that these foods have a stimulating effect on the bowels).

The first great episode of the war, the defense of the abbey close by Friar John, also contains a travestied allusion to communion. We see the blood transformed into wine, while the ruthless beating suggests the *vendange*. In French winegrowers' folklore *vendange* is connected with *bon temps,* the "propitious time."[17] The figure of propitious time symbolizes in folklore the end of evil days and advent of general peace. For this reason Rabelais develops a popular utopian theme: the triumph of peaceful labor and abundance over war and destruction. This is the fundamental theme of this entire episode of the Picrochole war.

Thus, the *vendange* atmosphere entirely permeates the second part of *Gargantua* and organizes the system of its images, just as the first part (Gargantua's birth) reflected the feast of cattle slaughter and carnival. The entire book is steeped in popular-festive atmosphere.[18]

[17] Two figures of the popular feast of *vendange* determine the entire character of this episode: the figure of *Bon Temps,* which inspired the basic idea of the chapter (the final victory of peace and general welfare and affluence); and the figure of his wife, *Mère Folle,* which is projected in the farcical, carnivalesque aspect of the Picrochole war.

[18] In his free translation of this book Fischart has considerably strengthened the festive element but offers it in the light of Grobianism. Grangousier is a passionate amateur of all festivities, because they imply banquets and clowneries. There is a long enumeration of German sixteenth-century feasts: the feast of Saint Martin, carnival, the blessing of palms, the consecration of a church, the fair, christening, etc. One feast follows the other, so that the entire cycle of the year in Grangousier's calendar consists exclusively of feast days. For Fischart, the moralist,

In the novel's Second Book, *Pantagruel,* there are also episodes related to the theme of feasts. In 1532, at the time when *Pantagruel* was written, the Pope proclaimed a Jubilee year in France, in addition to the usually scheduled celebrations. During the Jubilee certain churches were granted the right to sell papal indulgences, that is, absolutions from sin. In Rabelais' novel there is an episode directly related to this theme. Wishing to improve his financial status, Panurge tours the churches and buys indulgences; at the same time, pretending to pick up his change from the plate he collects a hundred times more than he deposited. He interprets the Gospel words *Centuplius accipies* (thou shalt be rewarded a hundredfold), uttered in the present tense by the priest, as an imperative form: "receive a hundredfold," so that his conscience is satisfied. In other words, this episode travesties the festive theme of the Jubilee year and of the Gospel text.

In the Second Book we also find an episode describing Panurge's unsuccessful attempt to gain the attention of a noble lady. Being rejected by her, he avenges himself in a peculiar manner. The central event of this episode takes place on the feast of Corpus Christi. It is a monstrous parody of the ritual, depicting a procession of 600,014 dogs who follow the lady and besmirch her dress, Panurge having sprinkled it with the diced genital organs of a bitch.

Such a parody of a religious procession on the day of *Corpus Christi* may appear at first sight as sacrilegious as it is unexpected. However, the history of this feast in France, as well as in other countries, especially in Spain, proves that extremely free, grotesque images of the body were quite usual on these occasions and were consecrated by tradition. It can be said that the grotesque body prevailed in the popular marketplace aspect of this celebration and created its specific atmosphere. Thus, for instance, traditional representations of this grotesque body participated in the procession, which included a monster combining cosmic, animal,

---

feasts meant gluttony and idleness. Such an interpretation and appreciation are, of course, in contradiction with Rabelais' treatment of this subject. However, Fischart's own attitude in this matter is ambiguous.

and human features, "the Babylonian harlot" astride the monster,[19] as well as giants (traditionally symbolizing the great body), negroes and moors (a grotesque deviation from the bodily norm), and a group of youngsters performing folk dances (like the quasi-indecent Spanish sarabande). It was only after these grotesque figures had marched by that the clergy made its appearance, carrying the host. The procession was closed by decorated coaches with actors in their theatrical costumes. (Therefore, the feast was called in Spain *fiesta de los carros*.)

The traditional procession on the feast of *Corpus Christi* had a clearly expressed carnivalesque character with a prevailing bodily note. In Spain a dramatic performance called *Autos Sacramentalis* was staged on that day. We can surmise the contents of this show from the plays of a similar type of Lope de Vega which have been preserved for us. Grotesque-comic elements prevail in these plays and even permeate their serious parts. They contain a considerable amount of travesty and parody not only of antique but also of Christian themes and of the festive procession itself.

We may sum up by saying that the popular marketplace aspect of this feast was, to a certain extent, a satyrical drama which parodied the Church ritual of the Corpus Christi (the host).[20]

In the light of these facts, Rabelais' travesty is neither surprising nor monstrous. The author merely develops all the elements of satyrical drama already in existence: the monster with the harlot astride, the giants and moors, the indecent gestures of the dance. True, the author develops these images with bold awareness. In the setting of satyrical drama, we must not be surprised by the urinating dogs, nor even by the role of the bitch. Let us also recall the ambivalent character of drenching in urine, the element of fertility and procreating power contained in this image. As Rabelais tells us in this episode, the dog urine formed a stream which

---

[19] The composite body of the monster with the harlot astride is equivalent to the bowels of the feast of cattle slaughter, which devour, are devoured and give birth simultaneously.

[20] The antique satyrical drama was a drama of the body and of bodily life. Monsters and giants played a considerable role.

still flows by St. Victor (and he adds that the Gobelin manufacturers use this stream for the dyeing of their tapestries).

The episodes we have analyzed are directly related to a few feasts only (cattle slaughter, *vendange*, the papal Jubilee, *Corpus Christi*). In these episodes the theme of the feast influences the organization of all the images. But these examples do not exhaust our subject. Throughout Rabelais' entire novel we find allusions to other feasts as well: St. Valentine's day, the fair of Niort, for which Villon composed his diablerie, the carnival of Avignon at which the baccalaureates played the game of *rafa*, the fair of Lyon with its gay monster, the glutton Mâchecroute. Describing his hero's visits to the universities of France, Rabelais devotes special attention to the recreational amusements and games of the students and baccalaureates.

In the popular marketplace aspect of the feast a substantial place was held by games (cards and sports, as well as by various forms of fortune-telling, wishes, and predictions). These manifestations, closely related to the popular-festive atmosphere, play an important part in the novel. It suffices to say that the entire Third Book is constructed as a series of fortune-telling episodes, in which Panurge makes inquiries concerning his betrothed. These incidents will deserve our special attention.

Let us first point out the considerable role of games in Rabelais' work. Chapter 20 of *Gargantua* contains the list of games played by the young hero after his dinner. The standard edition (1542) lists 217 names of games (including a number of parlor and table games and many open-air sports).

This famous enumeration had a considerable resonance. Rabelais' first German translator, Fischart, completed the long list with 372 German card games and dance tunes. The English seventeenth-century translator, Thomas Urquhart, also increased the lists of recreations by adding English games. The Dutch version of *Gargantua* (1682) added some national material, namely 63 purely Dutch games. This proves that Rabelais' list stimulated the interest of other countries in their own amusements. The Dutch version initiated research in the field of children's games, resulting in the greatest work ever undertaken in world folk studies: "Children's Games and Amusements in the Netherlands."[21]

Rabelais' own interest in games was not purely accidental. He shared this interest with his contemporaries. Games were related not only outwardly but also by an inner essential link to the popular marketplace aspect of feasts.

Besides the list in *Gargantua*, Rabelais widely used the rich vocabulary of games, borrowing from it his metaphors and comparisons. He drew from this source a great number of erotic allusions, like the expression *joueurs de quille*, as well as many colorful images expressing success and failure (for instance, *c'est bien rentré de piques!*, this is an unfortunate move). We must add that these expressions taken from games were important in shaping the vernacular.

The images of two important episodes of the novel are built on games. The first is the "prophetic riddle" that concludes the First Book (*Gargantua*), and the second is the dice-casting of Judge Bridlegoose.

The "prophetic riddle" was written by Mellin de Saint-Gelais, probably in full. But Rabelais had good reasons for using it; the poem was closely related to all his images. The analysis of the "prophetic riddle" will disclose a number of new and important aspects of this system.

Two elements are closely interwoven in the poem: the parody of a prophecy concerning the historic future and the images of a ball game. This relation of play and prophecy reveals a carnivalesque conception of the historical process.

Mellin de Saint-Gelais has another short poem in which the struggle for Italy between Francis I, Pope Clement VII, and Charles V is pictured as a *jeu de prime*, a popular card game of that time. The political situation of the time, the distribution of

[21] Cock, Karel, and Isidoor Tierlinck, *Kinderspel & Kinderlust in Zuid-Nederland met Schema's Teekeningen.* Konklijke Vlaamse Academie Voor Taalen-Letterkunde, reeks 6, No. 29, Ghent, 1902–1908.

forces, and the respective assets and weaknesses of the rulers are presented in the precise terminology of this game.

We find a similar little poem in Des Périers entitled "Prediction for the Lyonnais, Hinne Tibaut." This poem describes in prophetic tones the destiny of "three comrades." The "comrades" are actually three dice.

Prophetic riddles were so popular at the time of Rabelais that Thomas Sebillet devoted to this genre a special section of his "Poetics" (Chapter 11, *De l'Enigme*).[22] Riddles are extremely characteristic of the artistic and ideological conception of that time. The sad and terrifying, the serious and important are transposed into a gay and light key, from the minor key to the major. Everything leads to a merry solution. Instead of being gloomy and terrifying, the world's mystery and the future finally appear as something gay and carefree. This, of course, is not philosophical affirmation; it is an expression of the artistic and ideological tendency of the time, seeking to hear the sounds of the world in a new key, to approach it not as a somber mystery play but as a satyrical drama.

The other aspect of this genre is the parodical prophecy, which was also widespread in those days. Of course, serious prophecies were popular as well. The struggle of Francis I against Charles V led to an immense number of historical and political prognostics. Many of them were related to religious movements and wars. In most cases these prophecies were of a gloomy and eschatological character. There were also regular astrological predictions. Popular prognostics were periodically printed in the form of calendars, for instance, "The Ploughman's Prognostics" which offered weather forecasts and agricultural predictions.[23] Side by side with the serious prophecies and forecasts there appeared parodies and travesties of this genre which enjoyed considerable success. The

[22] See Thomas Sebillet, *Art poétique François*, 1548 (commentary by F. Gaiffe, 1910) Droz, 1932.
[23] *Prognostication des Laboureurs*, reedited by Anatole de Montaiglon in his *Recueil de poésies françaises de XVème et XVI ème siècles*, Vol. 2.

best known of these parodies were the "General Prognostics,"[24] "The Prognostics of Friar Thibault,"[25] and "New Prognostics."[26]

These are all typical popular-festive creations. They mock not so much the naïve faith in forecasts and prophecies as their tone, their interpretations of life, history, and the times. The jocular and merry approach is opposed to the serious and gloomy one; the usual and commonplace to the strange and unexpected, the material and bodily to the abstract and the exalted. The main goal of the anonymous authors of these parodies was to give time and the future a different coloring, to transfer the accent to the material bodily life. Popular-festive images were often used for depicting changes in history and time.

Rabelais' own "Pantagruelesque Prognostic" is written in a similar spirit. In this short text we find material bodily images: "During Lent, lard will avoid peas," "the belly will go forward," "the bottom will sit down first." There are also popular-festive images: "On the feast-day, people will not find the bean-kings in the cake," as well as images of games: "the dice will not fulfill your wishes," "you will not win points as needed."

In the "Prognostic" 's fifth chapter, which parodies astrological predictions, Rabelais first of all democratizes them. He considers that it is the greatest folly to believe that stars are made only for kings, popes, and nobles, and the great events of the official world. Astrology must be concerned too with the life and destinies of the lower classes. This is, in a way, the uncrowning of the stars, the stripping of their royal robes.

Rabelais' "Prognostic" also contains what might be called a "carnivalesque picture of carnival": "Men will change their dress so as to cheat others, and they will run about in the streets like fools and madmen; nobody has yet seen such a disorder in nature."

We find here in a reduced form the "prophetic riddle" from *Gargantua*. The images of a social, historical, and natural catas-

---

[24] *Ibid.*, Vol. 4. It is possible that the "General Prognostics" was written by Rabelais.

[25] *Ibid.*, Vol. 13.

[26] *Ibid.*, Vol. 12.

trophe are represented as a carnival with its masquerades and disorderly conduct.

The genre of travestied prophecies are essentially related to time, to the new year, to the guessing of riddles, to marriage, birth, and procreative force. This is why food, drink, the material bodily life and the images of games play in this genre such an important part.

Games are also closely related to time and to the future. The basic accessories of games, dice and cards, are often used as the accessories of fortune-telling. It is needless to dwell on the roots of the imagery representing feasts and games. What is important is not their generic relationship but their *related meaning*. This relation was clearly felt in the time of Rabelais. There was in those days a vivid awareness of the universalism of this imagery, of its link with time and the future, destiny, and political power. These links were part of their philosophy and entered into the interpretation of chessmen, dice, and the figures and colors in cards. Kings and queens of the "feast of fools" were often elected by casting dice. The most successful winner at this game was called *basilicus* or "royal." The images of games were seen as a condensed formula of life and of the historic process: fortune, misfortune, gain and loss, crowning and uncrowning. Life was presented as a miniature play (translated into the language of traditional symbols), a play without footlights. At the same time games drew the players out of the bounds of everyday life, liberated them from usual laws and regulations, and replaced established conventions by other lighter conventionalities. This was true not only of cards, dice, and chess but also of sports and children's games (ninepins, ball games). As yet, there were not sharp divisions between them, as those that were later established. We have seen that the figures in card games represented world events, as in the *jeu de prime* representing the struggle for Italy in Saint-Gelais' poem. Ball games also fulfilled these functions, as well as dice in the "three comrades" poem of Des Périers. In his "Poliphila's Dream" Francesco Colonna describes a game of chess; the chessmen are represented as live people, wearing conventional costumes inspired by that game. Here chess is transformed on the one hand into a carnival masquerade, on the other hand into a grotesque image of military and political events. This game is repeated in the Fifth Book of Rabelais' novel and is possibly based on rough sketches of Rabelais himself who was familiar with "Poliphila's Dream." There is an allusion to this book in *Gargantua*.

The peculiar interpretation of games in Rabelais' time must be carefully considered. Games were not as yet thought of as a part of ordinary life and even less of its frivolous aspect. Instead they had preserved their philosophical meaning. Like all humanists, Rabelais was familiar with the ancient conception of games which held them to be far better than ordinary idle pastimes. Therefore, Ponocrates did not exclude them from young Gargantua's education. On rainy days they devoted themselves to painting and sculpture, or revived, as Rabelais tells us, the antique custom of playing dice, following the description of this game by Leonicus[27] or the example of Lascaris, the king's librarian. While playing, they would recall the ancient authors who mentioned this game (Book One, Chapter 24).

The fate of the imagery of games is similar, in part, to that of abuses and improprieties. Having been absorbed by the sphere of private life, the images of games lost their universal relationship and were deprived of the meaning they formerly conveyed. The Romanticists sought to restore these images in literature (as they sought to restore the forms of carnival), but they understood them subjectively within the structure of personal destinies.[28] The tonality is entirely different in the Romantic period; it is usually in the minor key.

What has been said explains how it happens that the images of games, prophecies (as parodies), and riddles are combined with

[27] Nicolas Léonicène, a contemporary of Rabelais, Italian humanist, who published a dialogue concerning dice.

[28] The opinion here offered by us can also be extended, with certain reservations, to the images of games in Lermontov's works: "The Masquerade," "The Lady-Treasurer," "The Fatalist." These images also bear a special character in Dostoevsky's "Gambler" and "Raw Youth."

folk elements to form an organic whole. Their common denominator is gay time. They all transform the eschatology of the Middle Ages into a "gay monster." They humanize the development of history and prepare a sober and fearless knowledge of this process.

In the "prophetic riddle" historic events are represented with the help of all these forms (games, prophecies, and others) presented in a carnivalesque aspect. Let us take a closer look at it.

The author of the "riddle" declares that if it is possible to foretell the future with the help of stars and divine inspiration, he will predict what is going to happen next winter in this very place. There will appear "unquiet men" (*las du repos et fachez du séjour*). They will bring strife and rebellion among friends and relatives, they will divide all men into hostile parties, they will arm children against parents; all order will be disrupted, all social differences erased. Inferiors will lose respect for their superiors. Never has history, which has witnessed many wonders, told of such dreadful happenings.

Let us stress in this prophetic picture the complete destruction of the established hierarchy, social, political, and domestic. It is a picture of utter catastrophe threatening the world.

The historic calamity is increased by a cosmic disaster. The author predicts a flood, which will drown all mankind, followed by a terrible earthquake. Then a gigantic flame will appear, and finally calm and gladness will once more descend upon earth. In this picture we dimly see the threat of a universal crisis, of a fire that is to burn the old world, and of the joy brought by a world renewed. This image is in a way related to the one we have already seen, the transformation of the funeral pyre into a kitchen hearth and banquet.

Gargantua and Friar John discuss the "prophetic riddle." Gargantua takes the prognosis seriously and relates it to contemporary events, sadly foreseeing the persecution of the Evangelists. Friar John refuses to accept this gloomy interpretation. He swears by Saint Goderan that this is the style of the prophet Merlin. He means Mellin de Saint Gelais. Let Gargantua seek in the prophecy the deepest implications, all that the Friar sees is the description of a game of tennis, rather obscure, it is true (Book One, Chapter 58).

Friar John then offers his own interpretation: Social disintegration and rebellion mean the division of the ball players into two camps; the flood is the sweat pouring from their bodies, the universal conflagration is merely the fire near which they are resting after the game; there follows the banquet and rejoicing of the winners.

The second important episode built on the imagery of games is the scene in which old Judge Bridlegoose solved all lawsuits by casting dice. The legal term *alea judiciorum* (meaning the arbitrariness of court decisions) was understood by the judge literally, since *alea* means "dice." Basing himself on this metaphor, he was fully convinced that since he pronounced his judgments by dicing, he was acting in strict accordance with legal requirements. He gave a similar interpretation to the term *in obscuris minimum est sequendum,* "in obscure matters it is better to make the minimum decision" (as the most prudent one). Following this rule, Bridlegoose solved obscure matters by using the smallest dice. The entire order of this peculiar court procedure is built on the metaphors used by the judge in his court decisions. When induced to weigh the testimony of both parties, he places the plaintiff's file opposite the file of the defendant and then casts his dice. Thus all the cases judged by Bridlegoose are transformed into a gay parody, with the dice as the central image.[29]

These are two of the episodes related to games, and there are many others. The basic artistic purpose of the parodied and travestied prophecies and riddles is to uncrown gloomy eschatological time, that is, the medieval concept of the world. The parodies renew time on the material bodily level, transforming it into a propitious and merry notion. The images of games, also, are usually subjected to this purpose. In the Bridlegoose episode

[29] We are not discussing the entire meaning of this remarkable episode of Bridlegoose. We are here concerned only with the image of dice.

games have an additional function: they offer a gay parody of the legal methods of establishing truth. This travesty is similar to the one applied to the ecclesiastical and scholastic method, as told in the prologues and in various episodes of the novel.

We must here pause to examine more closely the soothsayings in the Third Book of Rabelais' work.

This book was a live echo of the dispute which stirred France, especially in 1542–1550. This was the *querelle des femmes,* which concerned the nature of women and wedlock. Nearly all French poets, writers, and philosophers participated in this dispute, which had a vivid repercussion at the royal court and in wide circles of the reading public. The dispute did not present a new topic of controversy; it had already caused some agitation in the fifteenth century. The problem under discussion was considerably complex, more complex than commentators generally believed it to have been.

Concerning women's nature and marriage, two opposing lines of thought were confronted. These two lines run through the entire Middle Ages and Renaissance. The first one is usually called "the Gallic tradition" (*tradition gauloise*); this is the medieval concept, a negative attitude toward woman. The second line, which Abel Lefranc calls the "idealizing tradition,"[30] exalts womanhood. At the time of Rabelais, this second line was supported by the "Platonizing" poets and was based in part on the tradition of chivalry of the Middle Ages.

Rabelais belonged to the Gallic tradition which was supported and renewed by a number of authors; it was especially defended by Gratien Dupont who published in 1534 a poem in three books entitled "The Controversy of the Masculine and Feminine Sex." Rabelais, as we have said, did not take the women's side. How can his position be explained?

[30] The *Querelle des femmes* is analyzed in detail by Abel Lefranc in his introduction to the Third Book. See Vol. 5, pp. 30 ff. of the critical edition, *Oeuvres,* ed. Abel Lefranc and Robert Marichal *et al.,* 7 vols., E. Champion and E. Droz, Paris and Geneva, 1912–1965.

The fact is that the Gallic tradition is a complex and contradictory phenomenon. Actually, it represented not one but two lines of thought: the popular comic tradition; and the ascetic tendency of medieval Christianity, which saw in woman the incarnation of sin, the temptation of the flesh. The latter often borrowed its symbols from the comic line; this is why scholars frequently combine and confuse the two lines in their research. We must add that in a number of medieval writings, hostile to women and to marriage (especially in encyclopedic works), the two tendencies are mechanically combined.

In reality, the popular comic tradition and the ascetic tradition are profoundly alien to each other. The popular tradition is in no way hostile to woman and does not approach her negatively. In this tradition woman is essentially related to the material bodily lower stratum; she is the incarnation of this stratum that degrades and regenerates simultaneously. She is ambivalent. She debases, brings down to earth, lends a bodily substance to things, and destroys; but, first of all, she is the principle that gives birth. She is the womb. Such is woman's image in the popular comic tradition.

But when this image is treated trivially (in the *fabliaux, facéties,* early novellas, and farces) woman's ambivalence acquires an ambiguous nature; it presents a wayward, sensual, concupiscent character of falsehood, materialism, and baseness. But these are not abstract moral traits of the human being. They cannot be taken out of the general pattern of images, for in this pattern womanhood performs the functions of debasement and at the same time of renewal of life. Womanhood is shown in contrast to the limitations of her partner (husband, lover, or suitor); she is a foil to his avarice, jealousy, stupidity, hypocrisy, bigotry, sterile senility, false heroism, and abstract idealism. The woman of Gallic tradition is the bodily grave of man. She represents in person the undoing of pretentiousness, of all that is finished, completed, and exhausted. She is the inexhaustible vessel of conception, which dooms all that is old and terminated. Like the Sybil of Panzoult in Rabelais' novel, she lifts her skirts and shows the parts through which everything passes (the underworld, the grave) and from which everything issues forth.

On this level the "Gallic tradition" develops the theme of cuckoldry. This is the uncrowning of the old husband and a new act of procreation with the young husband. In this system of images the cuckolded husband assumes the role of uncrowned old age, of the old year, and the receding winter. He is stripped of his robes, mocked, and beaten.

We must note that the image of the woman in the "Gallic tradition," like other images in this tradition, is given on the level of ambivalent laughter, at once mocking, destructive, and joyfully reasserting. Can it be said that this tradition offers a negative, hostile attitude toward woman? Obviously not. The image is ambivalent.

But as considered by the ascetic tendencies of Christianity and the moralistic abstract thought of modern satirists, the Gallic image loses its positive pole and becomes purely negative. It cannot be transferred from the comic to the serious level without distorting its very nature. Therefore, in most encyclopedic writings of the Middle Ages and the Renaissance which sum up the Gothic accusations against womanhood, the authentic Gallic images are disfigured. This is true of the second part of the *Roman de la Rose,* although the ambivalence of love and woman is preserved to a certain extent.

The Gallic tradition suffers another distortion in the literature of manners. In this case the image of woman appears entirely negative; or else the ambivalence degenerates into a mixture of positive and negative elements. This took place especially in the eighteenth century, when such static combinations of good and evil were offered as a true realistic picture, "resembling life."

But let us go back to the controversy of the sixteenth century and to Rabelais' part in it. The dispute was mainly conducted in the terms of the new, narrow conception: moralizing and scholastic humanist philosophy. Rabelais alone represented the authentic Gallic tradition. He did not join the enemy camps of the moralists or of the Epicurean followers of Castiglione. Neither did he take sides with the Platonizing idealists. However, the latter, as defenders of woman and love, were closer to him than the abstract moralists. A certain degree of ambivalence was still preserved by the Platonist's idea of "exalted womanhood"; this image was symbolically broadened and the regenerating element brought forward. But the Platonizing poets' abstract, idealistic, and serious approach was unacceptable to Rabelais. He clearly realized the novelty of this type of seriousness and exaltation which the Platonists had brought into literature; he was well aware of the difference of their approach from the gloomy seriousness of the Gothic age. But he did not believe that this new philosophy could survive in the crucible of laughter without being burned up. This is why Rabelais' voice remained completely isolated in the famous controversy. It was the popular voice of the marketplace and of carnival, of the *fabliaux, facéties,* anonymous jokes and anecdotes, *soties* and farces; but this voice made itself heard at the highest level of artistic forms and philosophic thought.

We shall now be able to analyze Panurge's fortune-telling, which fills the major part of the Third Book. Why is he testing his fortune? Because he wants to get married but at the same time fears being cuckolded. He wants to find out whether this has to happen.

All his inquiries give him the same answer; his future wife will cuckold, beat, and rob him, and his fate is inevitable. All his friends' advice, all the novellas about women which they quote, all the studies of the nature of women by the learned physician Rondibilis lead to the same conclusion. The woman's bowels are inexhaustible and never satisfied. She is organically hostile to all that is old (she is the principle of the new to be born). Panurge will inevitably be uncrowned and beaten (killed, at the worst). This fate is not related to any specific individual; it is symbolized by woman ("the promised spouse").

However, Panurge does not want to accept his fate. He believes that he can somehow escape his doom. In other words, he wants to be the eternal king, the eternal new year and youth. But woman is naturally opposed to eternity and unmasks it as senile presumptuousness. Cuckoldry, thrashing, and mockery are unavoidable. In vain does Panurge in his talk with Friar John (Book Three, Chapters 27 and 28) boast of the wondrous power of his phallus. Friar John gives him a firm answer: "I quite understand that, but time softens everything. No marble and porphyry but suffers old age and decay. If you have not at present reached this stage, then a few years hence, I shall hear you confessing that your cods are dragging in the dust." At the end of this conversation Friar John retells the famous novella of Hans Carvel; like all the other stories of this genre inserted in the novel it was not created by Rabelais but is fully in tune with his system of images and style. The ring is the symbol of eternity but is here also the sign of woman's sexual organ (a common folkloric interpretation); an endless torrent of conceptions and renewals flows through it. Panurge's hope to avoid his doom, the doom of the uncrowned, mocked, and destroyed old man, is as absurd as Hans's attempt, suggested by the devil, to stem the flow with his finger.

Panurge's fear of the inevitable cuckoldry and mockery is in tune with the fear of the son, the preordained robber and murderer, which is a feature of high-level drama. In the myth of Chronos the woman's womb plays a considerable role (the womb of Rhea, Chronos' wife and mother of the gods). Rhea not only gives birth to Zeus but hides the child from Chronos' persecutions; she thus ensures the new life of the world. Another well-known example of the fear of the son who is to seize the throne is the myth of Oedipus. Here once more, the mother's womb of Jocasta plays a dual role; it gives birth to Oedipus and is fecundated by him. Yet another example is found in Calderón's "Life is a Dream."

If on the high dramatic plane it is the son who kills and robs, it is the wife who plays this role on the plane of comic Gallic tradition. She will cuckold the husband, beat him, and chase him away. In the Third Book Panurge symbolizes obstinate old age (actually he has scarcely reached it) which does not accept change and renewal. He fears cuckoldry, the "promised spouse"; fate is represented by the young woman who kills the old and generates the new.

Thus, the basic theme of the Third Book is closely connected with time and with popular-festive forms: uncrowning (cuckoldry), thrashing, and mockery. Fortune-telling concerning the future bride and cuckoldry is linked with the theme of individual death, change, and renewal, but on the comic level death and renewal serve the purpose of humanizing time, of giving it a bodily substance, of creating its gay image. Looking into the future hazards of matrimony is a grotesque debasement of higher-level soothsaying: the inquiries of kings and pretenders about the fate of their crowns (symbolized on the comic level by horns, the emblem of cuckoldry). Such a scene of soothsaying is presented in *Macbeth*.

We have especially brought out the festive theme of Panurge's fortune-telling, contained in the Third Book. But this theme is the axis around which a wide circle of other images rotates. They are a carnivalesque revision of all the comic aspects presented by the obstinate old forms as well as by the new trends of philosophic thought. The leaders of theology, philosophy, medicine, law, and magic pass before our eyes. In this respect the Third Book reminds us of Rabelais' prologues. It is a magnificent piece of Renaissance journalism, founded on the grotesque elements of the marketplace.

We have analyzed the considerable influence of popular-festive forms on a number of important episodes of Rabelais' novel: scenes of battles, thrashings, uncrownings, as well as games and fortune-telling. The influence of the carnival forms is far from being exhausted by these scenes. We shall see other projections of the carnivalesque spirit in our next chapters. Here we shall be content with the discussion of two subjects: the basic philosophic meaning of the folk carnival and its special functions in Rabelais' novel.

What is the general world outlook expressed in the popular-festive carnival forms?

As a starting point, we shall turn to the description of the Roman carnival as given by Goethe. This remarkable picture deserves attentive study. Goethe captures with great depth and simplicity nearly all that is essential in this phenomenon. The fact that his description refers to the carnival of 1788, a comparatively late event, is of no importance in this case. The central philosophy of the carnival system was preserved long after Goethe's time.

Goethe was prepared better than anyone else for the event he was to describe. He showed throughout his life an interest and love for popular-festive forms and for the special element of realistic symbolism manifested by them. One of the most vivid impressions of his youth was the election and coronation of the head of the "Holy Empire of the German Nation" which he attended in Frankfurt. Although he described this festivity much later, his presentation of the topic and a number of other considerations convince us that this was one of the formative experiences of his youth. In other words, it was one of those events that to a certain extent determine the artistic vision of a lifetime. The Frankfurt festivity offered a popular semisymbolic spectacle displaying the signs of power, authority, elections, coronation, triumph. It was a political drama without footlights, in which it was difficult to trace any clear dividing line between symbol and reality. True, this pageant did not deal with national uncrowning but with a coronation. But the generic, formal, and artistic relation between election, coronation, and triumph on the one hand, and uncrowning and mockery on the other cannot raise any possible doubts. Originally, all these ceremonies and the images that composed them were ambivalent; the crowning of the new always followed the uncrowning of the old, as triumph succeeded mockery.

We have said that Goethe loved popular-festive forms, for example, masquerades and mystifications. He engaged in them in his youth and described them in *Dichtung und Wahrheit*. In his mature years he liked to travel incognito through the duchy of Weimar and was greatly amused by such masquerades and shows as he saw on these journeys. But this was not a mere diversion. He was aware of a deeper and more essential meaning of these travesties, of these changes of costume and social status.

Goethe was also attracted by the comic, carnivalesque spirit of

Hans Sachs.[31] Finally, during the Weimar period of his life Goethe was officially put in charge of court festivities and masquerades; for that purpose he studied the carnivalesque forms and masques.

Let us now follow Goethe in his description of the Roman carnival in his "Italian Journey," bringing out all that suits our own purpose. The poet first of all stresses the popular character of the carnival and the people's initiative in its celebration. It is a festival offered not by some exterior source but by the people to themselves. Therefore the people do not feel as if they were receiving something that they must accept respectfully and gratefully. They are given nothing, but they are left alone. This festivity demands no sanctimonious acknowledgment or astonishment such as official occasions usually expect. There are no brilliant processions inviting the people to pray and admire. Instead a signal is given to each and every one to play the fool and madman as he pleases.

This is extremely important for the carnival atmosphere—that even in its beginning it has no serious or pious tone. Nor is it set in motion by an order; it opens simply with a signal marking the beginning of merriment and foolery.

Further, Goethe stresses the suspension of all hierarchic differences, of all ranks and status; carnivalesque revelry is marked by absolute familiarity. Differences between superiors and inferiors disappear for a short time, and all draw close to each other. Nobody cares what may happen to him, while freedom and lack of ceremony are balanced by good humor. "During this time, even to this day, the Roman rejoices because, though it postponed the festival of the Saturnalia with its liberties for a few weeks, the birth of Christ did not succeed in abolishing it."[32]

[31] The works written in the Hans Sachs style by the young Goethe are "The Fair in Plunderweilerne," "Hans Wurst's Wedding," "The Show of Father Brey, the False Prophet." In one of these popular-festive works (the unfinished "Hans Wurst's Wedding") we even find such aspects of the carnivalesque genre as the transformation of oaths into personal nouns.

[32] ("The Roman Carnival" in *Italian Journey*, translated by W. H. Auden and Elizabeth Mayer, Pantheon, 1962, p. 446. Reprinted by permission of Random House, Inc.)

At the given signal the serious Roman citizen, who all year round feared to make a *faux pas,* immediately put aside his circumspection. Let us stress this complete liberation from the seriousness of life. In the atmosphere of carnivalesque freedom and familiarity, impropriety also has its place. The masker impersonating Pulcinella often permits himself indecent gestures in the presence of women: "As he talks to women, he manages to imitate with a slight impudent movement the figure of the ancient God of Gardens— and this in Holy Rome!—but his frivolity excites more amusement than indignation."[33]

Goethe also introduces the theme of historic uncrowning. In the midst of the dense and milling crowd: ". . . the Duke of Albany made this drive every day, to the great inconvenience of the crowd, reminding Rome, ancient ruler of kings, throughout these days of universal mummery, of the Carnival comedy of his kingly pretensions."[34]

Still further on, Goethe describes the battles of confetti, which acquire at times an almost realistic character. He also pictures mock disputes and verbal tournaments between the maskers, as between the Captain and Pulcinella. There is also the picture of Pulcinella being elected the king of clowns. He receives the jester's staff and rides down the Corso in a decorated carriage to music and loud shouting.

Finally, the author presents an extremely characteristic scene which takes place in a side street. A group of masquerading men appears. Some of them are disguised as peasants, others as women; one of them displays the signs of pregnancy. A quarrel breaks out among the men, and daggers made of silver foil are drawn. The women separate the fighters; the pregnant masker is terrified and her labor starts in the street. She moans and writhes while the other women surround her. She gives birth to a formless creature under the eyes of the spectators. Thus ends the performance.

The mimicking of the knifing and of the act of birth need no special explanation, after all that has already been said; the slaugh-

33 *Ibid.,* p. 451.
34 *Ibid.,* p. 457.

ter of cattle, dismemberment, and the act of birth form, as we may recall, the indissoluble unity of the first episode in *Gargantua*. The combination of killing and birth is characteristic of the grotesque concept of the body and bodily life. The entire little scene played in the Roman side street is a miniature comedy of the body.

The Roman carnival ends with the Fire Festival, or *moccoli,* which in Italian means "candle stumps." This is a grandiose pageant of fire along the Corso and the adjacent streets. Each participant in the parade carries a lighted candle: *Sia ammazzato chi non porta moccolo!* "Death to anyone who is not carrying a candle!" With this bloodthirsty cry, each one tries to blow out his neighbor's candle. Thus fire is combined with the threat of death, but the louder the cry, the more does the threat lose its direct threatening meaning. The deeply ambivalent nature of the wish for death is disclosed. Describing this gradual change of tone, Goethe quite correctly broadens its nature: "Just as in other languages curses and obscene words are often used as expressions of joy or admiration, so, on this evening, the true meaning of *sia ammazzato* is completely forgotten, and it becomes a password, a cry of joy, a refrain added to all jokes and compliments."[35]

The ambivalent character of all abusive expressions is correctly understood by Goethe. But his assertion that the initial meaning is gradually lost can scarcely be justified. The expressions he cites in which the wish of death is meant to express joy, good-natured mockery, flattery, or compliments are far from losing their initial intention; indeed it is this intention that creates the peculiar character and charm of these carnivalesque interjections, which would not be possible at any other time. The heart of the matter is the ambivalent combination of abuse and praise, of the wish for death and the wish for life, projected in the atmosphere of the festival of fire, that is, of burning and rebirth.

Beyond the formal contrast of meanings presented by these interjections, beyond their subjective interplay, there stands the objective ambivalence of being. This objective convergence of contrasting elements is not clearly realized, but is somehow dimly felt by the participants in the festival. •

[35] *Ibid.,* p. 467.

The combination of *sia ammazzato* with joyful intonation, with friendly, caressing greetings, with compliments and praise, is completely equivalent to the combination of killing and the act of birth in the previously mentioned side-street comedy. Actually, the same drama of pregnant and birth-giving death is enacted in the side-street show and in the *moccoli* closing the Roman carnival. The festival of fire revives the ancient ambivalence of the death wish, which also sounds like a wish for renewal and rebirth: die, and live again. This ancient ambivalence is not a dead remnant of the past; it is alive and finds a subjective echo among the participants in the festival precisely because it is objective, even if this objectivity is not completely grasped.

During carnival the ambivalence of being is revived; it is expressed in the ancient, traditional images (daggers, birth, fire). The same objective ambivalence of becoming was expressed by Goethe on the high level of lyric and philosophical consciousness in his immortal poem *Sagt es niemand*:

Und so lang du das nicht hast,
Dieses stirb und werde,
Bist du nur ein trüber Gast
Auf der dunkeln Erde.[36]

Goethe's poem expresses the same carnival cry of the fire festival: *sia ammazzato,* combined with joy, greetings, and praise. During carnival season the wish for death *stirb* sounds at the same time as *werde*. The participants in the celebration are not gloomy guests. Actually, they are not guests at all. Goethe correctly stressed that carnival is the only feast the people offer to themselves; they do not receive anything and have no sanctimonious regard for anyone. They are the hosts and are only hosts, for there are no guests, no spectators, only participants. And they are anything but gloomy. At the signal announcing the beginning of the festival, all those present, even the most serious, have put aside their austerity (Goethe stresses this). Finally, it would be scarcely appropriate to

[36] And as long as you do not possess
   This: die and become,
   You are but a gloomy guest
   On the dark earth.

speak of "darkness" during *moccoli* when the entire Corso is flooded with fire, with the flames of lighted candles and torches. Thus, there is here a complete parallelism: the protagonist of carnival (the people) are the absolutely merry hosts of the earth flooded with light, because they know that death is pregnant with new life, because they are familiar with the gay image of becoming and of time and are in full possession of this *stirb und werde*. The heart of the matter is not in the subjective awareness but in the collective consciousness of their eternity, of their earthly, historic immortality as a people, and of their continual renewal and growth.

But the first two lines of Goethe's poem:

Sagt es niemand, nur den Weisen,
Denn die Menge gleich verhöhnet![37]

were not written by the man who took part in the Roman carnival but rather by the Goethe who was a grand master of the Masonic lodge. He seeks to transform into esoteric wisdom the awareness that in its fullness and concreteness was accessible in his time only to the great masses. Actually, it was *die Menge* (the masses) who taught their own truth and who in their own language, their poetry, their carnivalesque images, imparted it to the wise Goethe, who was wise enough not to deride it.

Let us quote another parallel passage, which confirms our proposition: In Eckermann's "Conversations with Goethe," concerning the night of St. John, Goethe quotes his poem:

Let the children enjoy
The fires of the night of Saint John,
Every broom must be worn out,
And children must be born

and comments upon it as follows:

It is enough for me to look out the window to see in the brooms which are used to sweep the streets and in the children running

---

[37] "Tell no one, only the wise,
For the masses will despise!"

about in the streets the symbols of life ever to be worn out and renewed.
("Conversations with Goethe," January 17, 1827)

Goethe understood the language of the popular-festive images.
His sense of style was not offended by the carnivalesque combination of the images of the broom sweeping the streets and of children, the most universal of all symbols, representing the ever-dying
and renewed life.

But let us return to Goethe's description of the Roman carnival,
and in particular, to the ambivalent curse that is also a confirma-
tion, *sia ammazzato!* In the world of carnival all hierarchies are
canceled. All castes and ages are equal. During the fire festival a
young boy blows out his father's candle, crying out, *sia ammazzato
il signor Padre!* "Death to you, sir father!" This admirable carnivalesque interjection of the boy merrily threatening his father with
death and blowing out his candle needs no further comment.

Thus ends the Roman carnival. Around midnight there is a supper in every home; meat, which will be forbidden during Lent, is
consumed in great quantities.

The last day of the festive season is followed by Ash Wednesday.
For this occasion Goethe gives us, one might say, his philosophy of
carnival, trying to disclose its serious meaning:

> In the course of all these follies our attention is drawn to the
> most important stages of human life: a vulgar Pulcinella recalls
> to us the pleasures of love to which we owe our existence; a Baubo
> profanes in a public place the mysteries of birth and motherhood,
> and the many lighted candles remind us of the ultimate cere-
> mony.[38]

Goethe's reflections are somewhat disappointing. They do not
give all the elements of carnival; for example, there is no election
of the king of fools, and no mock wars or killings. The meaning
of the celebration is limited to the aspect of individual life and
death. The main collective and historic element is not disclosed.
"World conflagration" is reduced almost to the dimension of fu-

[38] *Aschermittwochbetrachtung.* "Ash Wednesday" in "The Roman
Carnival." *Op. cit.* ftn. 32, p. 469.

neral candles in an individual burial procession. Pulcinella's indecencies, the scene of childbirth enacted in the streets, the image
of death symbolized by fire are correctly tied together as a whole,
as one meaningful and universal pageant, but Goethe's view is
based on a narrow, individual conception of life and death.

So the admirable initial picture of carnival presented by Goethe
is transferred in his *Aschermittwochbetractung* to the sphere of an
individual subjective experience. And thus were these images to be
interpreted during the Romantic era. They were seen as symbols
of individual destiny, while instead it was precisely the people's
destiny that was revealed in them, indissolubly linked to earth and
permeated by the cosmic principle. Goethe himself did not seek in
his artistic creation to individualize the carnivalesque images, but
his Ash Wednesday meditations opened the way to this process.[39]

Goethe's merit in the pages quoted from "Italian Journey" and
from the "Conversations" is great: he saw and was able to disclose
the unity and the deep philosophical character of carnival. Beyond
the isolated, apparently unrelated foolish pranks, obscenities,
and coarse familiarity of carnival, and also in its complete lack of
seriousness the poet sensed a single viewpoint on the world and a
single style. He discovered this unity, even though he did not find
a clear, theoretic expression for it in his concluding lines.

In connection with Goethe's conception of realist symbolism in
popular-festive forms, we will quote two of his comments from
his talks with Eckermann. Concerning Correggio's picture "The
Weaning of a Child" Goethe says:

Yes, this, indeed is a picture! here we have spirit, naïveté, sensual
imagery, all combined. The sacred theme becomes all-human and

[39] Compared to Romanticism, the carnivalesque element (grotesque,
ambivalent) becomes more objective in the works of Heine, though the
subjective note inherited from Romanticism still prevails in his writings.
Here are some of Heine's lines from *Atta Troll* which prove his aware-
ness of ambivalence:
This wise madness,
This maddened wisdom,
The sigh preceding death
Suddenly changed to laughter.

is a symbol of a phase of life through which we have all passed. Such a picture is eternal because it goes back to the earliest times of mankind and foretells the most distant future.
("Conversations with Goethe," December 13, 1826)

Concerning "Myron's Cow" Goethe wrote: "Here we have a representation of highest art. This beautiful image shows us the principle of nourishment, on which the entire world relies and which penetrates all nature. I call this and all similar works the true symbols of God's omnipresence."[40]

As we can see, Goethe fully understood the symbolically extended meaning of the images of feeding: in the first example the nursing of a child, in the second the suckling of a calf.

We shall quote two more excerpts from the talks with Eckermann which reflect Goethe's almost carnivalesque conception of the idea of death and renewal presented both by separate individuals and by all of humanity:

You may note in general that in human life there is often a turning point; if everything favored a man in his youth and he was successful in everything, now all is changed of a sudden; defeats and misfortunes follow each other. Do you know what I think? Man must again be destroyed. Every outstanding person is called to fulfill a mission. Once he has fulfilled it, he is no longer needed upon earth, and Providence predestines him for something else.
(*Ibid.*, March 11, 1828)

I foresee the time when humanity will no longer please the Creator, and He will have to destroy everything once more, in order to renew creation. I am firmly convinced that everything is moving in this direction and that the exact term and time for this renewal have already been ordained, But we still have, of course, sufficient time before this and we may still enjoy ourselves for thousands and thousands of years upon this dear old earth."
(*Ibid.*, October 23, 1828)

We must add that Goethe's view of nature as a *whole*, as "all," including man also, was penetrated by carnivalesque elements. About 1782 he wrote a remarkable poem in prose entitled "Na-

[40] Eckermann, J. P., "Conversations with Goethe," May 29, 1831.

ture" and composed in the spirit of Spinoza. Here is an excerpt from this poem:

Nature. . . . Surrounded and embraced by it, we cannot emerge from it, nor penetrate deeper into it. Unwanted, unexpected, it draws us into the whirlwind of its dance and flies on with us, until we drop wearily out of its hands.

It has no speech, no language, but it creates thousands of languages and hearts, through which it speaks and feels. . . .

It is all. It rewards and punishes, gladdens and torments. It is stern and gentle, loves and terrifies, is impotent and all-powerful.

All men are in it, and it is in all men. It conducts a friendly game with all, and the more they win in it, the more it rejoices. With many, it plays so secretly, that the game ends unwittingly for them.

Its spectacle is always new, for it creates continually new spectators. Life . . . is its best invention; death means greater life to it. . . . It is whole and eternally unfinished. As it creates, so can one create eternally.

We can see from this quotation that "Nature" for Goethe has a deeply carnivalesque spirit. At the end of his life, 1828, he wrote an additional "explanation" of his poem "Nature." In this piece we find the significant words: "One may see a sort of pantheism, while at the base of world phenomena one presupposes the imponderable, humorous, self-contradictory creature which can be taken for a doubly serious game."

Goethe understood that seriousness and fear reflect a *part* that is aware of its separation from the whole. As to the whole itself in its "eternally unfinished" condition, it has a "humorous" character; that is, it can be understood in a comic aspect.

We shall now return to Rabelais. To a certain extent Goethe's description of carnival can serve as a picture of Rabelais' world, of the Rabelaisian system of images. Do we not find in Rabelais' novel all the elements depicted in Goethe's "Roman Carnival": the peculiar festive character without any piousness, complete liberation from seriousness, the atmosphere of equality, freedom, and familiarity, the symbolic meaning of the indecencies, the clownish crownings and uncrownings, the merry wars and beatings, the mock disputes, the knifings related to childbirth, the abuses that are affirmations? All of these are contained in Rabelais' world, and they have all the same philosophic meaning. What is this meaning?

The carnivalesque crowd in the marketplace or in the streets is not merely a crowd. It is the people as a whole, but organized *in their own way*, the way of the people. It is outside of and contrary to all existing forms of the coercive socioeconomic and political organization, which is suspended for the time of the festivity.

This festive organization of the crowd must be first of all concrete and sensual. Even the pressing throng, the physical contact of bodies, acquires a certain meaning. The individual feels that he is an indissoluble part of the collectivity, a member of the people's mass body. In this whole the individual body ceases to a certain extent to be itself; it is possible, so to say, to exchange bodies, to be renewed (through change of costume and mask). At the same time the people become aware of their sensual, material bodily unity and community.

During his Italian journey Goethe visited the amphitheater of Verona. It was, of course, deserted. Apropos of this visit, Goethe expressed an interesting idea concerning the self-awareness which this amphitheater brought to the people; thanks to it, they could perceive the concrete, sensual, visible form of their mass and unity.

Crowded together, its members are astonished at themselves. They are accustomed at other times to seeing each other running hither and thither in confusion, bustling about without order or discipline. Now this many-headed, many-minded, fickle, blundering monster suddenly sees itself united as one noble assembly, welded into one mass, a single body animated by a single spirit. (*Op. cit.* ftn. 32, p. 35)

A similar sense of unity was brought to the people by all the forms and images of medieval popular-festive life. But the unity did not have such a simple geometric character. It was more complex and differentiated; most important of all, it had an historic nature. The body of the people on carnival square is first of all aware of its unity in time; it is conscious of its uninterrupted continuity within time, of its relative historic immortality. Therefore the people do not perceive a static image of their unity (*eine Ge-stait*) but instead the uninterrupted continuity of their becoming and growth, of the unfinished metamorphosis of death and renewal. For all these images have a dual body; everywhere the genital element is emphasized: pregnancy, giving birth, the procreative force (Pulcinella's double hump, the protruding belly). We have pointed this out and will resume this subject in another chapter. Carnival with all its images, indecencies, and curses affirms the people's immortal, indestructible character. In the world of carnival the awareness of the people's immortality is combined with the realization that established authority and truth are relative.

Popular-festive forms look into the future. They present the victory of this future, of the golden age, over the past. This is the victory of all the people's material abundance, freedom, equality, brotherhood. The victory of the future is ensured by the people's immortality. The birth of the new, of the greater and the better, is as indispensable and as inevitable as the death of the old. The one is transferred to the other, the better turns the worse into ridicule and kills it. In the whole of the world and of the people there is no room for fear. For fear can only enter a part that has been separated from the whole, the dying link torn from the link that is born. The whole of the people and of the world is triumphantly gay and fearless. This whole speaks in all carnival images; it reigns in the very atmosphere of this feast, making everyone participate in this awareness.

In connection with the realization of the whole (eternally unfinished) we would like to quote another excerpt from Goethe's "Nature." ". . . Its crown is love. Only through love can we draw near to it. It has placed abysses between creatures, and all creatures long to merge in the universal embrace. It divides them, in order to bring them together. It atones for a whole life of suffering, by the mere pressing of lips to the cup of life."

We shall conclude by stressing that the carnival awareness of the people's immortality is intimately related to the immortality of the becoming of being and is merged with it. In his body and his life man is deeply aware of the earth and of the other elements, of the sun and of the star-filled sky. The cosmic nature of the grotesque body will be analyzed in our fifth chapter.

Let us now turn to our second question concerning the functions of popular-festive forms in Rabelais' novel.

Our starting point will be a brief analysis of the French comic drama "The Play in the Bower" (*Jeu de la Feuillée*) of the troubadour Adam de la Halle from Arras. This drama was written in 1262, almost three hundred years before Rabelais. The first comic play, it presents a feast of carnival type, using this theme and all the privileges implied by it: the right to emerge from the routine of life, the right to be free from all that is official and consecrated. The theme is treated simply, but directly. It is typically carnivalesque from beginning to end.

The "Play in the Bower" has scarcely any footlights, one might say, to separate it from real life. The performance was given in Arras and the action is also set in Arras, the author's hometown. The characters are the author himself (the young troubadour), his father Maître Henri, and other citizens of Arras who appear under their real names. The topic of the play is Adam's intention to leave Arras and his wife to study in Paris. This episode actually took place in the troubadour's life. However, there is a fantastic element interwoven with the many features of real life. The play was performed on the first of May, which was the time of the fair and of a popular festival, and the drama's entire action is coordinated with these events.

"The Play in the Bower" is divided into three parts. The first part could be defined as carnivalesque and biographical, the second part as carnivalesque and fantastic, and the last part as a carnivalesque banquet.

In the first part of this play the personal family affairs of the author, Adam, are presented with utmost freedom and familiarity. There follows a no less frank presentation of the other citizens of Arras, in which their private lives and their boudoir secrets are disclosed.

The play starts with Adam appearing in a scholastic gown (this is a masquerade, since he is not yet a student). He declares that he is leaving his wife, Marie, to go to Paris and improve his education. He intends to place his wife under his father's care. He tells how much Marie attracted him before their marriage. This leads to a detailed, very frank and free enumeration of her charms. Enter the father, Maître Henri. Asked by Adam to give him some money, the father says that he is unable to do so, being old and sick. The physician diagnoses the father's disease as "avarice" and names several other townfolk afflicted with this disease. Then the physician is consulted by a prostitute (Dame Douce). Apropos of this consultation the play offers a "survey" of the boudoir life of Arras and names other young women of shady reputation. During this medical dialogue, urine figures as the determining factor of human character and destiny.

The images of the physician and of the diseases and vices are treated here in the carnivalesque spirit. Enter a monk collecting a donation for St. Acarius, who cures madness and folly. Some people wish to be helped by this saint. Enter a madman accompanied by his father. The role of the madman, as well as the theme of insanity and folly in general, is important in the play. The madman freely criticizes a decree of Pope Alexander IV which reduces the privileges of scholastics (among them those of Maître Henri). Thus ends the first part of the play. The free talk and obscenities of these scenes are usually interpreted by scholars as the "coarseness of the times." Actually, this coarseness has a system and a style of its own. They represent the grotesque aspect of the world with which we are already familiar.

The boundaries between the play and life are intentionally erased. Life itself is on stage.

The second part with its fantastic theme starts after the monk, symbolizing the official Church and the official truth, falls asleep near a bower which forms the main section of the stage. A table is set in the bower, awaiting the visit of three fairies who are allowed to appear only on the eve of May Day and only when the official world is absent. Before their entrance "Harlequin's army" marches by with a jingle of bells. Enter King Harlequin's messenger, a comic devil. Then the three fairies enter. The next scene presents the fairies' supper in the bower, their conversation among themselves and with King Harlequin's messenger. His name is Croquesots, "fool-eater." The fairies predict the future, good or evil, and some of it concerns the author, Adam.

They spin the "wheel of fortune." At the end of the supper Dame Douce enters. Fairies protect prostitutes, who also reign supreme on May Day eve with its license and revelry. Dame Douce and the fairies represent the unofficial world, which that night is granted full liberty and impunity.

The last part, a carnivalesque banquet, takes place before sunrise in a tavern where the participants in the May Day festivities and the characters of the play are assembled. All drink, laugh, sing, and roll dice. They play for the monk who has fallen asleep once more. The host of the tavern takes the monk's reliquary and parodies his curing of fools; his antics provoke loud laughter. At the end of this scene the madman breaks into the tavern. But at that moment dawn breaks and church bells begin to ring. May Night with its freedoms is over. Upon the monk's invitation the guests betake themselves to church.

Such are the main elements of the first French drama. Strange as it might seem, it contains the embryo of almost all of Rabelais' world.

Let us stress first of all the close relation of the play to May Day. It springs, up to its minutest detail, from this feast's theme and atmosphere, which determine its form and character as well as its content. The authority of the official realm of Church and state is suspended, with all its norms and values. The world is permitted to emerge from its routine. The end of festive freedom is clearly heralded by the ringing of the morning church bells; while earlier in the play the bells of the marching harlequins begin to tinkle as soon as the monk has made his exit. The banquet theme plays an essential role in the play, with feasting in the bower and in the tavern. Let us also stress the theme of dice; not only are dice a common form of recreation but they are also intimately linked with the feast. Games are extra-official and are governed by rules contrary to the current laws of life. Further, the suspension of the Church's exclusive power brings back the uncrowned pagan gods: marching harlequins, the messenger Croquesots, and the fairies directing the dance of the prostitutes. The theme of Dame Douce merits our special attention. On May Day eve prostitutes enjoy special privileges and even authority; in our play Dame Douce prepares to settle accounts with her enemies. Finally, an important element in the play is represented by the wheel of fortune and the predictions and curses of the fairies. The feast looks into the future, and this future acquires not only a utopian character but also the primitive archaic form of prophecies, curses, and blessings (which initially concerned the future harvest, the increase of cattle, etc.). The theme of the relics is also characteristic, related as it is to the dismemberment of the body. A typical role is played by the physician and the attribute of his profession: urine. The theme of madness and folly is very important. Something like the market place *cri,* but addressed to fools, is introduced into the play and determines in part its atmosphere. The feast grants a right to folly.

Folly is, of course, deeply ambivalent. It has the negative element of debasement and destruction (the only vestige now is the use of "fool" as a pejorative) and the positive element of renewal and truth. Folly is the opposite of wisdom—inverted wisdom, inverted truth. It is the other side, the lower stratum of official laws and conventions, derived from them. Folly is a form of gay festive wisdom, free from all laws and restrictions, as well as from preoccupations and seriousness. Let us recall the apology of the fifteenth-century "feast of fools" in Chapter One. The defenders of this feast understood it as a gay and free expression of "our second nature" in which gay folly was opposed to "piousness and fear of God." Thus the champions of the festival considered it a "once-a-year" liberation, not only from routine but also from the religious outlook. It permitted the people to see the world with "foolish eyes," and this right belonged not to the "feast of fools" alone but to every feast in its popular marketplace aspect.

This is why the theme of folly and the image of the incurable fool are so important in the festive atmosphere of the "Bower."

The play ends with the fool appearing just before the church bells start ringing.

We may recall that in his description of carnival Goethe also stressed more than once that every participant in the festival, however serious and important he might be all the year round, permits himself once a year every kind of foolishness and clownery. And Rabelais, speaking of the fool Triboulet in Pantagruel's words, discusses wisdom and folly thus:

"Well, let us say a man who watches over his private affairs and domestic business . . . who attends to his household . . . who keeps his nose to the particular grindstone he works . . . who understands thoroughly how to avoid the pitfalls of poverty . . . . That, according to the world, should constitute a wise man. Yet, in the eyes of the celestial spirits, he may be the most unmitigated ass.

And whom do those spirits consider wise? Ha, that is a horse of another color. For them, a wise man, a man not only sage but able to presage future events by divine inspiration, is one who forgets himself, discards his own personality, rids his senses of all earthly affection, purges his spirit of all human care, neglects everything. All of which qualities are popularly supposed to be symptoms of insanity!"

Thus, Faunus, son of Picus, king of Latium, and a great soothsayer, was called Fatuus by the common herd.

Thus, when the various roles were distributed among a company of mummers, that of the Fool or Jester invariably went to the most talented and experienced actor.

Thus, mathematicians declared that the same horoscope applied for kings and zanies.
(Book 3, Chapter 37)

This comment is written in a high scholarly style. Official piousness is observed in the choice of words and in the concepts. Such words as "divine inspiration" and "celestial spirits" are used in relation to foolishness. In the first part Rabelais presents the saint as a fool; at that time there was nothing bizarre in such a conception; Rabelais himself was a Franciscan. The rejection of the world by such a fool or madman has here an almost traditional Christian connotation. But in Rabelais' mind this actually implies the rejection of the official world with its philosophy, system of values, and seriousness. And such is the image of Triboulet himself as shown in the novel. In the eyes of Rabelais the fool's truth presupposes freedom from personal material interests, from the unholy gift of managing family and personal affairs; but the language of this foolish truth is at the same time earthly and material. This principle did not have, however, a private selfish nature, but a wide popular quality. If we turn away from the official ideology expressed in this passage, we shall see the Rabelaisian praise of folly as a form of the unofficial truth. By "unofficial" is meant a peculiar conception free from selfish interests, norms, and appreciations of "this world" (that is, the established world, which it is always profitable to serve). The concluding lines of the excerpt directly point to fools and jesters on the festive theater stage.

Let us look once more at Adam de la Halle's comic drama. What is the role of the feast and festive folly displayed in it? They grant the author the right to treat an unofficial subject. Even more, he obtains the right to express unofficial views of the world. In spite of its simple unpretentious character, this play offers a special aspect of the world, completely alien to medieval philosophy and the established way of life. It offers first of all a gay and light aspect. Considerable roles in the drama are played by the banquet, the procreative force, the game of dice, the parodied character of the monk with the relics, the uncrowned antique gods (fairies, harlequins). The world appears in a more material bodily form; it is more gay and human, in spite of all the phantasmagoria. This is a festive view of the world, and it is legal as such. On May Day eve one is permitted to look at the world fearlessly and impiously.

The "Play in the Bower" makes no pretense of being a problem play. At the same time its scope is universal. It contains no abstract, moralizing element; it presents no comic characters, no comic situations or pictures of private, isolated elements of the world and social life. Neither does the play contain any abstract negations. The entire world is shown in its gay and free dimension, and the author sees this dimension as universal, all-embracing. True, this world is restricted, not by this or that phenomenon of life but exclusively by the limits of the feast of May Day eve. The morning bells bring the world back to seriousness and piousness.

Rabelais' novel was written nearly three centuries after the "Play in the Bower," but the functions of the popular-festive forms are similar. True, they have become broader, deeper, more aware, complex, and radical.

In the Fourth Book of Rabelais, after the beating of the Catchpoles, we find the "tragic farce" played by Master François Villon.

The aging Villon, who lived in Saint Maixent, decided to produce a passion play that was to contain an extensive diablerie. Everything was ready for this production, the only costume missing being the garment of God the Father. The local sacristan, Tappecoue (Ticklepecker), refused to lend any vestments from the sacristy, considering that to give them out for a theatrical show would be a sacrilege. Since he would not be persuaded, Master Villon decided to avenge himself. He knew when Tappecoue toured the parish on his filly and scheduled the diablerie dress rehearsal precisely at that time. Rabelais describes the devils and their costumes and "weapons," which were actually kitchen utensils. The rehearsal was held in town, in the marketplace. Villon took the devils to a feast at a nearby tavern. When Tappecoue rode by, the devils surrounded him with shouts and clanging, threw burning tar at him, and frightened the filly with a terrible blaze and smoke:

> The filly, scared out of her wits, started, reared, plunged forward, bucketed, galloped, jerked and curvetted. . . . Very soon (though he clung to the saddle with might and main) Ticklepecker lost his seat.
> Yet his stirrup straps were so many ropes, binding him to the beast; and his right sandal, caught in the stirrup, as in a vise, prevented his freeing his foot. The filly, meanwhile, charged along the road, shying and then darting, hellbent with terror, through hedge, briar and ditch, with Friar Ticklepecker dragged, peelarse, in her wake. Her progress bashed his head so hard against the road that his brains spurted out somewhere near the Hosanna . . . . Both arms and both legs were crushed to a pulp; his intestines were

pounded to a jelly; and when the filly reached her monastery stable, the sole trace of Friar Ticklepecker was a right sandal and the stump of a foot inside.
(Book 4, Chapter 13)

Such is the "tragic farce" played by Villon. Its theme is the rending of a body on the marketplace and near a tavern, during a banquet, in the carnivalesque setting of a diablerie. This is a tragic farce indeed, since Ticklepecker was torn to pieces.

The story is told by Lord Basché who relates it to the beating of the Catchpoles in his house and hopes it will encourage his household to even more vigorous thrashings.

Where lies the resemblance between Villon's prank and Lord Basché's thrashing? In both cases the carnival rights and freedoms are used to secure impunity but not for that purpose only. In one case freedom is granted for a nuptual ritual, in the other case for a diablerie. As we have seen, the custom of *nopces à mitaines* permitted behavior quite inadmissible in ordinary life: to cuff all persons present, regardless of their status and titles. The usual order and way of life, and especially the social hierarchy were suspended at the wedding feast. Rules of politeness among equals and of respect for the hierarchy among inferiors were canceled for that short period. Conventions vanished, the distance between men disappeared, and all this was symbolically expressed by the right to strike one's important and esteemed neighbor. During the short time of the wedding feast all participants entered, as it were, the utopian kingdom of absolute equality and freedom.[41]

This utopian element acquires here, as in all popular-festive

[41] Let us here mention as a parallel the interesting Saturnalian and carnivalesque folk legend of King Petot and his court. This legend is recalled by Rabelais (Book 3, Chapter 6). It is also mentioned in the "Menippus Satire" and in Molière's *Tartuffe* (Act 1, Scene 1). This is the explanation given of King Petot by Oudin in his *curiosité* "The court of King Petot": "Here all are masters, in other words, this is the place where all give orders, where nobody knows the difference between masters and servants." In the anonymous "Essay on Proverbs" of the first half of the sixteenth century, we have the following explanation: "This is the court of King Petot, where all are equal."

utopias, a sharply defined material bodily form. Freedom and equality are expressed in familiar blows, a coarse bodily contact. Beatings are, as we have seen, a tangible equivalent of improper speech. In the example given the ritual is nuptial; during the night the full physical contact of bride and bridegroom will be realized, the act of conception will be consummated, the reproductive force will triumph. The atmosphere of the celebration's central act spreads over all and everything; the cuffing, so to speak, radiates from it. Further, as in all popular-festive forms of that type, the utopian element has a gay character (the cuffing is light, playful). Finally, and this is important, this utopia is enacted without footlights; it is presented within life itself. True, the scene is strictly limited by time, the time of the banquet, but during that period there are no footlights, no separation of participants and spectators. Everybody participates. While the usual world order is suspended, the new utopian order which has come to replace it is sovereign and embraces all. Therefore the Catchpoles who have inadvertently joined the wedding feast must submit to the laws of the utopian kingdom and cannot complain of the beatings. There is no clear dividing line between this play and life, so that the one is passed on to the other. Lord Basché could use the mock cuffing in order to settle his accounts with the Catchpoles.

The absence of clearly established footlights is characteristic of all popular-festive forms. The utopian truth is enacted in life itself. For a short time this truth becomes to a certain extent a real existing force. With the help of this force it is possible to punish the sworn foes of this truth as did the Lord of Basché.

In the setting of Villon's "tragic farce" we find the same elements as in Basché's *nopces à mitaines*. The diableries represented the popular-festive part, the marketplace element of the mysteries. The latter, of course, had footlights and, being part of the play, the diableries also had them. But it was customary to permit the devils to run loose around the streets wearing their costumes; sometimes they were free to do so for several days before the performance.

As an example of this practice, in 1500 several clerics and laymen of the city of Amiens asked permission for the production of a passion play; they especially requested to *faire courir les personnages des diables* (to let the characters representing the devils run loose). One of the most famous and popular diableries of the sixteenth century was produced at Chaumont in the Haute-Marne as part of the "Mystery of St. John."[42] The announcement of the performance mentioned that the male and female devils would run loose in the streets of the city and of the nearby villages several days before the opening. The actors, disguised as devils, felt that they were somehow out of bondage and communicated this feeling to those who came into contact with them. They created an atmosphere of unbridled carnivalesque freedom. They considered themselves exempt from the law and, being mostly recruited among poor people (hence the expression "poor devil"), they often took advantage of their role to rob the peasants and mend their financial affairs. Regulations were often issued to restrict the devils' behavior off stage.

But even when these actors remained within the limits of the parts assigned to them, they still preserved their extra-official character. Their roles permitted both abuse and obscenities. They spoke and acted in contradiction to official Christian mores, shouted and made a great deal of noise on stage, especially if it was a "grand diablerie" of four or more devils. (Hence the French expression *faire le diable à quatre*.) Indeed, most of the curses and abuses containing the word "devil" are related to the mystery. In Rabelais' novel there are many expressions that can be traced back to this origin: *la grande diablerie à quatre personnages* (Book 1, Chapter 4); *faire d'un diable deux* (Book 3, Chapter 1); *crioit comme tous les diables* (Book 1, Chapter 13); *crient et urlent comme diables, pauvre diable* in various places. The link of these words with the diableries is quite understandable: they all belong to the same system of forms and images.

But the mystery devil is not only an extra-official figure. He is also an ambivalent image, like the fool and the clown, representing the destroying and renewing force of the material bodily lower

---

[42] See Emile Jolibois, *La Diablerie de Chaumont*, 1838.

stratum. The devil usually appeared in the mystery as a carnivalesque character. For instance, we see that the devils' weapons in Villon's farce were kitchen utensils (confirmed by other accounts). In his book "The Origin of Harlequin" O. Driesen undertakes a detailed comparison of the diableries and charivari in the *Roman du Fauvel* and discovers a striking resemblance of the images they contain. Charivari was also related to carnival.[43]

These typical traits of the devil, and above all his ambivalence and his material bodily element, make us clearly understand the meaning of his transformation into a popular comic figure. The devil Erl-King (who does not appear in the mysteries, however) is transformed into the carnivalesque figure of Harlequin. Let us recall that Pantagruel was also initially a mystery-play devil.

Thus, though a part of the mystery, the diablerie was related to carnival. It crossed the footlights to merge with the life of the marketplace and enjoyed similar privileges of freedom.

This is why the diablerie, let loose in the streets, permitted Master Villon to avenge himself on the sacristan Tappecoue with impunity. Just as in the Lord Basché episode, utopian freedom without footlights offers Villon the opportunity of dealing realistically with the enemy of this freedom.

But why did Tappecoue deserve such cruel punishment? It could be said that from the purely Dionysan point of view the sacristan became the enemy of Dionysus by refusing on principle to furnish the costume for the play. He therefore deserved to suffer the death of Penpheus, to be torn to pieces by the Bacchantes.[44] Further, from Rabelais' point of view Tappecoue was the worst of all enemies: he was the very incarnation of that which the author most detested. He was what Rabelais has called an agelast, a man who does not know how to laugh and who is hostile to laughter. True, Rabelais does not use these words directly, but the sacristan's behavior is typical of that sect. He manifested that blunt pious seriousness which was loathed by Rabelais. Tappecoue feared to

[43] See Otto Driesen, *Der Ursprung des Harlekin*, 1904.

[44] In sixteenth-century literature, we find the carnivalesque and culinary expression: "Penpheus' stew."

use a sacred vestment for a spectacle; he refused to make a gift to popular merrymaking, to serve the people, and he did so out of moral considerations, being filled with the Church's traditional hostility to shows, to mimes, and hilarity. More than that, he would not lend a garment for a masquerade; that is, he would not condone a change of dress for a renewed life. Tappecoue represents the kind of old age that refuses to give birth and to die. This is the sterile and obstinate senility so repulsive to Rabelais. The old man is the enemy of gay, popular truth about change and renewal which inspired Villon's diablerie. And so truth, which was in power for one day, had to destroy him. He died a truly carnivalesque death by dismemberment.

The image of Tappecoue, reflected in one symbolic act, incarnated the spirit of the Gothic age, with its one-sided seriousness based on fear and coercion—a seriousness which conceived everything *sub specie aeternitatis*, outside real time. This point of view tended to underwrite the static, unshakable hierarchy; it conceded no exchange of roles. Actually, in Rabelais' time all that remained of that Gothic age were vestments good for merrymaking. But these vestments were jealously guarded by the blunt and gloomy sacristan. It was the sacristan that Rabelais dealt with, but he used the vestments for rejuvenating carnival merriment.

In his novel, and by means of his novel, Rabelais behaves exactly as did Villon and the Lord of Basché. He acts according to their methods. He uses the popular-festive system of images with its charter of freedoms consecrated by many centuries; and he uses them to inflict a severe punishment upon his foe, the Gothic age. It is a merry play and therefore immune, but a play without footlights. In this setting of consecrated rights Rabelais attacks the fundamental dogmas and sacraments, the holy of holies of medieval ideology.

We must admit that Rabelais' "prank" in the style of Master Villon was fully successful. In spite of the frankness of his writings, he not only avoided the stake but suffered no serious persecution or vexation. To be sure, he had to take certain precautions, to disappear for a time and even cross the French border. But, generally speaking, everything ended well for him, apparently without much worry and anxiety. Rabelais' friend Etienne Dolet perished at the stake because of his statements, which although less damning had been seriously made. He did not use Rabelais' methods.

Rabelais was attacked by the agelasts who granted no special rights to laughter. All his books were condemned by the Sorbonne. (This did not, however, stop their distribution and reprint.) At the end of his life he was violently attacked by the monk du Puits-Herbault; he was also attacked from the Protestant side by Calvin. But the voices of all these agelasts remained isolated; the rights of laughter proved to be stronger. We repeat: his prank "à la Villon" was entirely successful.[45]

But the use of the system of popular-festive images must not be understood as an exterior, mechanical method of defense against censorship, as an enforced adoption of Aesop's language. For thousands of years the people have used these festive comic images to express their criticism, their deep distrust of official truth, and their highest hopes and aspirations. Freedom was not so much an exterior right as it was the inner content of these images. It was the thousand-year-old language of fearlessness, a language with no reservations and omissions, about the world and about power. It is obvious that such a fearless and free language lent a rich positive content to the new outlook.

The Lord of Basché used the popular-festive tradition of *nopces à mitaines,* not only to secure impunity for the beating of the Catchpoles but also in a symbolic sense. We saw that the beatings were carried out as a ritual, as a comic play, systematically organized in every detail, a "beating up" in grand style. The blows showered on the Catchpoles were creative, nuptial blows; they were showered on the old world, represented by the Catchpoles, and contributed at the same time to the conception and birth of the new

[45] The legend still current today concerning the cruel persecution supposedly suffered by Rabelais on the eve of his death has been completely discredited by Abel Lefranc. It seems that Rabelais died in peace, having lost neither the protection of the court nor the support of his high-ranking friends.

world. Exterior freedom and impunity are inseparable from the inner positive meaning of these forms and their philosophical content.

Tappecoue's carnivalesque dismemberment was similar in character. It too was treated in grand style and organized in minutest detail. The sacristan represented the old world, and his dismemberment was shown in a positive form. Here, too, freedom and impunity are inseparable from the positive content of all the images of this episode.

These carnivalesque forms must not surprise us. Even the great economic and sociopolitical changes of those historic times could not avoid a certain grotesque presentation. I will recall two well-known episodes of Russian history: one having to do with Ivan the Terrible and one with Peter the Great.

Ivan the Terrible struggled against Russian feudal sanctimonious traditions and the methods of distribution of estates to the boyars. He broke up the old political and social structure and moral code, and in doing so could not escape the influence of popular forms of mockery and derision: travesties and masquerades that turned the hierarchy "inside out," uncrownings and debasements.

While not breaking with the tradition of church bells, Ivan could not do without the jingle of the fools' bells; even the outward attributes of the *opritchina* had some carnival elements, for instance, the broom.[46]

The *opritchniks'* inner way of life and the banquets in the *Alexandrovskaya Sloboda* had a distinct grotesque aspect, as well as an extraterritorial character, similar to the freedom of the marketplace. Later, during its period of stabilization, the *opritchina* was suppressed and disavowed, and an attack was made on its very spirit, hostile to stabilization.

All these elements emerged once more at the time of Peter the Great. The jingling of the jester's bells almost entirely drowned the

[46] The *opritchina* was Ivan's special police and bodyguard which he had organized in order to fight against the feudal castes that opposed him. Their emblem was a broom (to sweep out corruption). (Translator's note.)

sound of church bells. Peter's importation to Russia of the later forms of the "feast of fools" is well known; never during the thousand years of its existence did this festival enjoy so wide an official recognition. The clownlike crownings and uncrownings of this feast directly invaded political life, even combining carnivalesque honors with real political power, as in the case of Romadonovsky.[47] Also, the new way of life in Russia made its appearance in masquerade attire, since Peter's reforms were interwoven with elements of travesty (the enforced shaving off of beards, European dress, Western polite manners). However, these carnival forms were an importation rather than a native manifestation. At the time of Ivan the Terrible, they were more popular and live, more complex and contradictory in nature.

Thus the exterior freedom of popular-festive forms was inseparable from their inner freedom, and from their positive outlook on the world. Together with this new positive outlook, they brought the right to express it with impunity.

We have already seen the philosophical meaning of popular-festive forms and will not return to them. But now we can also clearly see their special functions in Rabelais' novel.

These special functions become even more obvious in the light of the problem that all Renaissance literature was trying to solve, namely, to find forms that would make possible and would justify the most extreme freedom and frankness of thought and speech. The exterior, so to say, censored right and the interior right were undivided. Frankness was understood, of course, not in a narrowly subjective sense as "sincerity," the "soul's truth," or "intimacy." The Renaissance concept of frankness was far more serious; it meant a completely loud, marketplace frankness that concerned everyone. Thought and speech had to be placed under such conditions that the world could expose its other side: the side that was hidden, that nobody talked about, that did not fit the words and forms of prevailing philosophy. America was still to be discovered, the Antipodes reached, the Western hemisphere explored, and the

[47] Romandonovsky, a powerful boyar, was elected "all fools' pope." (Translator's note.)

question arose: "What is under our feet?" Thought and word were searching for a new reality beyond the visible horizon of official philosophy. Often enough words and thoughts were turned around in order to discover what they were actually hiding, what was that other side. The aim was to find a position permitting a look at the other side of established values, so that new bearings could be taken.

One of the first to pose this problem with full awareness was Boccaccio. The *Decameron* was written in a time of plague, which was to create new conditions for frank, unofficial words and images. At the end of the *Decameron*, Boccaccio stresses that the conversations put down in his book did not take place in church.

. . . 'twas not in Church, of matters whereto pertaining 'tis meet we speak with all purity of heart and seemliness of phrase, albeit among her histories there are to be found not a few that will ill compare with my writings; nor yet in the schools of the philosophers, where, as much as anywhere else, seemliness is demanded, nor in any place where clergy or philosophers congregate, but in whorehouses and among folk, young indeed, but not so young as to be seducible by stories, and at a time when, if so one might save one's life, the most sedate might without disgrace walk abroad with his breeches for headgear.
(Boccaccio, *Decameron*, Vol. 2, p. 347. Translated by J. M. Rigg and reproduced by courtesy of E. P. Dutton & Co., Inc., Everyman's Library Edition.)

And in another passage, one of the storytellers, Dioneo, says:
For in sooth, as you may know, so out of joint are the times that the judges have deserted the judgement-seat, the laws are silent, and ample license to preserve his life as best he may is accorded to each and all. Wherefore, if you are somewhat less strict of speech than is your wont, not that aught unseemly in act may follow, but that you may afford solace to yourselves and others. . . .
(*Ibid.* p. 91)

The end of this passage is composed with the reservations and toning-down that are characteristic of Boccaccio, but the beginning correctly depicts the role of the plague in his conception: it grants the right to use other words, to have another approach to life and to the world. Not only have all conventions been dropped, but all laws "both human and divine" are silenced. Life has been lifted out of its routine, the web of conventions has been torn; all the official hierarchic limits have been swept away. The plague has created its own unique atmosphere that grants both outward and inward rights. Even the most respected man may now wear his "breeches for headgear." And in accord with the general turnover, the problems of life may be discussed not in churches and schools but in whorehouses.

Furthermore, the plague as a condensed image of death is the indispensable ingredient of the *Decameron*'s entire system of images, in which the regenerating material bodily stratum plays the leading role. The *Decameron* is the high point of grotesque realism but in its poorer, petty form.

Another solution of the same problem is offered by Boccaccio in his hero's madness. An outward and inner freedom was sought from all the dogmas of the dying yet still prevailing philosophy—a freedom that would permit one to see the world with different eyes. Madness or folly, in the ambivalent sense of the word, granted this right to the *Decameron*'s hero.

The Rabelaisian solution was a direct appeal to the popular-festive forms. They bestowed upon both thought and word the most radical freedom, an outward and inner freedom that was also the most positive.

The influence of carnival, in the broadest sense of this word, was great during all periods of literary development. However, this influence was in most cases hidden, indirect, and difficult to detect. During the Renaissance it was not only exceptionally strong but direct and clearly expressed, even in its exterior forms. The Renaissance is, so to speak, a direct "carnivalization" of human consciousness, philosophy, and literature.

The official culture of the Middle Ages was evolved over many centuries. It had its heroic, creative period and was all-embracing and all-penetrating. This culture enveloped and enmeshed the entire world and every segment, even the smallest, of human consciousness. It was supported by an organization unique of its kind, the Catholic Church. In the time of the Renaissance the feudal structure was nearing its end, but its ideological domination of the human mind was still extremely powerful.

Where could the Renaissance find support in the struggle against the official culture of the Middle Ages, a struggle which was as intense as it was victorious? The ancient literary sources could not per se offer a sufficient basis, because antiquity was also still seen by many through the prism of medieval ideology. In order to discover humanist antiquity, it was necessary at first to be free from the thousand-year-old domination of medieval categories. It was necessary to gain new ground, to emerge from ideological routine.

Such support could be offered only by the culture of folk humor which had developed throughout thousands of years. The progressive leaders of the Renaissance participated directly in this culture and first of all in its popular-festive, carnivalesque aspect. Carnival (and we repeat that we use this word in its broadest sense) did liberate human consciousness and permit a new outlook, but at the same time it implied no nihilism; it had a positive character because it disclosed the abundant material principle, change and becoming, the irresistible triumph of the new immortal people. This was indeed a powerful support for storming the stronghold of the Gothic age; it prepared the way for a new, free, and sober seriousness.

In one of his articles, Dobrolyubov expressed a thought that deserves our notice: "It is necessary to work out in our soul a firm belief in the need and possibility of a complete exit from the present order of this life, so as to find the strength to express it in poetic forms."[48] At the base of Renaissance progressive literature there existed such a "firm belief." It was only thanks to this conviction that a radical change and renewal of all that exists became "necessary and possible," that the initiators of the Renaissance movement could see the world as they did. But this conviction also inspired the culture of folk humor; it was no abstract thought but a living

[48] Dobrolyubov: "Poems of Ivan Nikitin." Collected works in nine volumes, Goslitisdat Leningrad, 1963. Vol. 6, p. 167.

experience that determined this culture's forms and images. Official medieval culture tried to inculcate the exactly opposite belief in a static unchanging world order and in the eternal nature of all existence. This teaching, as we have said, was still powerful. It could not be overcome by individual thinking or scholarly perusal of antique sources (not seen in the light of "carnival consciousness"). Popular culture alone could offer this support.

This is the reason why in all the great writings of the Renaissance we clearly sense the carnival atmosphere, the free winds blowing from the marketplace. We find this element in the very structure of Renaissance writings and in the peculiar logic of their images, although nowhere more clearly than in Rabelais.

The analysis we have applied to Rabelais would also help us to discover the essential carnival element in the organization of Shakespeare's drama. This does not merely concern the secondary, clownish motives of his plays. The logic of crownings and uncrownings, in direct or in indirect form, organizes the serious elements also. And first of all this "belief in the possibility of a complete exit from the present order of this life" determines Shakespeare's fearless, sober (yet not cynical) realism and absence of dogmatism. This pathos of radical changes and renewals is the essence of Shakespeare's world consciousness. It made him see the great epoch-making changes taking place around him and yet recognize their limitations.

Shakespeare's drama has many outward carnivalesque aspects: images of the material bodily lower stratum, of ambivalent obscenities, and of popular banquet scenes.

The carnivalesque basic element in Cervantes' *Don Quixote* and in his novellas is quite obvious: his novel is directly organized as a grotesque play with all its attributes. The depth and consequent nature of his realism are also typical of this pathos of change and renewal.

Renaissance literature still needs special study in the light of correctly understood popular-festive forms.

Rabelais' novel is the most festive work in world literature. It expresses the very essence of the people's gay spirit. This is why this novel stands out so sharply against the background of the humdrum solemn literature of the following periods, especially of the nineteenth century. This is why it is impossible to understand him if we adopt the nonfestive posture that prevailed during those later years.

However, even within bourgeois culture the festive element did not die. It was merely narrowed down. The feast is a primary, indestructible ingredient of human civilization; it may become sterile and even degenerate, but it cannot vanish. The private, "chamber" feast of the bourgeois period still preserves a distorted aspect of the ancient spirit; on feast days the doors of the home are open to guests, as they were originally open to "all the world." On such days there is greater abundance in everything: food, dress, decorations. Festive greetings and good wishes are exchanged, although their ambivalence has faded. There are toasts, games, masquerades, laughter, pranks, and dances. The feast has no utilitarian connotation (as has daily rest and relaxation after working hours). On the contrary, the feast means liberation from all that is utilitarian, practical. It is a temporary transfer to the utopian world. The feast cannot be reduced to any specific content (for instance to the historical event commemorated on that day); it transgresses all limited objectives. Neither can it be separated from bodily life, from the earth, nature, and the cosmos. The sun shines in the festive sky, and there is such a thing as "feast-day" weather.[49] All these elements have been preserved in the bourgeois truncated forms of these celebrations.

Characteristically enough, modern Western philosophy of anthropology has sought to discover the festive awareness of man and this special aspect of the world, in order to overcome the pessimistic conception of existentialism. However, philosophical anthropology with its phenomenological method, alien to the historic, social

[49] An interesting task is the analysis of etymons and nuances in various languages. They also offer a study of festive images in popular speech and folklore, as well as in belles lettres. Put together, they form a unified picture of the festive universe.

element, cannot solve this problem. Moreover, this philosophy is guided by the narrow spirit of the bourgeois period.[50]

[50] The most interesting attempt to study the festive sense of man was made by O. H. F. Bollnow: *Neue Geborgenheit. Das Problem einer Uberwindung des Existentialismus.* Stuttgart, 1955. At the end of his book, Bollnow gives a piece of additional research devoted to the feast: *Zur Anthropologie des Festes,* pp. 195–243. The author does not use any historical material, makes no differentiation between popular (carnival) and official feasts, ignores the world's comic aspect and the popular and utopian character of the feast. His book, however, contains many valuable observations.

CHAPTER FOUR

Banquet Imagery in Rabelais

Here we have a representation of highest art.
This beautiful image shows us the principle
of nourishment, on which the entire world relies
and which penetrates all nature.
(GOETHE, *"CONCERNING MYRON'S COW"*).

The banquet images—food, drink, swallowing—are closely linked in Rabelais' novel with the popular-festive forms we have discussed in the previous chapter. This is no commonplace, privately consumed food and drink, partaken of by individuals. This is a popular feast, a "banquet for all the world." The mighty aspiration to abundance and to a universal spirit is evident in each of these images. It determines their forms, their positive hyperbolism, their gay and triumphant tone. This aspiration is like yeast added to the images. They rise, grow, swell with this leaven until they reach exaggerated dimensions. They resemble the gigantic sausages and buns that were solemnly carried in carnival processions.

Rabelaisian banquets are organically combined with all other popular-festive forms. Feasting is part of every folk merriment. Not a single comic scene can do without it. We saw that in Lord Basché's castle the Catchpoles are beaten during the wedding banquet. Tappecoue is also dismembered while the diablerie players are feasting at the inn. All this is, obviously, no mere coincidence.

Banquet images play an important role in Rabelais' novel. There is scarcely a single page in his book where food and drink do not figure, if only as metaphors and epithets. These images are closely interwoven with those of the grotesque body. At times it is difficult to draw a line between them, so strong is their original tie. An example is the episode of cattle slaughter previously described, representing the fusion of the devouring and devoured body. If we turn to *Pantagruel* (chronologically the first book) we immediately see how intimately these images are connected. The author relates that after Abel's killing the earth absorbed his blood and became fertile. Further, the people eat boxthorn berries and thanks to them their bodies reach gigantic dimensions. The wide-open mouth is the leading theme of *Pantagruel,* with the theme of swallowing, which is on the borderline between body and food images. Another image is the open womb of Pantagruel's mother in the throes of childbirth, from which issued a caravan of wagons loaded with salted food. We see how closely food images are connected with those of the body and of procreation (fertility, growth, birth).

Let us examine the role of the banquets throughout the novel.

Pantagruel's first heroic feats, accomplished when he was still in the cradle, are connected with food. The roast on a spit is the main image in Panurge's Turkish episodes. The scene of litigation between Lords Kissarse and Bumfondle, as well as the Thaumastes episode, ends with a feast. We saw the leading role played by the banquet in the burning of the knights. The entire episode of King Anarchus is filled with banquet imagery, especially with scenes of drunken bouts. The war ends with the saturnine feast in the capital of the Amaurotes. Epistemon's visit to the underworld also presents many banquet scenes.

The role of banquets is also considerable in *Gargantua,* chronologically the second book of the novel. The story begins with the cattle-slaughtering feast. Images of eating and drinking also play a substantial part in Gargantua's education. When he comes home at the beginning of the Picrochole war, he holds a banquet, and there is a detailed enumeration of all the dishes and game appearing on the table. We saw the role played by bread and wine at the start of the Picrochole war and in the fight in the monastery close. This book abounds in metaphors and comparisons borrowed from the vocabulary of food and drink and ends with the words: *"et grande chère."*[1]

There are fewer of these images in the Third Book, but we find them scattered here and there in various episodes of the story. Let us stress that Panurge's consultations with the theologian, the physician, and the philosopher are held during a dinner; the free discussion concerning women and matrimony which takes place during this meal is typical of such prandial conversations.

We find an increasing number of banquet scenes in the Fourth Book. They dominate in the carnivalesque war of sausages. We also find in this book the episode of the Gastrolaters and the longest list of foods of all world literature, not to mention the famous praise of Master Gaster and of his inventions. Food and the swallowing of food are vividly presented in the description of the giant Bringuenarilles and in the episode of Windy Island where the winds are the only nourishment. There is a chapter devoted to "Why Monks Love Kitchens." The book ends with feasting aboard a ship, thanks to which Pantagruel and his companions "rectify the weather." The concluding words of this book, ending Panurge's long scatological tirade, are "let us drink." And these are the last words of the novel written in Rabelais' own hand.

What is the meaning of these banquet images? We have already said that they are indissolubly linked with festivities, comic scenes,

[1] Our attention is drawn to the fact that banquet imagery is almost entirely absent from the Abbey of Thélème episode. All the abbey's rooms are enumerated and described in great detail, but curiously enough no kitchen is mentioned; there would be no space for it available in this building.

and the grotesque body. Moreover, they are intimately connected with speech, with wise conversation and gay truth. We have also pointed out their inherent tendency toward abundance and toward an all-embracing popular element. How can such an exceptional and universal role of the banquet theme be explained?

Eating and drinking are one of the most significant manifestations of the grotesque body. The distinctive character of this body is its open unfinished nature, its interaction with the world. These traits are most fully and concretely revealed in the act of eating; the body transgresses here its own limits: it swallows, devours, rends the world apart, is enriched and grows at the world's expense. The encounter of man with the world, which takes place inside the open, biting, rending, chewing mouth, is one of the most ancient, and most important objects of human thought and imagery. Here man tastes the world, introduces it into his body, makes it part of himself. Man's awakening consciousness could not but concentrate on this moment, could not help borrowing from it a number of substantial images determining its interrelation with the world. Man's encounter with the world in the act of eating is joyful, triumphant; he triumphs over the world, devours it without being devoured himself. The limits between man and the world are erased, to man's advantage.

In the oldest system of images food was related to work. It concluded work and struggle and was their crown of glory. Work triumphed in food. Human labor's encounter with the world and the struggle against it ended in food, in the swallowing of that which had been wrested from the world. As the last victorious stage of work, the image of food often symbolized the entire labor process. There were no sharp dividing lines; labor and food represented the two sides of a unique phenomenon, the struggle of man against the world, ending in his victory. It must be stressed that both labor and food were collective; the whole of society took part in them. Collective food as the conclusion of labor's collective process was not a biological, animal act but a social event. If food is separated from work and conceived as part of a private way of life, then nothing remains of the old images: man's encounter with the world and tasting the world, the open mouth, the relation of food and speech, the gay truth. Nothing is left but a series of artificial, meaningless metaphors. The original system of images symbolized the working people, continuing to conquer life and food through struggle and labor and to absorb only that part of the world that has been conquered and mastered. In such a system the banquet images preserve their intial meaning: their universalism, their essential relation to life, death, struggle, triumph, and regeneration. This is why banquet imagery went on living in the creative life of the people. The images continued to developed, to be renewed and filled with a richer meaning. They grew and were regenerated together with the people who created them.

Therefore, in contradiction to the opinion of some ethnographers and folklorists, banquet images are not the vestiges of dead ages, when collective hunting was followed by collective feasts, when the defeated animal was torn to pieces and devoured. Such simplified pictures of the primitive hunt seem to explain the origin of images related to dismemberment and devouring, but even these images, belonging to the remotest past (like those of the grotesque body), are far more complex than primitive concepts. They show a deep awareness; they are purposeful, philosophical, rich in nuances. They have a living connection with the surrounding context and are quite unlike the extinct remains of forgotten concepts. But those images that survive in the cults and rites of the official religious systems are different. Here the more ancient stage of development has been fixed in a sublimated form, while in the popular-festive system the development continued over thousands of years. At the time of Rabelais the banquet images still had a meaningful and artistically creative life.

The creative and rich life of banquet images was expressed especially in grotesque realism. It is in this sphere that we must seek the main source of Rabelais' banquet images. The influence of the ancient symposium is of secondary importance.

In the act of eating, as we have said, the confines between the body and the world are overstepped by the body; it triumphs over the world, over its enemy, celebrates its victory, grows at the world's expense. This element of victory and triumph is inherent in all banquet images. No meal can be sad. Sadness and food are incompatible (while death and food are perfectly compatible). The banquet always celebrates a victory and this is part of its very nature. Further, the triumphal banquet is always universal. It is the triumph of life over death. In this respect it is equivalent to conception and birth. The victorious body receives the defeated world and is renewed.

This is the reason why the banquet as a triumphal celebration and renewal often fulfills the function of completion. It is equivalent to nuptials (an act of procreation). Two epilogues are combined in the image of the wedding feast that concludes folktales. The fact is that "a feast" and "a wedding," put together in the nuptial banquet, offer a completed picture: the potentiality of a new beginning instead of the abstract and bare ending. Characteristically enough, death is never such a completion in the folktale. Even if it appears at the end of the story, it is followed by the funeral banquet (as in the *Iliad*) which forms the true epilogue. This form is related to the ambivalence of all folk images. The end must contain the potentialities of the new beginning, just as death leads to a new birth.

The triumphant nature of every banquet renders it not only a fit conclusion but also a framework for a number of essential events. Thus the Rabelaisian banquets may represent either an epilogue or a stage setting, as in the beating of the Catchpoles.

But the banquet is even more important as the occasion for wise discourse, for the gay truth. There is an ancient tie between the feast and the spoken word. The antique symposium presents this relation in its clearest and most classic form. But medieval grotesque realism had its own original symposium, that is, the tradition of festive speech.

One would be tempted to seek the origin of this connection of food with the spoken word at the very cradle of human language. But this ultimate origin, even if established with a certain measure of probability, would offer but little to the understanding of the later development and meaning of such a connection. Even for the authors of the antique symposium, for Plato, Xenophon, Plutarch, Athenaeus, Macrobius, Lucian, and others, the link between eating and speaking was not an obsolete remnant of this past but had a living meaning. Such was also the form of the grotesque symposium, and the work of Rabelais was the last link to present and to complete this heritage.[2]

Rabelais speaks directly of the connection in his prologue to *Gargantua:*

> I may add that in composing this masterpiece I have not spent or wasted more leisure than is required for my bodily refection—food and drink to you! Is that not the proper time to commit to the page such sublime themes and such profound wisdom? Homer, the paragon of all philologists, knew it perfectly well and Ennius also, the father of the Latin poets, as Horace testifies, though a certain sorry clown has said that his poems smelled more of wine than of oil.
>
> So, too, spoke a third-rate cynic about my books, but a ripe turd to the fellow! Oh, the sweet fragrance of wine! How much more reconciling, smiling and beguiling wine is than oil! Let the world say that I spent more on wine than on oil: I shall glory in it like Demosthenes when they accused him of the opposite. For my part, I consider it honorable and noble to be a sportsman and a wit, for as such I am welcome wherever two or three Pantagruelists are gathered together. (Book 1, Prologue)

In the beginning of this prologue the author intentionally debases his work. He can write only while eating; in other words, he spends but little time on his work, which is, as it were, a mere joke. Therefore, the expressions "sublime themes" and "profound wisdom" can be understood ironically. But this debasement is immediately effaced by allusions to Homer and Ennius who did the same.

Prandial speech is a free and jocular speech. The popular-festive right of laughter and clowneries, the right to be frank was extended to the table. Rabelais covers his novel with the fool's cap. But at the

[2] The tradition of the grotesque symposium in a reduced form continued to live in later years. We find its various aspects in the nineteenth century, as in Beethoven's table talk. It has actually survived up to our time.

same time the inner meaning of this table talk satisfies him. He actually does prefer wine to oil, oil being the symbol of Lenten, pious seriousness.

He was convinced that free and frank truth can be said only in the atmosphere of the banquet, only in table talk. Outside all considerations of prudence, such an atmosphere and such a tone corresponded to the very essence of truth as Rabelais understood it: a truth inwardly free, gay, and materialistic.

Behind the sanctimonious seriousness of all exalted and official genres, Rabelais saw the receding authority of the past: of characters like Picrochole, Anarchus, Janotus, Tappecoue, the Catchpoles, the plotters and slanderers, the executioners and agelasts, and the cannibals, who barked instead of laughing. In the eyes of Rabelais seriousness was either the tone of that receding truth and doomed authority, or the tone of feeble men intimidated and filled with terror. The grotesque symposium, the carnivalesque, popular-festive or antique "table talks" provided him with the laughing tone, the vocabulary, the entire system of images which expressed his own conception of truth. The banquet with its variations was the most favorable milieu for this absolutely fearless and gay truth. Bread and wine (the world defeated through work and struggle) disperse fear and liberate the word. The merry triumphant encounter with the world in the act of eating and drinking, in which man partakes of the world instead of being devoured by it, was profoundly congenial to Rabelais' outlook. This victory over the world in the act of eating was concrete, tangible, bodily. It gave the very taste of the defeated world, which had fed and would feed mankind. In this image there was no trace of mysticism, no abstract-idealistic sublimation.

This image materializes truth and does not permit it to be torn away from the earth, at the same time preserving the earth's universal and cosmic nature. The themes of table talk are always "sublime," filled with "profound wisdom," but these themes are uncrowned and renewed on the material bodily level. The grotesque symposium does not have to respect hierarchical distinctions; it freely blends the profane and the sacred, the lower and the higher, the spiritual and the material. There are no *mésalliances* in its case.

Let us stress in the previously quoted excerpt the opposition of wine and oil. As we have said, oil is the symbol of official bigoted seriousness, of the sanctimonious fear of God. Wine liberates from fear and sanctimoniousness. *In vino veritas.*

We must point out another important element: the link with the future of the words pronounced at the banquet, as well as with the praise-mockery complex. This element has survived in toasts and festive speeches; one might say that they belong to time itself, which kills and gives birth in a single act. (Hence its ambiguity and ambivalence.) Even within the rigid framework of Plato's and Xenophon's classical symposia, praise maintains its ambivalence, though in a mitigated form. The eulogy of Socrates permits the speaker to mention his ugliness, and Socrates may eulogize himself (in Xenophon) as a go-between. Old age and youth, beauty and ugliness, death and childbirth are often combined in a single two-faced image. But the festive voice of time speaks first of all about the future. The festive occasion inevitably suggests looking into better days to come. This lends a special character to table talk, liberated from the shackles of the past and present. In the Hippocrates collection there is a treatise on "Winds" with which Rabelais was well acquainted. It contained the following description of inebriety at banquets: "due to a sudden increase of blood, there is a change in the soul and in the thoughts it contains; then men forget their present misfortunes and are inspired with the hope of a happy future." But this utopian nature of prandial speeches does not separate men from earth; future triumphs are presented in material bodily images of abundance and rebirth.

The meaning and function of banquet images in Rabelais' novel become clearer when seen against the background of grotesque tradition.

This tradition starts with the famous *Coena Cypriani,* "Cyprian's Supper." The history of this peculiar work still remains problematical. It has doubtless no relation at all to St. Cyprian, bishop of Carthage (died in A.D. 258), in whose works the *Coena* was usually included. Neither is it possible to establish at what time it was written; it can be roughly dated between the fifth and the eighth century. Nor can we be sure of the exact goal and purpose pursued by the *Coena's* author. Some scholars (for instance, Brewer) assert that the author pursued purely didactic and even mnemonic aims: to fix the names and events of the Scriptures in the minds of students and parishioners. Others (Lapôtre) interpret this work as a parody of the "Banquet" in honor of the goddess Ceres, composed by Julian the Apostate. There are finally those who (like P. Lehmann and others) believe the *Coena* to be a parody of the sermon of Zeno, Bishop of Verona. It is appropriate to say a few words about this bishop.

Bishop Zeno composed a bizarre sermon. He evidently strove to put some order into the wild, unchristian banquets held by his flock during the Easter holidays. For this purpose he selected from the Bible and the Gospels all passages concerning food and drink partaken of by various persons, in other words all banquet images in holy writ. The result was a kind of renewal of the sacred on the material bodily level. This sermon contains elements of the *risus paschalis,* the free jokes which ancient custom permitted in Easter homilies.

The *Coena* does resemble Zeno's sermon, but it goes considerably further. The author makes a vast selection not only of banquet scenes but of all festive images of the Bible and the Gospels. He combines all these images into the grandiose picture of a banquet, full of life and movement, presented with extraordinary carnival-esque, or rather saturnalian freedom. The relation of the *Coena* to the Saturnalia is admitted by nearly all scholars. The basic theme is taken from the parable of the king celebrating his son's wedding (Matthew 22:1–14). All the figures from the Old and New Testaments, from Adam and Eve to Christ, are assembled at the great banquet. They are seated according to their role in scriptures: Adam is in the middle, Eve is sitting on a fig leaf, Cain on a plow, Abel on a milk jug, Noah on the ark, Absalom on branches, and Judas on a money-box. The food and drink served to the guests are also chosen according to their role. For example, Christ is served raisin wine called "passus" (from the word *passio*, the Passion). All the other arrangements are also presented in grotesque form. After eating (which is the first part of the antique symposium) Pilate brings water for the washing of hands. Martha is in attendance, David plays the harp, Salome dances, Judas kisses his fellow guests, Noah is drunk, and a rooster prevents Peter from falling asleep. On the day following the feast the guests bring gifts to their host: Abraham offers a ram, Moses the tables of the law, Christ a lamb. This scene is followed by the theme of a theft. The king discovers that many gifts have been stolen. A search is started and all the guests are treated as thieves. Hagar is executed in atonement and solemnly buried. Such is the construction of a "Cyprian's Supper." It marks the beginning of the banquet tradition in medieval literature.

The *Coena* is an absolutely free play, involving sacred persons, objects, themes, and symbols. The author hesitates at nothing. The fancifulness of the images is striking; Rabelais alone could compete with such a mésalliance. The entire world of Scripture whirls around in a grotesque dance. The passion of God, Noah's ark, Eve's fig leaf, the kiss of Judas have all become the gay elements of a saturnalian banquet. This right to extraordinary freedom was obtained by the author of the "Supper" by means of the banquet images which he selected as his starting point. They created the setting for an absolutely merry interplay. The material bodily character of the banquet images offered the opportunity of embracing almost all the contents of the Scriptures, renewing them at the same time. (In this renewed aspect the Bible scene can be clearly remembered.) The banquet had the power of liberating the word from the shackles of piousness and fear of God. Everything became open to play and merriment.

Let us stress one of the *Coena's* peculiar traits, that it brings together persons from the most diverse periods of Biblical history. It is, as it were, the gathering together of all history, represented by the protagonists seated around the festive table. The banquet acquires a grandiose, universal character. Let us also stress the theme of theft, of the travesty of the atoning victim, Hagar, and the parodic funeral. These themes closely interwoven with banquet images were later often used in grotesque symposia.

"Cyprian's Supper" enjoyed a great success from the time of its revival, the ninth century, to the sixteenth. It spread in its original version as well as in various revised forms. We have several such revised editions by the famous Abbot of Fulda, Rabanus Maurus (855), by Pope John (877), and others.

Rabanus Maurus was a very strict and orthodox churchman; nevertheless, he saw nothing sacrilegious in the *Coena*. He prepared an abridged edition of this work and dedicated it to King Lothair. In his dedication he wrote that this work would serve the king as a "recreational" reading (*ad jocunditatem*). The Roman Pope John VIII rewrote the "Supper" in verse (the original version was in prose), adding a prologue and an epilogue. The prologue shows us that his revised work was intended for scholastic entertainment during the Easter holidays, while the epilogue says that the *Coena* enjoyed considerable success at the court of King Charles the Bald. These facts are characteristic. They prove how sacred were the rights and freedoms enjoyed at banquets and recreations of the ninth century. For Rabanus Maurus and his contemporaries the festive banquet justified such a playful handling of religious topics; at other times it would be considered sacrilege.

There are many manuscripts of the *Coena*, copied and recopied during the following centuries, proof of the medieval symposium's great influence. It is interesting to note that the *Coena's* universalism and several other traits are repeated in the grandiose sixteenth-century symposium "How to Succeed in Life," as well as in "Pantagruel's Dream."[3] The latter work under Rabelais' influence determined in its turn the Third Book of Rabelais' novel.

The next work of the medieval symposium tradition which comes to our attention was composed in the fifteenth century. In the so-called "Cambridge song manuscript" there is a poem telling the story of a thief who came to the court of Archbishop Göeringer of

---

[3] François Habert d'Issoudun, *Le Songe de Pantagruel.*

Mainz and swore that he had visited heaven and hell.[4] He said that Christ was feasting in heaven; his cook was Peter the apostle and his cellarer John the Baptist. The thief stole a piece of lung from the heavenly table and ate it. For this misdeed the Archbishop imposed a penance on his visitor. This short tale is in the medieval banquet tradition: here we find a travesty of the Last Supper. The image of the banquet permits the event to be transferred to the material bodily level, introducing real culinary details and transforming the apostle into a cook.

In the eleventh and twelfth centuries the medieval symposium becomes more complex by the introduction of a satirical element. A work of the eleventh century, entitled "The Treatise of Garcia of Toledo," is typical in this respect. The treatise represents the continuous feasting of the Roman curia, with the Pope and the cardinals. The Pope drinks from a large golden cup: he has an unquenchable thirst. He drinks to all and to everything: to the redemption of souls, to the sick, to the harvest, to peace, travelers, and sailors. This is a parody of the litany. Nor do the cardinals lag behind in the drinking. The description of this continuous feast, of the gluttony of the Pope and of the other prelates, is full of gross exaggeration and long speeches of praise and abuse. This work is often compared to Rabelais' novel as a model of grotesque satire. The Pope's insatiable appetite acquires cosmic dimensions.

The "Treatise of Garcia of Toledo" is quite obviously directed against the corruption, avidity, and disintegration of the Roman curia. The banquet images, exaggerated to extraordinary dimensions, have here what might seem a purely negative connotation. This is the exaggerated picture of "the improper." However, the matter is far more complex. Banquet images, like all popular-festive forms, are ambivalent. True, in the given case they are made to serve a satirical, negative goal. But even here the images preserve their positive nature, and indeed it is this positive element that

---

[4] This "comic vision of the underworld" was published in *The Cambridge Songs*, edited by Karl Breul, Cambridge, 1915, pp. 59–85.

creates the exaggerations, though they are put to a satirical use. Negation is not transferred to the matter of images: to wine, food, abundance. This matter remains positive. There is no serious, consistent, ascetic tendency. Wherever such a tendency appears (as it often does in Protestant satire of the second half of the fifteenth century) the material bodily images inevitably fade and are dryly and parsimoniously presented: the exaggeration becomes abstract. There is nothing of this in the "Treatise." The images used for a satiric purpose continue to live their own life, that of the banquet. They have not been exhausted by the purpose for which they were used. But this does not diminish the force of the satire; the author denounces the curia effectively and at the same time frankly submits himself to the positive force of his banquet images. They create a free atmosphere that permits him to travesty liturgical and gospel texts.

The splitting of the traditional (more often popular-festive) image is a widespread phenomenon in world literature. The general formula of this process is the following: the image that was built and has developed as a grotesque conception of the body, that is, of a collective body of the people as a whole, is transferred to the private bodily life of man in class society. In folklore the people feast with their representatives, their deputies (the heroes and giants); in the "Treatise of Garcia of Toledo" the Pope and the cardinals are also feasting. They feast heroically, but they are not heroes. They do not represent the people; indeed they feast at the people's expense and disadvantage. Wherever the image is directly or indirectly borrowed from folklore and yet pictures the life of a class, there inevitably arises an inner contradiction and tension. Of course, our formula rationalizes and simplifies this phenomenon, which is actually complex, presenting many nuances and revealing the struggle of opposed tendencies. There is no clear solution, just as there is none (nor can there be one) in the living process of becoming. Bread stolen from the people does not cease to be bread, wine is always wine, even when the Pope drinks it. Bread and wine have their own truth, their own irresistible tendency toward superabundance. They have the indestructible connotation of victory and merriment.

This tendency contained in the popular-festive images encounters and is ambiguously interwoven with individual and class gluttony and cupidity. In both cases there is the desire of "much" and "more" abundance, but their philosophies are entirely different. The soul of the people as a whole cannot coexist with the private, limited, greedy body. There is the same complex and contradictory character in the bodily images related to the banquet; the fat belly, the gaping mouth, the giant phallus, and the popular positive image of the "satisfied man." The fat belly of the demons of fertility and of the heroic popular gluttons (for instance, Gargantua in folklore) are transformed into the paunch of the insatiable simonist abbot. The image, split between these two extremes, leads a complex and contradictory life.

In the seventeenth century one of the most popular figures of comic folklore was Gros Guillaume (Fat William), one of the three Turlupins. He was unusually obese and had to make well-planned contortions to reach his own navel. He was girt with two belts: one under his chest, the other under his belly, so that his body resembled a wine barrel. His face was thickly powdered with flour, which he shed on all sides when he gesticulated. Thus his figure was the symbol of bread and wine in bodily form. This two-legged creature representing the abundance of earthly goods was extremely popular. Gros Guillaume was the incarnation of the people's utopia and feasting, the "age of Saturn" returned to earth. The sanctity and the purity of his abundant belly raises, of course, no doubt regarding interpretation. Somewhat different is Mr. Pickwick's fat little paunch. There is much of Gros Guillaume in this character, or rather, there is much of his English equivalent, the popular clown. The English applaud Pickwick and will always applaud, but his paunch is far more ambiguous than Gros Guillaume's barrel of wine.

The splitting and inner contradictions of popular banquet images are found in many variations in world literature. One variation is the "Treatise of Garcia," already discussed. Let us mention still other examples.

Among the "Latin Poems Commonly Attributed to Walter Mapes"[5] there is a piece entitled "Magister Golias About a Certain Abbot" (*Magister Golias de quodam abbate*). This is the description of one day in the life of an abbot, a day filled exclusively with activities of a material bodily order and first of all with excessive eating and drinking. All these pictures of material life (the abbot knows no other existence) have an obviously grotesque character; everything is grossly exaggerated, with many enumerations of the various dishes consumed by the abbot. First there is a description of the different ways in which the abbot relieves himself (this marks the beginning of his day). Here, too, the material bodily images lead a complex double life. The pulse of the great collective body from which they sprang[6] is still beating in them. But this giant pulse is weak and intermittent, for the images are torn away from all that justified their growth and excessive dimensions. The abbot's triumphal banquet is an empty triumph, for it brings nothing to a conclusion. The positive "feast for all the world" and the negative parasitical character are blended into an inwardly contradictory whole.

We find a similar construction in another work contained in the *Golias Apocalisis*. But here it is stressed that the abbot who drinks the good wine leaves the poor wine to his monks. We hear the protesting voice of Friar John accusing his superior of drinking good

[5] Ed. T. Wright, London, 1841.

[6] The author of this piece is called "Magister Golias." This is the nickname of a libertine, a man who has abandoned routine and has transgressed the limits of official philosophy. The name was also applied to drunkards and rakes who waste their lives. We know that the *vagantes* also were called *goliards*. Etymologically, this name had two meanings, from its resemblance to the Latin word *gula* (gluttony) and to the name Goliath. Both meanings were current and did not contradict each other semantically. The Italian scholars F. Neri and F. Ermini proved the existence of a special "Goliath cycle." The Biblical giant was seen by St. Augustine and Bede as a contrast to Christianity, as an incarnation of the antichristian principle. Goliath's character inspired legends and songs about his gluttony and drunkenness. This name apparently became a substitute for the names of giants in folklore symbolizing the grotesque body.

wine while fearfully refusing to fight in defense of the monastery close.

In Latin recreational literature of the twelfth and thirteenth centuries, banquet images as well as those linked with procreative force are usually centered around the figure of a monk, portrayed as a drunkard, glutton, and lecher. The character of the monk is either complex or intermittent. First, as a devotee of material bodily life he sharply contradicts the ascetic ideal that he serves. Second, his gluttony represents the parasitism of a sluggard. But, third, he also expresses the positive, "shrove" principles of food, drink, procreative force, and merriment. The authors offer these three aspects concurrently, and it is difficult to say where praise ends and where condemnation starts. Certainly the authors are not in favor of the ascetic ideal; the accent is nearly always placed on the "shrove" element of the stories. We hear the voice of the democratic cleric who tries to eulogize the material bodily values while remaining within the confines of the ecclesiastical system of philosophy. These writings were, of course, related to recreation, to festive merriment, to the shrove days and to the freedom permitted during these periods.

Let us look at one of these stories which enjoyed great popularity. Its content is extremely simple. A monk spent his nights with a married woman until he was caught by the woman's husband, who castrated him. The author's sympathy is extended rather to the monk than to the husband. While the lady's "chastity" is ironically presented, the list of her lovers exceeds all probability. Actually, this story is nothing but a tragic farce about the destruction of the monastic phallus. The popularity of this story is proved by the considerable number of its manuscript copies, first published in the thirteenth century. In some of the manuscripts the story is offered as a "gay sermon," and in the fifteenth century it was even given the form of a "passion." Thus in the Paris codex it is called *Passio cuisdem monachi*; it is offered as a gospel reading and begins with the words "At that time...." It is actually a "carnivalesque passion."

One of the most widespread themes of Latin recreational literature of the twelfth and thirteenth centuries was the advantage of the cleric over the knight in amorous affairs. We have, for instance, "The Council of Remiremont," dating from the second half of the twelfth century and featuring a conference of women, who praise the superiority of clerics over knights. Similar themes are found in many writings of that period describing councils and synods of clerics in defense of their right to have wives and concubines. This right is sustained by a number of parodies of the gospel and other sacred texts.[7] In all these works the figure of the cleric or monk is the contradictory symbol of procreative force and material bodily superabundance. The character of Friar John is already in preparation, as well as that of Panurge (in part). But we have digressed from our subject of banquet images proper.

During the same period the tradition of the medieval symposium was developed along two other lines: the "drunkards' masses" and the Latin *vagantes*' lyrics. These works are well known and do not need a detailed analysis. Beside the parodical "drunkards' masses" (*missa de potatoribus*) there were the "gamblers' masses" (*officium lusorum*), and sometimes both themes, wine and gambling, were combined in a single ritual. These masses often strictly observed the original liturgical texts. Images of wine and drunkenness were almost devoid of ambivalence. These works were close to the superficial forms of modern parodies and travesties. In *vagante* poetry, images of food, wine, love, and gambling are manifestly linked with popular-festive forms. They also reflect the influence of the antique tradition of prandial songs. But generally speaking, the *vagante* banquet images initiate a new line of individual lyric development.

Such is the banquet tradition of Latin recreative literature. There can be no doubt whatever as to the influence of this tradition on Rabelais. Moreover, the works in this category play an important clarifying role as parallel or related manifestations.

What are the functions of the banquet images in the medieval tradition described above?

From "Cyprian's Supper" and Zeno's sermon to the later satires

7 The debate of clerics and knights was also presented in the vernacular. See Charles Oulmont, *Les Débats du Clerc et du Chevalier*, Paris, 1911.

and parodies of the fifteenth and sixteenth centuries, the banquet images liberate speech, lending it a fearless and free tone. In most cases the medieval symposium contains no philosophical discourses and disputes. But the work as a whole, all its verbal mass, is penetrated with the banquet spirit. Free play with the sacred—this is the basic content of the symposium of the Middle Ages. This does not represent nihilism, nor the primitive enjoyment of debasing the higher level. We will not understand the spirit of grotesque feasting if we do not take into account the deeply positive element, the victorious triumph inherent in every banquet image of folklore origin. The awareness of a purely human material bodily power fills this genre. Man is not afraid of the world, he has defeated it and eats of it. In the atmosphere of this victorious meal the world acquires a different aspect; it becomes an abundant harvest, a superabundant increase. All mystical fears are dissipated. (During banquets ghosts appear only to usurpers or to the representatives of the old dying world.) The banquet speech is universal and materialistic at the same time. This is why the grotesque symposium travesties and debases the purely idealistic, mystic, and ascetic victory over the world (that is, the victory of the abstract spirit). In the comic banquet there are nearly always elements parodying and travestying the Last Supper. These traits are preserved even in the works subjected predominantly to narrowly satiric tendencies.

The power of food and drink to liberate human speech is proved by the fact that schoolmen's and clerics' talks were invaded by a wide range of "colloquial" parodies and travesties of sacred texts related to wines and food. Such colloquial travesties were used at every feast. These texts, liturgical terms, and fragments of prayers turned inside out and debased accompanied every goblet of wine, every morsel of food. In Rabelais' novel this is vividly illustrated by Friar John's talk, and especially by the "Palaver of the Potulent." We have already quoted Henri Estienne's opinion. All these prandial parodies (still alive in our days) are the heritage of the Middle Ages; they are fragments of the grotesque symposium.

Some of Rabelais' contemporaries, Calvin, Charles de Sainte-Marthe, Voulté, and others, directly related the atheist and materialist movements of their time to the banquet atmosphere; they characterized these movements as a certain kind of "prandial libertinism."

In the Middle Ages and in the days of Rabelais this "prandial libertinism" had a democratic spirit. To a certain extent this spirit pervaded English prandial tradition as well, in the time of Shakespeare, Thomas Nash, Robert Greene, and their circle. In France the libertine poets Saint-Amant, Théophile Viau, and d'Assouci were related to this genre. In later years the prandial tradition acquired the form of aristocratic atheism and materialism, which found its striking expression in France, in the eighteenth-century orgies of the Vendôme circle.

The role of the banquet form of speech, liberated from fear and piousness, cannot be underestimated in literary history, nor in the history of materialist thought.

We have retraced only the Latin line of the medieval symposium. But banquet images also played an important role in medieval vernacular literary works as well as in oral folk tradition. The significance of banquet images is considerable in all the legends about giants (for instance, in the Gargantua story and in the chapbook relating it, which were the direct source of Rabelais' novel). There was a popular cycle of legends about the utopian land of gluttony and idleness (for instance, the *fabliau* of the *pays de Cocagne*[8]). We find the reflection of these legends in a number of medieval literary monuments. *Aucassin et Nicolette* describes Torelore, a world "turned inside out." The king of Torelore bears children while the queen fights a war. The war is conducted in pure carnivalesque fashion: with cheeses, baked apples, and mushrooms (the childbearing king and the foods used as weapons are typical popular-festive images). In the novel *Guyon de Bordeaux* the land produces an abundant harvest that belongs to nobody. The book entitled "Travels and Voyages of Panurge, Pantagruel's Disciple, to Unknown and Wondrous Islands"[9] (1537) pictures a utopian

[8] Published in Méon's *Recueil*.

[9] At the time of Rabelais this book was reprinted seven times, some of it with different titles. It was written under the influence of the two

country with mountains of butter, rivers of milk, and hot pies sprung from the soil like mushrooms.

This cycle is reflected in Rabelais' description of Alcofribas' journey in Pantagruel's mouth and the theme of payment for salvation, as well as in the war of sausages.[10]

Banquet images play a leading part in one of the most popular medieval themes, "The dispute between non-Lenten and Lenten foods" (*La Dispute du Gras et du Maigre*). This theme was often treated and had many variations.[11] Rabelais used these images in his enumeration of Lenten and non-Lenten foods offered by the Gastrolaters to their god and in the sausage war. Rabelais' source was the thirteenth-century poem, "The Fight of Lent with the Meat-Eater." (In the fifteenth century this theme was used by Molinet in the "Dispute of Fish with Meat.") The thirteenth-century poem tells of the struggle of two potentates, one symbolizing abstinence, the other non-Lenten foods. The "meat-eater's" army consists of large and small sausages, and fresh cheese, butter, and cream take part in the fighting.

Let us finally point out the essential meaning of banquet images in the *soties*, farces, and all forms of popular comic entertainments. We know that national clownish characters are even called by the names of national dishes (Hanswurst, Pikkelherring, and others).

In the sixteenth century a farce entitled "The Living Corpses" was produced at the court of Charles IX. A lawyer loses his mind

---

first books of Rabelais' novel and was used in turn by Rabelais for his Fourth Book, in the episodes of the war of the sausages and of the giant Bringuenarilles.

[10] Hans Sachs described in his *Schlaraffenland* a country where gluttony and idleness are held in esteem. Those who make progress in both fields are rewarded; those who fight against liverwursts are knighted; sleep is compensated with wages, etc. We find here images parallel to Rabelais' sausage war and Alcofribas' journey in Pantagruel's mouth. But Hans Sachs has a moralizing tone completely alien to Rabelais.

[11] It was still very much alive in the sixteenth century as shown in the pictures of Peter Breughel the Elder: two prints of the "Lenten" and the "non-Lenten" kitchen, and the "Tournament between Lent and Carnival." (All these works were done circa 1560.)

and imagines that he is dead. He gives up eating and drinking and lies motionless on his bed. In order to cure him, one of his relatives pretends that he too is dead and gives orders to be laid out on a table in the lawyer's room. All weep for the "dead" relative. Then he makes comic grimaces, and everybody laughs, including the supposedly dead man himself. The lawyer is surprised but is told that dead men laugh, so he forces himself to laugh; this is the first step in regaining his sanity. Then his relative begins to eat and drink. The lawyer is now persuaded that dead men also nourish themselves. He does so, too, and is completely cured. Thus, laughter, food, and drink defeat death. This theme recalls the novella "The Chaste Matron of Ephesus" by Petronius (from the *Satyrikon*).[12]

Banquet images are so closely interwoven with the grotesque body in medieval written and oral literature that many of these works will have to be examined in our next chapter, devoted to the grotesque concept of the body.

A few words about the Italian banquet tradition. In Pulci's, Berni's, and Ariosto's poems these images play an important part, especially in the case of the first two authors. The tradition is even more significant in Folengo's Italian works and especially in his macaronic writings. Various "edible" metaphors and comparisons acquire in his works an almost importunate character. Olympus in macaronic literature is a fat land with mountains of butter, seas of milk, and pâtés and dumplings floating in them. The muses are cooks. Nectar is a thick brew of bacon and spices. Folengo describes the kitchen of the gods in all detail, filling 180 verses. The debasing and renewing role of this grotesque is obvious, but no less obvious is its weakened and narrowed aspect. The element of narrow literary parody predominates in these writings. The victorious merriment of the banquet themes has degenerated; there is no more authentic universalism, and little remains of the popular utopian theme. A certain influence of Folengo on Rabelais cannot be

---

[12] Concerning this farce, see Louis Guyon, *Les Diverses Leçons*, Lyon, 1604, Vol. 1, Chapter 25.

denied, but it concerns superficial elements and, generally speaking, is not essential.

Such is the tradition of banquet images of the Middle Ages and the Renaissance, as inherited and perfected by Rabelais. The positive, triumphant, liberating element prevails in his images; their tendency to embrace all the people and to present abundance is fully and powerfully disclosed by him.

But Rabelais is also familiar with the image of monks as sluggards and gluttons. This aspect of the banquet is shown in the Fourth Book, in the chapter "Why Monks Love Kitchens." When describing Gargantua's education in the scholastic spirit, Rabelais satirically depicts his hero's gluttony. This passage resembles the day of the "certain abbot." But this narrowly satirical aspect acquires under his pen a limited and secondary meaning.

Rabelais' eulogy of Gaster is complex in character. This eulogy, like the chapters about the Gastrolaters which precede it, is filled with the struggle between contradictory tendencies. The abundance of food is here combined with gluttony of the Gastrolaters who adore the belly as a god. Gaster himself sends his "apes," that is, the Gastrolaters, to mediate upon his excrement and see what kind of divinity is contained in them. But against this background of trivial images of gluttony (the negation, however, does not concern the food and wine served by the Gastrolaters) there arises the mighty figure of Gaster himself, inventor and creator of all mankind's technology.

In Rabelaisian literature we find the assertion that the eulogy of Gaster contains the seed of historic materialism. This is both true and untrue. There can be no doubt concerning this assertion as it concerns the stage of historic development in Rabelais' time. But we do not find in this eulogy a primitive "materialism of the belly." Gaster, who invented agriculture, the conservation of grain, military weapons to defend it, the means for its transportation, the building of cities and fortresses and the art of destroying them, is eulogized in connection with these technological achievements. He was also the creator of the sciences (mathematics, astronomy, medicine, and others). Therefore, rather than representing the biological bowels of the animal, he is the incarnation of the material needs of the organized human collectivity. The bowels study the world in order to conquer and subjugate it. The eulogy has the triumphant banquet tone and ends with fantastic vistas of Gaster's future conquests and inventions. But this triumphant tone is mingled with elements of negation: Gaster is covetous, greedy, and unjust. He has not only invented the building of cities but also the methods for their destruction, that is, war. This combination creates the complex character of Gaster's image, a deep inward antinomy, which Rabelais was unable to solve. Neither did he try to find a solution. He left antinomy and the complexity of life as they were, for he was certain that almighty time would solve the problem.

Let us stress that the victorious banquet images in Rabelais' novel always have a historic coloring. This is most clearly seen in the episode of the fire that burned the knights and was then turned into a kitchen hearth. The banquet takes place, as it were, in a new epoch. And one might say that the carnival banquet was also held in the utopian future, in the Saturnian age come back to earth. Gay, triumphal time speaks in the language of banquet images. This element survives in our modern toasts.

There is still another significant aspect of the banquet images, which we have not as yet mentioned. This is the special relation of food to death and to the underworld. The word "to die" had among its various connotations the meaning of "being swallowed" or being "eaten up." The image of the underworld in Rabelais was also meant by him as the topographical lower stratum, that which represented hell in carnival forms. The underworld is one of the essential points of junction in Rabelais' novel as in all medieval literature (initiated by Dante). But we shall devote a chapter to these images of the lower stratum and the underworld and at that time will return to the aspects of banquet images which served as links to death and to hell.

Let us again stress in conclusion that banquet images in the popular-festive tradition (and in Rabelais) differ sharply from the images of private eating or private gluttony and drunkenness in early bourgeois literature. The latter express the contentment and satiety of the selfish individual, his personal enjoyment, and not the triumph of the people as a whole. Such imagery is torn away from the process of labor and struggle; it is removed from the marketplace and is confined to the house and the private chamber (abundance in the home); it is no longer the "banquet for all the world," in which all take part, but an intimate feast with hungry beggars at the door. If this picture of eating and drinking is hyperbolic, it is a picture of gluttony, not an expression of social justice. It is a static way of private life, deprived of any symbolic openings and universal meaning, no matter whether it is represented as satire that is, as purely negative, or as a positive state of well-being.

The popular-festive banquet has nothing in common with static private life and individual well-being. The popular images of food and drink are active and triumphant, for they conclude the process of labor and struggle of the social man against the world. They express the people as a whole because they are based on the inexhaustible, ever-growing abundance of the material principle. They are universal and organically combined with the concept of the free and sober truth, ignoring fear and piousness and therefore linked with wise speech. Finally, they are infused with gay time, moving toward a better future that changes and renews everything in its path.

This characteristic trait of the popular banquet images has not as yet been properly understood. They were interpreted on the level of the private way of life and were defined as "vulgar realism." Therefore, neither the extraordinary charm of these images nor their immense role in the literature, art, and philosophy of past ages could be grasped and explained. Neither was their antinomy studied as they developed within the system of class ideology, where they were subject to individualization and degeneration. These processes went on in different degrees, according to the various stages of class development. For instance, in Flanders, in spite of bourgeois development, banquet images still retained their positive popular aspect, though in a weakened form. This explains the forceful quality and the fascination of this genre in Flemish painting. In this sphere, too, a deeper study of folk culture will permit us to pose and solve in a new light a number of essential problems.

CHAPTER FIVE

The Grotesque Image of the Body and Its Sources

In the banquet images discussed in the previous chapter we have seen gross exaggeration and hyperbole. Such exaggeration is also inherent in other images of the body's life but is most strongly expressed in picturing the body and food. Here we must seek the deepest source and the creative principle of all other hyperbole of the Rabelaisian world, the source of all that is excessive and superabundant in it.

Exaggeration, hyperbolism, excessiveness are generally considered fundamental attributes of the grotesque style.

The most consistent and well-documented endeavor to give the history and, in part, the theory of the grotesque was made by the German scholar G. Schneegans in his *Geschichte der Grotesken Satyre,* "The History of Grotesque Satire," 1894. About half of this book is devoted to Rabelais, and indeed it can be said that the author centered his attention on Rabelaisian studies. His interpretation of the grotestque image is clear and systematic but appears, however, radically incorrect in our eyes. At the same time, his mistakes are typical; they are repeated in the majority of works devoted to this subject, preceding, or especially, following his own. Schneegans ignores the deep ambivalence of the grotesque and sees it merely as a negation, an exaggeration pursuing narrowly satirical aims. Because such an approach is typical, we shall begin the present chapter by a criticism of Schneegans' work.

The author of "The History of Grotesque Satire" insists upon the strict differentiation of three types or categories of the comic: the clownish, the burlesque, and the grotesque.

As an example of the clownish, Schneegans presents a scene from the Italian *commedia dell'arte* (a scene that was first discussed by Flögel and then by Fischer). A stutterer talking with Harlequin cannot pronounce a difficult word; he makes a great effort, loses his breath, keeping the word down in his throat, sweats and gapes, trembles, chokes. His face is swollen, his eyes pop; "it looks as if he were in the throes and spasms of childbirth." Finally Harlequin, weary of waiting, relieves the stutterer by surprise; he rushes head forward and hits the man in the abdomen. The difficult word is "born" at last.

The example of the burlesque is taken from Paul Scarron's parody of Virgil *Virgile Travesti,* 1653. In order to degrade the high images of the *Aeneid,* Scarron stresses the trivial material bodily images. Hecuba washes diapers, and Dido is presented as a blunt-nosed African negress.

Examples of the grotesque are taken from Rabelais. Friar John asserts that even the shadow of a monastery belfry bears fruit; the monastic habit restores to the dog the reproductive force it has lost; Panurge proposes to build the walls of Paris with genital organs.

Schneegans demonstrates the different character of the laughter provoked by these three types of the comic. In the first example (clownery) the laughter is direct, naïve, and devoid of anger. The stutterer can laugh at himself. In the second example (burlesque) irony is added to laughter, arising from the degradation of high literature. Moreover, the laughter is indirect, since it is necessary to be familiar with the *Aeneid* to enjoy the parody. In the third example (the grotesque) specific social phenomena are berated: monastic depravity and the venality of Parisian women are treated with extreme exaggeration. Here again the satire is indirect, for it is necessary to know the social phenomena that are being berated.

Schneegans founds the difference between these three types of laughter upon formal psychological aesthetics. The comic, in general, is based upon the contrast between the feeling of pleasure and displeasure. All types of the comic have this common ground. The differences between the three types Schneegans describes are determined by the various sources of pleasure and displeasure and the various combinations of these feelings.

In the first instance displeasure is caused by the unexpected and unusual method of healing the stutterer; pleasure is caused by the happy result of Harlequin's trick.

In the second example pleasure is caused by degrading high literature. All that is high wearies in the long run. The more powerful and prolonged the domination of the high, the greater the pleasure caused by its uncrowning. Hence the great success of parodies and travesties, when they appear at the right time, that is, when the reader wearies of high matters. Thus, Scarron's travesties directed against the despotism of Malherbe and classicism were opportune in his time.

In the example of grotesque, displeasure is caused by the impossible and improbable nature of the image: It is unimaginable that a woman could conceive from a monastery belfry, and such an absurdity creates a strong feeling of vexation. But this feeling is overcome by two forms of pleasure: first, we see the truly existing monastic corruption and depravity as symbolized in the hyperbolic image; in other words, we find some place for this exaggeration within reality. Second, we feel a moral satisfaction, since sharp criticism and mockery have dealt a blow to these vices.

In the clownery example no one is mocked, neither the stutterer nor Harlequin. In the example of burlesque the high style of the *Aeneid* and classicism in general are the object of mockery, but there is no moral incentive for irony. This is merely a *boutade*. In the example of grotesque the object of mockery is a specific negative phenomenon, something that "should not exist" (*nichtsein-sollendes*). Schneegans sees precisely in this fact the basic nature of the grotesque: it exaggerates and caricatures the negative, the inappropriate. In the author's mind this distinguishes the grotesque from the *clownish* and from burlesque. In the first two forms of the comic there can also be exaggeration, but they lack the satiric orientation toward the inappropriate. Moreover, exaggeration in the grotesque acquires an extreme, fantastic character.

In art, according to Schneegans, the grotesque is first of all a caricature but a caricature that has reached fantastic dimensions. Schneegans discusses a series of caricatures of Napoleon III based upon the exaggeration of the emperor's nose. The grotesque is manifested in the caricatures that lend the emperor's nose extraordinary dimensions, transforming it either into a pig's snout or a crow's beak.

The exaggeration of the inappropriate to incredible and monstrous dimensions is, according to Schneegans, the basic nature of the grotesque. Therefore, the grotesque is always satire. Where there is no satirical orientation there is no grotesque. From this definition Schneegans deduces all the peculiarities of Rabelais' images and verbal style: excessiveness, superabundance, the tendency to transgress all limits, endless enumerations, and accumulations of synonyms.

Such is Schneegans' concept. It is typical. The interpretation of the grotesque image as purely satirical, that is, negative, is widespread. Rabelais has always had the reputation of a satirist, although he is no more a satirist than Shakespeare and less than Cervantes. Schneegans transfers to Rabelais his own narrow modern interpretation of satire as a negation of separate individual phenomena, not as a negation of the entire order of life (including the prevailing truth), a negation closely linked to the affirmation of that which is born anew.

Schneegans' concept is, as we have said, typical but radically erroneous. It is founded on the complete neglect of a series of essential aspects of the grotesque and first of all neglect of its ambivalence. Moreover, Schneegans ignores the folklore sources of the grotesque.

Schneegans is forced to admit that even with considerable effort it is impossible to find the satirical orientation in all of Rabelais' exaggeration. He explains this by the very nature of exaggeration, which always tends to transgress its own limits; the author of grotesque is carried away, is "drunk" with hyperbole, at times forgetting the true role of exaggeration and losing his grasp on satire.

As an example of such exaggeration forgetful of its initial satiric goal, Schneegans cites the fantastic growth of body members in *Pantagruel*. True, hyperbole is one of the attributes of the grotesque (especially in the Rabelaisian system of images). However, it is not its essential attribute. It is even more inadmissible to reduce to mere satire the entire substance of the grotesque image. Schneegans incorrectly interprets the pathos of exaggeration and the principle that is its moving force.

We may inquire: whence comes this pathos, this "drunkenness," if something negative and inappropriate is exaggerated? Schneegans does not answer this question in his book. He fails to analyze the character of exaggeration, which often undergoes sharp transformations in quality.

If the nature of grotesque satire consists in the exaggeration of the improper, where can that joyful lavishness described by Schneegans come from? How can we explain the quality, wealth, and variety of the image, its often unexpected relation to the most distant and, it may seem, unrelated phenomena? At best, the purely satirical exaggeration of the negative could account for the merely quantitative, not qualitative element of the image and its various relations.

A grotesque world in which only the inappropriate is exaggerated is only quantitively large, but qualitatively it is extremely poor, colorless, and far from gay. (Such is, in part, Swift's gloomy world.) What would such a world have in common with Rabelais' merry and rich universe? Satire alone would not suffice to explain even the positive pathos of the quantitative exaggeration, not to speak of the qualitative wealth.

Because Schneegans relied on the idealistic aesthetics of the second part of the nineteenth century and on the narrow artistic and ideological norms of his time, he could not find the right path to the grotesque. He could not understand the possibility of combining in one image both the positive and the negative poles. Even less was he able to understand that an object can transgress not only its quantitative but also its qualitative limits, that it can outgrow itself and be fused with other objects. The pregnant and two-bodied images could not be grasped by Schneegans; he did not see that, in the grotesque world of becoming, the limits between objects and phenomena are drawn quite differently than in the static world of art and literature of his time.

Let us return to Schneegans' point of departure, to his examples of clownery, burlesque, and grotesque. He sought to discover through analysis the purely formal psychological mechanism of their perception, instead of concentrating on the objective content of these images. But if we start with this objective content, and not with the formal psychological elements, we shall find the essential similarity and relationship of the three examples. The differences established by Schneegans will appear artificial and accidental.

What is the objective content of the first example? Schneegans himself describes it in such a way that we cannot be left in doubt: the stutterer enacts a scene of childbirth. He is pregnant, bearing the word that he is unable to deliver. Schneegans says that "it looks as if he were in the throes and spasms of childbirth." The gaping mouth, the protruding eyes, sweat, trembling, suffocation, the swollen face—all these are typical symptoms of the grotesque life of the body; here they have the meaning of the act of birth. Harlequin's gesture is also quite obvious: he helps to deliver the word, and the word is actually born. We specify that it is the word that is born, and we stress this fact: a highly spiritual act is degraded and uncrowned by the transfer to the material bodily level of childbirth, realistically represented. But thanks to degradation the word is renewed; one might say reborn. (We are still within the cycle of delivery and childbirth.) We further see the essential topographical element of the bodily hierarchy turned upside down; the lower stratum replaces the upper stratum. The word is localized in the mouth and in the head (thought); from there it is transferred to the abdomen and is pushed out under the impact of Harlequin's head. This traditional gesture of the head ramming the abdomen or the buttocks is essentially topographical. Here once more we have the logic of opposites, the contact of the upper and the lower level. We have also an exaggeration: the symptoms produced by the stutterer's distress (tension of the eyes, sweat) are increased to such an extent as to typify childbirth. Thus the entire mechanism of the word is transferred from the apparatus of speech to the abdomen. An objective analysis of this brief scene discloses the fundamental and essential traits of the grotesque. It reveals a great wealth and fullness of meaning, worked out to the smallest detail. It has at the same time a universal character; it is a miniature satyrical drama of the word, of its material birth, or the drama of the body giving birth to the word. The extraordinary realism, the wealth of meaning are inherent in this excellent sketch, as in all comic folk images.

An objective analysis of Scarron's parody will reveal the presence of similar elements. But Scarron's images are poorer, more simplified; they contain many artificial, literary, accidental traits. Schneegans merely sees the degradation of the high style, which had reached the point of wearying the reader. He explains this degradation by a formal psychological consideration: it is necessary to lower the eyes in order to rest them from looking up. Actually, we have here the uncrowning of the *Aeneid*'s images by transferring them to the material bodily level, to the level of food, drink, sexual life, and the bodily phenomena linked with them. This sphere has a positive meaning. It is the generating lower stratum. Therefore, the *Aeneid*'s images are not only uncrowned, they are renewed.

Let us now look at the third example offered by Schneegans, at his Rabelaisian images. Friar John asserts that even the shadow of the monastery belfry can render women more fertile. This image immediately introduces us to the logic of the grotesque. This is no mere exaggeration of monastic "depravity." The object transgresses its own confines, ceases to be itself. The limits between the body and the world are erased, leading to the fusion of the one with the other and with surrounding objects. It must be recalled that the belfry (a tower) is the usual grotesque symbol of the phallus.[1] The entire context creates an atmosphere justifying this metamorphosis. We must quote the Rabelaisian text in the original:

C'est (dist le moyne) bien rentré de picques. Elle pourroit estre aussi layd que Prosperpine, elle aura, par Dieu, la saccade puisqu'il y a moynes autour, car un bon ouvrier mect indifferentement toutes pièces en oeuvre. Que j'aye la vérolle en cas que ne les trouviez engroissées à vostre retour, car seulement l'ombre du clochier d'une abbaye est feconde.[2]
(Book 1, Chapter 45)

Friar John's speech is filled with unofficial and degrading elements that prepare the atmosphere for our grotesque image. First of all, we have an expression borrowed from the game of cards (*rentré de picques*, in the sense of an unfortunate turn). Then there is the image of the ugly Proserpine, queen of the underworld. This, of course, is not the antique mythological figure, but the "devil's

---

[1] The tall tower interpreted as the phallus was well known to Rabelais and to his contemporaries, from antique sources. Here is an excerpt from Lucian, ("The Syrian Goddess"): "In these propylaea there stand phalli thirty fathoms high. A man climbs on one of these phalli twice a year and remains on its summit seven days. And it is from his summit that this man can enter into closer conversation with the gods and pray for the welfare of all Syria."

[2] "That's incompatible, it holds no water, the cap won't fit . . . Were your wife uglier than Proserpine, by God, she'd find herself jerkthumped as long as there was a monk within a thousand miles. Good carpenters use every kind of timber. The pox riddle me if you don't all find your wives pregnant on your return. The very shadow of an abbey spire is fecund."

mother" of the medieval diableries. Moreover, this image was topographically set, since in Rabelais' novel the underworld is always
linked with the bodily lower stratum. Further, we have the oath
(*pardieu*) and the curse related to the bodily lower stratum (*que
j'ay la vérolle*). There follows two metaphors for the sexual act;
one is taken from horsemanship (*saccade* "jerk," or "jolt"), the
other is a proverb about a good craftsman using every kind of wood.
In both cases there is a degradation and renewal of objects of a
different order: horsemanship and the carpenter's craft. These, too,
are the preparations for the grotesque image.

All these elements of speech create a specific, free atmosphere.
Most of them are directly linked to the lower stratum; they lend a
bodily character to objects and degrade them, fuse the body and the
world, thus introducing the concluding theme: the transformation
of the belfry into a phallus.

Is this grotesque image merely a satire of monastic depravity, as
Schneegans tells us? The passage just analyzed is part of an extensive episode of the pilgrims who were swallowed by Gargantua with
his salad but later managed to escape. Actually, this scene is directed against the pilgrims and against the belief in the miraculous
power of the relics that cure diseases (in this case the plague). But
this definite private orientation of satire by no means exhausts the
meaning of the episode and does not determine all the images that
compose it. At the center we find the typical grotesque picture of
the swallowing of the pilgrims, followed by their no less typical
immersion in urine. Finally, there is the parody of the psalms,
which seem to have predicted all the pilgrim's misfortunes. This
travesty is a degrading interpretation of certain images of the
psalms. The themes have a vast universal connotation; it would be
absurd to believe that they have been mustered only in order to
denounce the pilgrims' parasitism and their primitive faith in
relics. This would be like shooting sparrows with heavy guns. The
discountenancing of pilgrimages and crude superstition is the official angle of the episode. In his speech to the pilgrims Grangousier
uses the formal language of a wise government. He speaks like the
royal pamphletists expressing the official point of view on the

abuses of pilgrimages. He does not deny faith but only the pilgrims' uncouth superstition.[3]

This, then, is the official thought openly expressed in the episode. But the nonofficial, popular-festive language of the marketplace speaks here of very different things. The mighty material bodily element of these images uncrowns and renews the entire world of medieval ideology and order, with its belief, its saints, its relics, monasteries, pseudoasceticism, fear of death, eschatologism, and prophecies. In this world to be swept away the pilgrims are only tiny, pitiful figures, which can be swallowed down unnoticed in salad and almost drowned in urine. The material bodily element has here a positive character. And it is precisely the material bodily image that is exaggerated to disproportionate dimensions: the monastic phallus as tall as a belfry, the torrents of Gargantua's urine, and his immeasurably large, all-swallowing gullet.

This is the reason why the monastic belfry, uncrowned and renewed in the form of a giant phallus, with its shadow that impregnates women, is least of all an exaggeration of the monks' depravity. It uncrowns the entire monastery, the very ground on which it stands, its false ascetic ideal, its abstract and sterile eternity. The belfry's shadow is the shadow of the phallus that generates new life. Nothing remains of the monastery; there remains only the living man, Friar John—glutton and drunkard, pitilessly sober, mighty and heroic, full of inexhaustible energy, and thirsting for the new.

We must add that like all similar images the belfry has a topographic character: the tower pointing upward, to heaven, is transformed into the phallus (the bodily lower stratum) and impregnates women (again the body's lower parts).

Another example of the grotesque, chosen by Schneegans from Rabelais, is Panurge's proposal to build walls from genital organs of women. It is prepared thus:

[3] The criticism of this superstition is expressed in the spirit of moderate evangelism, which, it seems, was supported by the royal authority when Rabelais wrote the pilgrim episode.

"Do you know what Agesilaus said?" Pantagruel answered. "They asked him why the great city of Lacedaemon was not girded with walls. Pointing to the citizens, expert in military discipline, strong and so admirably equipped: 'These are the walls of the city!' he said. He meant that cities need no stouter or safer walls than the valor of their citizens."
(Book 2, Chapter 15)

In this antique reminiscence, rendered in high style, the grotesque image of walls turned into flesh is introduced. It is prepared by the conceit that the strongest walls are made of the bones of soldiers. The human body becomes a building material. The limits between the body and the world are weakened (true on the high metaphoric plane). All this precedes Panurge's project:

"I have observed that the pleasure-twats of women in this part of the world are much cheaper than stones. Therefore, the walls should be built of twats, symmetrically and according to the rules of architecture, the largest to go in front. Next, on a downward slope like the back of an ass, the medium-sized, and last of all, the least and smallest. These should all be made to dovetail and interlace, diamond-shape, like the great tower of Bourges, with as many horny joy-dinguses, which now reside in claustral codpieces.

"What devil could possibly overthrow these walls; what metal on earth could stand up as well against punishment? . . . What is more, no lightning could strike them. Why? Because they are consecrated."
(*Ibid.*)

It is clear that the cheapness of Paris women is merely a secondary theme, and that even here there is no moral condemnation. The leading theme is fecundity, as the greatest and safest array of strength. It would be a mistake to rationalize this image by saying, for example, that the citizens' fecundity and the increase of population are the city's best military defense. This idea is not extraneous to the image, but such a narrowing of the grotesque metaphor is inadmissible.

Panurge's metaphor is broader and more complex, and above all it is ambivalent. It contains an element of topographic negation, since Panurge's walls uncrown and renew the fortified walls, as well as military valor, bullets, and even lightning, which is powerless to crush them. Military power and strength are helpless against the material bodily procreative principle.

In another part of the novel (Book Three, Chapter 8) we find Panurge's long dissertation stating that the first and most important armor is the codpiece protecting the genital organs. He states that when a man's head is cut off he alone perishes, but if he loses his genital organs all the human race will be destroyed. And he adds that these organs were the stones with which Deucalian and Pyrrha reestablished mankind after the flood. Here, once more, we find the image of the procreative principle as the best building material.

Panurge's dissertation is interesting from yet another point of view: the utopian principle is well expressed in it. Panurge declared that, wishing to preserve all the species of the vegetable kingdom, nature armed the seeds and germs of plants with sheaths, husks, shells, thorns, bark, and spikes, while man is born naked with his genitals unprotected. This passage of Rabelais' novel was inspired by Pliny's reflections from the seventh book of his "Natural History." But Pliny's gloomy world outlook led him to pessimistic conclusions concerning the weakness of mankind, while Panurge's deductions are extremely optimistic. He believes that if man is born with unprotected genitals, this proves that he is called to peace and a peaceful rule over nature. It was only the "Iron Age" that incited him to be armed, and he started arming, according to Biblical legend, with the first codpiece, a fig leaf. But sooner or later man will return to his peaceful vocation and will fully disarm.[4] Here explicitly, but in a somewhat narrowed rationalized form, we find the theme that implicitly was contained in the indestructible bodily wall uncrowning military power.

It suffices to consider Panurge's reflections, previously quoted, to be convinced of the irrelevancy of the satirical interpretation: the

[4] We find a similar theme in Erasmus (*Adagia* III, 10:1). He also begins by saying that man is born naked and draws the conclusion that man is begotten not for war but for friendship.

cheapness of Paris women. We shall then see that the stones suggested by Panurge for the city walls are the same stones used by Deucalion and Pyrrha to rebuild the ruins of mankind.

Such is the true objective content of the examples given by Schneegans. From the point of view of this objective content, the similarity between the examples appears far more obvious than the dissimilarity. The latter exists, of course, but not where Schneegans is looking for it. The artificial theory of the psychological mechanism of perception on one hand and the narrow aesthetic norms of his time on the other prevented Schneegans from seeing the true essence of the phenomenon he had undertaken to study , that is the grotesque. First of all, the examples we have examined, the scene from the *commedia dell'arte*, Scarron's travesty of the *Aeneid*, and finally Rabelais' images, are to a smaller or greater extent related to the medieval folk culture of humor and to grotesque realism. We find this heritage in the very construction of these images and especially in the concept of the body; this special concept binds together the quoted examples and essentially relates them to one another. In all three cases we find the same mode of representation of the bodily life, which differs sharply from the classical mode, as well as from the naturalist picture of the human body. This permits us to include all three examples (without, of course, ignoring their differences) in the common concept of the grotesque.

We find at the basis of grotesque imagery a special concept of the body as a whole and of the limits of this whole. The confines between the body and the world and between separate bodies are drawn in the grotesque genre quite differently than in the classic and naturalist images. We have already seen this difference in a number of Rabelaisian images. In the present chapter we must broaden our observations, systematize them, and disclose the sources of Rabelais' grotesque concept of the body.

But let us first have a look at another example cited by Schneegans: the caricature of Napoleon and the exaggeration of the size of his nose. According to Schneegans, the grotesque starts when the exaggeration reaches fantastic dimensions, the human nose being transformed into a snout or beak. We shall not discuss the nature of these caricatures per se; it is but superficial satire, deprived of true grotesque character. We are interested in the theme of the nose itself, which occurs throughout world literature in nearly every language, as well as in abusive and degrading gesticulations. Schneegans correctly points out the grotesque character of the transformation of the human element into an animal one; the combination of human and animal traits is, as we know, one of the most ancient grotesque forms. But the author does not grasp the meaning of the grotesque image of the nose: that it always symbolizes the phallus. Laurent Joubert, the famous sixteenth-century physician and a contemporary of Rabelais, whose theory of laughter we have already mentioned, wrote a book on popular superstitions in medicine.[5] In Part 5, Chapter 6 of this book he speaks of the popular belief that the size and potency of the genital organs can be inferred from the dimensions and form of the nose. Friar John also expresses this belief in his monastic jargon. Such is the usual interpretation of this image in the literature of the Middle Ages and the Renaissance, linked with the popular-festive system. The most widely known example of this symbolism is the famous carnival "Dance of the Noses" of Hans Sachs (*Nasentanz*).

Of all the features of the human face, the nose and mouth play the most important part in the grotesque image of the body; the head, ears, and nose also acquire a grotesque character when they adopt the animal form or that of inanimate objects. The eyes have no part in these comic images; they express an individual, so to speak, self-sufficient human life, which is not essential to the grotesque. The grotesque is interested only in protruding eyes, like the eyes of the stutterer in the scene described earlier. It is looking for that which protrudes from the body, all that seeks to go out beyond the body's confines. Special attention is given to the shoots and branches, to all that prolongs the body and links it to other

[5] Laurent Joubert, *Erreurs populaires et propos vulgaires touchant la médecine et le régime de santé*. Bordeaux, 1579.

bodies or to the world outside. Moreover, the bulging eyes manifest a purely bodily tension. But the most important of all human features for the grotesque is the mouth. It dominates all else. The grotesque face is actually reduced to the gaping mouth; the other features are only a frame encasing this wide-open bodily abyss.

The grotesque body, as we have often stressed, is a body in the act of becoming. It is never finished, never completed; it is continually built, created, and builds and creates another body. Moreover, the body swallows the world and is itself swallowed by the world (let us recall the grotesque image in the episode of Gargantua's birth on the feast of cattle-slaughtering). This is why the essential role belongs to those parts of the grotesque body in which it outgrows its own self, transgressing its own body, in which it conceives a new, second body: the bowels and the phallus. These two areas play the leading role in the grotesque image, and it is precisely for this reason that they are predominantly subject to positive exaggeration, to hyperbolization; they can even detach themselves from the body and lead an independent life, for they hide the rest of the body, as something secondary (The nose can also in a way detach itself from the body.) Next to the bowels and the genital organs is the mouth, through which enters the world to be swallowed up. And next is the anus. All these convexities and orifices have a common characteristic; it is within them that the confines between bodies and between the body and the world are overcome: there is an interchange and an interorientation. This is why the main events in the life of the grotesque body, the acts of the bodily drama, take place in this sphere. Eating, drinking, defecation and other elimination (sweating, blowing of the nose, sneezing), as well as copulation, pregnancy, dismemberment, swallowing up by another body—all these acts are performed on the confines of the body and the outer world, or on the confines of the old and new body. In all these events the beginning and end of life are closely linked and interwoven.

Thus the artistic logic of the grotesque image ignores the closed, smooth, and impenetrable surface of the body and retains only its excrescences (sprouts, buds) and orifices, only that which leads beyond the body's limited space or into the body's depths.[6] Mountains and abysses, such is the relief of the grotesque body; or speaking in architectural terms, towers and subterranean passages.

Grotesque images may, of course, present other members, organs and parts of the body (especially dismembered parts), but they play a minor role in the drama. They are never stressed unless they replace a leading image.

Actually, if we consider the grotesque image in its extreme aspect, it never presents an individual body; the image consists of orifices and convexities that present another, newly conceived body. It is a point of transition in a life eternally renewed, the inexhaustible vessel of death and conception.

As we have said, the grotesque ignores the impenetrable surface that closes and limits the body as a separate and completed phenomenon. The grotesque image displays not only the outward but also the inner features of the body: blood, bowels, heart and other organs. The outward and inward features are often merged into one.

We have already sufficiently stressed the fact that grotesque imagery constructs what we might call a double body. In the endless chain of bodily life it retains the parts in which one link joins the other, in which the life of one body is born from the death of the preceding, older one.

Finally, let us point out that the grotesque body is cosmic and universal. It stresses elements common to the entire cosmos: earth, water, fire, air; it is directly related to the sun, to the stars. It contains the signs of the zodiac. It reflects the cosmic hierarchy. This body can merge with various natural phenomena, with mountains, rivers, seas, islands, and continents. It can fill the entire universe.

The grotesque mode of representing the body and bodily life prevailed in art and creative forms of speech over thousands of years.

---

[6] This grotesque logic is also extended to images of nature and of objects in which depths (holes) and convexities are emphasized.

From the point of view of extensive use, this mode of representation still exists today; grotesque forms of the body not only predominate in the art of European peoples but also in their folklore, especially in the comic genre. Moreover, these images predominate in the extra-official life of the people. For example, the theme of mockery and abuse is almost entirely bodily and grotesque. The body that figures in all the expressions of the unofficial speech of the people is the body that fecundates and is fecundated, that gives birth and is born, devours and is devoured, drinks, defecates, is sick and dying. In all languages there is a great number of expressions related to the genital organs, the anus and buttocks, the belly, the mouth and nose. But there are few expressions for the other parts of the body: arms and legs, face, and eyes. Even these comparatively few forms of speech have, in most cases, a narrow, practical character; they are related to the nearby area, determine distance, dimensions, or number. They have no broader, symbolic meaning, nor are they especially expressive. They do not participate in abuse and mockery.

Wherever men laugh and curse, particularly in a familiar environment, their speech is filled with bodily images. The body copulates, defecates, overeats, and men's speech is flooded with genitals, bellies, defecations, urine, disease, noses, mouths, and dismembered parts. Even when the flood is contained by norms of speech, there is still an eruption of these images into literature, especially if the literature is gay or abusive in character. The common human fund of familiar and abusive gesticulations is also based on these sharply defined images.

This boundless ocean of grotesque bodily imagery within time and space extends to all languages, all literatures, and the entire system of gesticulation; in the midst of it the bodily canon of art, belles lettres, and polite conversation of modern times is a tiny island. This limited canon never prevailed in antique literature. In the official literature of European peoples it has existed only for the last four hundred years.

We shall give a brief characterization of the new canon, concerning ourselves less with the pictorial arts than with literature. We shall build this characterization by comparing it to the grotesque conception and bringing out the differences.

The new bodily canon, in all its historic variations and different genres, presents an entirely finished, completed, strictly limited body, which is shown from the outside as something individual. That which protrudes, bulges, sprouts, or branches off (when a body transgresses its limits and a new one begins) is eliminated, hidden, or moderated. All orifices of the body are closed. The basis of the image is the individual, strictly limited mass, the impenetrable façade. The opaque surface and the body's "valleys" acquire an essential meaning as the border of a closed individuality that does not merge with other bodies and with the world. All attributes of the unfinished world are carefully removed, as well as all the signs of its inner life. The verbal norms of official and literary language, determined by the canon, prohibit all that is linked with fecundation, pregnancy, childbirth. There is a sharp line of division between familiar speech and "correct" language.

The fifteenth century was an age of considerable freedom in France. In the sixteenth century the norms of language become more strict, and the borderline between the different norms grew more evident. This process intensified at the end of the century, when the canon of polite speech that was to prevail in the seventeenth century was definitely formed. At the end of the century Montaigne protested in his "Essays" against these prohibitions.

What harm has the genital act, so natural, so necessary, and so lawful, done to humanity, that we dare not speak of it without shame, and exclude it from serious and orderly conversation? We boldly utter the words, *kill, rob, betray*: and the other we only dare utter under our breath. Does this mean that the less of it we breathe in words, the more are we at liberty to swell our thoughts with it? For it is amusing that the words which are least used, least written, and most hushed up should be the best known and the most generally understood. There is no person of any age or morals but knows them as well as he knows the word *bread*. They are impressed upon each of us, without being expressed, without voice and without form. (And the sex that does it most is charged to hush it up.)

(Montaigne, "Essays," III, Chapter 5. Translated by George B. Ivez, copyright Harvard University Press, 1925. Reproduced by permission.)

In the new canon, such parts of the body as the genital organs, the buttocks, belly, nose and mouth cease to play the leading role. Moreover, instead of their original meaning they acquire an exclusiveness; in other words, they convey a merely individual meaning of the life of one single, limited body. The belly, nose, and mouth, are of course retained in the image and cannot be hidden, but in an individual, completed body they either fulfill purely expressive functions (this is true of the mouth only) or the functions of characterization and individualization. There is no symbolic, broad meaning whatever in the organs of this body. If they are not interpreted as a characterization and an expressive feature, they are referred to on the merely practical level in brief explanatory comments. Generally speaking, all that does not contain an element of characterization in the literary image is reduced to a simple bodily remark added to speech or action.

In the modern image of the individual body, sexual life, eating, drinking, and defecation have radically changed their meaning: they have been transferred to the private and psychological level where their connotation becomes narrow and specific, torn away from the direct relation to the life of society and to the cosmic whole. In this new connotation they can no longer carry on their former philosophical functions.

In the new bodily canon the leading role is attributed to the individually characteristic and expressive parts of the body: the head, face, eyes, lips, to the muscular system, and to the place of the body in the external world. The exact position and movements of this finished body in the finished outside world are brought out, so that the limits between them are not weakened.

The body of the new canon is merely one body; no signs of duality have been left. It is self-sufficient and speaks in its name alone. All that happens within it concerns it alone, that is, only the individual, closed sphere. Therefore, all the events taking place within it acquire one single meaning: death is only death, it never coincides with birth; old age is torn away from youth; blows merely hurt, without assisting an act of birth. All actions and events are interpreted on the level of a single, individual life. They are enclosed within the limits of the same body, limits that are the absolute beginning and end and can never meet.

In the grotesque body, on the contrary, death brings nothing to an end, for it does not concern the ancestral body, which is renewed in the next generation. The events of the grotesque sphere are always developed on the boundary dividing one body from the other and, as it were, at their points of intersection. One body offers its death, the other its birth, but they are merged in a two-bodied image.

In the new canon the duality of the body is preserved only in one theme, a pale reflection of its former dual nature. This is the theme of nursing a child.[7] But the image of the mother and the child is strictly individualized and closed, the line of demarcation cannot be removed. This is a completely new phase of the artistic conception of bodily interaction.

Finally, the new canon is completely alien to hyperbolization. The individualized image has no place for it. All that is permitted is a certain accentuation of expressive and characterized features. The severance of the organs from the body or their independent existence is no longer permitted.

We have roughly sketched the basic outlines of the modern canon, as they generally appear in the norms of literature and speech.[8]

[7] Let us recall Goethe's remarks as reported by Eckermann in "Conversations with Goethe" concerning Correggio's painting "The Weaning of a Child." Goethe is attracted by the duality of the image, preserved in an attenuated form.

[8] Similar classical concepts of the body form the basis of the new canon of behavior. Good education demands: not to place the elbows on the table, to walk without protruding the shoulder blades or swinging the hips, to hold in the abdomen, to eat without loud chewing, not to snort and pant, to keep the mouth shut, etc.; in other words, to close up and limit the body's confines and to smooth the bulges. It is interesting to trace the struggle of the grotesque and classical concept in the

The comic conception, inherited from folk culture of humor, from grotesque realism and from elements of familiar speech, culminates in Rabelais' novel. In all the episodes that we have analyzed, and in their separate images, we have seen the grotesque body. Its mighty torrent flows through the entire novel: the dismembered parts, the separate organs (as in Panurge's wall), the gaping mouths devouring, swallowing, drinking, the defecation, urine, death, birth, childhood, and old age. The bodies are merged with each other or with objects (as in the image of *carême-prenant*) and with the world. A tendency toward duality can be glimpsed everywhere. Everywhere the cosmic, ancestral element of the body is stressed.

The tendency to duality can be found to a greater or smaller extent in the episodes we have examined. Let us offer an example of a more external and uncouth projection of duality.

The emblem in his (Gargantua's) hat? Against a base of gold weighing over forty pounds was an enamel figure very much in keeping. It portrayed a man's body with two heads facing one another, four arms, four feet, a pair of arses and a brace of sexual organs, male and female. Such, according to Plato's *Symposium*, was human nature in its mystical origins.
(Book 1, Chapter 8)

The androgyne theme was popular in Rabelais' time. In the sphere of pictorial art I will recall a similar presentation in Leonardo da Vinci's "Coitus," showing this act in its inner bodily aspect.

Rabelais not only represents the grotesque image of the body in its essential forms. He also offers the theory of the body in its ancestral aspect. Panurge's arguments quoted previously are typical in this respect. In another passage he says that in the realm of Salmagundi:

. . . no malefactor would be put to death by law, without friggling like a pelican (as lustily as belly can), until his spermatic vessels

---

history of dress and fashion. Even more interesting is this struggle in the history of dance.

were drained of the few drops required to trace a Greek Υ, the letter sacred to Priapus. After all, here was a wealth too rich to waste. Your criminal, begetting a male, would die content, forfeiting his life, he would have left the world another.
(Book 3, Chapter 26)

In his famous speech about debtors and creditors, describing the utopian world where all lend money and receive loans, Panurge also develops the theory of the ancestral body:

The interdependent universe was so beautifully organized that, the problem of nutrition perfected, it went on to lend to those unborn—a loan, by means of which it sought to perpetuate and multiply itself in its own image: children.
"To this end, each particular elects and pares off the most precious elements of its food to dispatch them downward into vessels and receptacles most suitably contrived by nature. These elements flow down long circuits and flexuosities into the genitories; receive a competent form; find chambers designed, in both male and female, for the preservation and perpetuation of humankind. And all of it is done by loans and debts, a fact proved by the phrase 'the obligations of wedlock.' "
(Book 3, Chapter 4)

Again, in the Third Book, there is an explanation of why newly married men are not forced to go to war. Here the ancestral theory is developed once more. This is one of the leading themes of the entire Third Book.

We shall resume this theme in our next chapter, examining it in its historic aspect as the growth and immortality of the human race, as expressed in Gargantua's famous letter to Pantagruel. The relative immortality of the semen is seen here in its intimate relation to mankind's historic progress. The human race is not merely renewed with each new generation, it rises to a new level of development. This theme, as we shall see, is also found in the praise of "Pantagruelion."

Thus, in Rabelais' book the image of the ancestral body is merged with the people's vivid awareness of historic immortality. We have seen that this awareness forms the very nucleus of the entire system of popular-festive imagery. The grotesque conception of the body is interwoven not only with the cosmic but also with the social, utopian, and historic theme, and above all with the theme of the change of epochs and the renewal of culture.

In all the episodes and images discussed in the preceding chapters, the material bodily lower stratum was most often represented in the narrow sense of the word. But in these images a leading role is also played, as we have said, by the gaping mouth. This is, of course, related to the lower stratum; it is the open gate leading downward into the bodily underworld. The gaping mouth is related to the image of swallowing, this most ancient symbol of death and destruction. At the same time, a series of banquet images are also linked to the mouth (to the teeth and the gullet).

These are some of the central images of the popular-festive system. The exaggeration of the mouth is the fundamental traditional method of rendering external comic features, as pictured by comic masks, various "gay monsters" (Mâchecroûte of the Lyon carnival), devils in diableries, and Lucifer himself.

It is obvious why the gaping mouth, the teeth, the swallowing have an essential meaning in the Rabelaisian system of images. The gaping mouth plays a specially important part in *Pantagruel*. One may say that it is the hero of this book.

Neither Pantagruel's name nor the nucleus of his image was created by Rabelais. The name existed before him in literature as that of a character of the diableries; it also existed in spoken language as a colloquial term for a hoarseness caused by excessive drinking. The colloquialism referred to the mouth, throat, to overindulgence and disease, in other words, to the characteristic grotesque complex. Pantagruel's character is also linked to the broader, cosmic complex of the diableries.

We already know that the diableries were part of the mysteries and that their images had a popular-festive character. The body they presented had a distinctly grotesque form. It was in this grotesque atmosphere that the figure of Pantagruel appeared on the scene.

We first encounter him in a mystery of the second part of the fifteenth century, "The Acts of the Apostles," by Simon Gréban. In the diablerie of this play Proserpina, mother of the devils, brings four of her sons (*petits dyables*) to Lucifer. Each little devil represents one of the four elements: earth, water, air, and fire, and each exercises his specific activity in his own sphere. A broad picture of the elements is thus unfolded. One of the four devils, whose name is Pantagruel and who represents water, says: "I fly over the seas, more sprightly than a bird of prey." During his flights he becomes saturated with sea salt and is therefore related to the substance that causes thirst. In this mystery Lucifer says that at night, awaiting other activities, he throws salt into the mouths of drunkards.

The devil Pantagruel appears in a similar role in another play, *Saint Louis*. He delivers a monologue, relating in great detail that he spent the night among some young men who had been reveling all evening; with great precaution not to awaken them he threw salt into their mouths, and so "Glory be to God, when they awoke they were more thirsty than before!"

This image of Pantagruel as a mystery-play devil is linked on one hand with the cosmic elements water and sea salt and on the other hand with the grotesque image of the body (open mouth, thirst, drunkenness). Finally, he is linked with a purely carnivalesque gesture of throwing salt into an open mouth. All these features, which are the basis of the image of Pantagruel, are closely related to one another. This traditional nucleus was fully retained by Rabelais.

We must specially point out that *Pantagruel* was conceived and written by Rabelais during the unusual heat wave and drought of 1532. Men actually walked with their mouths wide open. Abel Lefranc is right in surmising that the little devil's name and his tricks of causing thirst were often mentioned in Rabelais' entourage, provoking jokes and curses. The weather conditions rendered this image popular. It is quite possible that Rabelais made use of Pantagruel's character because of the drought.

Pantagruel's first chapter immediately introduces the grotesque body with all its characteristic traits. It describes the origin of the giant race to which Pantagruel belongs. After the killing of Abel,

the earth, saturated with his blood, became exceptionally fertile.
Here is the beginning of this first chapter:

You must therefore remember that I speak of the beginning of
the world, of long ages since, of more than forty times forty nights
ago, to reckon as the Druids did.
A little while after Cain slew his brother Abel, the earth, imbued
with the blood of the just, was one year extremely fertile in all
fruits. Medlars were particularly plentiful and large, just three
to the bushel. So that year was recorded in the memory of men as
the year of the great medlars.
(Book 2, Chapter 1)

Such is the first bodily theme of this chapter. Its grossly carnivalesque traits are obvious. The first death (according to the Bible,
Abel was the first man to die) renewed the earth's fertility. Here
we have the combination of killing and birth with which we are
familiar. Death, the dead body, blood as a seed buried in the earth,
rising for another life—this is one of the oldest and most widespread themes. A variant is death inseminating mother earth and
making her bear fruit once more. This variant often produces a
flowering of erotic images (of course, not in the narrow, specific
sense of the word). Rabelais speaks elsewhere of the "sweet, much-
desired embrace of . . . Mother Earth, which we call burial." (Book
Three, Chapter 48). This image of a burial is probably inspired by
Pliny, who gives a detailed picture of the earth's motherhood and
of burial as a return to her womb. ("Natural History," II, 63.)
Rabelais is inclined to conceive this image in all its variations and
nuances, not in the high style of the antique mysteries but in the
carnivalesque, popular-festive spirit: a gay and sober belief in the
relative historic immortality of the people and of himself within
the people.

Thus, the theme of death-renewal-fertility was Rabelais' initial
theme, the opening of his immortal novel (since *Pantagruel* was
the first book to be written). We stress this fact.

The earth became especially rich in medlars (*en mesl*). But men
who ate these medlars began to develop abnormally; one part of
the body would grow to monstrous dimensions. Rabelais presents

a number of typical grotesque forms of exaggerated body parts that completely hide the normal members of the body. This is actually a picture of dismemberment, of separate areas of the body enlarged to gigantic dimensions. First of all, we see men with monstrous bellies (a typical grotesque hyperbola); Saint Pansard (St. Paunchman) and Mardi Gras belong to this gay race. Saint Pansard's ironic name was associated with carnival, and King Carnival, himself, is related to the family of fat paunches. Next, Rabelais depicts hunchbacks with humps of huge proportions, or monstrous noses, abnormally long legs, gigantic ears. There are men with disproportionate phalli (wound six times around their waists) and others with unusually large testes. We have a picture of a giant grotesque body and at the same time an array of carnival figures.

Directly preceding this gallery of grotesque human members, Rabelais pictures cosmic perturbations in the skies, which also have a carnivalesque nature: the star Spica is transferred from Virgo to Libra. But these phenomena are so difficult to understand that the astrologers would merely break their teeth on them. The grotesque image of teeth reaching up to the skies was inspired by the common expression "to chew" a difficult astrological problem.

Further, Rabelais gives a long enumeration of the giants who were Pantagruel's ancestors. We find here a great number of Biblical, antique, medieval, and imaginary names. Rabelais was a connoisseur, possessing a wealth of information on this subject, for the ancient giants had already been listed by the scholar Ravisius Textor, whose works were used by Rabelais. The giants and their legends are closely related to the grotesque conception of the body. We have already pointed out the role of giants in antique satyric drama (which was precisely a drama of the body). Most local legends connect such natural phenomena as mountains, rivers, rocks, and islands with the bodies of giants or with their different organs; these bodies are, therefore, not separated from the world or from nature. We have also pointed out that giants were an indispensable part of popular-festive carnival images.

Such is the content of *Pantagruel*'s first chapter. Grotesque figures are interwoven with cosmic phenomena. The entire array of

the novel's images starts with the theme of death-renewal-fertility.
This theme also opens the second chapter:

> At the age of four hundred fourscore and fourty-four years, Gargantua begat his son Pantagruel upon his wife named Badebec, daughter to the king of the dimly-seen Amaurotes in Utopia. She died in the throes of childbirth. Alas! Pantagruel was so extraordinarily large and heavy that he could not have possibly come to light without suffocating his mother.
> (Book 2, Chapter 2)

This is the theme already familiar to us from the Roman carnival of combined killing and childbirth. Here, the killing is done by the newborn himself, in the very act of his birth.

Birth and death are the gaping jaws of the earth and the mother's open womb. Further on, gaping human and animal mouths will enter into the picture.

The terrible drought which occurred at the time of Pantagruel's birth is described in the novel:

> . . . beasts were found dead in the fields, their mouths agape.
> As for the men, their state was very piteous. You should have seen them with their tongues dangling like a hound's after a run of six hours. Not a few threw themselves into the wells. Others lay under a cow's belly to enjoy the shade . . . . It was hard enough, God knows, to save the holy water in the churches . . . scores of parched, unhappy wretches followed the priest who distributed it, their jaws yawning for one tiny driblet . . . . Ah! thrice happy that year the man who had a cool, well-plenished wine cellar underground.
> (*Ibid.*)

We must point out that the images of the "well," the "cow's belly," and the "cellar" are equivalent to the "gaping mouth." The latter corresponds in grotesque topography to the belly and to the uterus. Thus, side by side with the erotic image of the *trou* (the "hole") the entrance to the underworld is represented: the gaping mouth of Satan, the "jaws of hell." The "well" is a current medieval image of the fruit-bearing womb. The cellar has a similar connotation, with the theme of death, of swallowing down, more strongly accentuated. Thus, the earth and its orifice acquire here an additional grotesque element. This picture prepares the further assimilation of earth and sea as a bodily category.

Rabelais goes on to recall the ancient myth of Phaeton who, driving the sun's chariot, came too near to earth and almost set it on fire; the earth was covered with sweat so that the seas became salty. (Plutarch attributes this explanation to Empidocles.) Rabelais transfers these images from the high mythical level to the gay level of popular-festive degradation:

> Earth at that time was so excessively heated that it broke into an enormous sweat which ran over the sea, making the latter salty, since all sweat is salt. If you do not admit this last statement, then taste of your own sweat. Or savor the perspiration of your pox-stricken friends when they are put in sweat-boxes for treatment. It is all one to me.
> (*Ibid.*)

The entire complex of images composing this passage is extremely characteristic. The typical grotesque image of sweating (similar to other elimination) plays a leading role, and even a cosmic role, since the earth itself sweats and pours its sweat into the sea. Further, we have the image of the merry disease, syphilis, related to the bodily lower stratum. Finally, sweat is related to eating (the taste of sweat); this weakened form of scatophagy is characteristic of medical grotesque (as early as Aristophanes). This passage implicitly contains the traditional nucleus of the little devil Pantagruel, related to the sea element and causing thirst. At the same time, the hero of this passage is the earth. In the first chapter the earth, saturated with the blood of Abel, became fertile and gave birth; in the second chapter it sweats and thirsts.

Rabelais goes on to give a bold parody of a religious procession. During a ceremony organized by the Church, the faithful who were praying for rain suddenly saw drops of heavy sweat appearing on the ground as on the brow of a human being. They thought it was dew sent by heaven in answer to their prayers. But they were mistaken, for when they tried to quench their thirst, they found the liquid was a pickled solution even saltier than sea water. Thus, the miracle deceived the pious people. Here once more, the material bodily element appears in its role of uncrowning.

Precisely on that day and at that hour Pantagruel was born. His name in Rabelais' burlesque etymology means "the all-thirsting one." The hero's birth itself occurs in a grotesque atmosphere; before he emerges from his mother's womb, he is preceded by a caravan of wagons loaded with salted (thirst-arousing) food. Only then does the child Pantagruel appear, "shaggy as a bear." The third chapter develops the ambivalent death-birth theme. Gargantua does not know whether to weep over his wife's death or to laugh with joy at the birth of his son. He now laughs "like a calf" (a newborn animal), or moos "like a cow" (birth-giving and dying).

The fourth chapter tells of Pantagruel's early feats when he was still in his cradle; all of these exploits are acts of devouring and swallowing. At each feeding he sucked the milk of 4,600 cows. He was served his gruel in a gigantic bell. His teeth were already so strong and solid that he chewed off a big portion of his bowl. One morning, wishing to suck one of the cows, he freed one hand from his swaddling clothes and, seizing the cow by its legs, chewed off the udder and half the stomach, as well as the liver and kidneys. The cow was taken away from him, but he held on to one of the legs and swallowed it like a sausage. Another time Gargantua's pet bear came near Pantagruel; he seized it, tore it to pieces and devoured it as if it were a chicken. He was so strong that he had to be chained to his cradle, but one day he appeared carrying the cradle on his back in the hall where Gargantua was presiding over a huge banquet; the child's hands were tied, so he put out his tongue and licked the food off the table.

All these feats are related to sucking, devouring, swallowing, tearing to pieces. We see the gaping mouth, the protruding tongue, the teeth, the gullet, the udder, and the stomach.

We shall continue to analyze some of the more typical banquet images.

In the episode of the Limousin student, Pantagruel seizes him by the throat, which a few years later causes the man to "die the death of Roland," that is, death of thirst. The traditional character of the little devil Pantagruel appears in this episode.

In Chapter 14 we find the following image: During a feast, offered at the end of the lawsuit of My Lords Kissarse and Bumfondle, the drunken Panurge declares:

"God help me, mate, if I could rise up as fast as I swallow down, I would long ago have been above the sphere of the moon with My Lord Empedocles, who was hoisted thither by an eruption of Aetna. But I can't tell what's the matter. This wine is strong and delicious, yet the more I drink, the thirstier I get. I think the mere shadow of My Lord Pantagruel engenders thirst even as the moon produces catarrhs."
(Book 2, Chapter 14)

Let us here point out the topographic content: the highest sphere of the sky and the lower part of the stomach. Once more we also find the traditional nucleus of Pantagruel's image, the arousing of thirst. But in this passage the leading role is played by Pantagruel's shadow (note the similarity to the shadow of the belfry). The grotesque element also appears in the ancient, traditional idea of the influence of the moon (or other heavenly bodies) on diseases.

During the banquet Panurge relates the story we already know, how he was almost roasted alive in Turkey but instead roasted a Turk on a spit, and how he was almost torn to pieces by dogs. He was cured from "toothache" (caused by the dog's teeth) by throwing to the animals the lard in which he had been wrapped. We also find here the image of fire that burned down the Turkish town and an image of a cure by fire: roasting on a spit cured Panurge of rheumatism. This purely carnivalesque scene ends by Panurge's eulogy of the spit and of the roast.

Pantagruel's traditional image reappears in the Thaumastes episode. After his first interview with Pantagruel, Thaumastes was so thirsty that he had to drink wine all night long and rinse his throat with water. During the dispute, when the public began to applaud, Pantagruel shouted at them to hold their peace:

At which they sat there, struck of a heap and blinking like owls. Had they swallowed fifteen pounds of feathers, they would not have

dared cough. The mere sound of his voice so parched their throats that their tongues hung a half-foot out of their mugs. It was as though Pantagruel had salted their throats.
(Book 2, Chapter 18)

In the burning of the knights episode and in the banquet with which we are already familiar we see Pantagruel's gaping mouth. The knight whom he captured was afraid that Pantagruel was going to swallow him up. The giant's gullet was so large that he could have swallowed his prisoner like "a sugared almond," and the knight would appear in his captor's mouth no bigger than a grain of millet in the mouth of an ass.

The war against King Anarchus clearly presents all the leading images of the first chapter: the gaping mouth, the gullet, salt, thirst, and urine (instead of sweat). Pantagruel sends to King Anarchus a captured knight with a casket of euphorbium syrup and red pepper in order to make him thirsty:

King Anarchus barely swallowed one spoonful when a terrific burning seared his mouth, ulcerated his uvula and peeled the whole surface of his tongue. No remedy offered him seemed to bring the slightest relief save incessant drinking; the moment he took the cup from his lips, his tongue scorched. So they kept pouring wine down his throat through a funnel.... Whereupon, the whole host began to booze, guzzle and swill until in the end they fell into a dead sleep, grunting and snoring like hogs.
(Book 2, Chapter 28)

At the same time Pantagruel and his companions made their own preparations in view of the battle. He took 237 casks of wine, filled the ship's dinghy with salt, and attached it to his belt. He then took a dose of a diuretic. Finally, King Anarchus' camp was set on fire while the enemy was asleep after a drunken orgy. The further development of this episode is so characteristic that we quote it in full:

Meanwhile Pantagruel scattered the salt from his dinghy into their gaping mouths in such quantities that the poor wretches barked like foxes.
"Oh, oh, Pantagruel," they hawked. "Why do you add further heat to the firebrands in our throats?"

Suddenly Panurge's drugs began to take effect and Pantagruel felt an imperious need of draining his bladder. So he voided on their camp so freely and torrentially as to drown them all and flood the countryside ten leagues around. We know from history that had his father Gargantua's great mare been present and likewise disposed to piss, the resultant deluge would have made Deucalion's flood seem like a drop in a bucket. A mare of the first water, Gargantua's; it could not relieve itself without making another Rhone or Danube.

The soldiers sallying from the city saw the whole thing.

"The enemy has been hacked to pieces," they exulted. "See the blood run."

But they were mistaken. What they believed in the glow from the burning camp and the dim moonlight to be blood of slaughtered enemies was but the wine from our giant's bladder.

The enemy now awakened thoroughly to see their camp blazing on one hand and Pantagruel's urinal inundation on the other. They were, so to speak, between the fiery devil and the deep Red Sea. Some vowed the end of the world was at hand, bearing out the prophecy that the last judgment would be by fire. Others were certain they were persecuted by the sea-gods Neptune, Proteus, Triton and others. Certainly the waters flowing over them were salty.

(Book 2, Chapter 28)

We see once more all the fundamental images of the book's first chapters, but here the salt liquid is not sweat but urine, and it is not eliminated by the earth but by Pantagruel. However, as a giant Pantagruel acquires a cosmic meaning. The traditional nucleus of the Pantagruel image is hyperbolized: an entire army of gaping mouths, a boat full of salt poured into them, the element of water and the gods of the sea, a flood of salted urine. This is a characteristic interplay of images: urine-blood-seawater. All these images are put together to form the picture of a cosmic catastrophe, the destruction of the world by flood and fire.

Medieval eschatology in this episode is degraded and renewed in the absolute material bodily lower stratum. It is turned into carnivalesque fire that causes the world's rebirth. Let us recall Goethe's feast of fire in the "Roman Carnival," with its cry "Death to thee!" Let us also recall the vision of a world catastrophe in the "prophetic riddle": a flood that is actually nothing but sweat and a world conflagration that turns out to be a kitchen hearth. In our episode all the dividing lines between bodies and objects are erased, even the boundaries between a banquet and war. The banquet, salt, and thirst are the means used for war. Blood is substituted by torrents of urine after a drunken orgy.

We must not forget that urine (as well as dung) is gay matter, which degrades and relieves at the same time, transforming fear into laughter. If dung is a link between body and earth (the laughter that unites them), urine is a link between body and sea. This is why the little devil Pantagruel, who in the mystery play is the incarnation of the salt sea element, becomes in Rabelais' novel the incarnation of the gay element of urine. (Pantagruel's urine, as we shall later see, possesses certain curative properties.) Dung and urine lend a bodily character to matter, to the world, to the cosmic elements, which become closer, more intimate, more easily grasped, for this is the matter, the elemental force, born from the body itself. It transforms cosmic terror into a gay carnival monster.

We must take into consideration the importance of cosmic terror, the fear of the immeasurable, the infinitely powerful. The starry sky, the gigantic material masses of the mountains, the sea, the cosmic upheavals, elemental catastrophies—these constitute the terror that pervades ancient mythologies, philosophies, the systems of images, and language itself with its semantics. An obscure memory of cosmic perturbations in the distant past and the dim terror of future catastrophes form the very basis of human thought, speech, and images. This cosmic terror is not mystic in the strict sense of the word; rather it is the fear of that which is materially huge and cannot be overcome by force. It is used by all religious systems to oppress man and his consciousness. Even the most ancient images of folklore express the struggle against fear, against the memories of the past, and the apprehension of future calamities, but folk images relating to this struggle helped develop true human fearlessness. The struggle against cosmic terror in all its forms[9] and manifestations did not rely on abstract hope or on the eternal spirit, but on the material principle in man himself. Man assimilated the cosmic elements: earth, water, air, and fire; he discovered them and became vividly conscious of them in his own body. He became aware of the cosmos within himself.

This assimilation of cosmic elements within the body was most acutely felt at the time of the Renaissance. It found its theoretical expression in the idea of the microcosm, which was used by Rabelais in Panurge's comments about creditors and debtors quoted earlier. We shall further discuss these aspects of Renaissance philosophy. We must here stress that it was in the material acts and eliminations of the body—eating, drinking, defecation, sexual life —that man found and retraced within himself the earth, sea, air, fire, and all the cosmic matter and its manifestations, and was thus able to assimilate them. Indeed, the images of the material bodily lower stratum have a prevailingly cosmic connotation.

In the sphere of imagery cosmic fear (as any other fear) is defeated by laughter. Therefore dung and urine, as comic matter that can be interpreted bodily, play an important part in these images. They appear in hyperbolic quantities and cosmic dimensions. Cosmic catastrophe represented in the material bodily lower stratum is degraded, humanized, and transformed into grotesque monsters. Terror is conquered by laughter.

[9] The images reflecting this struggle are often interwoven with images of a parallel struggle in the individual body against the memories of an agonizing birth and the fear of the throes of death. Cosmic fear is deeper and more essential. It is hidden in the ancestral body of mankind; this is why it has penetrated to the very basis of language, imagery, and thought. This cosmic terror is more essential and stronger than individual bodily fear of destruction, though both voices often mingle in folklore and especially in literature. Cosmic terror is the heritage of man's ancient impotence in the presence of nature. Folk culture did not know this fear and overcame it through laughter, through lending a bodily substance to nature and the cosmos; for this folk culture was always based on the indestructible confidence in the might and final victory of man. Official culture, on the contrary, often used and even cultivated this fear in order to humiliate and oppress man.

Let us return to the episode of the war against Anarchus. We have a detailed description of Pantagruel's single combat with Werewolf. This is an interplay of similar images. Werewolf advanced with gaping jaws (*la gueule ouverte*), and Pantagruel poured over his enemy some eighteen casks and one tub of salt which stuffed his throat, nose, and eyes. Then Pantagruel hit Werewolf in the groin and spilled some wine; his opponent thought that his bladder was pierced, mistaking the wine for urine.

The next chapter describes the resurrection of Epistemon and his visit to the underworld. If we recall that in bodily topography hell is represented as Lucifer's gaping jaws and that death swallows up and returns the body to the bosom of the earth, it will then become clear that we are still within the sphere of familiar images: the open mouth and womb. The visit to the underworld will be analyzed in detail in the next chapter.

The episode of the war against King Anarchus ends in two images of a purely carnivalesque type.

The first image is a grotesque-utopian banquet "for all the world." When the victors arrived in the land of the Amaurotes, bonfires were lighted everywhere, and tables with tasty food were spread in the streets. It seemed, writes Rabelais, that the times of Saturn had returned. The second image is the uncrowning of King Anarchus in which he is made into a green-sauce crier. Thus the war ends in a carnivalesque banquet and degradation.

The chapter that follows (Book Two, Chapter 32) relates how, during a torrential rain, Pantagruel covered a whole army with his tongue. We have next the description of the journey of the author (Alcofribas) into Pantagruel's mouth. Finding himself inside these gaping jaws, Alcofribas discovers an entirely new unknown world: wide fields, woods, fortified cities, and more than twenty-five kingdoms. The citizens living in Pantagruel's mouth are convinced that their world is more ancient than the earth. Alcofribas spends six months in the giant's mouth; he feeds on the morsels of food that enter it and defecates in Pantagruel's throat.

This episode, inspired by Lucian ("True Stories"), is an excellent conclusion to the series of images of the gaping mouth already described. Pantagruel's mouth contains an entire universe, a kind of buccal underworld. Like Epistemon's Hades, this hell is also organized as a world "turned inside out." Here, for instance, men are paid not for working but for sleeping.

The story of a universe older than earth expresses the idea of the relativity of the evaluation of time and space, presented in its grotesque aspect.

Chapter 33 tells about Pantagruel's sickness and recovery. He had stomach trouble, and during his sickness his abundant urine formed hot springs, of therapeutic value, in various parts of France and Italy. Here, once more, Pantagruel symbolizes a gay cosmic element.

The episode further relates the story of the descent into Pantagruel's stomach in order to clean it. Men armed with picks, shovels, and baskets are enclosed in a copper globe that Pantagruel swallows like a pill. (Note the image of swallowing.) Once inside the stomach, the visitors climb out of their globe and do their cleaning operation. Like Pantagruel's mouth in the preceding chapter, his stomach has enormous, almost cosmic dimensions.

In the concluding chapter of the Second Book we find more grotesque images of the body. The chapter contains a plan of the next parts of the novel. Among the projected episodes is the destruction of the underworld by Pantagruel, who tosses Proserpina into the fire and breaks Lucifer's four teeth and one horn. Further, the plan includes Pantagruel's journey to the moon in order to ascertain whether during its decline the three quarters of the moon are hidden in the heads of women.

Thus, from beginning to end this book of the novel presents as its main theme the images of the open mouth, the gullet, the teeth, and the tongue. The gaping jaws belong to the traditional nucleus of the devilkin Pantagruel in the mystery.

This image is organically combined on the one hand with swallowing and devouring, on the other hand with the stomach, the womb, and childbirth. At the same time the banquet images, as well as those of death, destruction, and hell are also related to this system.

Finally, the open mouth is linked with another basic element of Pantagruel's traditional image, a composite of thirst, water, wine, and urine.

All the main organs and areas, as well as all the basic acts of the grotesque body, are pictured and developed around the central image of the gaping jaws. This is the most vivid expression of the body as not impenetrable but open. Further, the gaping jaws are a wide entrance leading into the depths of the body, and these characters are accentuated by the fact that an entire inhabited universe is located in Pantagruel's mouth and that people can descend into the stomach as into an underground mine. The same features (gaping jaws and depths) also appear in the open womb of Pantagruel's mother, as well as in the image of the earth that has absorbed the blood of Abel and the image of the underworld. The bodily depths are fertile; the old dies in them, and the new is born in abundance. The entire Second Book is saturated with pictures of procreative force, fertility, abundance. The phallus and the codpiece (as a substitute for the phallus) constantly appear within this open sphere. The grotesque body has no façade, no impenetrable surface, neither has it any expressive features. It represents either the fertile depths or the convexities of procreation and conception. It swallows and generates, gives and takes.

Such a body, composed of fertile depths and procreative convexities is never clearly differentiated from the world but is transferred, merged, and fused with it. It contains, like Pantagruel's mouth, new unknown spheres. It acquires cosmic dimensions, while the cosmos acquires a bodily nature. Cosmic elements are transformed into the gay form of the body that grows, procreates, and is victorious.

Pantagruel was conceived and written during the misfortunes suffered by France in 1532. True, these misfortunes were not catastrophic, but they were serious enough to affect the people's consciousness and to awaken their cosmic terror and eschatological expectations. Rabelais' book was a merry answer to these fears and pious moods. Once again we have a remarkable example of a Renaissance piece of journalism based on the popular tradition of the marketplace. It is a militant echo of the events and thoughts of that historic period.

In 1532, as we have said, there was a long and intense spell of hot weather and drought which lasted for six months, until September. The dry weather threatened the crops and especially the vineyards. Because of these conditions, the Church organized many religious ceremonies and processions, reflected in the parodies at the beginning of the novel. In the autumn of the year the plague broke out in various parts of France and lasted throughout the following year. There is an allusion to the plague in *Pantagruel,* where it is explained as the result of lethal vapors arising from Pantagruel's sick stomach.

The unfortunate weather conditions and the plague awakened a cosmic terror, like that of the fourteenth century, a terror related to a system of eschatological images and mystical ideas. But natural catastrophes, like other catastrophes, usually also awaken historical criticism and lead to a revision of all dogmatic positions (as in the case of Boccaccio and Langland in the fourteenth century). Something similar, though in a less drastic form, took place when *Pantagruel* was written. The historic events served as a starting point for Rabelais' novel. It is quite possible that the image of the devilkin Pantagruel, who makes men thirsty, and the very tonality of this figure were born from the free colloquial element of the marketplace and from the familiarity of table talk. For the devilkin was the object of gay curses intended for the world and for nature; he was the hero of the free parodies of eschatology, divine providence, and world catastrophes. But around this central figure Rabelais accumulated an enormous mass of material from the culture of folk humor developed during thousands of years: a culture that reflected the struggle against cosmic terror and created the image of the gay, material bodily cosmos, ever-growing and self-renewing.

The Second Book is the most cosmic. This element is not as strong in the other books in which the historic, social and political themes are emphasized. But the overcoming of cosmic fear and eschatology still remains a leading theme to the end of the novel.

In the development of this theme the grotesque body plays a most important part. It is the people's growing and ever-victorious body that is "at home" in the cosmos. It is the cosmos' own flesh and blood, possessing the same elemental force but better organized. The body is the last and best word of the cosmos, its leading force. Therefore it has nothing to fear. Death holds no terror for it. The death of the individual is only one moment in the triumphant life of the people and of mankind, a moment indispensable for their renewal and improvement.

Let us now examine some of the sources of the grotesque body, confining ourselves to Rabelais' immediate source material. The grotesque concept of the body lived especially in the familiar and colloquial forms of the language. The grotesque was the basis of all the abuses, uncrownings, teasing, and impertinent gestures (as pointing at the nose or the buttocks, spitting, and others). Finally, this conception of the body is contained in the most varied types of folklore. These patterns were scattered everywhere and were easily understood and familiar to all Rabelais' contemporaries. The groups of sources we intend to examine are but the separate characteristic expressions of this prevailing form, directly related to the theme of Rabelais' novel.

Let us first look at the legend of the giants. This is an essentially grotesque image of the body, but of course the theme can be more or less developed.

In the *roman de chevalerie,* which was widely known, the giants had almost entirely lost their grotesque character. They symbolized in most cases unusual physical strength and allegiance to the lord who had conquered them.

In the Italian heroic-comic tradition of Pulci (*Il Morgante Maggiore*) and especially of Folengo (*Fracassus*), the grotesque features of the giants, transferred from the genre of chivalry, reappear once more. The Italian tradition of comic giants was well known to Rabelais and must be considered as one of his sources.

But the direct source was, as we know, the chapbook entitled "The Great Chronicles of Gargantua" (1532). This anonymous work contains certain travestied elements reflecting the King Arthur cycle; it does not represent, however, a parody in the modern sense of the word. The giant image has here a strong grotesque bodily character. The chapbook was inspired by the oral folk legend of Gargantua, which lived in folk tradition up to the time of the "Great Chronicles" and continues to live in its oral form even today, not only in France but also in England. The different versions of the "Chronicles" were written down in the nineteenth century and collected in the book of Paul Sébillot, *Gargantua dans les traditions populaires*, 1883. Contemporary *berrichon* legends of Gargantua and other giants are contained in the book of Jean Baffier, *Nos Géants d'autrefois, Récits berrichons*, Paris, 1920. Even in the late oral tradition Gargantua's image preserves a completely grotesque bodily character. The giant's enormous appetite is brought out first of all. Even today we hear the French expression *quel Gargantua!* (what a glutton!).

All the legends of giants are closely related to the relief of the locality where the story is told. The legend always finds a visible, obvious support in the physical setting; the dismembered, scattered, or flattened body of the giant is discovered in the natural landscape. Even in modern France a great number of rocks, stones, megalithic formations, dolmens, and menhirs have been named after Gargantua; we have Gargantua's finger, tooth, cup, armchair, stick, etc. This is actually a Rabelaisian complex of the giant's chopped members, of his kitchen utensils and other paraphernalia. In Rabelais' time this world of rock and stone was, of course, much larger.

The parts of the giants' dismembered bodies and their houseware, scattered throughout France, had an obviously grotesque character; they could not fail to exercise an influence on Rabelais' images. Thus mention is made in *Gargantua* of the gigantic bowl in which the young hero ate his gruel, and the author adds that the bowl can still be seen at Bourges. There is nothing which reminds us of Gargantua in the modern city, but a sixteenth-century document states that there was in Bourges an immense rock scooped out like a bowl which was known as *Scutella gigantis*, the giant's cup. Once a year wine merchants filled it with wine for the poor. Rabelais borrowed his image from true life.[10]

Besides the bodily grotesque of the "Great Chronicles," we must also recall "Pantagruel's Disciple," an anonymous book published in 1537. This work reflected the influence of Rabelais' novel as well as of Lucian's "True Stories." But we also find in it popular-festive elements and the influence of the oral tradition of legendary giants. This work had in its turn an influence on Rabelais.

We must stress the role of popular-festive giants. They were common figures in the shows produced at fairs, in which they still appear in our days together with midgets. The giant was also the protagonist of carnival parades and of the processions of Corpus Christi. At the end of the Middle Ages a number of cities that employed permanent "town jesters" also had permanent "town giants" and even "families of giants," paid by the city and obliged to take part in all the pageantries. This institution of town giants in a number of cities and villages of Northern France and Belgium, for instance, in Lille, Douai, and Kassel, was maintained up to the nineteenth century. In Kassel a celebration was held in 1835 to commemorate the famine of 1638; on that feast a giant distributed free soup to the people. This connection of the giant with food is characteristic. In Belgium there were festive "giants' songs" closely relating the giant to the family hearth and to cooking.

The figure of the giant as part of folk festivals and carnivals was, of course, familiar to Rabelais. He also knew the local legends that have not survived in our time. His novel mentions the names of giants connected with eating and swallowing: Happemousche, Engolevent, Maschefain, and others.

Finally, he was familiar with the giants of antiquity, especially with Euripides' cyclopes, which are twice mentioned in his novel.

Such are Rabelais' sources. We may conjecture that the popular-

[10] Considerable folklore material concerning the broken body of stone and the stoneware of the giant is given by Salomon Reinach, *Cultes, Mythes et Religions*, Vol. 3: *Les monuments de pierre brute dans le langage et les croyances populaires*, pp. 364–433; see also P. Sébillot, *Le Folklore de France*, Vol. 1, pp. 300–412.

festive giants were the most important in his eyes. They enjoyed immense vogue, were familiar to everyone, and were saturated with the free atmosphere of the marketplace. They were closely connected with the popular conception of material-bodily wealth and abundance. The image and the atmosphere of the giant appearing at the fairs doubtless contributed to the shaping of the Gargantuan legend of the "Great Chronicles." The influence of popular giants of fairs and marketplaces on the first two books of Rabelais' novel is quite obvious.

As to the "Great Chronicles," its influence was mainly external and was actually reduced to a few topical themes.

An important source for grotesque-bodily images is the cycle of legends and literary works related to the so-called "Indian Wonders." This cycle had a definite influence on all medieval works of fantasy. We also find this direct or indirect influence in Rabelais' novel. Let us briefly recall the history of this tradition.

The first collector of tales about the wonders of India was Ctesias, a Greek who lived in Persia in the fifth century before Christ. Ctesias assembled all the stories concerning India, its treasures, wondrous flora and fauna, and the extraordinary bodily forms of its inhabitants. This collection has not been preserved, but it was used by Lucian in his "True Stories," by Pliny, Isidore of Seville, and others.

In the second century of our era the *Physiologus* was compiled in Alexandria; this was a natural history book combined with legends and "wonders." The *Physiologus* describes minerals, plants, and animals. The natural kingdom is presented in a most grotesque combination. The book was widely used during the following centuries, especially by Isidore of Seville, whose work served as a source for the medieval bestiary.

A compilation of all this legendary material was made in the third century by Callisthenes. There are two Latin versions of his work, one by Julius Valerius composed about A.D. 300 and the other entitled "The History of the Wars of Alexander the Great," dating from the tenth century. A further compilation of the Callisthenes legends was included in all cosmographic works of the Middle Ages, by Brunetto Latini and Gautier of Metz, among others. All these works are deeply imbued with the grotesque conception of the body basically inherited from the "Indian Wonders."

These legends were later included in the stories of travels, real (as in the case of Marco Polo), or imaginary (as in Sir John Mandeville's popular book). In the fourteenth century all these travels were collected under the title of *Merveilles du monde*, "Wonders of the World." This manuscript contains interesting miniatures representing typical grotesque human figures. Finally, the "wonders" were incorporated in a poem, *Le Roman d'Alexandre*, composed in Alexandrian verse.

Thus was this legend built and spread. It determined the themes of numerous works of medieval pictorial art.

What are the main features of the "Indian Wonders"? The legend describes India's fantastic wealth and extraordinary natural resources, as well as its purely fictitious phenomena: devils spitting fire, magic herbs, enchanted woods, fountains of youth. The description of animals is quite extensive. In addition to real species are fantastic beasts much as harpies, unicorns, and phoenixes. Mandeville depicts a griffin in great detail and Brunetto Latini a dragon.

But most important of all in our mind is the description of extraordinary human beings. These creatures have a distinctive grotesque character. Some of them are half human, half animal: the hippopods with hoofs instead of feet, sirens with fishtails, "sinucephalics" who bark like dogs, satyrs, and onocentaurs. This is an entire gallery of images with bodies of mixed parts. There are also giants, dwarfs, and pygmies. There are various monsters: the "scipedes" who have only one leg, "leumans" without a head and with a face on the chest, cyclopes with one eye on the forehead, others with eyes on their shoulders or on their backs, creatures with six arms, and others who feed through their noses, and so forth. All this constitutes a wild anatomical fantasy, so popular in the Middle Ages.

Rabelais loved this fantasy, this free play with the human body and with its organs, one recalls the pygmies born from Pantagruel's flatus, whose hearts were located in the rectal area, or the monstrous children of Antiphyses and the famous Carême-prenant. In all these images we find a fanciful anatomy.

An important feature of the "Indian Wonders" is their relation to the underworld. The numerous demons who appear in India's woods and valleys, according to the legend, led medieval writers to believe that the entrance to hell was hidden in this land. They were also convinced that the earthly paradise, the first abode of Adam and Eve, was located in India, some three days' journey from the Fountain of Youth. It was said that Alexander the Great had found there "the abode of the just," in which they would be enclosed until the Day of Judgment. The legend of Prester John and his kingdom (which was also set in India) tells of the roads leading to the underworld and to the earthly paradise. The river Phizon flowed from paradise through Prester John's kingdom. The roads and the orifices or holes (*trous*) leading respectively to paradise and hell lend a special character to these wondrous lands and reflect the peculiar artistic and ideological conception of space in the Middle Ages. The earth, consisting of mountains and precipices, was constructed like a grotesque body. The impenetrable surface of the earth was constantly broken up by a tendency to rise or descend into the depths, into the underworld. In these depths and orifices another world was believed to exist, like the one contained in Pantagruel's mouth. While traveling on earth, men sought the gates or doors to these "other" dimensions. The classic expression of this search is the remarkable "Journey of Saint Brendan," which will be discussed in our next chapter. In popular legends mountains and precipices acquired more or less bodily features.

All this created the specific character of medieval topography and a peculiar interpretation of the cosmos. We shall return later to this subject.

The cycle of legends contained in the "Indian Wonders" was extremely popular in the Middle Ages. This cycle not only influenced the cosmographic literature in the broad sense, including the travelogues, but also affected all medieval writings. Moreover, the "Indian Wonders" were strongly reflected in pictorial art; the legends inspired the miniatures that illustrated the manuscripts, as well as frescoes and sculptures in churches and cathedrals.

Thus because of the "Indian Wonders" the eyes and imagination of medieval man were accustomed to the grotesque body. Both in literature and pictorial art, the body of mixed parts and the strangest anatomical fantasies, the free play with the human limbs and interior organs were unfolded before him. The transgression of the limits dividing the body from the world also became customary.

The "Indian Wonders" are therefore an important source of the grotesque conception of the body. We must add that these legends were still alive and stimulated interest in the time of Rabelais.

In the last chapter of *Pantagruel* Rabelais tells the story of his hero's voyage to the land of Prester John (India). This journey was to be immediately followed by the destruction of the underworld, and the entrance to hell was precisely located in the Prester's land. In the novel's initial plan the "Wonders" were to play an important part. The direct and indirect influence of this legend is clearly reflected in anatomical fantasies.

Another important source of the grotesque concept was the medieval mystery and, of course, the diablerie that was part of it. This genre often concerned itself with dismembered bodies, their roasting, burning, and swallowing. For instance, in the mystery "The Acts of the Apostles" we meet for the first time the devilkin Pantagruel. Lucifer orders his devils to burn several heretics, adding a long description of the methods to be used for their roasting. In "The Mystery of St. Quentin" there is a long enumeration of verbs (more than one hundred of them) referring to bodily tortures: the victims were to be burned, mutilated, torn apart, and so forth. We have here a grotesque dismemberment, an anatomization. Rabelais describes a devouring of sinful souls which is obviously inspired by the diablerie. We have already mentioned the grotesque bodily character of the devils and of their gestures, as shown in these medieval performances.

The very structure of the sets used in the mysteries was an im-

portant source of the concept of the grotesque body. In these plays
the stage reflected the medieval idea of the world's position in
space. The front of the stage presented a platform that occupied
the entire first floor of the structure and symbolized the earth. The
backdrop was formed by an elevated set which represented heaven
or paradise.[11] Beneath the platform representing the earth there
was a large opening, indicating hell, covered by a broad curtain
decorated with a huge mask of the devil (Harlequin). When the
curtain was pulled back, the devils jumped out of Satan's gaping
jaws, or sometimes out of his eyes, and landed on earth. In 1474
the author of a mystery gave these stage directions, "Hell must be
represented in the form of huge jaws which open and shut when
needed."[12]

Thus the gaping jaws, located in the very center of the stage and
at the level of the spectators' eyes, were familiar to every mystery-
play audience. The medieval public centered its curiosity on them,
expecting the most amusing and comic protagonists to emerge from
them. (The diableries, as the popular billingsgate part of the mysteries, always enjoyed great success and sometimes eclipsed the rest
of the performance.)

Considering the immense intrinsic value of this three-level stage
in the artistic and ideological life of the Middle Ages, we may assert that the "jaws of hell" were merged with the image of the
world itself, as well as with its dramatic, theatrical conception.

Otto Driesen devoted some excellent pages of his book "The
Origins of Harlequin"[13] to the dramatic projection of this figure;
he presents on page 149 a sketch of a seventeenth-century ballet
preserved in the archives of the Paris Opera. At the very center of

[11] This word is still used in French and Russian for the top gallery
of the theater.

[12] See also the description of a scene of the Passion performed in
Valencienne in 1547, in an addendum to *Histoire de la langue et de la
littérature française, des origines à 1900,* Petit de Julleville, 1896–1899,
Vol. 2, pp. 415–417.

[13] Otto Driesen, *Der Ursprung des Harlekin,* 1904.

the stage we see a gigantic head with gaping jaws. Inside the jaws sits a female devil, two devils look through the monster's eyes, a devil sits astride each of its ears, while devils and clowns dance around it. The sketch proves that this image and the dramatic events related to it were still quite usual and fully understood. Among other things, Driesen points out that even in his own times the expression "Harlequin's cloak" (*manteau d'Arlequin*) was still used in the Paris theaters, meaning the entire front of the stage.

The topography of the medieval stage had, as we see, a basically grotesque bodily connotation. It is obvious that the gaping mouth, as a leading image in *Pantagruel,* is not only related to the traditional symbolism of this hero (scattering of salt, for example) but also to the structure of the stage. Rabelais' organization of the novel's imagery reflects this topography. As far as we know, no author of Rabelaisiana has stressed the leading role of the gaping mouth in the novel's First Book or compared it with the organization of the mystery stage. Yet this comparison is of great importance for the correct understanding of these books, since it proves the influence of the popular theatrical forms on Rabelais' initial work as well as on the entire character of his artistic and ideological vision and thought. It also proves that the gaping mouth in its grotesque cosmic meaning, which may appear so strange and difficult to understand for the modern reader, was quite familiar and understandable for Rabelais' contemporaries. It was completely ordinary in their eyes; equally familiar was its universal, cosmic connotation. Neither were the men of that time surprised to see grotesque figures jump out of this mouth and land on the stage, on which events from the Bible and the Gospels were dramatized. The topographical meaning of this image was also understood as representing the gates of the underworld. Such was the influence of the mystery and the diablerie on Rabelais' own concept of the body.

A certain influence on the grotesque concept of the body was exercised by relics, which had great significance in the medieval world. It can be said that various parts of the saints' bodies were scattered over France and indeed throughout the medieval Christian world. There was no small church or monastery that did not preserve a relic, at times a quite unusual one (a drop of milk from the Blessed Virgin's breast or the sweat of a saint, as mentioned by Rabelais). Arms, legs, heads, teeth, hair, and fingers were venerated. It would be possible to give a long grotesque enumeration of all these parts of a dismembered body. At the time of Rabelais the ridiculing of relics was common, especially in Protestant satire. Even the agelast Calvin wrote a pamphlet about relics with a certain comic overtone.

In medieval literature the dismembered bodies of saints were often an occasion for grotesque images and enumerations. In one of the best medieval parodies, "The Treatise of García of Toledo," which we have already mentioned, the hero, a wealthy simonist bishop from Toledo, brings to Rome a present for the Pope, the miraculous relics of the saintly martyrs Ruphinus and Albinus. In the language of medieval travesties the names of these nonexistent saints mean gold and silver. The story describes the Pope's particular devotion to the martyrs. He praises them and asks that all their precious remains should be brought to him; there follows a grotesque enumeration of the various parts of the dismembered bodies: "from Ruphinus' kidneys, Albinus' intestines, from stomach, back, rump, ribs, chest, legs, and arms; and all the members of the saints." We see that, as early as the eleventh century, relics were the object of parody.

Medieval recreational literature was rich in anatomical grotesque. We have already spoken of the parodies in which grammatical categories were listed in terms of the lower stratum. The renewal of abstract categories and philosophical conceptions was characteristic of the recreational genre. In the famous dialogue of Solomon and Morolf (quoted by Gargantua), Solomon's exalted proverbs are countered by the clown Morolf's answers; the latter transfers most of the questions to a coarse material bodily level.

Let us cite another interesting example of medieval grotesque anatomy. From the thirteenth century on, a poem entitled "The Ass's Will" was widely known over Europe. A dying ass bequeaths the parts of his body to various social and professional groups, beginning with the Pope and cardinals. The dismemberment here corresponds to the divisions of the social hierarchy: the ass's head is for the Pope, the ears for the cardinals, the voice for the choir, the feces for the peasants, etc. The source of this parody is very ancient. According to Jerome, a satire called "The Pig's Will" (*Testamentum porcelli*) was popular among schoolmen as early as the fourth century. This parody was copied in the Middle Ages and has been preserved. It was apparently the source of "The Ass's Will."

In these satires it is interesting to note the combination of the dismemberment of the body and of society. This is a travesty of the widespread mythical concept of the origin of various social groups from various parts of a god's body. (The oldest monument of this social topography is the *Rig-Veda*.) In most cases this is a dismembered body.[14] But here, instead of a god's body, we have the body of an ass; this is an ancient traditional travesty of the divinity. In medieval parodies its organs and its braying, as well as the shouts of its drivers play an important part. We hear these shouts in Rabelais' novel. There are several mentions of the abusive term: "*viédaze,*" the ass's phallus. The topographical character of this abusive expression is quite obvious. Let us recall Rabelais' remark: "This is as difficult as to extract a certain sound (*pet*) from the bottom of

14 The *Rig-Veda* pictures the birth of the world from the body of the man Purusha; the gods sacrificed him and cut up his body, according to the method of sacrificial dismemberment. Various social groups were thus created from the various parts of Purusha's body, as well as from certain cosmic phenomena. From his mouth appeared the Brahmans, from his arms soldiers, from his eyes the sun, from his head the sky, from his feet the earth, etc. In the christianized Germanic mythology we find a similar conception, but here the body is composed of the various parts of the universe. Adam's body is composed of flesh from the earth, bones from the stones, blood from the sea, hair from plants, and thoughts from clouds.

a dead ass." This is a peculiar method of raising to the highest degree the topographical lowest level: the rump of an ass and moreover of a dead ass. Such abuses are often found in Rabelais.

Oaths, curses, and various abusive expressions are a source of considerable importance for the grotesque concept of the body. We have already spoken at length of these forms of speech and will limit ourselves to a few additional considerations.

Each abusive expression always contains in some topographical and bodily aspect the image of pregnant death. Our analysis of *Pantagruel* showed that one of the main themes of this book is the theme of birth-giving death: for instance, the first death renewing the earth's fertility and the birth of Pantagruel which caused his mother's suffocation. This theme presents continual variations of bodily topographical images. It was further transposed, without losing its bodily character, into the theme of historic death and renewal: the burning of the knights, the transformation of death and war into a banquet, the uncrowning of King Anarchus. Strictly speaking, and however paradoxical this may seem, the episodes are but a widely developed form of abusive language. The entire world is shown as a pregnant and regenerating death.

In the popular-festive carnival atmosphere in which Rabelais' images were constructed, the abusive expressions were like sparks flying in different directions from the great conflagration that renewed the world. Ominously enough, each extinguished candle of the *moccoli* festival was accompanied by the cry of "Death to thee," which had a joyous overtone. The gay abuses and curses and the mocking of cosmic forces had initially a cultic character, but they were later to play an essential role in the system of images reflecting the struggle against cosmic terror and every other kind of fear of superior powers. For the ancient cultic abuse and derision were precisely directed against these superior powers of the sun, the earth, the king, the military leader. This defiance was preserved in the billingsgate of Rabelais' time.

The comic performers of the marketplace were an important source of the grotesque image of the body. They formed a huge and motley world that we can only touch upon here. All these jugglers, acrobats, vendors of panaceas, magicians, clowns, trainers of monkeys, had a sharply expressed grotesque bodily character. Even today this character has been most fully preserved in marketplace shows and in the circus.

Unfortunately, the popular French comic forms are better known in their later manifestations (starting with the seventeenth century) when they were already influenced by the Italian improvised comedy. True, this comedy also preserved the comic concept of the body, but in a weakened form determined by purely literary trends. On the other hand, in the *lazzi* (the nontopical tricks of this comedy) the grotesque was fully developed.

We analyzed at the beginning of this chapter the scene from the Italian comedy presenting Harlequin and the stutterer. The comic nature of this scene consists in the fact that the utterance of a difficult word is enacted as childbirth. This is typical of popular comic creation. The entire logic of the grotesque movements of the body (still to be seen in shows and circus performances) is of a topographical nature. The system of these movements is oriented in relation to the upper and lower stratum; it is a system of flights and descents into the lower depths. Their simplest expression is the primeval phenomenon of popular humor, the cartwheel, which by the continual rotation of the upper and lower parts suggests the rotation of earth and sky. This is manifested in other movements of the clown: the buttocks persistently trying to take the place of the head and the head that of the buttocks.

Another expression of this principle is the important role of the inside out and upside down in the movements and acts of the grotesque body. A deeper and more subtle analysis would disclose in many traditional popular comic gestures and tricks a mimicking of childbirth such as we observed in the little Italian scene. Moreover, the great majority of these traditional gestures and tricks is based on the mimicking of the three main acts in the life of the grotesque body: sexual intercourse, death throes (in their comic presentation—hanging tongue, expressionless popping eyes, suffocation, death rattle), and the act of birth. Frequently these three acts are transformed or merged into each other insofar as their exterior symptoms and expressions coincide (spasms, tensions, popping eyes, sweat, convulsions of arms and legs). This is a peculiar mimicking of death-resurrection; the same body that tumbles into the grave rises again, incessantly moving from the lower to the upper level (the usual trick of the clown simulating death and revival). Bodily topography of folk humor is closely interwoven with cosmic topography. The organization of the stage of the show and the circus ring displays the same topographical structure as the stage of the mystery: the earth, the underworld, and heaven (but, of course, without the Christian connotation of the mystery setting). We also find the cosmic elements in these shows: the air (acrobatic feats and stunts), water (swimming), earth, and fire.

The grotesque character is also seen in the form of the body. We have mentioned Gros Guillaume, symbolizing bread and wine. The forms of Fat William typify the usual tendency of the popular comic figure to efface the confines between the body and surrounding objects, between the body and the world, and to accentuate one grotesque part, stomach, buttocks, or the mouth.

In the oral popular comic repertory we also find everywhere the reflection of the grotesque concept of the body: specific obscenities, debasing parodies, abuse and cursing, and dismembered parts. It is obvious that the comic folk element was one of Rabelais' main sources.

A few words about epic grotesque anatomy. The ancient and medieval epics and the *roman de chevalerie* did not ignore the grotesque concept of the body. Images of dismemberment and detailed anatomic descriptions of wounds and deaths became *de rigeur* in these epics influenced by Homer and Virgil. Ronsard writes in his preface to *La Franciade*, "If you wish a soldier or an officer to die on the battlefield, he must be smitten at the most sensitive part of his body and you must be a good anatomist to draw such a picture."

Rabelais was considerably influenced by Pliny, Athenaeus, Macrobius, and Plutarch, that is, by the representatives of ancient prandial talks. In these talks we find scattered the main images of the grotesque body and of grotesque bodily processes; they contain such leading themes as copulation, pregnancy, birth, eating, drinking, and death.

But of all the ancient authors, Hippocrates, or more correctly speaking, the "Hippocratic anthology" exercised the greatest influence on Rabelais, an influence that extended not only to his philosophic and medical views but even to his imagery and style. This was because Hippocrates' thought and that of the other authors of the anthology contain more images than conceptual traits.

The "Hippocratic anthology" is far from homogeneous. It contains works representing different schools; from the philosophic and medical point of view we find essential differences in the understanding of the human body, the nature of diseases, and methods of treatment. But in spite of these differences, all the works contained in the anthology present a grotesque image of the body; the confines dividing it from the world are obscured, and it is most frequently shown open and with its interior exposed. Its exterior aspect is not distinct from the inside, and the exchange between the body and the world is constantly emphasized. The organism's various eliminations, which so often appear in the grotesque, also acquire here a great significance.

It was in the doctrine of the four elements that the confines of the body and the world are effaced. Here is an excerpt from the work entitled "The Winds" (De flatibus):

The bodies of men and other living beings are sustained by three kinds of nourishment; the names of these nourishments are as follows: food, drink, spirit [pneuma]. The spirits which live in the bodies are called winds, and those outside are called air. The latter is the greatest master of all and everything and it is important to consider its strength. In fact, the wind is the current and flow of air. Therefore, when abundant air produces a strong current, its breath unroots the trees from the earth, the waves rise on the sea, and huge, heavily-laden ships are tossed to and fro. . . . In truth, that which lies between heaven and earth is filled with spirit, which is the cause of winter and summer; it is cold and concentrated in winter, soft and calm in summer. Moreover, the spirit directs the way of the sun, moon, and stars. For the spirit is the fuel of fire, and the latter cannot exist without it, so that the spirit, which is eternal and subtle per se causes the eternal course of the sun. Why the air has so much power over everything else has already been said. But for mortals too, it is the cause of life, and for the sick the cause of sickness. And for all, so great is the need of spirit that if a man abstains from food and drink, he can still go on living for two or three days and more; but if he closes the path of the spirit to his body, he will die on that very day, so great is the need of that spirit for the body. . . . But air must also enter with many foods, for with all that is eaten and drunk, the spirit penetrates in a more or less large quantity. This is obvious from the fact that many persons belch when eating and drinking, doubtless because the imprisoned air escapes, breaking the bubbles in which it was enclosed.

The author of this work considers air the basic element of the body. But he conceives this element, of course, not in its depersonalized physicochemical form but in its concrete and obvious manifestations: wind tossing heavily laden ships, air directing the movement of the sun and stars. Cosmic life and the life of the human body are drawn intimately together by this element of man's existence. They are offered in their obvious unity of imagery; both the movement of the sun and belching are caused, for example, by the same concrete and perceptible air. In other works contained in the anthology, water and fire are presented as intermediaries between the body and the cosmos.

In the essay "Air, water and localities" (*De aere, aquis, locis*) we find the following passage:

Concerning the earth, conditions are similar to those of human beings. Indeed, wherever seasons bring about considerable and frequent changes, the locality also presents wild and contrasting aspects: many wooded hills as well as fields and meadows. But wherever seasons do not vary too much, the land is uniform. Similar conditions prevail among men. Indeed, some people are like mountains, others have the nature of meadows and lakes, while still others resemble valleys and bare regions, because the seasons which bring external variety to nature differ from each other, and if they differ among themselves, they will also produce many different men.

In this passage the confines between the body and the world are eased along yet another line: the relationship and concrete resemblance of man to the natural landscape. In one part of the anthology entitled "The number seven" we find an even more grotesque image. This essay represents the earth as a huge human body; the head is formed by the Peloponnesus, the spine by the Isthmus, and so on. Each geographical part of the earth and each land corresponds to a definite part of the body; all the physical and spiritual features and way of life of the population depend on their anatomical localization.

Ancient medicine, as reflected in the "Hippocratic anthology," lent great importance to bodily eliminations. In the physician's eyes the body was first of all represented by the elimination of urine, feces, sweat, mucus, and bile. Further, all symptoms were linked with the last moments of the patient's life and with his death and were interpreted as the issue of the struggle within the patient's body. As signs of this struggle between life and death, the smallest bodily manifestations were placed on the same level and were conferred the same importance as the heavenly constellations, and as the mores and customs of various peoples. Here is an excerpt from the first book of "Epidemics":

Concerning the circumstances of the diseases on which the diagnoses must be founded, we shall discover them from the general nature of all the people as well as from the particular nature of each man . . . and, moreover, from the general and individual condition of the heavenly bodies and of each land, from the customs, diet, way of life of each patient, from his speech, silence, thoughts, sleep or insomnia, dreams, their nature and when they occur, from rash, tears, paroxysms, eliminations, urine, mucosities, vomit. It is also necessary to observe the crisis occurring in diseases, to find out from where they stem and what is their nature, to study the chemical deposits leading to death or damage, sweat, aigue, low bodily temperature, coughing, sneezing, hiccups, breath, winds, either silent or with sound, hemorrhages, hemorrhoids.

This excerpt is characteristic of the "Anthology"; it places on one level the symptoms of life and death; these symptoms vary in rank of importance and in cosmic overtones, from the patient's sneezing and winds to the condition of the heavenly bodies. No less characteristic is the dynamic list enumerating the body's eliminations. Such lists, doubtless inspired by Hippocrates, are found in Rabelais' novel. Panurge praises the virtues of "greensauce" in just this manner:

... finally, it set the belly in apple-pie order, so a man could belch, fart, poop, piddle, shit, sneeze, sob, cough, throw up, yawn, puff, inhale, exhale, snore, snort, sweat and wangle the ferrule to his heart's content. ...
(Book 3, Chapter 2)

Let us recall the famous *facies hippocratica* (the Hippocratic features). Here the face has no subjective expression, it does not reflect the patient's thoughts but only the objective fact of the approach of death. Life and death speak in it; it belongs to the supraindividual sphere of the ancestral life of the body. The face and body of the dying man lose their identity. The degree of the face's resemblance to itself determines the degree of death's proximity or remoteness. Here is a remarkable excerpt from the "Prognostics":

In acute diseases it is necessary to make the following observations: first of all as to the patient's face: does it resemble or not the face of persons in good health, and especially does it resemble itself? For the latter sign should be considered the best, and the lack of this resemblance presents the greatest danger. The face will then offer the following aspect: sharp nose, sunken eyes and hollow temples, ears cold and taut, the ear-lobes twisted, the skin on the forehead taut and dry, the color of the face greenish, dark or leaden.
... If the eyelid is wrinkled or turns blue or pale, as well as lips and nose, it must needs be understood that this is a lethal sign.

Let us finally quote the no less remarkable picture of death throes, from the "Aphorisms." (Section 8, Aphorism 18):

Death is near when the warmth of the soul rises above the umbilic to the diaphragm, and all the humors are burned out. When the lungs and the heart lose their moisture and warmth is concentrated in the lethal parts, the spirit of warmth evaporates, leaving the regions from which it entirely ruled over the entire organism. Then the soul escapes, in part through the skin, in part through all the apertures of the head, out of which, as we say, life issues forth. Then the soul, together with bile, blood, phlegm and flesh, leaves its bodily abode, which is grown cold and has already acquired the aspect of death.

In these last moments and in the language of the expiring organism, death becomes a moment of life, receiving an expressive reality and speaking with the tongue of the body itself; thus, death is entirely drawn into the cycle of life. The burning up of all bodily moisture, the concentration of warmth in the lethal parts, its evaporation, the departure of the soul with bile and phlegm through the apertures of the head—all these images demonstrate the grotesque open character of the body and the cosmic elements moving within it. The Hippocratic *facies* and this description of the death throes had, of course, an essential significance for the system of images of pregnant death.

We have already pointed out that for the complex image of the physician in Rabelais, Hippocrates' conception of the representative of the medical profession had great importance. Let us quote a significant definition of the physician from the treatise "Of Good Manners" (*De habitu decenti*):

Summing up all that has been separately said, we needs must transfer wisdom into medicine, and medicine into wisdom. For the physician-philosopher is equal to God. Indeed there is but little difference between wisdom and medicine, and between all that is sought in wisdom and all that exists in medicine: contempt of money, honesty and modesty, simplicity in dress, respect, sound judgment, the spirit of decision, neatness, thoughtfulness, the knowledge of all that is necessary for life, hate of vice, the negation of superstitious fear of the gods, divine excellence.

We must stress that the time of Rabelais in France was the only time in the history of European ideology when medicine was the center not only of the natural sciences but of the humanities as well; indeed it was assimilated into philosophy. This phenomenon was observed not in France alone; many famous humanists and scientists of that time were physicians: Cornelius Agrippa, Paracelsus, Cardano, Copernicus. This was the only age that attempted to orient the entire picture of the world toward medicine (there were a few individual attempts at other times).[15] There was a tendency to obey Hippocrates' demand to transfer wisdom to medicine and medicine to wisdom. Nearly all French humanists of the Renaissance were to some extent associated with medicine and studied the ancient medical treatises. The dissection of corpses, which was a rare novelty, attracted wide circles of cultured society. In 1537 Rabelais performed a public dissection of a man who had been hanged and accompanied the autopsy by a scientific explanation. This demonstration of the dismembered body enjoyed great success. Étienne Dolet devoted a short Latin poem to the event, in which he praised the good fortune of the executed man: instead of becoming the prey of the birds, his corpse helped to demonstrate the harmony of the human body, and the face of the greatest physician of his time was bent over it. Never was the influence of medicine on literature and art stronger than during the Renaissance.

We must finally say a few words about the famous "Hippocratic novel." This work was included in the supplements to the "Hippocratic anthology." It was the first European novel in the form of letters and the first to have an ideologist (Democritus) as its hero. It is also the first work to develop the "maniac theme" (the madness of the laughing Democritus).

Strangely enough, historians and theoreticians almost entirely ignored this work, despite its immense influence on Rabelais' theory of laughter and on the general theory of laughter in his time. The Rabelaisian apology of folly (as expressed by Pantagruel) was inspired by Democritus' comments concerning the madness of men who are wise in the practical sense, covetous and devoted to material goods, who consider him mad because he laughs at their seriousness. These men "consider that madness is

[15] Lote correctly characterizes the exceptional position of medicine: "Medicine became the science of the sixteenth century, it exercised a great influence and inspired confidence which it no longer retained in the seventeenth century." Georges Lote, *La Vie et l'oeuvre de François Rabelais*, Paris: Droz, 1938, p. 163.

wise and that wisdom is madness." The wisdom-madness ambivalence is here quite obvious, although stated in rhetorical form.

Yet another feature of this novel must be pointed out as important in our context. When Hippocrates visited the "mad Democritus" in Abders, he found him sitting in front of his house surrounded by dead, disemboweled birds. He was writing a treatise on insanity and was dissecting the birds in order to localize the center of bile, which he believed to be the source of madness. We find here laughter, madness, and the dismembered body. The elements of this complex are, it is true, rhetorically abridged, but their ambivalence and mutuality have been sufficiently preserved.

As we said, the "Hippocratic anthology" had an immense influence on medical and philosophical thought of the Renaissance. Of all the literary sources of Rabelais' grotesque concept of the body, this anthology is one of the most important.

In Montpellier, where Rabelais completed his medical studies, the Hippocratic method prevailed. Rabelais himself gave a course in 1531 on the Greek Hippocratic text, still considered a novelty in that school. At the end of 1537 he published Hippocrates' "Aphorisms" with commentaries (in the "Grif" edition). At the end of 1537 he wrote a commentary on the Greek text of the "Prognostics." The Italian physician Manardi, whose medical letters were published by Rabelais, was also a devotee of Hippocrates. All of this proves how great a place was occupied in Rabelais' life by Hippocratic studies; this was especially true at the time when he wrote the two first books of his novel.

Let us conclude by recalling as a parallel the medical views of Paracelsus, in whose mind the basis of the entire medical theory was the complete concordance of the macrocosm (the universe) and the microcosm (man).

The first foundation of medicine, according to Paracelsus, is philosophy, the second is astronomy. The starry sky is also contained in man himself, and the physician who ignores the sky cannot know man. In this theory the body of man has an extraordinary wealth, being rich with all that exists in the universe. The universe is, so to speak, reassembled in all its diversity within the human body; all its elements are found and are connected in the sphere of the individual body.[16]

Abel Lefranc links Rabelais' philosophic thought (especially in connection with the immortality of the soul) with the Paduan school of Pomponazzi. In his treatise "Of the Soul's Immortality" (*De immortalitate animi*), Pomponazzi proved the identity of body and soul. The soul cannot be separated from the body that creates it, individualizes it, directs its activity, lends it content. Outside the body the soul would be completely empty. In Pomponazzi's mind the body is a microcosm that assembles in one single entity all that is scattered and alienated in the rest of the cosmos. Rabelais was familiar with Pomponazzi's school. Étienne Dolet, Rabelais' intimate friend, was the Italian philosopher's pupil and follower.

The grotesque concept of the body in some of its essential elements represented the humanist and, above all, the Italian philosophy of that period. It had conceived, as we have seen, the idea of the microcosm (based on ancient tradition) as adopted by Rabelais. The human body was the center of a philosophy that contributed to the destruction of the medieval hierarchic picture of the world and to the creation of a new concept. We shall now examine this new picture.

The medieval cosmos was built according to Aristotle. It was based on the precept of the four elements (earth, water, air, and fire), each of which had its special rank in the structure of the universe. According to this theory all the elements were subject to a

16 At the time of Rabelais the conviction that the parts of the body had corresponding signs in the zodiac enjoyed general recognition. Man was commonly pictured with his anatomical parts thus labeled. Such pictures had a philosophic grotesque character. G. Lote adds to his monograph (*Ibid.*, Table 8, pp. 252–253) three such drawings of the fifteenth and sixteenth centuries, presenting the connection of each part of the body with one of the zodiacal signs.

definite order from top to bottom. The nature and the movement of each element were determined according to its position in relation to the center of the cosmos. Nearest of all to this center is the earth, and any part separated from the earth tends to move back to the center along a straight line; in other words, it falls. Fire moves in the opposite direction; it continually tends upward, therefore away from the center. Water and air lie between earth and fire. The basic principle of all physical phenomena is the transformation of one element into the element nearest it. Thus fire is transformed into air, air into water, water into earth. This transformation is the law of creation and destruction to which all earthly things are subject. But above the earthly world there rises the world of celestial bodies, not ruled by this law. The celestial bodies are composed of a special kind of matter, *quinata essentia,* which is not subject to transformation. Celestial bodies, as the most perfect, are endowed with pure movement only, the circular movement around the center of the earth. Concerning the sky's "substance," that is, "quintessence," there were endless scholastic debates, which found their expression in Rabelais' Fifth Book in the episode of the Queen of Quintessence.

Such was the medieval picture of the cosmos. The characteristic trait of this picture was that all degrees of value correspond strictly to the position in space, from the lowest to the highest. The higher the element on the cosmic scale (that is, the nearer to the "immovable motor") the more nearly perfect was this element's quality. The conceptions and the images of the higher and lower stratum as expressed in space value became the flesh and blood of medieval man.

The Renaissance destroyed this hierarchical picture of the world; its elements were transferred to one single plane, and the higher and lower stratum became relative. The accent was placed on "forward" and "backward." This transfer of the world from the vertical to the horizontal was realized in the human body, which became the relative center of the cosmos. And this cosmos was no longer moving from the bottom to the top but along the horizontal line of time, from the past to the future. In bodily man the hierarchy of the cosmos was reversed and canceled; he asserted himself outside it.

This reconstruction of the cosmos from vertical to horizontal in man and the human body was strikingly expressed in Pico della Mirandola's famous speech, *Oratio de hominis dignitate* ("Of the Dignity of Man"). This oration was Pico's introduction to the defense of the 900 theses to which Rabelais alludes by having Pantagruel undertake the defense of the 9764 theses. Pico asserted in his speech that man is superior to all beings, including the celestial spirits, because he is not only being but also becoming. He is outside all hierarchies, for a hierarchy can determine only that which represents stable, immovable, and unchangeable being, not free becoming. All the other beings remain forever what they were at the time of their creation, for their nature is ready-made and unchanging; it receives one single seed which can and must develop in them. But man receives at his birth the seeds of every form of life. He may choose the seed that will develop and bear fruit. He grows and forms it in himself. Man can become a plant or an animal, but he can also become an angel and a son of God. Pico preserves the language of the hierarchy, he preserves in part the old values (he is cautious), but essentially the hierarchy is suspended. Such concepts as becoming, the existence of many seeds and of many possibilities, the freedom of choice, leads man toward the horizontal line of time and of historic becoming. Let us stress that the body of man reunites in itself all the elements and kingdoms of nature, both the plants and the animals. Man, properly speaking, is not something completed and finished, but open, uncompleted. Such is Pico della Mirandola's basic idea.

In Pico's *Apologia* we find the theme of the microcosm (in connection with the idea of natural magic) and the form of "universal sympathy," thanks to which man can combine in himself the higher and the lower, the near and the distant, and can penetrate into all the secrets hidden in the depths of the earth.

Ideas of "natural magic" and of "sympathy" between all phenomena, were widespread during the Renaissance. These ideas, as expressed by Giambattista Porta, Giordano Bruno, and especially Campanella, played a considerable role in destroying the medieval notion of hierarchical space in which natural phenomena had their own distinct levels. The new ideas brought together that which was divided, effacing false boundaries, contributing to the transfer of all to one horizontal plane of the becoming of the cosmos in time.

We especially stress the extreme popularity of the idea of "universal animatization." This idea was defended by Ficino, who sought to prove that the world is not an aggregate of elements but an animate being in which each part is an organ of the whole. Patrizzi proved in his *Panpsychia* that everything in the universe is animate, from the stars to the simplest element. This idea was also shared by Cardano, who considered all natural phenomena as similar in some respect to organic matter. For example, metals are "buried plants" leading their life underground; stones experience youth, growth, and maturity.

All these ideas could exercise some direct influence on Rabelais, since all of them stem from the general tendencies of the Renaissance. All things in the universe, from heavenly bodies to elements, had left their former place in their hierarchy and moved to the single horizontal plane of the world of becoming, where they began to seek a new place and to achieve new formations. The center around which these perturbations took place was precisely the human body, uniting all the varied patterns of the universe.

For all the Renaissance philosophers mentioned previously—Pico della Mirandola, Pomponazzi, Porta, Patrizzi, Bruno, Campanella, Paracelsus, and others—two tendencies appear characteristic. First is the tendency to find in man the entire universe with all its elements and forces, with its higher and lower stratum; second is the tendency to think of the human body as drawing together the most remote phenomena and forces of the cosmos. This philosophy expressed in theoretical terms the new awareness of the cosmos as man's own home, holding no terror for him. It was reflected by Rabelais in the language of images and on the plane of laughter.

In most Renaissance philosophies astrology and "natural magic" play a more or less important role. Rabelais took neither seriously. He brought together the separate, infinitely remote phenomena of the medieval hierarchy, making them collide, uncrowning and renewing them on the material bodily level; but he used for this purpose neither "magic" sympathy nor astrological "concordance." He was consistently materialistic, and moreover approached matter only in its bodily aspect. In his mind the body was the most nearly perfect form of the organization of matter and was therefore the key to all matter. The material components of the universe disclose in the human body their true nature and highest potentialities; they become creative, constructive, are called to conquer the cosmos, to organize all cosmic matter. They acquire a historic character.

In the eulogy of Pantagruelion, a symbol of man's entire technical culture, we find the following striking passage:

. . . those heavenly intelligences we call the gods, both terrestrial and maritime, took fright, when they perceived how, thanks to the blessed herb pantagruelion, the Arctic peoples, under the very eyes of the Antarctic, crossed the Atlantic Ocean, passed the twin tropics, pushed through the torrid zone, spanned the zodiac, frolicked beneath the equinox, and held both poles within sight on the horizon.

Faced with such a situation, the gods, terrified, said:

"Pantagruel has, by this mere herb, caused us more worry and labor than ever the Aloides or Giants, Otus and Ephialtes, when they sought to scale Olympus. He will soon marry and beget children by his wife. This is a fate we cannot forestall, for it has been woven by the hands and shuttles of the three fatal sisters, daughters of Necessity. Who knows but Pantagruel's children will discover some herb equally effectual? Who knows but humans may, by its means, visit the source of hail, the springs of the rain, the forge where lightning is produced. Who knows but they will invade the regions of the moon, intrude within the territories of the celestial signs? Some, then, will settle at the sign of the Golden Eagle, others at the Ram, others at the Crown, others at the Harp, others at the Silver Lion. They will sit down at our divine board, take our goddesses to wife, and thereby themselves become divine." (Book 3, Chapter 51)

In spite of the somewhat rhetorical and official style of this excerpt, the idea it expresses is far from having official implication. We find here the divinization and apotheosis of man. Earthly space is defeated; all peoples who were scattered throughout the world are united. Thanks to navigation and the invention of the sail, men have entered into material contact. Mankind has become one. After the invention of aviation (which Rabelais foresees), man will direct the weather, will reach the stars and conquer them. This entire image of the triumph of mankind is built along the horizontal line of time and space, typical of the Renaissance. Nothing remains of the medieval hierarchic vertical.

The movement in time is guaranteed by the birth of generation after generation, a never-ending succession that fills the gods with fear. Pantagruel, too, intends to get married and to have children, and this is the relative immortality of which Gargantua speaks in his letter to his son. The immortality of the ancestral body of mankind is rhetorically proclaimed. As we have seen, this living and deep awareness gives form to all the popular-festive images of the Rabelaisian novel. Not the biological body, which merely repeats itself in the new generations, but precisely the historic, progressing body of mankind stands at the center of this system of images.

Thus, in the grotesque concept of the body a new, concrete, and realistic historic awareness was born and took form: not abstract thought about the future but the living sense that each man belongs to the immortal people who create history.

CHAPTER SIX

Images of the Material Bodily Lower Stratum

Your philosophers who complain that the ancients
have left them nothing to write about or invent
are obviously very much mistaken. The phenomena you
see in the sky, the wonders earth, sea, and river offer
you are not to be compared to what is hidden in
the womb of earth.
(PANTAGRUEL, *BOOK 5, CHAPTER 48*).

Everywhere eternity is stirring
And everything tends toward non-being
In order to participate in being.
(GOETHE, *"ONE AND ALL"*).

The words of the first epigraph, from the Fifth Book, were probably not written by Rabelais himself. But if we turn our attention
away from the style, certainly not Rabelaisian, these lines are typical not only of his work but of similar examples of Renaissance
thought and thought of the preceding period. (The author of the
Fifth Book may have had the draft and the rough sketches made by
Rabelais.) In these words of the priestess of the Holy Bottle the
center of the world is transferred into the depths, the underground
world. The new elements, the riches hidden in this underground,
are superior to all that is in heaven, on the surface of the earth, or

in the seas and rivers. True wealth and abundance are not on the highest or on the medium level but only in the lower stratum.

The quoted words are preceded by the declaration of the priestess:

"Go, my good friends; may you depart under the protection of that intellectual sphere, whose centre is everywhere, whose circumference is nowhere, and whom we call God. When you return to your world, bear witness to your fellow men that the greatest treasures and most wonderful things lie hidden underground—and not without reason."
(Book 5, Chapter 48)

The famous definition of the divinity as "the sphere, whose centre is everywhere, whose circumference is nowhere" does not belong to Rabelais. It is taken from *Hermes Trismegistes,* is found in the *Roman de la Rose,* in Saint Bonaventure of Beauvais and in other authors; this definition was current in the days of Rabelais. Both Rabelais and the author of the Fifth Book, as well as the majority of their contemporary authors, saw in the definition the decentralization of the universe. Its center was not in heaven but everywhere; all places were equal. This new aspect permitted the author to transfer the relative center of the universe from heaven to the underground, that is, to the underworld, which according to the medieval conception was farthest removed from God.[1]

Immediately before uttering the words quoted in the epigraph, the priestess relates that Ceres had a foreboding that her daughter would find in the underworld more happiness and wealth than on earth. The mention of the images of Ceres, the goddess of fertility, and of Proserpina, goddess of the underworld, as well as the allusion to the Elysian mysteries are also typical of praise addressed to the bowels of the earth. The entire episode of the visit to the oracle of the Holy Bottle is a travestied allusion to the Elysian mysteries.

The words of the priestess are an excellent introduction to our

[1] In Dante's picture of the world, this point of extreme remoteness from the divinity is expressed by Lucifer's triple jaws munching Judas, Brutus, and Cassius.

present chapter. The mighty thrust downward into the bowels of the earth, into the depths of the human body, is reflected in Rabelais' entire world from beginning to end. This downward movement animates all his images, all the leading episodes, all the metaphors and comparisons. Rabelais' world in its entirety, as in every detail, is directed toward the underworld, both earthly and bodily. We have already said that according to Rabelais' initial plan the novel's central topic was to be the search for the underworld and Pantagruel's descent into hell (Dante's topic presented on the comic level). Moreover, we must admit that although the novel was written over a period of twenty years and with considerable interruptions, Rabelais did not digress from his original plan and indeed almost fulfilled it. Thus, the journey into the underground was in the novel from its conception and was elaborated in every detail.

This downward movement is also inherent in all forms of popular-festive merriment and grotesque realism. Down, inside out, vice versa, upside down, such is the direction of all these movements. All of them thrust down, turn over, push headfirst, transfer top to bottom, and bottom to top, both in the literal sense of space, and in the metaphorical meaning of the image.

We also see the downward movement in fights, beatings, and blows; they throw the adversary to the ground, trample him into the earth. They bury their victim. But at the same time they are creative; they sow and harvest (let us recall the bridal cuffing in Lord Basché's house, the transformation of the battle into a harvest or a banquet).

The downward movement is also expressed in curses and abuses. They, too, dig a grave, but this is a bodily, creative grave.

Debasement and interment are reflected in carnival uncrownings, related to blows and abuse. The king's attributes are turned upside down in the clown; he is king of a world "turned inside out."

Finally, debasement is the fundamental artistic principle of grotesque realism; all that is sacred and exalted is rethought on the level of the material bodily stratum or else combined and mixed with its images. We spoke of the grotesque swing, which brings together heaven and earth. But the accent is placed not on the upward movement but on the descent.

The downward movements, scattered throughout the forms and images of popular-festive merriment and grotesque realism, are reassembled by Rabelais; they are understood anew and merged in one single movement directed into the depths of the earth, the depths of the body, in which "the treasures and most wonderful things lie hidden" (never described by the ancient philosophers).

We shall examine in detail two episodes of the novel which reveal most strikingly the meaning of the downward movement in all Rabelais' images, as well as the special character of the Rabelaisian underworld. We have in mind the famous episode of Gargantua's swabs in the First Book (Chapter 13) and the episode of the resurrection of Epistemon and his story of hell in the Second Book (Chapter 30).

In the first episode little Gargantua tells his father about the new and most efficient kind of swab, which he has discovered after many preliminary experiments. There follows a long enumeration of swabs, as follows:

"Once I mopped my scut with the velvet scarf of a damozel. It was pleasurable: the soft material proved voluptuous and gratifying to my hindsight. Once, too, I used a hood, from the same source and with the same results. The next time it was her neckerchief; again, her crimson satin earpieces, but they were bespangled and begilt with beshitten jewelry that scraped my tailpiece from end to end (Saint Anthony's fire roast the bumgut of the decorator and the decorated!)

I recovered from this, thanks to a page's cap with plume to it like those the Swiss Guards sport.

Next, spirting behind a bush, I came upon a March cat (Spring birds are best, runs the rune!) and I put it to excellent advantage though its claws mildly lacerated my perinaeum.

But I was fit again on the morrow, for I employed the gloves of my charming mother; they bore odors of sanctity and scuttling.

Sage, then, which is capital stuffing for a goose . . . fennel, a fine umbelliferous herb for sauces . . . dill, also yellow and umbelliferous . . . sweet marjoram . . . rose leaves and gourd leaves . . . cabbage, which I define as various kinds of cultivated vegetables with round heart or head . . . beets, vine branches and mallow, that wild and garden plant with hairy stems and leaves and purple flowers . . . mullein, woolly of bud and scarlet to the butt . . . lettuce and spinach leaves . . . all of which was fit for the dusthole and amounted to kicking against the pricks . . .

What more? Mercury and purslane, a low succulent herb used in salads and pickled . . . nettles and comfrey—a tall, rough-leaved ditch plant from which I caught the bloody Lombardy gripe, but I cured it by applying my codpiece for bum-wad!"
(Book 1, Chapter 13)

Let us look at this first excerpt and analyze it.

The transformation of an object into a swab is essentially its debasement, uncrowning, and destruction. Abusive expressions such as "not good enough for a swab" are current even in modern languages; they preserve merely the negative and destroying element.

On the contrary, in the passage quoted from Rabelais the element of renewal is not only present but even prevails. All these various objects used as swabs are uncrowned in order to be regenerated. Their half-effaced image reappears in a new light.

In this long list every object emerges quite unexpectedly; its appearance is completely unprepared. The images of objects succeed each other, without logic, with almost as much freedom as in a *coq-à-l'âne*, an intentionally absurd jumble of words and sentences (as is also the case in the speeches of Lords Kissarse and Bumfondle).

But having reappeared in this bizarre sequence, the object is evaluated in accord with its efficacy as a swab, completely apart from its original function. This new standard invites the reader to look at the object in a different light, to measure it, so to speak, for its new use. In this process the object's form, material, and size are reconsidered.

What actually matters, however, is not the formal renewal of each individual swab. If we take a closer look at the choice of swabs, we shall see that this choice is not merely capricious; it has its own logic, though an unusual one. The first five objects: the scarf, the hood, the neckerchief, the earpieces, the cap, are apparel for the face and head, that is, for the upper part of the body. Their function as swabs is literally a transfer of the upper to the lower bodily stratum; the body turns a cartwheel.

These five swabs belong to the wide category of themes and images related to the substitution of the face by the buttocks, the top by the bottom. The rump is the "back of the face," the "face turned inside out." World literature and language abound in an infinite variety of these turnabouts. One of its most common forms, expressed in word or gesture, is *baise-cul*, a variant often found in Rabelais' novel. Gymnastes' sword that he uses in the carnivalesque war of sausages is called *Baise-mon-cul*, and the name of one of the contending gentlemen in the trial is *Baise-cul*, Lord Kissarse. The Sybil of Panzoult shows her "scut" to Panurge and his companions. The grotesque gesture of displaying the buttocks is still used in our day.[2]

Thus, the first five swabs belong to the cycle of themes in which the face is replaced by the rump. The movement from top to bottom is here quite obviously bodily. This downward thrust is also stressed by the fact that abuse erupts between the fourth and fifth image and is hurled at the jewelry, the jeweler, and the lady. This eruption of billingsgate lends dynamic force to the downward thrust.

In this dense atmosphere of the material bodily lower stratum,

[2] This is one of the most common uncrowning gestures throughout the world. It appears in the oldest description of the fourteenth-century charivari in the *Roman du Fauvel;* this charivari contains a song about the *baise-cul* and the various participants display their bottoms. We must recall that the Rabelais legend relates that Rabelais had offered to perform this gesture, provided the part had been washed clean. In the novel the inhabitants of Papimania promise to observe the "ritual" during their audience with the pope.

In "Solomon and Morolf" we find the following episode: One day, Solomon refused to receive Morolf in audience; to take his revenge, Morolf lured the king to his house and received him sitting on the stove, turning his rump to him and saying, "You did not want to see my face, then look at my behind."

the formal renewal of half-effaced images takes place. Objects are reborn in the light of the use made of them. They reappear before our eyes; the softness of silk, the "beshitten jewelry" emerge in all their concrete, tangible form. As we have said, they are renewed in the sphere of their debasement.

The same logic directs the further choice of swabs. The sixth is the March cat. This unexpected choice of something completely unforeseen for such a use sharply brings out the feline character, the flexibility, and the claws of the animal. This is the most dynamic image. A gay farce is offered to the reader's imagination, a scene with two protagonists (the cat and the *cul*). Such a farce is contained in almost all the scenes. In this one the object plays an unusual part and, thus shown, comes alive in a new light. Such a revitalizing effect on objects, positions, professions, or masks is characteristic of the *commedia dell'arte*, farces, pantomimes, and other comic popular genres. The object or the person is assigned an unusual, even paradoxical role (due to absentmindedness, misunderstanding or intrigue); this situation provokes laughter and renewal in the sphere of extraordinary reactions.

We shall not examine all the swabs, since Rabelais constructs these images according to the principle of classification. The queen's gloves are followed by a long list of plants divided into subgroups: spices, vegetables, salads, medicinal plants (though classification is not strictly observed). This enumeration is a botanical demonstration. Each name in Rabelais' mind was related to a definitely visualized image of the leaf, its specific structure and breadth. Rabelais measures each plant in connection with its new use, and makes its form and size obvious to the reader. The botanical description of species (without morphological analysis) was fashionable at that time. Rabelais himself gives examples of such descriptions in the discussion of pantagruelion. In the swab episode he does not describe the plants but only names them; yet their unexpected new function conjures up their visible, material outline. In describing "Pantagruelion," he uses the opposite method, giving a detailed picture of the plant and inviting the reader to guess what it is (hemp).

We must add that the images of plants used as swabs are marked, though to a lesser degree, by the movement from top to bottom. These are mostly greens used in food or drugs (salads, spices, medicinal plants, leaves and stalks of vegetables) which have to be eaten and swallowed. The substitution of the top by the bottom and of the face by the buttocks can also be detected here.

We shall quote with some abridgment the next series of swabs:

"I utilized sheets, blankets, curtains, cushions, carpets, rugs. . . . I went on with hay, straw, oakum, floss, wool and paper. . . . Next I wiped myself with a hat, . . . then in turn with a pillow, a slipper, a gamebag and a basket—faugh! What a thorny, unpleasant bumduster. . . . In this connection let me tell you that some hats are smooth, others soft as velure, others shiny as satin, still others crisp as taffeta. But the best of the lot is the beaver, for it makes a finished abstersion of the faecal matter.

I tried a hen, a rooster, a pullet, a hide of calfskin, a hare, a pigeon, a cormorant, a lawyer's briefcase, a woolen hood, a coif and the feathers of a falconer's lure."
(*Ibid.*)

Swabs are chosen again in groups. In the first group are objects of bedding and dining-room accessories, once more the upside-down movement. There follows the group of hay, straw, etc.; their material character is clearly seen in their new destination. In the next, more motley group, the lack of concordance between the various objects and the way in which they are used (a farcical discrepancy) is sharply brought out, especially in the case of the basket, which is particularly stressed. In the group of hats the material is analyzed in accordance with its new utilization. In the last group the unexpected appearance of the object and the farcical use made of it are stressed once again. The very length and variety of the list of swabs are not without significance. This is the intimate world of one's immediate surroundings: apparel related to face and head, bedding and dining-room accessories, fowl, and food. This intimate world is regenerated in the dynamic, abusive choice of swabs; it emerges anew in the gay farce of its transformation. The positive aspect of this uncrowning is, of course, the prevailing one. Rabelais enjoys all these objects in their concrete variety. He plays with them, touches them, testing again and again their material, form, individuality, and the very sound of their names. This is a page from the great inventory performed by Rabelais at the end of the old and at the beginning of the new era of world history. As in every annual inventory, it is necessary to test every object separately, to weigh and measure it, to determine its wear and tear, to establish the damage and deterioration, to evaluate and reevaluate. Many fictions and illusions have to be written off the new balance sheet, which must be realistic and clear.

The new-year inventory is first of all a gay inventory. Things are tested and reevaluated in the dimensions of laughter, which has defeated fear and all gloomy seriousness. This is why the material bodily lower stratum is needed, for it gaily and simultaneously materializes and unburdens. It liberates objects from the snares of false seriousness, from illusions and sublimations inspired by fear. This is, as we shall see, the final goal of the episode just examined. The long string of uncrowned and renewed household objects prepares for another kind of uncrowning.

We shall now come to the last swab, considered best by the hero.

"But to conclude: I affirm and maintain that the paragon arsecloth is the neck of a plump downy goose, provided you hold her head between your legs. Take my word of honor on this score and try it for yourself. You will experience a most marvelously pleasant sensation in the region of your scutnozzle, as much because of the fluffy under plumage as because the bird's warmth, tempering the bumgut and the rest of the intestines, actually reaches your heart and brain.

Do not believe the old women here when they prattle that the felicity of the heroes and demigods in the Elysian fields lies in their asphodel or ambrosia or nectar. On the contrary, they are happy, to my mind, because they swab their rumps with a goose. Duns Scotus, the learned philosopher, holds the same opinion."
(*Ibid.*)

The picture of the last swab presents an element of delight and beatitude. The physiological path of this delight is also shown; it is born in the anal region from the softness and warmth of the goose, makes its way up the rectum and the intestines, reaching the heart and then the brain. And this delight is precisely the beatitude after death; true, it is not enjoyed by the saints of the Christian paradise but by the heroes and demigods in the Elysian fields. Thus, the swab episode brings us right into the underworld.

The cycle of themes and images of the turnabout face and the substitution of the upper by the lower parts is linked with death and the underworld. This link was still alive and recognized in the time of Rabelais.

When the Sibyl of Panzoult showed her backside to Panurge he exclaimed: "I see the Sibyl's hole" (*trou de la Sybille*), as the entrance to the underworld was called in antiquity. Medieval legends describe many of these holes in various parts of Europe. They were believed to be the entrances to purgatory or hell, but in familiar speech the word had an obscene connotation. The most commonly known landmark was "Saint Patrick's hole" in Ireland, believed to be the entrance to purgatory. Pilgrimages were made to this site as early as the twelfth century, and it was surrounded by legends to which we shall later return. At the same time, the name Saint Patrick's hole had indecent overtones. Rabelais used this interpretation in his "Antidoted Flummeries" (*Fanfreluches antidotées*), in which he mentions the "hole of Saint Patrick," the "hole of Gibraltar," and thousands of other "holes." Gibraltar was also known as "trou de la Sybille" (a pun on Seville) and this, too, was an improper expression.

When visiting the dying Raminagrobis, who chased away all the monks, Panurge begins to curse. He makes the following suppositions as to the fate of the soul of the sinful poet:

"... His soul is headed for thirty thousand basketfuls of devils. ... Would you like to know where?. ... Why right under Proserpine's cacking stool ... in the selfsame infernal bucket into which she voids her enema-induced fecalities ... to the left of the giant cauldron of hell ... three fathoms from the claws of Lucifer ... very close to the dark chamber of Demigorgon."
(Book 3, Chapter 22)

The Dante-like precise comic topography of hell presents a

striking picture. However, the most terrifying place in it for Panurge is not Satan's jaws but Proserpine's stool. Proserpine's rump is, so to say, an underworld in the underworld, the lower depths in the lower depths, and Raminagrobis is headed for this region.

Thus it is not surprising that the swab episode, with its constant movement from top to bottom, brings us finally into hell. Rabelais' contemporaries saw nothing extraordinary in this picture. True, we are brought not so much to hell as to heaven, since Gargantua spoke of the beatitude of demigods and heroes, that is, of the ancient underworld. Obviously this is a parody of Christian teachings concerning the eternal bliss of saints and of the just in paradise.

In this travesty the downward is opposed to the upward movement. The entire spiritual topography is turned upside down. It is possible that Rabelais had in view the doctrine of Thomas Aquinas concerning beatitude. In the swab episode bliss does not start on the top level but in the lower stratum, in the anal region. As we have seen, the path is clearly indicated, through the rectum to the heart and brain. The parody of the medieval topography is obvious; the soul's beatitude is deeply immersed in the body's lowest stratum. Such is the conclusion of the downward thrust of all the images of this episode.

This travesty of one of the basic teachings of Christianity is, however, far removed from cynical nihilism. The material bodily lower stratum is productive. It gives birth, thus assuring mankind's immortality. All obsolete and vain illusions die in it, and the real future comes to life. We have already seen in the Rabelaisian microcosmic picture how this body is concerned with "those who are not yet born" (*qui ne sont encore nés*) and how each organ sends "down" the most valuable part of its nourishment to the procreative region. This lower stratum is mankind's real future. The downward movement that penetrates all Rabelaisian images is ultimately directed toward this gay future. At the same time the author mocks the pretenses of the isolated individual who wants to be perpetuated and who is ridiculous in his senility. Both these elements—the debasement of the obsolete and the real, gay future of the human race—are merged in one ambivalent image. In Rabelais' world we must not be surprised by the fact that the debasing swab is not only able to renew the images of separate real objects but can be referred to the future of mankind.

The entire character of the Rabelaisian novel confirms our interpretation of the episode's conclusion. In his work Rabelais consistently parodies all the elements of medieval teachings and sacraments. As we shall see, the episode of Epistemon's resurrection travesties the essential Gospel miracles. The peculiar parody of the passion and of the sacrament of communion (the Last Supper), however cautious, can be clearly traced throughout the novel. But this travesty plays its most important, organizing role in the first two books. Its main features can be defined as an inverted transubstantiation: the transformation of blood into wine, of the dismembered body into bread, of the passion into a banquet. We have seen various parts of this travesty in the episodes previously discussed. Rabelais also shows in this microcosmic picture of the body how bread and wine ("the essence of all food") are transformed into blood in the human organism. This is the other side of the travesty. We shall find in the novel a series of other parodies of various religious teachings and cults. We have already mentioned Panurge's martyrdom and miraculous escape in Turkey. Abel Lefranc considers Pantagruel's genealogy a parody of Biblical texts. We have seen in the prologues the parody of ecclesiastical systems of persuasion and methods of establishing truth. This is why the swab-episode parody of the beatitude of the saints and the just in heaven should not surprise us.[3]

Let us briefly sum up our analysis of this peculiar episode. Against the background of modern literature, this chapter appears strange and coarse. However, the swab is a traditional humorous theme of debasement. We have already mentioned a number of examples from world literature, but nowhere was this theme developed and differentiated in so great detail as in Rabelais' work.

[3] But, of course, this should not be interpreted as abstract rationalist atheism. It is a humorous corrective of all unilateral seriousness. It is a gay satyrical drama, which restores the ambivalent "ever uncompleted whole" of being.

It is characteristic of Rabelais' method of treating this theme that he presented not only its ambivalence but an obviously positive pole of regeneration. It is a gay and free play with objects and concepts, but it is a play that pursues a distant, prophetic goal: to dispel the atmosphere of gloomy and false seriousness enveloping the world and all its phenomena, to lend it a different look, to render it more material, closer to man and his body, more understandable, and lighter in the bodily sense.

It can thus be spoken of in gay, familiar, fearless tones. In other words, the episode is not an isolated commonplace obscenity of our modern times but an organic part of a large and complex world of popular marketplace forms. Only if torn away from this world and seen per se in the modern sense will these images appear vulgar and dirty. For Rabelais, as always, this is but a spark from the gay carnival bonfire in which the old world is burned.

The episode is constructed in an ascending scale. The uncrowning by transformation into swabs and the renewal in the material bodily sphere start with trivia and rise to the very epitome of medieval philosophy. The liberating process is applied to the seriousness of petty human preoccupations, to cupidity and practical life, to the didactic gloom of moralists and bigots; it is applied to that great seriousness of fear that is reflected in the dark picture of the end of the world, the last judgment and hell, as well as in the images of heaven and beatitude.

Speech and gesture are gradually freed from the pitifully serious tones of supplication, lament, humility, and piousness, as well as from the menacingly serious tones of intimidation, threats, prohibition. All the official expressions of medieval man were infused with these tones alone and were poisoned by them. Official medieval culture did not know the fearless, free, and sober forms of seriousness. The familiar popular, carnivalesque gesture of little Gargantua, transforming everything into swabs, uncrowning and renewing, purifies and prepares the soil for this new bold and sober *human* seriousness.

The familiar conquest of the world, exemplified in the swab episode, also prepared a new, scientific knowledge of this world, which was not susceptible of free, experimental, and materialistic knowledge as long as it was alienated from man by fear and piousness and penetrated by the hierarchic principle. The popular conquest of the world, as symbolized in the episode, destroyed and suspended all alienation; it drew the world closer to man, to his body, permitted him to touch and test every object, examine it from all sides, enter into it, turn it inside out, compare it to every phenomenon, however exalted and holy, analyze, weigh, measure, try it on. And all this could be done on the one plane of material sensual experience.

This is why the folk culture of humor and the new experimental science were organically combined at the time of Rabelais. They were also combined in Rabelais' entire activity as writer and scholar.

Let us now turn to the episode of Epistemon's resurrection and of his visions in the underworld (Book 2, Chapter 30).

This is one of the boldest episodes of Rabelais' novel. Abel Lefranc has proved convincingly enough that this chapter is a travesty of the main Gospel miracles: the resurrection of Lazarus and of the daughter of Jairus. Some features are borrowed from one of these two stories and some from the other. Moreover, Lefranc found in this chapter some elements of the Gospel stories about the cure of the deaf and dumb and of the blind.

This parody is constructed by mixing the corresponding Gospel texts with images of the material bodily stratum. Panurge warms Epistemon's head by placing it on his codpiece; this is an obvious material debasement but at the same time a curative contact with the genital organs. Further, Epistemon's body is brought to the place where the banquet is held and where the resurrection takes place. His neck and head are washed with "good white wine." There follows an anatomizing image (*veine contre veine*). Panurge's oath must be especially stressed: he is ready to lose his own head if he does not succeed in resurrecting Epistemon. Let us note that the theme of this oath ("I hope to lose my own head") coincides with the actual decapitation of Epistemon. Such a coincidence is typical for Rabelais' entire system of images; the theme of curses, abuses, oaths, often repeats the incidents described in the story (rending and dismemberment of bodies, thrusts into the bodily lower stratum, drenching in urine). Let us note yet another trait: Panurge declares that the loss of the head is the wager of a fool. But the "fool" (*fol, sot*) in the context of Rabelais and of all the Renaissance never had the purely negative meaning of common stupidity. "Fool" is an ambivalent abuse; moreover, it is closely related to the image of festive fools of the *soties* and popular marketplace humor. The loss of a head is a minor loss for a fool, but this is said by the fool himself, and the loss is as ambivalent as his foolishness (the inverse side, the lower part of official wisdom). This theme of a fool's play is inherent in the entire episode. To lose his head is a purely comic act, and all the incidents that follow, the resurrection and the ghostly visions, are presented in the aspect of carnival or of a show in a marketplace booth.

Here is the scene of Epistemon's awakening:

> Epistemon began to breathe, then he opened his eyes, yawned, sneezed. . . . Finally he let go a great household fart.
> "He's healed now all right!" Panurge exclaimed, giving him a glass of strong white wine with a slice of sugared toast. And healed he was, though for the next three weeks very hoarse and sorely afflicted with a dry cough he could dispel only by drinking. (Book 2, Chapter 30)

All the symptoms of return to life are here described in succession from the top downward. First, there is breath from the mouth and opening of the eyes. Then comes debasement: yawning (a lower sign of life), sneezing (still lower, a kind of elimination), and finally, breaking wind (the bodily lower stratum, the anus). The last symptom is decisive: *A ceste heure est il guery*, Panurge declares.[4] Thus we have here a complete turnabout, the replacement of the higher by the lower level: it is not the breath of the mouth, but the flatus that appears as the symbol of life and the true sign

---

[4] Panurge's words are a travestied allusion to the Gospel, where the sign of the resurrection of the daughter of Jairus is the partaking of food.

of resurrection. The episode of the swabs pictured beatitude; here the anus symbolizes resurrection.

In the concluding part of this excerpt, wine becomes the leading image (a banquet symbol); it confirms the victory of life over death and further helps Epistemon to cure his dry cough.

Such is the first part of the resurrection episode. As we see, all the images reflect the thrust downward. Let us also note the accompanying banquet images. The second part of the episode is devoted to Epistemon's ghostly visions, that is, to the underworld. This part is also accompanied by banquet images. Here is the beginning of his story:

> Epistemon started to speak. He had seen the devils, he told them, he had spoken familiarly with Lucifer, he had a rolicking time in hell and in the Elysian Fields. The devils, he testified, were such excellent fellows and jovial company that he regretted Panurge's recalling him back to life so soon.
> "I enjoyed seeing them immensely."
> "How so?" Pantagruel asked.
> "They are not so badly treated as you suppose," Epistemon explained. "The only thing is that their conditions are changed very curiously. I saw Alexander the Great, for instance ... he earns the barest living by darning old hose. Xerxes is a crier of mustard, Romulus a saltmaker; Numa Pompilius, the royal Roman lawgiver, is a nailsmith; Tarquin a porter; Piso, the successor of Galba, a peasant clod ..."
> (*Ibid.*)

The image of the underworld is related from its very beginning with that of a banquet; Epistemon feasts in hell and in the Elysian fields. Further, the underworld offers Epistemon an amusing picture of the ghostly life of the doomed. This life is organized as a typical carnival. Everything here is inverted in relation to the outside world. All who are highest are debased, all who are lowest are crowned. The enumeration offered by Rabelais is nothing but a carnivalesque travesty of antique and medieval heroes. The position and profession of each of the doomed inmates is a debasement in the topographical sense of the word; for instance, Alexander the Great is darning old hose. Sometimes the situation of the doomed hero is pictured by a physical trait, as by referring to Achilles as "scrofulous."

From the formal point of view this enumeration (and we have merely cited its beginning) recalls the list of swabs; the new assignments and occupations of the heroes emerge just as unexpectedly. The inconsistency of these new situations produces a similar effect of farcical topsy-turvy and turnabout. One of these new occupations is of peculiar interest: Pope Sixtus IV treats syphilis in the underworld. This leads to the following dialogue:

> "What!" exclaimed Pantagruel. "Do they have the pox in hell?"
> "Of course," Epistemon informed him. "I never saw so many pox-bloods in my life. There must be over a hundred million. You see, those who never caught it in this world contract it in the other!"
> "God's body! I'm safe!" cried Panurge. "I've been all the way to the hole of Gibraltar and the utmost bounds of the Pillars of Hercules, and I've gathered of the ripest, too!"
> (*Ibid.*)

Let us stress, first of all, the logic of this reversed situation; those who did not have syphilis on earth must contract it in hell. We must recall the character of this "gay" disease, which strikes the lower stratum. And finally, we must note in Panurge's words the topographical connotation of the "Hole of Gibraltar" and the "Pillars of Hercules," symbolizing these lower bodily regions. These geographical landmarks were located on the western boundaries of the antique world, which also pointed the way to Hades and to the Islands of the Blessed.

The carnivalesque spirit is also sharply defined in the following excerpt:

> "It was the rule in hell," Epistemon explained, "that all who had been great lords and ladies on earth were condemned to struggle for the most ignoble, precarious and miserable livelihood below. On the contrary, philosophers and such as had been needy on this planet became puissant lords in the inferno . . . .
> "I saw Diogenes . . . enjoying the most magnificent luxury. He wore a rich purple robe and held a sceptre in his right hand. When Alexander the Great failed to patch Diogenes' breeches, he abused

him until the ex-monarch trembled with fury. And Diogenes never failed to beat him for his incompetence.

"I saw Epictetus, too, most gallantly dressed in the French fashion. He was sitting under a cool pleasant arbor with a bevy of comely ladies . . . I almost had a sunstroke looking at old Sol engraved on Epictetus' golden crowns."
(*Ibid.*)

The philosophers Diogenes and Epictetus play here the role of carnivalesque fools elected kings. The royal purple robes and golden scepter of Diogenes are stressed as well as the beating inflicted on the old uncrowned king, Alexander the Great. The image of Epictetus is presented in a different, more gallant style; he is the feasting, dancing king.

The other scenes of Epistemon's visions are depicted in a similar spirit. The writer Jean Lemaire, leader of the school of Rhetoricians, who was an enemy of the popes during his life, plays the role of clownish pope in the underworld. His cardinals are former clowns, Caillette and Triboulet. Former kings and popes kiss Lemaire's slipper, and he orders his cardinal to beat them.

The scene is not devoid of ritualistic debasing gestures. When Xerxes, who is a mustard vendor, demands too high a price, Villon drenches his merchandise in urine. A man called Perceforest urinates against a wall on which Saint Anthony's flames are painted. The Franc-Archier of Baignolet, who has become an inquisitor in hell, wants to burn him as a heretic.

A banquet forms the setting of the entire episode. Pantagruel invites everyone to eat and drink, and the feast is to last for a whole month. During the feast, to which Pantagruel and his companions immediately proceed, the fate of the defeated King Anarchus is decided, and Pantagruel and Panurge prepare the king for the position he will occupy in hell. That is, they train him for a low profession.

The carnivalesque uncrowning of King Anarchus, which we have already mentioned, is pictured in Chapter 31. Panurge clothes the king in a clownish costume, which is minutely described, each detail of the attire being explained by Panurge in terms of a *jeu de mot.* Anarchus is to be vendor of greensauce. This carnivalesque uncrowning imitates the rituals performed in the underworld.

It remains for us to sum up briefly our analysis of the episode of Epistemon's resurrection and ghostly visions.

The image of the underworld offered in this episode has a sharply defined popular festive character. Hell is a banquet and a gay carnival. We find here all the familiar debasing ambivalent images of drenching in urine, beating, travesty, abuse. The downward thrust, inherent in all Rabelaisian images, brings us to the underworld, but the underworld also symbolizes this descent.

In the Rabelaisian system of images the underworld is the junction where the main lines of this system cross each other: carnivals, banquets, fights, beatings, abuses, and curses.

How can one explain this "crossroads" character of hell, and what is its philosophic meaning?

It is, of course, impossible to answer this question by means of abstract argument. It is first of all necessary to turn to Rabelais' sources and to the traditional representation of hell which existed throughout the Middle Ages and culminated in Renaissance literature. Second, we must disclose the popular elements of this tradition. Finally, we must seek to understand its meaning and that of the image itself, in the light of the major problems of Rabelais' times.

But first of all, let us say a few words about the antique sources. The literary works of antiquity that pictured hell are these: the eleventh chapter of "The Odyssey"; *Phaedrus, Phaedo, Georgias,* and "The Republic" of Plato; "Scipio's Dream" of Cicero; Virgil's *Aeneid,* and a series of Lucian's works, especially "Menippus or the Descent into Hades."

Rabelais knew all these works, but nothing can be said about their impact on his novel. Even Lucian's influence is usually much exaggerated. Actually, the resemblance of "Menippus" to the episode of Epistemon's visions is limited to merely external traits.

Lucian describes the underworld as a gay picture. He stresses the element of travesty and exchange of roles. This picture prompts Menippus to compare the life of man to a pageant.

Looking at all of this I decided that the life of man is like a long process, in which Fate is the leader who assigns each his place and dress. Taking anyone who chances along, he clothes him in royal robes and tiara, gives him a bodyguard of lance-bearers, places a diadem on his head; he clothes another one in a slave's garb, bestows beauty on a third, while yet another one is rendered hideous and ridiculous. For, of course, the spectacle must be varied.

The powerful on earth, the kings and the rich, in Lucian's Hades have changed position:

And you would laugh even more seeing the kings and satrapes begging among the dead and forced because of their poverty to sell dried meat or teach grammar; every passerby mocks them, slapping them in the face as the least of slaves. I could not control myself when I saw Philip of Macedonia in a corner: he was mending rotten footware for a small fee. Yes, you can see many others there on the crossroads, collecting alms: Xerxes, Darius, Policrates...

Compare this to Epistemon's account of the underworld (Book Two, Chapter 30): "The only thing is that their conditions are changed very curiously. I saw Alexander the Great, for instance. Do you know what he does?... Well, he earns the barest living by darning old hose. Xerxes is a crier of mustard, Romulus a salt-maker; Numa Pompilius, the royal Roman lawgiver, is a nail-smith ...."

In spite of this external resemblance, there is a deep essential difference between Rabelais and Lucian. Lucian's laughter is always abstract, ironical, devoid of true gaiety. Scarcely anything remains of the ambivalence of the saturnalian symbols. The traditional images are bloodless and made to serve the abstract moral philosophies of stoicism (moreover, degenerate and distorted by late cynicism). His kings are slapped "in the face, as the least of slaves." But these are commonplace punishments of the regime of slavery, transferred to Hades. They are but a dim survival of the saturnalian ambivalent king-slave images. These are mere blows, devoid of all generating force; they do not contribute to birth and renewal. Lucian's banquet presents the same commonplace, superficial aspect; the inmates of Lucian's underworld also eat, but eating has nothing in common with Rabelaisian feasting. Former kings may not enjoy it, but neither can the former slaves and beggars. Everybody eats but nobody feasts, not even the philosophers, who only laugh ironically, mocking the uncrowned kings and the wealthy. This is what matters most. Lucian's material bodily principle merely serves to debase the higher images, to render them commonplace, with almost no ambivalence. It does not renew or regenerate. Hence the crucial difference between Lucian and Rabelais is in tone and style.

At the head of the medieval presentations of the underworld we must place the so-called "Apocalypse of Peter." This work was composed by a Greek author at the end of the first or the beginning of the second century and is a summary of the antique conceptions of Hades, adapted to Christian doctrine. "The Apocalypse of Peter" was not known in the Middle Ages in the original.[5] It determined the fourth-century *Visio Pauli* (The Vision of Paul), different versions of which were widespread in the Middle Ages. It strongly influenced the mighty torrent of Irish legends concerning paradise and hell, which played an immense role in the history of medieval literature.

Among the Irish legends those linked with "Saint Patrick's hole" play an important role. This opening leads into purgatory. According to the legend, it was first shown by God to Saint Patrick, who lived in the fifth century. In the middle of the twelfth century the monk Henri de Saltrais depicted the descent into purgatory of a knight; the work was entitled "The Purgatory of Saint Patrick." The famous "The Vision of Tungdal" was also written at about the same time. After his death, Tungdal undertook a journey into the underworld and returned to the world of the living to tell about the terrifying spectacles he had witnessed. These legends awakened an extraordinary interest and inspired a number of simi-

[5] It was first discovered in an Egyptian tomb in 1886.

lar works: "The Purgatory of Saint Patrick" by Marie of France, "Of the Contempt of the World" by Pope Innocent III, "The Dialogues of St. Gregory," Dante's "Divine Comedy."

The images of ghostly visions, borrowed from "The Vision of Paul," developed and enriched by powerful Celtic imagination, acquired extraordinary dimensions and ever-greater detail. The grotesque images of the body especially were multiplied. The number of sins increased as well as the forms of punishment (from seven to nine and more). In the structure of these images of torture it is easy to trace the specific logic of abuse, curses and oaths, and the logic of topographical bodily negation and debasement. These images are often organized as the realization of the metaphors contained in billingsgate expressions. The body of the doomed sinner is presented in a grotesque aspect. The relation to devouring is often apparent: some sinners are roasted on a spit, others are forced to drink molten metal. In "The Vision of Tungdal" Lucifer is pictured chained to a red-hot range while he himself devours sinners.

One cycle of legends about the underworld was linked to Lazarus. According to one of these ancient legends, Lazarus, sitting at the feast with Christ at the house of Simon the Leper, related his visions of the ghostly world. A sermon attributed to Saint Augustine stressed the exceptional position of Lazarus as the only living man to have beheld the secrets of the other world. In this sermon Lazarus also relates his visions during the feast. The theologian Pierre Comestor quoted Lazarus' testimony. At the end of the fifteenth century the figure of Lazarus appeared in the mysteries, but the banquet setting of his story was especially well known through the popular calendars.

All these legends of the ghostly kingdom, containing grotesque bodily elements[6] and banquet images, determined the theme and

---

[6] As we have seen, these grotesque-comic elements were already given in their initial form in the "Vision of Tungdal." They had an influence as well on pictorial art. For instance, Hieronymus Bosch painted a panel presenting the Tungdal theme (circa A.D. 1500) which stressed precisely the grotesque aspects of the "vision" (the sinners devoured by Lucifer). The frescoes of the Cathedral of Bourges also depict a comic hell.

imagery of the diableries and prevailed in this genre. The diableries also stressed the comic aspect of the images of hell.

What was the influence of these legends and literary works on Rabelais' underworld? As we have seen, Rabelais stressed two main elements: first, the banquet that forms the setting of Epistemon's tale (he feasts in the netherworld, and so do the philosophers; food is sold by the inmates) and second, the consistently carnivalesque aspect of the ghostly kingdom.

The banquet element is seen in the legends and writings of the Middle Ages to which we have alluded. In "The Vision of Tungdal" (twelfth century) Lucifer devours sinners while he himself roasts on a gigantic range. The mysteries sometimes presented Lucifer in this setting. We find a similar image in Rabelais when Pantagruel relates that Lucifer one day broke his chain because of frightful colic after having breakfasted on the fricassee of a sergeant. In the Fourth Book (Chapter 46) there is the devil's long discussion about the flavor of various souls: which are good for breakfast, which for dinner, and how they are to be served. Apparently, Rabelais' direct sources were two poems, *Salut d'Enfer* by an anonymous author and *Songe d'Enfer* by Raoul Houdenc. In both poems the authors describe their visit to Beelzebub and their feast with the devils and present a detailed cuisine of sinners. Thus, the hero of *Salut d'Enfer* is served a soup of usurers, a roast of forgerers, and a sauce of lawyers. Raoul Houdenc offers an even more detailed description of the infernal menu. Like Epistemon, the two poets enjoy a courteous welcome in hell and, like Rabelais' characters, have a familiar conversation with Beelzebub.

The influence on Rabelais of the cycle of legends related to Lazarus is no less obvious. We have already pointed out that the Epistemon episode is in part a parody of the resurrection of Lazarus in the Gospels. Epistemon's story about his ghostly visions has a banquet setting similar to that of the Lazarus legend.

Such are the sources of the first, banquet, theme in Rabelais' underworld. The origins of the second, carnival, theme can also be found in these sources.

The carnivalesque, festive element is clearly indicated in the two poems. But it exists even earlier, in the most ancient cultic legends. The underworld symbolizes the defeated and condemned evil of the past. True, this evil is interpreted and represented from the official, Christian point of view. The negation bears, therefore, a somewhat dogmatic character. But in the legends this dogmatic negation is interwoven with the folkloric conception of the depths of the earth as the maternal womb, which at the same time absorbs and gives birth; it is also combined with the idea of the past as a gay monster that is chased away. The folkloric conception of gay time could not but penetrate the images of hell, as the symbol of the defeated evil of the past. This is why as early as the Vision of Tungdal Lucifer is represented as a gay monster, the symbol of obsolete power and of fear that has been defeated. This theme with its incessant changes and varied nuances could create the gloomy images of Dante's inferno and Rabelais' gay netherworld. Finally, the very logic of the lower stratum, of the inside-out and turnabout, irresistibly drew these images into the sphere of grotesque interpretation.

But there is yet another element that must be taken into consideration. The gods of antique mythology which Christianity had turned into devils and the images of Roman Saturnalias which lived on during the Middle Ages were thrown by orthodox Christian consciousness into hell and brought their pagan spirit along with them.

One of the oldest descriptions of carnival is presented in the form of a mystic vision of the underworld. The eleventh-century Norman historian Orderic Vital pictured in detail the vision of the priest Goshelin, who on January 1, 1091, returning at night from a visit to the sick, saw "Erl-King's army" marching along the deserted road. Erl-King was described as a giant, armed with a huge mace (recalling Heracles). The army he led was motley, the front row formed by men wearing the skins of wild beasts and carrying all kinds of kitchen utensils and housewares, followed by men carrying fifty coffins. Tiny beings with large heads sat on the coffins holding big baskets in their hands. Then came two Ethiopians with a gibbet on which two men were tortured by a devil who dug his fiery spurs into their flesh. Next came a great number of women on horseback. Their saddles were studded with red-hot nails, onto which they fell as they rode. Among the women were noble ladies, some of them real people, alive at the time of the vision. Last came the clergy and soldiers enveloped in flames. All these marchers were souls of dead sinners. Goshelin talked to three of them, one of whom was his dead brother, and learned that they were migrants from purgatory expiating their sins.

Such is Goshelin's vision.[7] It does not, of course, refer to "carnival." The priest himself, and the author who relates the incident, consider that Goshelin saw Erl-King's Army. This mythological picture (similar to the "wild army," the "wild hunt," or "King Arthur's army") is here subject to a Christian interpretation. Christian conceptions determine the character and the separate details of Orderic's story: Goshelin's terror, the complaints and moans of the marching men and women. The man of the gibbet tortured by the devil is the murderer of a priest; the women astride the saddles studded with nails are being punished for their depravity. In a word, the atmosphere is far from carnivalesque.

And yet, the carnival character of the separate images and of the march is beyond question. In spite of the distorting influence of the Christian presentation, the traits of the Saturnalia appear quite clearly. We find here the image of the giant which is characteristic of the grotesque body and is the constant protagonist of all such processions. The image of Heracles and his mace is closely related to the underworld. The newborn babes sitting on the coffins are no less typical. Beyond the Christian *mise-en-scène* we clearly see the ambivalence of birth-giving death. The material bodily lower stratum is symbolized by the depraved women (*dames douces*), whose obscene gestures imitate those of coitus. (Let us recall the Rabelaisian metaphor of the sexual act borrowed from horseback riding, the *saccade*). The men wearing the skins of wild beasts and

7 Goshelin's visit is analyzed in detail by Otto Driesen in *Der Ursprung des Harlekin,* 1904, pp. 24–30.

armed with kitchen utensils are obviously carnivalesque images. The flame burning the soldiers is the fire that burns and renews the terrifying past (the *moccoli* of the Roman carnival). The vision also contains the element of uncrowning, since the sinners are former feudal lords, knights, noble ladies, clerics, who are now debased and deprived of their high positions. Goshelin converses with a viscount who is punished because he was a corrupt judge; another lord stole his neighbor's mill.

In this New Year's march there is something that reminds us of the "procession of the uncrowned gods," especially in the figure of Erl-King himself, armed with his mace. We know that in the Middle Ages the carnival processions, especially in Germany, were interpreted as the march of the rejected pagan gods. The idea of the deposed higher powers and truths had become part of the nucleus of carnival images. Neither can the influence of the Saturnalias be ignored here. The antique gods played in these parades the role of the saturnalian uncrowned king. It is characteristic that in the second part of the nineteenth century a number of German scholars insisted on the Germanic origin of the word "carnival," deriving it from *Karne* or *Harth,* which means a holy site, that is, a pagan community and its priests, and from *val* or *wal,* which means "dead," "killed." According to this theory, carnival meant the "procession of the dead gods." We quote this interpretation merely to show how persistent was the conception of the deposed divinities.

Orderic Vital's candid tale proves how closely these images of hell and carnival were interwoven in the minds of godfearing eleventh-century Christians. At the end of the Middle Ages the diableries emerged from this combination when the carnival element prevailed and transformed the underworld into a gay popular spectacle of the marketplace. We find a parallel process of "carnivalization" of hell in all the Renaissance festivals.

Carnival hell was seen in various forms. Its metamorphoses in the Nürnberg carnival parades of the sixteenth century, recorded in detail, were: a house, a tower, a palace, a ship, a windmill, a dragon spitting fire, an elephant with men astride, a giant devouring children, an old devil eating wicked wives, a store selling all kinds of rummage, the Venus mountain, an oven for the baking of fools, a cannon to shoot ill-tempered women, a trap to catch fools, a galley with monks and nuns, and the wheel of fortune spinning fools. The whole contraption, stocked with fireworks, was usually burned in front of the town hall.

All these variations of the carnivalesque hell are ambivalent and include in one way or another the symbols of fear defeated by laughter. All of them are carnivalesque dummies representing in a more or less harmless form the old, receding world. At times these are merely ridiculous monsters, and at other times they symbolize the obsolete character of that old world, its futility, absurdity, stupidity, ridiculous pomposity, and so forth. These images are similar to the debasing junk that fills Rabelais' netherworld: the old hose that Alexander the Great is darning or the piles of rags and garbage that the former usurers pick over. This world is doomed to the regenerating flames of carnival.

All that we have said above casts some light on the philosophical significance of the underworld images in medieval tradition as well as in Rabelais' novel. The organic link of hell with all the other images of the Rabelaisian system is made clear. Let us examine some aspects of these images.

For thousands of years folk culture strove at every stage of its development to overcome by laughter, render sober, and express in the language of the material bodily lower stratum (in an ambivalent sense) all the central ideas, images, and symbols of official cultures. In the preceding chapter we saw how cosmic fear and the images of world catastrophes and eschatological theories, cultivated in official philosophies, found their comic equivalents. The carnivalesque disasters and parodical prophecies freed man from fear, brought the world closer to him, lightened the burden of time, and turned it into a sequence of gay transformations and renewals.

The image of the underworld was also developed. We have seen that the process of carnivalization of the official conceptions of hell and purgatory took place throughout the Middle Ages. The elements of this process were contained even in the official "visions" of hell. At the conclusion of the medieval period the underworld became a central theme, the crossroads of two cultures: the official and the popular tradition. This theme disclosed most clearly the difference between these two cultures. The underworld is a peculiar balance sheet, the end of individual lives and destinies and at the same time the judgment dealt out to the separate life of man as a whole, based on the highest criteria of Christian philosophy (religious, metaphysical, ethical, social, and political). This synthesis revealed the fundamental medieval conception of good and evil, not in abstract form but in a strikingly intensified pictorial and emotional form. This is why the image of hell was a powerful instrument of ecclesiastical propaganda.

The basic traits of official medieval culture reached their extreme limit in the images of the underworld, an ultimate concentration of gloom, fear, and intimidation. The nonhistoric appreciation of the individual and his destiny was here most consistently exemplified. The vertical line of ascent and fall prevailed, while the horizontal line of historic time was obliterated. The concept of time in official medieval culture was here most strikingly revealed.

Folk culture strove to defeat through laughter this extreme projection of gloomy seriousness and to transform it into a gay carnival monster. Folk culture organized the inferno according to its own fashion, opposing sterile eternity by pregnant and birth-giving death; preserving the past by giving birth to a new, better future. If the Christian hell devalued earth and drew men away from it, the carnivalesque hell affirmed earth and its lower stratum as the fertile womb, where death meets birth and a new life springs forth. This is why the images of the material bodily lower stratum pervade the carnivalized underworld.

The image of the netherworld in folk tradition becomes the symbol of the defeat of fear by laughter. The fear is dual: the mystic terror inspired by hell and death and the terror of the authority and truth of the past, still prevailing but dying, which has been hurled into the underworld.

During the Renaissance the inferno was pictured as more and

more filled with kings, popes, clerical and political leaders, not only the dead, but also those still living. All that was denied, condemned, doomed was collected in this nether region. The satire of the Renaissance and of the seventeenth century used this imagery to portray a gallery of historic figures and political characters. But this satire often presented, as in the case of Quevedo, a purely negative aspect; the ambivalence of the images was considerably mitigated. The literary treatment of this theme entered a new period of development.

We know from *Pantagruel*'s last chapter that Rabelais intended to describe his hero's journey into the legendary land of Prester John, located in India, and thence into the underworld. This topic does not come as a surprise. Let us recall that *Pantagruel*'s leading image is the gaping mouth, the *gueule d'enfer,* of the medieval mystery. All of these images lead downward to the earthly and bodily lower stratum. Even the swab episode, as we have seen, leads us to the netherworld.

In Rabelais' basic source (the folk legend of Gargantua) there is an episode of the hero's descent into hell. True, the "Great Chronicle" does not contain this story, but a farce of 1540 alludes to the episode as to something commonly known. One of the new oral variants of the legend, recorded by Sébillot,[8] also contains this incident.

The heroes of folk humor often descend into hell. One of them was Harlequin, who, like Pantagruel, was a devil in his preliterary past. In 1585, in Paris, there appeared a work entitled "The Gay Story of the Feats and Adventures of the Italian Comedian, Harlequin," containing his dreams and visions, his descent into hell to bring back mother Cardina, and his escape after having deceived Cerberus, the infernal king himself, and other devils.

In hell Harlequin turns somersaults, leaps and skips, sticks out his tongue, and makes Charon and Pluto laugh. All these gay leaps

[8] Paul Sébillot, *Le Folklore de France,* 4 vols., Paris, 1904–1907, Vol. 1, pp. 52–53.

and bounds are as ambivalent as the underworld itself. Harlequin's somersaults are topographical; their points of orientation
are heaven, earth, the underworld, the top and the bottom. They
present an interplay, a substitution of the face by the buttocks; in
other words, the theme of the descent into hell is implicit in this
simple acrobatic feat. The figures of folk humor tend to descend.
The famous comic of the seventeenth century, Tabarin, went down
into the inferno. His story, entitled "Tabarin's Descent into Hell,"
was published in 1612.

To return to Pantagruel, his journey to the underworld, according to the plan of the novel, was to lead through the land of Prester John in India. This approach was in accord with legend,
which presumed the opening to heaven and hell to be located in
that region. But the route to be followed by Pantagruel to reach
India, as Rabelais projected it, was the route to the extreme West,
through the *Iles des Perles,* i.e., through Brazil. Thus the route to
the legendary land of death, thought to lie to the west of the Pillars
of Hercules, was also Rabelais' response to the geographical explorations of his time. In 1523-1524, Francis I had sent the Italian navigator Verrazano, to Central America in order to discover
the straits that would shorten the distance between China and
India, without sailing around Africa as did the Portuguese.

Rabelais almost fulfilled the program of the novel as planned
in the last chapter of *Pantagruel.* But the exterior aspect of the
novel was drastically changed; we do not find the land of Prester
John, and the underworld has been replaced by the island of the
"Oracle of the Holy Bottle" (though we do not know how Rabelais would have depicted this scene). As to the southwest route, it
was replaced by the route to the northwest, Pantagruel's journey
in the Fourth Book.

This new itinerary to the northwest was also an echo of contemporary exploration, of France's now revised colonial thrusts.
Since Verrazano did not discover the straits of Central America,
Rabelais' famous contemporary Jacques Cartier advanced a new
plan: to shift the itinerary to the north polar regions. In 1540 Cartier made his way to Canada. In 1541 Francis I sent him to colonize

this newly discovered territory of North America. So Rabelais, too, changed his hero's itinerary and made him sail to the northwest, to the polar regions, to which Cartier was pointing.

Cartier's itinerary was also the famous legendary route to hell and paradise. This northwestern route was enveloped in Celtic lore. To the northwest of Ireland the ocean was full of mystery. You could hear amid the roaring waves the moans of the dead; the waters were scattered with strange islands, full of wonders like those of India. We have seen that the "hole of Saint Patrick" was part of those Celtic legends of the sea. The Irish tales were absorbed by the literature of late antiquity, especially by Lucian and Plutarch. For instance, Rabelais' novel contains the episode of the words that froze and melted; this incident was directly borrowed by the author from Plutarch, but its images are doubtless of Celtic origin. The same can be said of the episode of the isle of the Macreons, inspired by Plutarch. Incidentally, Plutarch relates that Saturn, guarded by Briareus, lives on one of these northwestern islands.[9]

We shall mention here one legend of this Celtic cycle, which doubtless influenced the story of Pantagruel's journey; that is, the Fourth Book of the novel. This is the legend of St. Brendan's voyage, an ancient christianized Irish myth. "The Travels of St. Brendan" (*Navigation sancti Brendani*), written in the tenth century, enjoyed immense popularity in the Middle Ages in all European countries, both in prose and in poetic form. The most interesting version is the Anglo-Norman poem of the monk Benoît, written in 1125. It can be summarized as follows, noting similarities to Rabelais.

St. Brendan and seventeen monks of his monastery sailed from Ireland in search of paradise, to the northwest, toward the polar regions. (This is also Pantagruel's route.) The voyage lasted seven years. St. Brendan sailed from island to island, as did Pantagruel, ever discovering new wonders. On one of these isles he found white

---

[9] According to contemporary scholars (for example, Georges Lote), Rabelais had a special liking for Celtic fantastic tales. Even in ancient literature, he chose elements of Celtic origin (for instance, Plutarch).

sheep as large as deer. On another he saw gigantic trees with red leaves; white birds perched on their branches were singing the praise of God. On another isle one deep silence reigned, and lamps shone at the time of the holy office. The old man described in the legend is much like Rabelais' Macrobius. The travelers had to celebrate Easter on a shark's back, and there is in Rabelais an episode picturing a whale. St. Brendan witnesses a fight between a dragon and a griffin and observes a sea serpent and other monsters. The monks overcome all the dangers, thanks to their piety. At one time they see a great sapphire altar rising from the sea. They pass by the opening leading to hell from which a cloud of fire rises. Near the "jaws of hell" they find Judas sitting on a small rock surrounded by stormy waves. He rests from his torment on feast days. Finally, they reach the gates of paradise; its walls of precious stones glisten with topazes, amethysts, amber, and onyx. A heavenly messenger permits them to visit paradise. They see lush meadows, flowers, trees laden with fruit. A sweet fragrance fills the air. The woods are inhabited by gentle beasts; rivers of milk flow through the grounds, and the dew is made of honey. It is neither hot nor cold. There is no hunger, no sadness.

We have here a typical example of the medieval concept of earthly space and of movement within this space. Just as in the grotesque body, there is no opaque surface, only cavities and heights. An excellent symbol of this legendary relief is the hole of hell and next to it Judas' rock, or the sapphire altar rising from the depths of the sea. The opening to hell and the gates of paradise break up the earth's surface and disclose other worlds. In this legend Christian ecclesiastical ideas are combined with contrasting popular images. The images are still powerful and lend their charm to the legend. Paradise is a popular utopian kingdom of material bodily abundance and peace; it is the golden age of Saturn, where there are no wars, no suffering, but material wealth. Plutarch precisely located Saturn's abode on one of the isles of the Irish sea. Thus in this pious poem, as in Goshelin's mystic vision, we hear the ever-present overtones of the Saturnalias.

In Pantagruel's voyage to the Northwest, the legendary route to the utopian land of peace and abundance is interwoven with the real contemporary route, the last word in geographical exploration, the route of Jacques Cartier. Such a combination is characteristic of all Rabelais' basic images. We shall resume this topic in the next chapter.

The themes inspired by St. Brendan's voyage are combined in the Fourth Book with images of a different order. Actually, Pantagruel's entire voyage takes place in the underworld, the obsolete world of comic monsters. The isle of the Catchpoles, the isle of wild sausages and the carnivalesque war of its inhabitants, the figure of Carême-prenant (and its fantastic anatomization), the isles of Papimania and Popefiggery, the isle of Gaster and the festive offerings of the Gastrolaters, as well as the inserted tales and episodes, especially the stories about the beating of the Catchpoles by the Lord of Basché and Villon's tricks—all these are carnivalesque images of the old world and of the old truths; they are the gay monsters who fill the grotesque underworld and are the protagonists of the diableries. The downward thrust in its most varied forms and manifestations marks all the images of the Fourth Book. We must also note the great number of political allusions in this section of the novel.

The legendary wonders of the Irish sea are thus transformed into a gay carnivalesque underworld.

As we see, Rabelais' initial plan, suggested in his last book, (the fourth) was consistently carried out, in spite of all external transformations.

The philosophical meaning of the downward movement and of the underworld images which reflect it must be understood in the light of the radical reconstruction that the medieval picture of the universe underwent during the Renaissance. In the preceding chapter we described the hierarchical character of the medieval physical cosmos (the respective positions of the four elements and their movement). Such a gradation also existed in the metaphysical and moral world order. An important influence on the entire medieval philosophy was exercised by Dionysius the Areopagite. His works[10] contain a complete and consistent development of the idea of hierarchy. The teaching of the Areopagite is a combination of neoplatonism and Christianity. The idea of a graded cosmos, divided into higher and lower worlds was taken from neoplatonism. While Christianity brought the idea of redemption as an intermediary between these two levels, Dionysius offered a systematic description of his hierarchical scale, leading from heaven to earth. Between man and God there is the world of pure intelligences and heavenly powers. They are divided into three circles which, in turn, have three subdivisions. The Church's hierarchy faithfully reflects this heavenly pattern. The teaching of the Areopagite had a great influence on Erigena, Albert the Great, Thomas Aquinas, and others.

In the medieval picture of the world, the top and bottom, the higher and the lower, have an absolute meaning both in the sense of space and of values. Therefore, the images of the upward movement, the way of ascent, or the symbols of descent and fall played in this system an exceptional role, as they did also in the sphere of art and literature. Every important movement was seen and interpreted only as upward and downward, along a vertical line. All metaphors of movement in medieval thought and art have this sharply defined, surprisingly consistent vertical character. All that was best was highest, all that was worst was lowest. The horizontal line of movement, forward or backward, is absent; it was nonessential, since it brought no change to objects in the scale of values or in their true destiny. It was understood as static, or as a senseless rotation within a closed circuit. Even the medieval accounts of voyages and pilgrimages were devoid of the special pathos of advance along the world's horizontal; in these medieval tales the line of advance was distorted and replaced by the vertical concept of world-space. The concrete, visible model of the earth on which medieval thought was based was essentially vertical.

This hierarchial movement also determined the idea of time,

[10] "Of Divine Names," "Of Divine Hierarchies," "Of Ecclesiastical Hierarchy."

which was conceived as horizontal. Therefore, the hierarchy was considered outside of time, and time was not essential for hierarchical ascent. There was no conception of progress, of moving forward in time. It was possible to be instantly reborn in the highest spheres, even before "Mahomet's pitcher" would have time to spill. Medieval eschatology devalued time.

Dante's picture of the world is characteristic. In his world a considerable role is attributed to time, but all Dante's metaphors of spatial values have a purely vertical tendency of ascent and fall. He knows only the upward and the downward, not the forward movement. But he develops his system of vertical images with extraordinary depth and richness. His entire world is shown along the vertical line, from the lowest level, Satan's jaws, to the extreme heights that are the abodes of God and of beatified souls. The only movement that changes the position and the destiny of the soul is the upward or downward movement. We scarcely find any outstanding images of near or remote objects in time and space. Both in the *Divina Commedia* and in the *Vita Nuova* Beatrice's image is projected in the hierarchical light. The fall makes this image remote, while the soul that is raised draws it nearer. The infinite distance separating the poet from the beloved can be instantly overcome or can be made to last forever. Time and space seem to be entirely excluded from the story of this love; they exist only in their symbolic aspect. How different from popular folk lyrics, where remoteness from the object of love, the long and difficult roads leading to it, and the concrete time of expectation play such an essential role.[11] Time is devalued in Dante's world. In the hierarchical order every moment contains the extreme low degree and the high degree of perfection; real historic time can change nothing.

But the medieval picture of the world as it appears in Dante is already in a state of crisis and stands at the breaking point. In spite of his ideological intentions, individuality and variety appear in his work on a single hierarchical plane. Such images as Farinata,

---

[11] The famous Provençal image of the "far-away princess" is a hybrid between the official hierarchical medieval concept of distance and the true space of folk lyrics.

Ugolino, Paolo and Francesca are important and are differentiated but not according to their hierarchical position on the scale of the ascending souls. Dante's world is extremely complex. His exceptional artistic force is revealed in the powerful tension of opposed elements that pervades all his images. The mighty impact of the upward vertical movement is opposed by the no less mighty impulse to break through toward the horizontal of real space and historic time, the tendency to understand and form destiny outside the hierarchical norms and values of the Middle Ages. Hence the extraordinary tension of the balance created in his world by Dante's titanic power.

At the time of Rabelais the hierarchical world of the Middle Ages was crumbling. The narrow, vertical, extratemporal model of the world, with its absolute top and bottom, its system of ascents and descents, was in the process of reconstruction. A new model was being constructed in which the leading role was transferred to the horizontal lines, to the movement forward in real space and in historic time. Philosophy, scientific knowledge, human practice and art, as well as literature, all worked on this new model.

In the struggle for a new conception of the world and for the destruction of the medieval hierarchy, Rabelais continually used the traditional folklore method of contrast, the "inside out," the "positive negation." He made the top and the bottom change places, intentionally mixed the hierarchical levels in order to discover the core of the object's concrete reality, to free it from its shell and to show its material bodily aspect—the real being outside all hierarchical norms and values.

The mighty thrust of all folk images into the absolute lower stratum, the element of time they contain, and the ambivalent nature of the underworld are opposed in Rabelais to the abstract hierarchical tendency to ascend. Rabelais sought the real world and real historic time, not on the upper level but in the lower depths. In the words of the priestess of the Holy Bottle, "The greatest treasures are hidden underground, and the wisest of all is time, since it will reveal all riches and all secrets."

The material bodily principle, earth, and real time become the relative center of the new picture of the world. Not the ascent of the individual soul into the higher sphere but the movement forward of all mankind, along the horizontal of historic time, becomes the basic criterion of all evaluations. Having done its part upon earth, the individual soul fades and dies together with the individual body; but the body of the people and of mankind, fertilized by the dead, is eternally renewed and moves forever forward along the historic path of progress.

Rabelais gave to these ideas an almost direct theoretical expression in Gargantua's famous letter to Pantagruel (Book Two, Chapter 8). Let us examine the part of the letter related to this philosophy.

Among the gifts, graces and prerogatives with which our sovereign Creator, God Almighty, blessed and enriched humanity from the beginning, there is one that I deem supreme. By its means, though we be mortal, we can yet achieve a sort of immortality; through it we may, in the course of our transitory lives, yet perpetuate our name and race . . . .

I therefore have reason to give thanks to God, my Saviour, for having granted me the joy of beholding my old age blossom anew in your youth. When, by His pleasure, which rules and orders everything, my soul must abandon this human habitation, I shall not believe I am dying utterly, but rather passing from one place to another. For in you my visible image will continue to live on earth; by you, I shall go on frequenting honorable men and true friends, as I was wont to do.
(Book 2, Chapter 8)

This letter is written in high rhetorical style. It is a bookish speech externally loyal to the Catholic Church and delivered by a humanist obeying all the norms and conventions of eloquence. Neither does the tone of the letter, nor the rather archaic style, nor the correct, pious choice of words contain the slightest allusion to the marketplace jargon that characterizes the novel. Gargantua's admonition seems to belong to a different world, it is a model of official oration.

However, the letter's contents do not correspond to official ecclesiastic philosophy. In spite of all the pious forms of speech, marking the beginning and the end of nearly every paragraph, the ideas developed by Gargantua concerning earthly immortality belong to a dimension entirely different from the Church's teaching. Rabelais does not openly contest the eternal life of the soul outside the body, which he accepts as self-evident. But he is interested in the related idea: immortality linked with the body, with earthly life, accessible to a living experience. He is interested in the perpetuation of human culture and of the seed, the name, the deeds of men. He is not satisfied with the static survival of the soul departing from the senile body for another world. He wants to see himself, his old age and senility, flowering in the new youth of his son, grandson, and great-grandson.

We stress Rabelais' characteristic approach. He does not say that the son takes the place of the father; such an expression would break the tie between father and son, old age and youth, as two static, closed phenomena opposed to each other. Rabelais' image has a dual body: he says that old age flowers anew in youth (*mon antiquité charnue refleurit en ta jeunesse*). To express his idea he uses the rhetorical form, which is an adequate translation of the grotesque folk image of pregnant old age and birth-giving death. Rabelais' picture stresses the uninterrupted but contradictory unity of the vital process, which does not cease on death but on the contrary triumphs in it, for death is life's rejuvenation.

Let us take note of another typical expression in Gargantua's letter. He writes: "When my soul must abandon this human habitation, I shall not believe I am dying utterly, but rather passing from one place to another." It could be surmised that the ego will not die utterly because it will rise to the heavenly abodes together with the soul departing from the body. But it seems that the soul's destiny does not interest Gargantua; he thinks of the change of "habitation" in earthly terms and within earthly space; he is interested in the life of his son and in the destiny of all the future generations. The vertical line of the soul's ascent is here completely suppressed; there remains the bodily horizontal, the passing from one abode to another, from the old to the youthful body, from generation to generation, from the past to the future.

But Rabelais did not have in mind the biological renewal and rejuvenation of a man through his progeny. For him the biological element could not be separated from the social, historic, and cultural element. The father's new flowering in the son does not take place on the same level but on a higher degree of mankind's development. When life is reborn, it does not repeat itself, it is perfected. Gargantua further points out in his letter the great transformation that took place during his lifetime:

Now, by God's grace, light and dignity have been restored to letters, and I have lived to see it. Indeed, I have watched such a revolution in learning that I, not erroneously reputed in my manhood the leading scholar of the century, would find it difficult to enter the bottom class in a grammar school.
(Book 2, Chapter 8)

Let us note, first of all, Rabelais' clear awareness of the historical revolution that has taken place, of the changing times, and the advent of a new era. The author expresses this awareness in the other parts of his novel with the help of a system of folk images, celebrating the New Year, spring, or carnival; in Gargantua's letter he creates a theoretical basis.

Rabelais clearly defines the specific character of human rejuvenation. The son does not merely repeat the youth of his father. Although Gargantua is the most highly educated man of his time, his knowledge is now insufficient for a child in first grade. Mankind is incessantly progressing historically and culturally, and thanks to this progress, the youth of each new generation attains a higher degree of cultural development. This is not the youth of an animal, which simply repeats the pattern of the preceding generations; it is the growth of historic man.

The image of old age flowering in its progeny has also a historic character. This, once more, is not the rejuvenation of the biological individual but of historic man's culture.

Two centuries were to elapse before Rabelais' idea could be repeated (and not in its best version) by Herder and his teaching of the progress of human culture in each new generation. Herder's attempt to justify death is idealistic, and his optimism is somewhat farfetched. It lacks the quality of Rabelais' unconditional defense of life, which is also inclusive of death.

The idea that man becomes more nearly perfect is completely cut off from the vertical ascent. The new, horizontal movement forward in real time and space is the prevailing note here. Man's improvement is attained not by the rise of the individual soul toward the hierarchical higher spheres but by man's historical development.

In Rabelais' novel the image of death is devoid of all tragic or terrifying overtones. Death is the necessary link in the process of the people's growth and renewal. It is the "other side" of birth.

Rabelais expressed this idea clearly, though somewhat rationalistically and conventionally, in the third chapter of Pantagruel, when Gargantua's wife dies as their son is born. In this situation Gargantua suffers great embarrassment: "A terrible doubt racked his brain: should he weep over the death of his wife or rejoice over the birth of his son?" And so he cries "like a cow," but then, thinking of Pantagruel, exclaims:

"Ho, ho ho, ho, how happy I am! Let us drink, ho! and put away our melancholy! Bring out the best wine, rinse the glasses, lay the table, drive out those dogs, poke up the fire, light the candles, close that door there, cut the bread in sippets for our pottage, send away these beggar folk but give them anything they ask for! You, there, hold my gown! I shall strip to my doublet to entertain the gossips better."

As he said this, he heard the priests chanting litanies and mementos as they bore his wife off to burial.
(Book 2, Chapter 3)

Birth and death meet in this scene. Death is the "other side" of birth. Gargantua does not know whether he should laugh or cry, but the joy of renewal prevails. The father celebrates the triumph of life by a gay feast, but as in the entire Rabelaisian world we find here an element of a utopian future. All that is not in the banquet spirit must be eliminated; no beggars, no dogs asking for food are allowed. Clothes must be changed ("I shall strip to my doublet"). There is also a travesty of the liturgy (the last supper, wine, bread, a clean tablecloth, burning candles, closed doors). But the celebration marks a real triumph, for life has defeated death.

In Rabelais' system of images the combination of death and laughter is characteristic. The episode of Janotus de Bragmardo (which we have analyzed elsewhere) ends as follows:

The theologian had no sooner concluded than Ponocrates and Eudemon burst into such uproarious peals of mirth that they all but gave up the ghost. Theirs was almost the plight of Roman Crassus who died of laughter when he saw a mule eating thistles and Greek Philemon, an ass eating figs prepared for his own dinner. Master Janotus began to laugh too, and all vied in hilarity. Their eyes watered at the violent concussion of the cerebral substance which pressed out these lachrymal humidities and brought them flowing out through the optic nerves. Here was a picture of Democratus heraclitizing and Heraclitus democratizing. (Book 1, Chapter 20)

Death from laughter is one of the forms of gay death. Rabelais turns more than once to this theme. In the tenth chapter of *Gargantua* he enumerates the cases of death caused by happiness and joy. These examples are borrowed from antique sources. For instance, he takes from Aulus Gellius the death of Diagoras, whose three sons won the Olympic games and who died from joy when the three youths placed their laurel crowns on his head and the spectators showered flowers on him. In Pliny Rabelais found the death of the Lacedaemonian Chilon in similar circumstances.[12] There are nine cases of death from joy in Rabelais' listing. The author even gives a physiological explanation of these accidents, founded on Galen.

In the Third Book, Chapter 21, we find the story of the last moments of the poet Raminagrobis. When Panurge and his companions visited the good old man, he was in the agony of death but still smiling cheerfully.

In the Fourth Book Rabelais describes the strange death of the giant Widenostrils, "swallower of windmills," and cites a long list

---

[12] We must note that these deaths of old men from joy are linked to the triumph of their sons.

of unusual demises, some of them due to happy circumstances (as death from drowning in a barrel of *malvasie*). Rabelais had borrowed most of these stories from ancient and new anthologies of death, which presented their subject systematically and were extremely popular. Rabelais' main source was the anthology of erudite works collected by Ravisius Textor.[13] This collection's first chapter was devoted to death and one section was entitled: "Deaths from laughter and joy."[14] This interest in unusual and gay deaths was typical of Rabelais and of his time.

Death is an ambivalent image for Rabelais and for the popular sources from which he drew his material; therefore, death can be gay. While depicting an individual body in the throes of death, this image also shows a glimpse of another youthful body being born; even if it is not shown or directly named, it is implicit in the image. Where death is, there also is birth, change, renewal. The image of birth is no less ambivalent; it represents the body that is born and at the same time shows a glimpse of the departing one. In the first case we have the negative pole but without a break with the positive pole; in the second case, we have the reverse, the positive continuous with the negative. The image of the underworld also bears this ambivalent character; it contains the past, the rejected and condemned, as unworthy to dwell in the present, as something useless and obsolete. But it also gives us a glimpse of the new life, of the future that is born, for it is this future that finally kills the past.

All these ambivalent images are dual-bodied, dual-faced, pregnant. They combine in various proportions negation and affirmation, the top and the bottom, abuse and praise. We shall have to

[13] The first edition of this book was published in 1503. Two other editions were published before 1532. The book enjoyed great success.

[14] In the anthology of Valerius Maximus, which enjoyed immense success as early as the Middle Ages, there is also a chapter "Of Extraordinary Deaths." Rabelais took five examples from it.

In the erudite anthology of Baptista Fulgosus (1507) there is a similar chapter on unusual deaths from which Rabelais borrowed two examples. The anthologies prove the popularity of this theme in the Middle Ages and the Renaissance.

examine once more this ambivalence of Rabelais' images but mostly from the formal point of view.

We shall first discuss Rabelais' peculiar form of negation, with which we are already partly familiar; we shall then turn to the combination of praise-abuse in the words used in his novel.[15]

Negation in popular-festive imagery has never an abstract logical character. It is always something obvious, tangible. That which stands behind negation is by no means nothingness but the "other side" of that which is denied, the carnivalesque upside down. Negation reconstructs the image of the object and first of all modifies the topographical position in space of the object as a whole, as well as of its parts. It transfers the object to the underworld, replaces the top by the bottom, or the front by the back, sharply exaggerating some traits at the expense of others. Negation and destruction of the object are therefore their displacement and reconstruction in space. The nonbeing of an object is its "other face," its inside out. And this inside out or lower stratum acquires a time element; it may be conceived as the past, the obsolete, or the nonexistent. The object that has been destroyed remains in the world but in a new form of being in time and space; it becomes the "other side" of the new object that has taken its place.

Carnival celebrates the destruction of the old and the birth of the new world—the new year, the new spring, the new kingdom. The old world that has been destroyed is offered together with the new world and is represented with it as the dying part of the dual body. This is why in carnivalesque images there is so much turnabout, so many opposite faces and intentionally upset proportions.

[15] We have in mind the manifestations of popular artistic imagery which until now have not been understood and studied. These are elemental dialectic phenomena. Up to now, only phenomena expressing the relations of formal logic have been analyzed, or, better, only those that fit the framework of these relations: manifestations in one single plane, in one dimension, and in one tone, representing the static character of the object, not its becoming and ambivalence. The manifestation of the culture of folk humor reflects precisely these dialectics in the form of imagery.

We see this first of all in the participants' apparel. Men are trans-vested as women and vice versa, costumes are turned inside out, and outer garments replace underwear. The description of a charivari of the early fourteenth century, in *Roman du Fauvel,* says of its participants, "They donned all their garments backward."

This logic of the "wrong side out" and of "bottoms up" is also expressed in gestures and other movements: to walk backward, to ride a horse facing its tail, to stand on one's head, to show one's backside.[16]

We find a similar logic in the choice and use of carnival objects. They are, so to speak, turned inside out, utilized in the wrong way, contrary to their common use. Household objects are turned into arms, kitchen utensils and dishes become musical instruments. Useless and worn-out items are produced, such as a pierced bucket and a barrel with its bottom knocked out. We have already seen the role played by junk in the carnivalesque underworld.

We have also sufficiently discussed the part played by "bottoms up" in folk humor, from common somersaults to more complex comic situations.

The imagery of time and space is also marked by the element of negation in abuse; this element is usually topographical: the bot-tom of the earth, the bottom of the human body. Abuse is the most ancient form of ambivalent negative imagery.

In Rabelais' system of images a highly important role is played by negation in time and space expressed in forms of the contrary— the backside, the lower stratum, the inside out, and the topsy-turvy. We have already given a sufficient number of these examples.

As a matter of fact, the negative pole in this time-space play is not removed from the positive pole. This is not an abstract, abso-lute negation that clearly cuts off the object from the rest of the world. The time-space negation does not make such a division; it considers the phenomenon in its becoming, in its movement from the negative to the positive pole. It does not deal with an abstract

---

[16] In the same description of charivari (*Roman du Fauvel*) one reads, *Li uns montret son cul au vent.*

concept (for this is no logical negation), it actually offers a description of the world's metamorphoses, its remodeling, its transfer from the old to the new, from the past to the future. It is the world passing through the phase of death on the way to birth. This is not understood by those who see in such images a bare, purely negative satire of definite, strictly limited contemporary manifestations. It would be more correct (though not quite accurate) to say that these images are oriented toward the entire scope of the contemporary world, toward the present as such, and that they represent this present in the sequence of the past giving birth to the future, or in the past's pregnant death.

Side by side with the time-space form of negation we see a related form constructing the positive image by means of the negation of certain manifestations. This is a process similar to the opposite, inside-out logic but in a more abstract form, without the clear time-space exchange. This form was widely utilized in grotesque realism. Its most common aspect is the simple act of replacing a negation by an affirmation. This is the method used to a certain extent by Rabelais in his construction of the image of the Abbey of Thélème. Thélème is the opposite of a monastery; that which is forbidden in the monastery is permitted and even prescribed in Thélème. We find in medieval literature a number of similar constructions. "The Rules of Blessed Libertine," a parody of monastic law, is similarly built on sanctifying that which is forbidden. Another example is the so-called "Song of the Vagrant Order," which rejects the common prohibitions. During the Renaissance a picture of the "inside-out monastery" where everything is submitted to the cult of love was given by Jean Lemaire in his "Temple of Venus" and by Coquillart in his "New Rights." Both these works had a certain influence on Rabelais.

In this play with negation, the opposition to the official world and all its prohibitions and limitations is obviously revealed. It also expresses the recreative, festive suspension of these restrictions. It is a carnival game of negation, and this game may also serve utopian tendencies (though expressed in a rather formalistic aspect).

The most interesting example of this carnivalesque game of negation is the famous "History of Nemo," *Historia de Nemine*, one of the most unusual pages of Latin recreative literature.

Radulfus Glaber, a French monk, composed the *Historia de Nemine* in the form of a sermon. *Nemo* is a hero whose nature, position, and exceptional powers are equal to those of the second person of the Trinity, that is, the Son of God. Radulfus discovered the great *Nemo* in a number of Biblical, Evangelical, and liturgical texts, as well as in Cicero, Horace, and other writers of antiquity; the word *nemo*, (nobody) which in Latin is used as a negation, was interpreted by Radulfus as a proper noun. For instance, in the Scriptures *nemo deum vidit* (nobody has seen God) in his interpretation became "Nemo saw God." Thus, everything impossible, inadmissible, inaccessible, is, on the contrary, permitted for *Nemo*. Thanks to this transposition, *Nemo* acquires the majestic aspect of a being almost equal to God, endowed with unique, exceptional powers, knowledge (he knows that which no one else knows) and extraordinary freedom (he is allowed that which nobody is permitted).

Radulfus' work has not been preserved, but the character of *Nemo* which he created impressed some of his contemporaries to the extent of initiating a special sect, the *secta neminiana*. This movement was opposed by a certain Stephen from the monastery of St. George, who demanded that the followers of the sect be condemned by the Paris hierarchy and burned at the stake. Stephen's polemic, as well as a number of revised versions of *Nemo*, have been preserved. There are many manuscripts of these revisions dating from the fourteenth and the fifteenth centuries, proving *Nemo*'s immense popularity. What was the attraction of this extraordinary character?

We do not know what were the intentions of *Nemo*'s original creator, Radulfus. But he probably did not take his character seriously; probably *Nemo* was no more than a game, the diversion of a medieval cleric. But the limited and bluntly serious Stephen (an agelast like Rabelais' Ticklepecker) took the story at its face value and began to fight the heresy. However, his approach was not typical; all *Nemo*'s revised versions have the obvious and frank character of an amusing game.

We have no reason to believe that the *Nemo* story in its different versions was in any way connected with the "feast of fools" or any other definite festivity of the carnival type. But its link with the festive, recreational atmosphere of the shrove days is beyond question. *Nemo*'s story is a typical recreation of the medieval cleric (as is the majority of medieval parodies); in this genre, speaking like the eulogists of the "feast of fools," folly inherent in man (in the ambivalent sense) must freely express itself. This is the air that must be pumped into wine barrels in order to preserve them from the "continual ferment of piousness and fear of God."

Nemo is the free carnivalesque play with official negations and prohibitions. This image is spun from freedom; it is the liberation from all the restrictions that oppress man and are consecrated by official religion. Hence, the exceptional attraction of this game for medieval man. All the endless gloomy sentences: "no one may," "no one can," "no one knows," "no one dares" are transformed into gay words: "Nemo may," "Nemo can," "Nemo knows," "Nemo must," "Nemo dares." The authors of the revised texts heaped up more and more freedoms, liberties, and exceptions on behalf of their hero. The proverb says, "no one is a prophet in his own country" (*nemo est acceptus propheta in patria*), but *Nemo* is a prophet at home. No one can have two wives, but *Nemo* is allowed bigamy. According to the Benedictine rule, it was forbidden to talk after supper, but *Nemo* was an exception, he could talk (*post completorium Nemo loquatur*). Thus, from the highest divine commandments to minor restrictions and limitations of monastic life, *Nemo*'s independence, freedom, and power remained unrestrained.

The play with negation in *Nemo*'s image was not devoid of a certain utopian element, though this utopianism had a formal-anarchist character. In spite of the difference between this play and the previously mentioned time-space forms of negation (the opposite world, the inside out), these two genres have an important function in common. *Nemo*'s image is the incarnation of the opposite, of the world of limited human possibilities, of official obligations and prohibitions. This is why the two forms are often combined and confused.

The play with negation can be found often in the work of Rabelais. Besides the Thélème utopia, already mentioned, let us look at Gargantua's childish occupations, where proverbs are used in their opposite sense. The role of negation is also important in the description of the exterior and interior organs of Carême-prenant and of his way of life. We also find this play in the eulogy of Panurge's debts, in the picture of the isle of Ennasin, and in a series of other episodes. Moreover, the play with negation is scattered throughout the entire novel. It is difficult at times to draw the line between the time-space opposites and the play with opposite meanings; one form passes directly into the other, as in the description of Carême-prenant. Both body and meaning can do a cartwheel, and in both cases the image becomes grotesque and ambivalent.

The play with negation and its time-space expression both combine in one single image the old and the new, the dying and the generated. Both phenomena are the expression of one dual-bodied world and of that time element which simultaneously destroys and renews, replaces and substitutes.

Let us now look at the fusion of praise and abuse in Rabelais' language. We have discussed this phenomenon in a previous chapter, where we saw that abuse is the "other side" of praise. The popular-festive language of the marketplace abuses while praising and praises while abusing. It is a two-faced Janus. It is addressed to the dual-bodied object, to the dual-bodied world (for this language is always universal); it is directed at once to the dying and to what is being generated, to the past that gives birth to the future. Either praise or abuse may prevail, but the one is always on the brink of passing into the other. Praise implicitly contains abuse, is pregnant with abuse, and vice versa abuse is pregnant with praise.

Rabelais has no neutral words; we always hear a mixture of praise and abuse. But this is the praise and abuse of the whole, of gay time. The point of view of the whole is far from being neutral and indifferent. It is not the dispassionate position of a third party, for there is no place for a third party in the world of becoming. The whole simultaneously praises and abuses. Praise and abuse may be aligned or divided among private voices, but in the whole they are fused into ambivalent unity.

Praise and abuse are mixed in Rabelais not only in the author's words but often also in the words of his characters. They are directed at the whole as well as at every part, however insignificant (for no part is seen separately from the whole). The fusion of praise-abuse belongs to the very essence of the Rabelaisian language.

It would be superficial and radically false to explain this mixture by the fact that in every real part of the existing world, as well as in every real individual, positive and negative traits are always combined, because there is always a reason for praise as well as for abuse. Such an explanation has a static and mechanical character; it conceives parts of the world scene as isolated, immovable, and completed. Moreover, separate features are stressed according to abstract moral principles. In Rabelais' novel praise-abuse is aimed at the entire present and at each of its parts, for all that exists dies and is born simultaneously, combines the past and the future, the obsolete and the youthful, the old truth and the new truth. However small the part of the existing world we have chosen, we shall find in it the same fusion. And this fusion is deeply dynamic: all that exists, both in the whole and in each of its parts, is in the act of becoming, and therefore comic (as all that is becoming), but its nature is also ironic and joyful.

We shall examine two episodes of the novel in which this fusion of praise-abuse is expressed with the greatest clarity and simplicity. We shall then look at similar manifestations and at some of their common sources.

In the Third Book Panurge, depressed by the unsolved problem of whether to marry and puzzled by the unsatisfactory answers of fortune-telling, turns to Friar John for advice. He makes his request in the form of a litany. For his invocation he chooses the indecent word *couillon* and repeats it 153 times, accompanying it with praise concerning the excellent condition of the friar's genital organ.

Here is the beginning of this litany:

"O dumpy cod, stumpy cod, famous in birth, hamous in girth; O cod, rich in lactory secretions and heavy as lead; O cod, rose-red; O cod, above all things fair, cod covered with hair; O cod, caulked and dawked, veined and ingrained: Hear me, I beseech you!

O tuck, O cod, O stucco cod; O cod grotesque (what incunabula you scrawl in grottos!); cod humoresque, cod arabesque (with styles, devices, mottoes!)".
(Book 3, Chapter 26)

All the 153 epithets added to *couillon* are extremely varied. They are grouped, without strict order, either for their alliteration, rhyme, or even assonance, or according to the various fields from which these expressions are taken—terms of the pictorial arts (grotesque, arabesque), literary terms (tragic, satyric). But all these are purely exterior links, which have no relation whatever to the object itself. All the epithets are equally unexpected and fortuitous. The word *couillon*, like all indecent words, is isolated; it is not used in the pictorial arts, in architecture, or in trade; each epithet applied to it is unusual and forms a *mésalliance*. But all the 153 terms have one trait in common: they all have a positive character, represent the *couillon* in excellent condition, and are, in this sense, a form of praise and glorification.

After Panurge has explained his case, Friar John addresses him in turn. But he is displeased with Panurge and his tone is therefore quite different. He chooses a similar form of invocation and repeats it 150 times, but all his epithets depict the phallus in poor condition. Here is an excerpt of Friar John's litany: "O mouldy, mildewed, musty cod; O fusty cod; O reasty, rusty cod; cod frigid and numb, kneaded in ice-cold water; cod pendent and pendulous, O cod appellent, cod levelled, slack, relaxed and flapping cod: Hear me, I beseech you!" (Book Three, Chapter 28). Friar John's invocation is abusive. The outward principle of choosing the epithets is the same as that adopted by Panurge; as applied to the given object they are fortuitous, except perhaps a few that indicate the symptoms of venereal disease.

Such is this famous episode of the parodical invocations. Let us first of all point out certain traits these images have in common with the swabs we previously discussed. The similarities are obvious. The 153 epithets linked with the phallus are subject to the rite of uncrowning and lead to a new birth. Their meaning is renewed in a sphere of life unusual for them. We are already familiar with this method. Let us look at some new elements.

The very word *couillon,* or "cod," was current in familiar billingsgate as a form of address, as abuse, as caress (*couillaud, couillette*), as friendly encouragement, or simply as an overemphasized mode of speech. In Rabelais' novel this word is used frequently. The author offers a great number of derivations, some of them rather unexpected: *couillard, couillâtre, coullaud, couillette, couillonnas, couillonne, couilloniforme, couillonnicque, couillonniquement,* and finally the woodcutter's name, *Couillatris.* Such unexpected and unusual derivations revived and renewed the word (Rabelais likes extraordinary derivations from indecent words). We must note that *couillon* contained an element of familiar invocation much stronger than that of other similar expressions. This is why Rabelais chose it for the construction of his parodical litany.

The word was essentially ambivalent; it closely combined praise and abuse, it glorified and humiliated. In this sense it was similar to the word *fol* or *sot.* Just as the fool was the king of the other world, the inside-out world, so was *couillon* the main organ of procreative force, the center of the nonofficial, forbidden picture of the world, the king of the topographic bodily lower stratum. Rabelais developed this ambivalence in his litany. It is impossible to trace a sharp line of distinction between the praise and the abuse of this invocation, to find where the one ends and the other begins. In this case it is not important whether the one litany chooses only the positive, and the other only the negative epithets:

both these categories are related to the deeply ambivalent word *couillon,* and both of them only strengthen this ambivalence. The word is repeated 303 times in the litanies; the very fact that the prayerful, cordial tone is replaced by the contemptuous, ironic one only increases the ambivalence of this Janus-like, dual-faced billingsgate. Thus Panurge's praise and Friar John's abuse are equally two-faced, each in its own way; put together they form another two-faced Janus of what might be called second degree.

This ambivalent eulogy of *couillon* creates the peculiar atmosphere of the entire conversation of Friar John and Panurge, an atmosphere characteristic of the whole novel. The eulogy introduces the same tone of absolute familiar billingsgate frankness, where all things are named by their own name, shown from the front and from behind, from top to bottom, from inside and out.

To whom is the praise-abuse of the litanies addressed? To Panurge? to Friar John? Perhaps it is addressed to those 303 manifestations, which are hitched as epithets to the indecent word and are thus uncrowned and renewed?

Formally, the praise-abuse of the litanies is addressed to Friar John and Panurge, but actually they have no definite, restricted addressee. They spread in all directions, drawing all spheres of culture and reality after them (in the linked epithets). The ambivalent word *couillon* as a familiar combination of praise-abuse is universal. It was not mere chance that the ecclesiastical form of litany was chosen, for this form of pious, one-sided praise is here debased and drawn into the vast torrent of praise-abuse, reflecting the contradiction of the world of becoming. The ambivalent invocation thus loses its character of common familiarity; it reflects a universal point of view, an authentic counter-litany addressed to the material bodily lower stratum, symbolized by the image of *couillon.*

It must be noted that the two litanies are separated by Friar John's words about the birth of the Antichrist and the necessity of emptying the seminal ducts (*couilles*) before the Last Judgment, and by Panurge's project of letting every criminal conceive a new life before execution. Here the image of *couillon* (*couilles*) is shown in its universal cosmic meaning and is directly linked with the images of the Last Judgment and of the underworld.

The parodical litany thus presents a condensed expression of the basic peculiarity of Rabelais' language, which always combines, more or less clearly, the praise-abuse image and is always addressed to the dual-bodied world of becoming. These peculiar traits of Rabelaisian language were already contained in the popular speech of the marketplace, toward which Rabelais' style was oriented.

This style is characterized by the absence of neutral words and expressions. It is colloquial speech, always addressed to somebody or talking for him, or about him. For this other party there are no neutral epithets and forms; there are either polite, laudatory, flattering, cordial words, or contemptuous, debasing, abusive ones. But even regarding a third party, there are no strictly neutral tones; neither are there any neutral words concerning objects; they are also either praised or abused.

The more official the speech, the more are these tones differentiated, for the speech reflects the established social hierarchy, the official scale of evaluation concerning objects and concepts and the static lines dividing them, as fixed by official philosophy.

But the more unofficial and familiar the speech, the more often and substantially are those tones combined, the less distinct is the line dividing praise and abuse. Indeed the two coincide in one person or object as representing the world of becoming. The hard, official lines of division between objects, phenomena, and values begin to change and fade. There is an awakening of the ancient ambivalence of all words and expressions, combining the wish of life and death, of sowing and rebirth. The unofficial aspect of the world of becoming and of the grotesque body is disclosed. But this ancient ambivalence is revived in a free and gay form.

The survival of this ambivalence can be observed even in the familiar speech of cultured men of our modern times. We find in intimate letters certain coarse and abusive words used in friendly fashion. When certain limits in men's relations have been removed, so that these relations become quite intimate and frank, the usual speech patterns begin to break up. A new, familiar pattern is constructed in which the current polite words begin to appear false, stereotyped, narrow, and especially incomplete. They have a hierarchical overtone and are inadequate for free familiar use. Therefore, all these current words are discarded and are replaced either by terms of abuse or by words created according to this abusive pattern, which are more realistically complete and alive. Praise and abuse are combined in them to form an indissoluble whole. Thus Friar John's and Panurge's two-faced *couillon* begins to emerge. Wherever conditions of absolute extra-official and full human relations are established, words tend to this ambivalent fullness. It is as if the ancient marketplace comes to life in closed chamber conversation. Intimacy begins to sound like the familiarity of bygone days, which breaks down all barriers between men.

It would be grossly incorrect to transfer this phenomenon to the psychological sphere. It is a complex social and verbal manifestation. All peoples still have enormous spheres of unpublicized speech, nonexistent from the point of view of literary written language. Only a small and polished portion of these unpublicized spheres of speech reaches the printed pages, usually in the form of "colorful dialogue" of the protagonists of a story, as removed as possible from the author's own direct and serious speech patterns. To form a strict ideological evaluation and a full artistic picture of these dialogues is impossible, not because they usually contain a great number of obscenities (not always the case) but because they appear alogical. They transgress all distances between objects, manifestations, and values; they fuse and combine elements that the mind is accustomed to divide strictly and even to oppose to each other. In these unpublicized spheres of speech all the dividing lines between objects and phenomena are drawn quite differently than in the prevailing picture of the world. These lines seek as it were to reach another object at the next point of development.

All these alogical spheres of unpublicized speech are manifested in modern times only when the serious goals of language have been dropped, when men are placed in conditions of extreme familiarity and engage in an aimless and uncontrolled verbal game, letting their imagination run from serious lines of thought. Such patterns find but a feeble reflection in literary writings, and only in the lowest and most senseless comic verbal forms.[17]

Today these spheres of unpublicized speech have almost lost their original meaning, have broken with folk culture and have become in most cases obsolete vestiges of the past. But in the days of Rabelais the role of the unpublicized spheres was entirely different. They were far from being unknown; on the contrary they were closely linked with marketplace publicity. Their intrinsic value in folk speech, which became for the first time the language of literature and ideology, was considerable. And their role in breaking up medieval philosophy and the building of a new world picture was highly productive.

Let us here examine one of these phenomena, though it has no direct visible connection with ambivalent praise-abuse.

One of the popular forms of comic speech was the so-called *coq-à-l'âne*, "from rooster to ass." This is a genre of intentionally absurd verbal combinations, a form of completely liberated speech that ignores all norms, even those of elementary logic.

The forms of verbal absurdities were widespread during the Middle Ages. The element of intentional absurdity existed in various aspects of many genres, but there was also a special genre of this comic speech known as *fatrasie*. This was a form of verse composed of an absurd string of words, linked by assonance or rhyme

[17] An important role is usually played by the unpublicized spheres during the juvenile period of an author's development, when they prepare his creative originality (which is always related to a certain destruction of the prevailing world picture and to its revision at least in part). See, for instance, the role of these spheres of speech during the youth of Flaubert. In general, the letters of Flaubert and of his friends (during all periods of his life) offer rich material for the study of the phenomena discussed here (familiar forms of speech, indecencies, friendly abuse, and aimless comic forms). See especially the letters of Poitevin to Flaubert and of Flaubert to Feydeau.

but with no meaning and no single theme. In the sixteenth century these verbal absurdities were often found in *soties*.

The expression *coq-à-l'âne* had been established after Clément Marot wrote his first poem in that genre, entitled *Epître du coq-à-l'âne, dédiée à Lyon Jamet*.[18] This piece contains no unity of composition nor logical consistency in the presentation of facts and the development of ideas but is devoted to "news of the day" in the life of Paris and of the royal court. This theme determines the intentionally scattered choice of events and thoughts, held together merely by the fact that they all make news.

In Rabelais' novel *coq-à-l'âne* plays an important role. The speeches of Kissarse and Bumfondle in the eleventh, twelfth, and thirteenth chapters of *Pantagruel* are constructed as typical *coq-à-l'âne*. We find a similar construction in the eleventh chapter of *Gargantua* which presents the young giant's amusements in a series of proverbs, most of them turned inside out. Another example of this genre is offered in Chapter 2 of the same book, entitled "Antidoted Flummeries." All these are systematic, pure, and unbroken *coq-à-l'âne*. But many verbal absurdities and alogisms are scattered throughout the book. For instance, there are strong *coq-à-l'âne* elements in Chapter 9 of the Fourth Book, which lists the strange names and family relations of the inabitants of the Ennasin Island.

What is the artistic and ideological meaning of this genre?

First of all, it is a game of words, current expressions (proverbs and adages), and common sequences of terms deprived of their logic and meaning. It is as if words had been released from the shackles of sense, to enjoy a play period of complete freedom and establish unusual relationships among themselves. True, no new consistent links are formed in most cases, but the brief coexistence of these words, expressions, and objects outside the usual logical conditions discloses their inherent ambivalence. Their multiple meanings and the potentialities that would not manifest themselves in normal conditions are revealed.

---

[18] The expression *coq-à-l'âne*, meaning an absurdity and inconsequence of speech, existed of course before the creation of this genre.

But every separate case of this genre has its own functions and character. For instance, the "Antidoted Flummeries" are constructed as a riddle. This chapter depicts certain historic events but with a considerable admixture of obscenities and a few banquet images. The poem is written in such a way that the reader is induced to look in it for allusions to some contemporary or recent political events.[19] Thus a peculiar carnivalesque picture of political and historical life is created by the author. Events are conceived outside their traditional official interpretation and offer, therefore, new opportunities for interpretation and appreciation.

A different character is presented by Chapter 11 of the same book (*Gargantua*). Gargantua's childish amusements are here pictured with the aid of proverbs and various common expressions. But they follow each other without any logical sequence. Moreover, these expressions are turned inside out. Gargantua always acted in his own way, in spite of the proverb, that is, he acted contrary to the proverb's recommendation. For instance, he bit off more than he could chew, leapt before he looked, and struck the iron while it was cold. As a result of this game, the image of young Gargantua is built in the spirit of the folkloric fool, whose actions are contrary to reason, defying all norms of common sense.

Finally, the speeches of Kissarse, Bumfondle, and Pantagruel in the episode of the lawsuit offer the purest, one might say classic *coq-à-l'âne*. The speeches are not a parody of the legal eloquence of that time, nor are they, generally speaking, a parody at all. The images chosen for the speeches are devoid of all visible links. Here is the beginning of Kissarse's speech:

"My Lord, the truth is that a good woman of my house was taking her eggs to market . . . .
Whereas there passed between the twin tropics the sum of three-pence towards the zenith . . . and *whereas* the Riphaean Mountains had that year suffered a great sterility of paste and imitation stone . . . and *whereas* this was due to a warfare of fiddlefaddle seditiously

---

[19] The representatives of the historic-allegoric method attempted to decipher these allusions.

fomented between the tripegabblers and the Accursian maunder-mongers . . . and *whereas* the cause of the contention was the re-bellion of the Switzers, who had assembled to the number of three, six, nine, ten . . . and *whereas* they did this to get presents on New Year's day, at the season when soup is served to oxen and the keys of the coal cellar given to country wenches so they may feed the dogs plenty of oats. . . .

. . . all night long they kept their hands on the pot, dispatching Bulls on horseback and Bulls on foot to keep the ships in harbor, because the tailors insisted on making stolen tatters into

A peashooter to shoot a pea
Across the Oceanic Sea

which at the moment was pregnant with a potful of cabbage, ac-cording to the opinion handed down by the manufacturers of hay-bundles. On the contrary, the physicians maintained that the urine revealed no positive traces . . .'
(Book 2, Chapter 11)

As we pointed out, there is no link between these images; Kis-sarse's speech truly skips from "rooster to ass." It is built in the spirit of the Russian proverb: "In the vegetable garden grows the elder tree, and uncle is in Kiev." But all these jumbled images are offered according to the Rabelaisian system. We have here the typical grotesque picture of the world, in which the generating, devouring, and defecating body is fused with nature and with cosmic phenomena: the Riphaean mountains sterile of imitation stone, the sea pregnant with cabbage, physicians analyzing the urine of the sea ("the Pantagruel complex"). We further see vari-ous kitchen and household materials and activities in their carni-valesque aspect (soup served to oxen, the feeding of oats to dogs). Finally, all these grotesque bodily, cosmic, and carnivalesque im-ages are combined with historic events (the rebellion of the Switz-ers, the dispatching of Bulls to keep the ships in harbor). All these images and the very mode of their combination are typical of popu-lar-festive forms. We shall also find these images in the *soties* and farces of the time of Rabelais but subject, usually, to definite topical lines. In the quoted excerpt we find a completely free carni-valesque game of images, unrestricted by any framework of meaning. The divisions between the phenomena and the objects are completely effaced, and the grotesque aspect of the world is sharply outlined.

In a period of the radical breaking up of the world's hierarchical picture and the building of a new concept, leading to a revision of all old words, objects, and ideas, the *coq-à-l'âne* acquired an essential meaning; it was a form which granted momentary liberation from all logical links—a form of free recreation. It was, so to speak, the carnivalization of speech, which freed it from the gloomy seriousness of official philosophy as well as from truisms and commonplace ideas. This verbal carnival broke man's century-old chains of medieval philosophy, thus preparing a new sober seriousness.

Let us return to the problem of combined praise-abuse in Rabelais' work and examine another example.

The Third Book contains the famous episode in which Pantagruel and Panurge vie in their eulogy of the fool Triboulet. They give 208 epithets describing his *folie*, again a litany. The epithets are taken from various spheres: astronomy, music, medicine, legal and political relations, falconry, and others. The choice of these words is as unexpected and illogical as in the other parodical litanies analyzed previously. Here, too, everything is ambivalent. All these epithets expressing the highest degree of a certain quality refer to folly and praise it. But folly, as we know, is also ambivalent. The fool or clown is the king of the upside-down world. In the word *fol*, as in the word *couillon*, praise and abuse are merged into an indissoluble whole. To take the word "fool" as pure negation and abuse or as pure praise (as for instance, the word "saint") would destroy the entire meaning of this protean litany. In another part of the novel Triboulet is described as "morosophic," that is, foolish-wise. We know Rabelais' comic etymology of the word *philosophie* as *fin folie*. All these expressions toy with the word and image of *fol*.

Triboulet's eulogy is described by Rabelais himself as a *blason*, (blazon), a characteristic literary manifestation of the Renaissance. In addition to its special heraldic use, *blason* has the dual connotation of both praise and abuse. This dual meaning already existed in the old French language and was fully preserved at the time of Rabelais (though the negative element of this word, blame, is somewhat mitigated). Only later did *blason* express merely the idea of praise (*louange*).

Blazons were widespread in the literature of the first part of the sixteenth century. Everything was submitted to blazoning.

Clément Marot wrote two short humorous poems entitled "The Beautiful Breast" and "The Ugly Breast," thus creating a new type of *blason* which produced a great effect. Poets began to blazon women's mouths, ears, tongues, teeth, eyes, and eyebrows, performing a systematic dissection and anatomization of woman in a tone of humorous, familiar praise or denigration. The method was typical of those days, for it was rooted in popular speech, which was the source of avant-garde literature and of the poets of Clément Marot's school in particular. The blazon preserved the duality of its tone in its appreciation; in other words, it could render praise ironical and flatter that which was usually not to be flattered.[20] Blazons remained outside the official system of straight and strict evaluations. They were a free and ambiguous praise-abuse. Here is the definition of this genre, given by Thomas Sébillet in his *Art Poétique françois* in 1548: "The blazon is a continuous praise or constant abuse of the object to be blazoned . . . both the hideous and beautiful, the bad and the good can be equally well blazoned." This definition clearly stresses the blazon's ambivalence. Sébillet's *Art Poétique* represents the poetics of the school of Clément Marot; it belongs to the time of Rabelais.

We must point out that poetic blazons, and those of Clément Marot's school in particular, sometimes acquired the character of pure praise or denigration. This rhetorical degeneracy sharply increased toward the end of the century. The link with popular

---

[20] This is exemplified in the eulogy of Panurge's debts. Ambiguous praise was also widespread in Italian literature. See Berni, *Lode del debito* ("In Praise of Debt") and the praise of card games with which we are already familiar.

blazons and with the popular dual-faced praise of the marketplace was more and more attenuated, while the influence of antique (rhetorical) forms of praise was increased.[21]

Elements of the blazon were common in the great genres of the fifteenth and of the first part of the sixteenth century, in the mysteries and *soties*. Here we find the praise of fools (*sots*) in the form of a long list of epithets, similar to the Rabelaisian eulogy of Triboulet. We find blazons in the "Mystery of Saint Quentin," and the "Monologue of Fools"[22] contains approximately one hundred epithets and forty-eight verses filled with this blazoning. Finally, in the "New Monologue of Fools"[23] we find as many as one hundred and fifty epithets.

Thus Triboulet's blazoning eulogy had a traditional character and was thought by Rabelais' contemporaries to be self-explanatory. We have already pointed out the immense importance of the fool and clown and of the theme of folly.

Let us now have a look at the popular blazons in the narrow sense of the word. The popular tradition was mostly concerned with the praise and abuse of other nationalities, of various regions, provinces, cities, and villages. Definite epithets were attached to each, and these were more or less developed and given ambivalent connotations, although in some cases the abusive element prevailed.

The oldest collection of this genre dates from the thirteenth century. At the time of Rabelais a new collection appeared under the

---

[21] An interesting example of rhetorical praise-abuse is *Der Satyrische Pylgram* (1666) by Grimmelshausen. The subtitle of this work is *Kalt und Warm, Weiss und Schwarz* "Cold and Hot, White and Black." In his preface Grimmelshausen declares that there is nothing perfect in this world except God, and that there is nothing so bad, except the devil, that it cannot be praised in some way. He discusses twenty themes (man, money, dances, wine, women, weapons, gunpowder, war, masquerades, medicine, and others), praising each first, then denigrating it, until something like a synthesis is finally offered.

[22] Anatole de Montaiglon, *Recueil de poésies françaises de XVème et XVIème siècles*, Vol. 1, pp. 11–66.

[23] *Ibid.*, Vol. 3, pp. 15–18.

title of *Dict des Pays*.[24] It contained short characterizations in most cases of nationalities, provinces and cities.

Rabelais gives a number of characterizations repeating the popular blazons. For instance, he writes: *saoul comme un Anglais* (drunk as an Englishman). This was a persistent blazon of the English; even in the oldest, thirteenth-century collection England is defined by this trait: *Li mieldre buveor en Engleterre*, "the best drunkards are in England."[25] In the first chapter of *Pantagruel* Rabelais mentions the *couilles de Lorraine*. The inhabitants of Lorraine were blazoned for the unusual size of their *couilles*. Rabelais also mentions the swiftness of the Basques, love in Avignon, the Parisians' curiosity; all these are epithets from popular blazons. And still another ancient blazon is *Li plus sot en Bretagne*, "the most foolish are in Brittany."

We see that popular blazons are deeply ambivalent. Each nationality, province, or city is the best in the world in respect to one attribute: Englishmen are the best drunkards, people of Lorraine the most potent sexually, in Avignon there is the greatest number of prostitutes, the Bretons are the most foolish, and so on. But the special attribute has in most cases an ambiguous or, more correctly speaking, a dual character. Praise and abuse are merged into an indissoluble unity. The Breton's attribute "the most foolish" reminds us directly of Triboulet's blazon. Popular blazons are usually listed as ironical; this is true in the original Greek sense but untrue if we grant irony its new, more subjective and negative meaning. Popular blazons are two-faced.[26]

Rabelais' novel contains all the types of blazons of his time. *Pantagruel* offers a poem in the spirit of Clément Marot's school,

24 *Ibid.*, pp. 110–116.
25 It is interesting that this old blazon of the English is repeated by Maxim Maximovich in Lermontov's "Hero of our Time." We also find it in Shakespeare, spoken by Iago in *Othello*.
26 At the end of the last century interesting material concerning popular blazons of various provinces of France began to be published. See H. Gaidoz et P. Sébillot. *Blason populaire de la France*, Paris, 1884; Canel, *Blason populaire de la Normandie*, 1857; Banquier, *Blason populaire de la Franche-Comté*, Paris, 1897.

blazoning the University of Orléans. Popular blazons, that is, ethnic epithets, are scattered throughout the novel, and we have quoted some of them. The eulogy of the clown Triboulet and the blazoned parodical litanies of Friar John and Panurge disclose the deepest essence of this genre, its dual face, complete ambivalence, and contradictory fullness. Finally, blazoning tones pervade the entire novel, which is filled with ambiguous praise and abuse.

A certain duality is also inherent in pure abusive forms without any elements of praise. Here is an example of such abuse from Chapter 25 of *Gargantua*:

> The bakers not only turned a deaf ear to our shepherds' request, but worse, insulted them outrageously. Apparently our men were waifs, snaggleteeth, red-headed Judases, wastrels and shitabeds; they were stinkers and fly-by-night smoothsters—idlers, too, yet nicksters—belly-busters, proudsters, badsters, clots, sharpers, puts, scabbard-dragglers and sweets. (The latter mild epithet applies to one whose fly is lined with silk and satire.) Joke-smiths, they were, yet lazy, riffraff oaves, louts, wompsters, tonies, wonglers, fops and rattletooth almsters, and, for occupation, they herded petrified turds and shepherded stillicidious excrement. Such was the harvest of defamatory epithets our herders reaped and, hard upon it, the flat statement that they were unfit to taste dainty pastry. Let them be satisfied with coarse bread and hard loaf.
> (Book 1, Chapter 25)

Here we have a common string of abuse. The length of this string of derogatory expressions is striking; there are twenty-eight abusive words. This group of abuses is not ambivalent as a whole, it is purely negative. But within the group most of the expressions are ambivalent; they are related to animal traits, bodily defects, foolishness, gluttony, defecation—all characteristic of the popular system of images. Such an expression as *chienlicts, (chie-en-lit)* is used to designate one of the carnival masks. Thus even this group of abuses discloses the image of the unlimited and mixed human body and of bodily life (food, defecation) in its grotesque ambivalence. We see the peculiar two-faced aspect of the world, the peculiar character of men and objects, which does not exist in the system of literary speech imagery.

Let us look at yet another manifestation of praise-abuse in Rabelais' novel, the famous inscription on the gates of Thélème, in which some are expelled from the abbey while others are invited. This inscription in verse can be considered as belonging to the genre of the *cri*, that is to say, of those "cries" which opened the performances of mysteries and *soties* and were addressed to the representatives of various social groups and corporations, or to fools (in the *soties*). This is the loud cry of the marketplace composed in the official or in the parodical style. The inscription on the Thélème gates belongs to this genre but, of course, not in its construction and versification.

The inscription can be divided into two parts: the words that expel and those that invite. The first part has a purely abusive character, the second part contains words of pure praise. The abusive character of the first part is strictly observed. In the first stanza, for instance, Rabelais abuses hypocrites with fifteen different epithets, among them *hypocrites, bygotz, vieux matagotz, marmiteux*. Nearly all the other words of this stanza have an abusive nuance (*abus meschant, meschanceté, faulseté, troublez*). In the stanzas that proffer an invitation (starting with the fifth), all the words, on the contrary, have a positive connotation and are chosen to express praise and friendliness (*gentilz, joyeux, plaisans, mignons, serains, subtilz*). Thus the two strictly organized groups of praise and abuse are opposed to each other. As a whole, the inscription is ambivalent. But there is no ambivalence within it; each word has either a purely positive or purely negative meaning. This is a case of ambivalence that has become somewhat exterior and rhetorical.

The praise-abuse in Rabelais becomes rhetorical whenever he turns away from the popular marketplace forms and approaches official speech and official style. This was, in part, the case of the Thélème episode. True, we have here an element of opposites, of an interplay of negations and certain other popular-festive traits, but Thélème is essentially a humanist utopia reflecting the influence of literary (mostly Italian) sources.

We observe a similar phenomenon in the chapters where Rabelais speaks directly as an almost official "royal publicist."

In the Third Book, Chapter 48, there is a conversation between Gargantua and Pantagruel concerning a theme of special interest at that time: the refusal of the Church to consecrate a marriage concluded against the will of the parents. Here we see an example of the rhetorical nature of praise and abuse:

" . . . according to the laws of the country I cited, what happens? Take the most errant ruffian, villain or scoundrel; the most evil-smelling foul-breathing hangdog; the most scurvy and leprous stinkard; your most vicious footpad or brigand imaginable. Well, such a knave may abduct the most highborn, the richest, the most upright and the chastest maiden in the land; he may snatch her out of her father's house, out of the very embrace of her mother, and far beyond reach of kin and friend. All he needs is a priest to help him, by celebrating a secret marriage, and to share the future spoils."
(Book 3, Chapter 48)

The groups of abuse and praise are here devoid of all ambivalence; they are separated and opposed to each other as distinct phenomena that do not merge. This is a purely rhetorical speech that draws sharp static lines between the various manifestations and values. All that remains of the marketplace element is the rather exaggerated length of the string of abuses.

The phenomenon of praise-abuse that we have examined has an important theoretical, historical, and literary meaning. Positive and negative elements are, of course, inherent in every word of a living speech. There are no indifferent, neutral words; there can only be artificially neutralized words. In the most ancient forms of speech the merging of praise and abuse, that is, a duality of tone, is characteristic. In the subsequent development this duality of tone subsists; it acquires a new meaning in the nonofficial, familiar, and humorous popular spheres. Thanks to the duality of tone, the laughing people, who were not in the least concerned with the stabilization of the existing order and of the prevailing picture of the world (the official truth), could grasp the world of becoming as a whole. They could thus conceive the gay relativity of the limited class theories and the constant unfinished character of the world—

the constant combination of falsehood and truth, of darkness and light, of anger and gentleness, of life and death.[27] The dual tone of the people's speech is never torn away from this whole nor from the becoming; this is why the negative and the positive elements do not seek a separate, private, and static expression. The dual tone never wants to halt the spinning wheel, to find and outline the top and the bottom, the front and the back; on the contrary, it marks their continuous change and fusion. In popular speech the accent is always placed on the positive element (but we repeat, without tearing it away from the negative).

In the official philosophy of the ruling classes such a dual tone of speech is, generally speaking, impossible: hard, well-established lines are drawn between all the phenomena (and these phenomena are torn away from the contradictory world of becoming, of the whole). A monotone character of thought and style almost always prevails in the official spheres of art and ideology.

At the time of the Renaissance the dual tone of popular speech was waged in a tense struggle against the stabilizing tendencies of the official monotone. For a deeper understanding of the complex and varied manifestations of style of that great epoch, the study of this struggle is exceptionally important and interesting (as is the struggle of the grotesque against the classic canon, the two conflicts being related). This struggle, of course, continued during the following centuries, but it acquired new, complex, and sometimes hidden forms. However, this theme is outside the scope of our present work.

The ancient dual tone of speech is the stylistic reflection of the ancient dual-bodied image. As the ancient image disintegrated, an

[27] Goethe gives an interesting picture of the dual body in its serious philosophic aspect in his poem: "The Pariah." The fusion of praise and abuse in relation to the Divinity in the thematic (not stylistic) monotone is expressed as follows:
And I will murmur to him gently,
And I will shout to him angrily
That which clear reason orders,
That which weighs heavily on my chest.
These thoughts, these feelings—
Let them be an eternal secret.

interesting phenomenon in the history of literature and spectacle took place: the formation of images in pairs, which represent top and bottom, front and back, life and death. The classic example of such pairs is Don Quixote and Sancho, but similar images are still seen today in circus sideshows and other comic productions. The dialogue of these pairs is of considerable interest, since it marks the as yet incomplete disintegration of the dual tone. In reality, it is a dialogue of the face with the buttocks, of birth with death. We find a similar manifestation in the antique and medieval debates between winter and spring, old age and youth, fasting and abundance, old times and new, parents and children. These debates are an organic part of the system of popular-festive forms, related to change and renewal. (Such a debate is recalled by Goethe in his description of the Roman carnival.) The debates were known as *agons* in ancient literature; for instance, we have an interesting fragment of a debate between three choirs—old men, adults, and boys—in which each choir proved the value of its age.[28] *Agons* were most common in Sparta and Italy (and in modern Sicily they are still the indispensable feature of popular feasts). The *agons* of Aristophanes are complex and literary in character. Similar debates in Latin (for instance, *conflictus veris et hiemis*), and especially in the vernacular, were popular in all countries.

All these *agons* and debates are dialogues of the forces and phenomena of different times, of two poles of becoming, of the beginning and the end of a metamorphosis. They unfolded and to a certain extent rationalized or rhetoricized the dialogue element inherent in the dual-tone speech. These popular-festive debates of time and age, as well as the dialogues in pairs, of face and buttocks, top and bottom, were apparently one of the folkloric roots of the novel and of its specific dialogue. But this theme is also outside the scope of our work.

It remains for us to sum up some of the elements of the present chapter.

[28] See Bergk, Fr., *Carmina Popularia,* 18.

The last phenomenon we examined, the combination of praise-abuse, reflects ambivalence on the stylistic plane, duality of the body and incompleteness (the eternal unfinished nature) of the world which we found expressed in all the peculiarities of the Rabelaisian system of images. The old dying world gives birth to the new one. Death throes are combined with birth in one indissoluble whole. This process is represented in the images of the material bodily lower stratum; everything descends into the earth and the bodily grave in order to die and to be reborn. This is why the downward movement pervades Rabelais' entire imagery from beginning to end. All these images throw down, debase, swallow, condemn, deny (topographically), kill, bury, send down to the underworld, abuse, curse; and at the same time they all conceive anew, fertilize, sow, rejuvenate, regenerate, praise, and glorify. This general downward thrust, which kills and regenerates, unifies such different phenomena as blows, abuses, the underworld, and the act of devouring.

We must add that even Dante's images of the inferno sometimes are obvious reflections of abusive metaphors. At times he openly brings in the theme of devouring (Ugolino gnawing Ruggieri's skull, Satan's jaws gnawing Judas, Brutus, and Cassius); at other times abuse and devouring are implicit in his images. But their ambivalence is almost completely toned down in Dante's world.

During the Renaissance all these images of the lower stratum, from cynical abuse to the image of the underworld, were filled with a deep awareness of historic time, of the change of epochs in world history. In Rabelais this element of time and of historic change deeply pervades all his images of the material bodily lower stratum and lends them historic coloring. In his work the dual body becomes a dual world, the fusion of the past and future in the single act of the death of the one and the birth of another, in the image of the grotesque historic world of becoming and renewal. Time itself abuses and praises, beats and decorates, kills and gives birth; this time is simultaneously ironic and gay, it is the "playing boy" of Heraclitus, who wields supreme power in the universe. Rabelais builds an extraordinarily impressive image of historical becoming within the category of laughter. This was not possible before the Renaissance, when it had been prepared by the entire process of historical development. "History acts fundamentally and goes through many phases when it carries obsolete forms of life into the grave. The last phase of the universal historic form is its comedy. . . . Why such a march of history? This is necessary in order that mankind could say a gay farewell to its past."[29]

This Rabelaisian system of images, which is universal and all-embracing, permits and even demands both an exceptional concreteness and fullness; it looks for detail, exactness, actuality, the sense of reality in the presentation of historical facts. Each of these images combines an extreme breadth and a cosmic character with an exceptionally concrete feeling of life, with individuality and a journalistic response to the events of the day. Our last chapter will be devoted to this remarkable aspect of Rabelaisian realism.

[29] K. Marx and F. Engels, *Collected Works.* Vol. 1, p. 418.

CHAPTER SEVEN

Rabelais' Images and His Time

We have examined Rabelais' images mostly in relation to folk culture. Our interest lay in the basic struggle between this culture and the official Middle Ages. But we have already pointed out that this main line was organically combined with the echoes of more or less important events that marked the years, months, or even days when the various parts of the novel were created. We may say with assurance that the entire novel, from beginning to end, grew out of the very depths of the life of that time, a life in which Rabelais himself was a participant or an interested witness. His images link the immeasurable depth and breadth of folk universalism with concreteness, individuality, and with a detailed presentation of living actuality. These images are far remote from abstract symbolism and schematism. We may say that in Rabelais' novel the cosmic breadth of myth is combined with the directness of a modern survey and the concrete precision of a realist novel. Beyond the images that may appear fantastic we find real events, living persons, and the author's own rich experience and sharp observation.

French Rabelaisiana has performed an important and assiduous task in order to discover this link of Rabelais' images with his own time. Thanks to this research, considerable and valuable factual material has been collected. But this material has been clarified and generalized according to narrow methodological positions. A faulty "biographism" prevails, in which social and political events lose their direct meaning and sharp implications, are minimized, blunted, and become mere facts in the author's own life story. They remain at the level of everyday trivialities. In the accumulation of this biographical data we lose sight of the portentous meaning of that time as well as of Rabelais' novel. Neither do we any longer see the genuine popular position that Rabelais upheld in the struggle of his time.

True, certain Rabelais scholars, and especially the late Abel Lefranc, devoted considerable attention to the political events reflected in the novel, but intepreting them, as well as their presentation by Rabelais, on the official plane. Abel Lefranc even considered Rabelais as a "royal publicist." True, our author was a "publicist" but not a "royal" one, though he did understand the relatively progressive spirit of the royal government and of some individual aspects of the king's policy. We have already said that Rabelais offered remarkable examples of the publicity of the marketplace, a publicity without an iota of officialdom. He did not adhere completely to any group within the framework of the ruling classes (including the bourgeoisie); he did not adopt any official point of view, nor did he agree with any proceeding or approve any current event. But at the same time he could very well grasp and appreciate the relative progressiveness of specific manifestations of his epoch, among them certain royal decrees that he welcomed in his novel. However, his appreciation never took on an official and unconditional character. For the popular, marketplace images, saturated with ambivalent laughter, disclosed all the limitations of this progressiveness. From the people's point of view, as expressed in the novel, there were always wider perspectives, reaching far beyond the limited progress of the time. Rabelais' basic goal was to destroy the official picture of events. He strove to take a new look at them, to interpret the tragedy or comedy they represented from the point of view of the laughing chorus of the marketplace. He summoned all the resources of sober popular imagery in order to break up official lies and the narrow seriousness dictated by the ruling classes. Rabelais did not implicitly believe in what his time "said and imagined about itself"; he strove to disclose its true meaning for the people, the people who grow and are immortal.

While destroying the official conception of his time and of contemporary events, Rabelais did not seek, of course, to submit them to a scholarly analysis. He did not speak in the conceptual language but in the tongue of popular comic images. While breaking up false seriousness, false historic pathos, he prepared the soil for a new seriousness and for a new historic pathos.

Let us now look at a number of examples from Rabelais' novel which reflect his time, from his immediate surroundings to great historical events.

The first chapter of *Pantagruel,* while describing the hero's birth, recalls the terrible heat and drought of that season and the thirst it caused among the people. According to Rabelais this drought lasted "thirty-six months, three weeks, four days and thirty hours or more." From the memoirs of Rabelais' contemporaries we learn that the year 1552, when *Pantagruel* was written, was marked by a severe drought that lasted six months. The author merely exaggerated the length of the drought. As we have said, the general suffering revived the image of the devilkin Pantagruel who made people thirsty, thus lending reality to this image. In the same book we find the episode of Panurge buying indulgences to improve his financial affairs. In that very year when Rabelais was writing his novel a Papal jubilee was proclaimed in France. The churches visited by Panurge were actually authorized to sell indulgences. As we see, the accuracy of every detail was here strictly observed by our author.

In the same book we find the following episode:

> Reading the noble *Chronicles* of his ancestors, Pantagruel discovered that Geoffroi de Lusignan, known as Geoffrey with the Great Tooth, his stepmother's daughter-in-law's uncle's son-in-law's aunt's eldest sister's cousin-in-law's grandfather, was buried at Maillezais, the abbey he had destroyed and later rebuilt. Accordingly, like a dutiful relative, Pantagruel took a day off to call on Ardillon, the noble abbot; then, passing through Sansay, Celles, Coulonges and Fontenay-le-Comte (where he saluted the learned Tiraqueau), he reached Maillezais and duly visited the sepulchre of Geoffrey with the Great Tooth.
> (Book 2, Chapter 5)

When Pantagruel saw Geoffrey's stone effigy erected on his tomb, he was impressed by the angry look the sculptor had lent his statue.

In this episode there are two fantastic traits: the image of the traveling giant Pantagruel and his comic, parodical relationship to Geoffrey. All the other elements of this episode—the names of the persons and localities, the various events, the statue's angry look, and other details—strictly correspond to reality and are intimately linked with Rabelais' own life and impressions.

In those days (1524–1527) when Rabelais was secretary of Geoffroi d'Estissac, bishop and abbot of Maillezais, he often traveled back and forth from Poitiers (Pantagruel's itinerary), riding past the localities he faithfully cites in his story. D'Estissac was at that time incessantly traveling throughout his diocese (like most prelates in those days, he was interested in building), and Rabelais accompanied him on these journeys. Therefore, he was thoroughly familiar with the province of Poitou and with its smallest localities. He names some fifty of these in his novel, some of them mere hamlets. All the names listed in our episode were well known to him. Rabelais' first years as a monk were spent in the Cordeliers' monastery at Fontenay-le-Comte; he attended the meetings of humanist lawyers held at the home of the scholar Tiraqueau, with whom he remained friendly to the end of his life. Near Legugé was the abbey where Rabelais often visited the learned Abbot Ardillon. Here, under the influence of Jean Boucher, he apparently wrote his first poems in French. Both Ardillon and Tiraqueau were Rabelais' well-known contemporaries.

Neither was Pantagruel's ancestor Geoffroi de Lusignan, nicknamed "Great Tooth," an imaginary person. He lived in the early thirteenth century and burned the abbey of Maillezais (for this crime Rabelais pictured him in the underworld as a vendor of flint, a carnivalesque punishment). Lusignan later repented, rebuilt the abbey, and richly endowed it. This is why a magnificent statue was erected in his honor in the church of Maillezais, although his body was buried elsewhere.

The angry look of the stone effigy described in the novel also strictly corresponds to reality. True, the statue has since been destroyed, but its head was found under the ruins of the church and is now preserved in the museum of Niort. Plattard describes this sculpture as follows: "Puckered brows, a severe and petrified expression, bristling whiskers, wide-open mouth and bared teeth; the entire sculpture is a naïve picture of anger."[1]

Let us stress in Geoffroi's portrait the wide-open mouth and bared teeth, the dominant grotesque image of Pantagruel in the Second Book. Is this why Rabelais, who so often beheld this sculpture in the abbey's church and retained it in his memory, made Geoffroi Pantagruel's ancestor?

The structure and content of this brief and minor episode are extremely typical of Pantagruel's fantastic and even cosmic image, woven from a reality intimately known to the author.

Pantagruel travels through an area with which Rabelais was familiar, meets the author's personal friends, and sees objects Rabelais had seen. The episode contains many real names of people and localities and even gives some personal home addresses, of Ardillon and Tiraqueau.

[1] Jean Plattard, *L'Invention et la composition dans l'oeuvre de Rabelais*, p. 58.

The world surrounding Pantagruel has therefore a realistic individual character; it presents familiar names of various people and objects. Abstract generalizations, typifications, and appellations are reduced to a minimum. We must also stress the local topographical character of this episode. We find this character throughout the novel. Rabelais always seeks to introduce into the texture of his story a real peculiar trait of some French province or town, some local curiosity or legend. We have already mentioned that the dish for Pantagruel's gruel was actually displayed in Bourges as "the giant's bowl." Little Pantagruel was chained to his crib, and Rabelais notes that one of the chains is preserved in La Rochelle, the other in Lyon, and the third in Angers. These chains were actually exhibited and were well known to the inhabitants of the three towns. In Poitiers young Pantagruel broke off a piece of rock and built a table for the students. This broken rock still exists in Poitiers but is split in two parts.

Such locally known items, scattered throughout the novel, strengthen the individual traits of things already familiar. These are characteristic elements of the Rabelaisian world. Even objects of common use, such as a bowl for gruel, acquire an individual character as relics belonging to historical figures and exhibited in museums. We shall later return to Rabelaisian individualizations.

Let us now look at the book of *Gargantua*. The events of this book (except the Paris episodes) take place in the region of Chinon, in Rabelais' native land. All the localities, large or small, are designated with absolute precision and can be traced on the maps or registers of lands of that time. At the center of events (topographically speaking) we find the royal residence of Gargantua's father, Grangousier. At the present time, Rabelais scholars have been able to identify Grangousier's home as La Devinière, the estate of the author's father, the lawyer Antoine Rabelais. François Rabelais was born on that estate. The modest house of the Rabelais family at La Devinière has been preserved. The ancient fireplace can still be seen, at which good Grangousier sat roasting chestnuts, waiting for them to burst, poking the fire with a charred stick, and telling his family the good tales of yore, when he was informed of Picrochole's sudden aggression.

All the other geographical names and topographical data given in the novel, and there are many, come to life. All are real to the minutest detail, and are merely exaggerated in their dimensions. Not far from Devinière, on the left bank of the Negron, there still exists the *prairie de la Soulsay* on which the "Palaver of the Potulent" took place. February fourth, during the carnivalesque festival of cattle-slaughtering, Gargantua was born. Abel Lefranc correctly figures that these were the place and date of Rabelais' own birth.

The entire topography of Picrochole's war is also absolutely realistic and precise: Seuilly and Lerné, and the road running between these localities where the battle of the winegrowers and the bakers took place, as well as the Negron valley where military operations were conducted around Devinière on the strip of land bounded by Lerné, La Roche Clermault, Vaugaudry, and La Vauguyon—all these sites are named in the novel and present a clear picture of these operations. The monastery close defended by Friar John is still in existence as well as a fragment of the wall that was there in the time of Rabelais.

The Picrochole war was itself based on real events. Rabelais pictured a conflict that broke out in his native land; the Rabelais family and their friends sided with one camp, while the lord of Lerné, Gauchet de Sainte-Marthe sided with the other. The lord of Lerné owned the fisheries on the river Loire, obstructing navigation, and because of this was involved in a lawsuit with the local communities interested in navigation. The lawsuit lasted a long time, was suspended, then once more resumed, to reach a climax in 1532, when François Rabelais visited his father at Devinière during the grape harvest. The lawyer Antoine Rabelais was for a time a friend of his neighbor, Gauchet de Sainte-Marthe, and was even in charge of his affairs. But he later sided with the communities whose interests were being jeopardized. They were defended by the lawyer Gallet, Antoine Rabelais' relative and close friend. Thus, during his summer visit to Devinière François found himself at the center of this conflict and possibly took part in it to a certain extent.

The description of the Picrochole war is full of allusions to this real conflict. Even some of the names correspond to real ones. Grangousier's envoy is Gallet, and we have seen that a lawyer of that name was in charge of the community's interests against Gauchet de Sainte-Marthe. The beaten-up standard-bearer of the bakers, who was the actual cause of the war, was Marquet, the name of Sainte-Marthe's son-in-law. In Chapter 47, Rabelais gives the list of the thirty-one feudal estates (one of the author's typical enumerations) that formed the "ancient confederation" and offered their assistance to Grangousier. Not one of these names is imaginary. They are real names of towns, boroughs, villages, and hamlets located on the banks of the Loire and the Vienne or nearby and interested in navigation on the Loire. They all actually formed an alliance in the lawsuit against Sainte-Marthe. It is quite possible that the episode of the Lerné bakers and the Seuilly winegrowers also actually took place. Abel Lefranc points out that the old competition still exists between the two communities, a dim memory of the ancient feud.

Thus the central theme of *Gargantua* is presented in an intimate, familiar world, in the author's homeland and its immediate surroundings. The topography of this land is described with remarkable precision. This world, with the persons and objects it contains, has an individual and concrete character. Such fantastic events as, for instance, the pilgrims being swallowed with the salad and drowned in urine are set in the courtyard and garden of the Devinière estate, which are realistically described and exist almost unchanged in our days.

The same is true of all the other episodes of this book, as well as those of the following books. Rabelaisiana has discovered in most of them real places, real persons and events. A number of characters of the Third Book can be identified as Rabelais' contemporaries: Herr Trippa was Agrippa of Nettesheim, the theologian Hippothadeus was Lefèvre d'Etaples, the poet Raminagrobis was

Jean Lemaire, and Doctor Rondibilis was the physician Rondelet.
The village of Panzoult (in the episode of the sibyl) existed and
still exists; a popular prophetess is said to have actually lived there,
and the cave that was her dwelling is still shown to tourists.

The same can be said of the Fourth Book, although the data are
not as abundant and precise as for the preceding sections. We shall
be content with one example, the anecdote concerning Villon's
prank. This "tragic farce" takes place at St. Maixent (in the province of Poitou with which Rabelais was so familiar). The roadside
cross mentioned in the novel (Ticklepecker's brains were spilled at
its foot) still stands in the suburbs of this little town. It is possible
that Rabelais' story was inspired by some local tale; one of the
parishes near St. Maixent is still known as the church "of the dead
monk."

These examples sufficiently point out that the immediate foreground of his images is the world he had lived in and the people
he closely knew. In this familar foreground of Rabelais' presentation, everything is individual, historically unique. The general is
minimized; each object is called by its own name. Characteristically
enough, even in his comparisons, Rabelais always seeks to mention
individual, historically singled-out objects and phenomena. Thus
at the banquet following the burning of the knights, Pantagruel
says that it would be good to hang church bells on the chewing jaws
of the guests; in this remark, he is not content with speaking of
church bells in general, but names well known churches of Poitiers,
Tours, and Cambrai. In Chapter 64 of the Fourth Book, we find
the following comparison: "Friar John with, in his wake, the ste-
wards, footmen, butlers, cupbearers, carvers, servers, caterers and
minor flunkies, brought on four tremendous ham pies, that looked
for all the world like the four bastions of the city of Turin."

Many similar examples could be cited. Rabelais continually tends
to use objects that he has seen and that are historically unique. A
similar characteristic trait is his interest, shared by his contemporaries, in curiosities, in rare and unusual objects. Most of the curiosities we have discussed can still be seen today: the sculptured

head of Geoffroi of the Great Tooth, the stone table for student feasts in Poitiers, the roadside cross of St. Maixent at which Ticklepecker spilled his brains.

But this immediate world (or more correctly speaking, microcosm) of familiar places, objects, and people by no means exhausts the reality reflected in the novel. Beyond this sphere we find another, broader perspective, more important historically. This sphere also belongs to reality, but it has a different dimension.

Let us turn once more to the images of the Picrochole war. They are based, as we have seen, on a local provincial conflict (almost a family quarrel) of the Loire communities with Antoine Rabelais' neighbor, Sainte-Marthe. The arena is the limited ground of Devinière's immediate neighborhood. This, as we have seen, is the foreground of the Picrochole war, the land that Rabelais had often covered in his travels, which was familar to his eyes, which he felt under his very fingertips, and which was linked with his relatives and friends.

However, Rabelais' contemporaries and their descendants did not recognize Picrochole as Gauchet de Sainte-Marthe, but as Charles V or other aggressive despots of that time, Lodovico Sforza or Ferdinand of Aragon. And they were right to make this association. Rabelais' entire novel is intimately connected with the political events and problems of that period. The first three books (especially *Gargantua*) reflect France's struggle against Charles V. The Picrochole war in particular is a direct echo of this struggle. For instance, in the striking picture of Picrochole's council of war there is an element of straight satire against the emperor's aggressive policy. This scene is Rabelais' answer to a similar scene in Thomas More's *Utopia* in which aggression and the goal of a world monarchy were attributed to Francis I. One might say that Rabelais "readdressed" these accusations to Charles V. The source of Gallet's speech in which he accuses Picrochole of aggression and defends Grangousier's peaceful policy is a speech on the causes of the war between France and Charles V, made by Guillaume du Bellay (Rabelais' future friend and protector) and addressed to the German princes.

The question of determining the aggressor was acutely and correctly felt in connection with the war between Charles V and Francis I. A number of anonymous writings were devoted to this problem by authors of du Bellay's entourage, to which Rabelais also belonged.

The images of the Picrochole war are a living echo of this actual political theme of the aggressor. Rabelais offered his own solution to this problem and created in Picrochole an immortal image of the militarist, aggressive politician. He doubtless lent him some of the traits of Charles V. This link with the political problems of his time creates the background of the Picrochole war, reflecting actual events.

But in the fifteenth and sixteenth centuries the problem of war and peace was posed in a broader sense than that of the aggressor in an isolated case of a given military conflict. It was a matter of principle concerning the rights of monarchs and nations to fight and the distinction between the just and unjust war. The organization of a general peace was under discussion. It suffices to recall Thomas More and Erasmus.

The images of the Picrochole war reflect these political principles, acquiring a second, broader and deeper meaning.

Of course, this second plane of images is concrete and historically individualized. There is absolutely no abstract generalization, no typification, but this individualized picture is presented in wider dimensions. From the minor we are transferred to the major individuality (not to an abstract type); the major repeats the minor structure.

Beyond this second plane we reach the last, third plane of the Picrochole images. The grotesque body of the giants, the banquet images, dismemberment, torrents of urine, the transformation of blood into wine, of the battle into a feast, and King Picrochole's uncrowning—these constitute the popular carnivalesque festive plane of the Picrochole war that we have previously discussed.

The third, popular dimension is also individual and concrete, but this is the broadest, all-embracing, universal individuality. At the same time, the festive popular images reveal the deepest meaning of the historic process, which extends not only beyond contemporary events in the narrow sense but beyond Rabelais' entire epoch. These images reveal the people's views concerning war and peace, the aggressor, political power, and the future. In the light of these views, formed and defended over thousands of years, we discover the gay relativity of events as well as of the entire political problem they presented. The distinction between the just and the unjust, the right and the wrong, the progressive and the reactionary is not lost as the framework of definite time and immediate relevance is lost, but these distinctions do lose their absolute character, their one-sided and limited seriousness.

A popular-festive universalism penetrates all Rabelais' images, lending meaning to every detail and relating it to the final whole. All these familiar individual objects and localities, which were actually seen by the author and which occupy the foreground, are related to the major individual whole of the world, a two-bodied whole in the state of becoming, as revealed in torrents of praise and abuse. In such conditions there cannot be any suggestion of a naturalist atomization of reality, of an abstract and tendentious approach.

We have discussed the images of the Picrochole war. But the second broadened plane of reality exists also in all the other images of the novel. All of them are related to actual political events and problems of the time.

Rabelais was well informed concerning all the great contemporary political problems. In 1532 he began close relations with the brothers du Bellay, who were at the very center of political events. Under Francis I, Cardinal Jean du Bellay headed what might be called the bureau of diplomatic and literary propaganda, which was considered of great importance. A considerable number of pamphlets published in Germany, the Netherlands, Italy, and, of course, France, were written or inspired by the two brothers. They created their own diplomatic and literary agencies in all countries.

Thanks to the du Bellays, Rabelais was at the very source of high-level political affairs. He was the immediate witness of their development and was probably initiated in the secret projects and plans of the royal government which were fulfilled by the two brothers. Rabelais accompanied Jean du Bellay on his three visits to Italy with important diplomatic missions to the Pope. He was in the service of Guillaume du Bellay during the French occupation of the Piedmont. He attended the historic meeting of Francis I and Charles V at Aigues-Mortes as a member of the French king's retinue. He was, therefore, an eyewitness of the most important political acts.

From *Gargantua* on, actual political problems play a considerable part in the novel. Besides the immediate political theme, the three books that follow (in the present sequence) are filled with more or less distinct allusions to events and persons belonging to that historic period.

Let us examine these themes in the Third and Fourth Books.

We have already pointed out that the central image of the Third Book's prologue, the defense of Corinth, reflects the military preparations of France and of Paris in particular, undertaken because of the deterioration of relations with the emperor. These measures were put in force by Jean du Bellay, and Rabelais could apparently observe them at close range. The first chapters of the Third Book, devoted to Pantagruel's wise and humane policy in the conquered territories of King Anarchus, represent an almost direct eulogy of Guillaume du Bellay's policy in the conquered territories of Piedmont under French occupation. During that period Rabelais was Guillaume du Bellay's confidential and faithful secretary and was, therefore, initiated in all his chief's activities.

Guillaume du Bellay, Seigneur de Langey, was one of the most remarkable men of his time. He was apparently the only person to whom the mercilessly sober and demanding Rabelais could grant a certain respect. The image of the Seigneur de Langey impressed him and left a mark in his novel.

Rabelais was closely connected with Guillaume du Bellay during the last period of the Seigneur's political activity. He was present at du Bellay's death, embalmed his body, and brought it to his burial vault. He recalls the last moments of the dying man in the Fourth Book of the novel.

The Seigneur de Langey's policy in the Piedmont had gained Rabelais' deep sympathy. Du Bellay strove first of all to draw the population of the occupied province to his side. He sought to raise the Piedmont's economic standard. The army was forbidden to oppress the population and was subjected to strict discipline. Moreover, he imported an enormous quantity of wheat to Piedmont and distributed it to the people, spending his entire personal income.[2] This was a completely new and unheard of method of military occupation. The Third Book's first chapter describes this policy. The prevailing note in this chapter is fertility and the people's abundance. The author starts with the fertility of the Utopians (Pantagruel's subjects) and then goes on to laud du Bellay's policy (in other words, Pantagruel's):

Here I draw the attention of my bibbing readers to a point of statesmanship. Certain despotic spirits, to their shame and loss, promulgate violence. What an error! On the contrary, in order to instill and maintain obedience in a newly-conquered people, the one thing a monarch must avoid is pillaging, harrying, vexing, oppressing, and tyrannizing them. The rod of iron will not work; woe to the conqueror who swallows the nation in his maw—a demovorous king, as Achilles called Agamemnon. . . . Conquered nations are newborn babes; as such they must be given suck, they must be rocked, fondled and amused. Like newly planted trees, they must be supported, propped up, protected from all tempests, injuries and calamities. Like convalescents from lengthy illness, they must be nursed, coddled and cherished.
(Book 3, Chapter 1)

This eulogy of an actual political method is deeply infused with a festive conception of the popular body which is born, feeds, grows, and is regenerated. Growth and renewal are the leading themes in the people's image. Rabelais compares them to a newly planted tree, to an organism restored to health. The ruler is the mother nursing her child, the gardener is the healing physician. The bad ruler is given the grotesque nickname of "people-eater."

These typically Rabelaisian and carnivalesque images of the

---

[2] After Du Bellay's death his heirs scarcely received anything. Even the pension that he willed to Rabelais was apparently not paid for lack of funds.

people and of their ruler broaden and deepen to an extraordinary degree the actual political problem of the Piedmont occupation. They link the historical event to the whole, to the constantly growing and renewed world.

The Seigneur de Langey, as we have said, left a deep mark on the entire Third and Fourth Books. The memories of his person and of his last moments play an essential role in the chapters of the Fourth Book devoted to the death of heroes. These almost absolutely serious lines stand out from the rest of the novel. The initial theme, borrowed from Plutarch, is combined with Celtic images from the cycle of the Northwestern land of death and with St. Brendan's voyage in particular. These chapters devoted to the death of heroes are like a requiem to the Seigneur de Langey.

Furthermore, the Seigneur determined the image of Pantagruel himself as presented in the Third and Fourth Books. In these books Pantagruel does not in any way resemble the devilkin of the mystery who causes thirst and is the hero of the gay *facéties*. He becomes the ideal image of the wise monarch. This is how he is described in the Third Book:

Was he not, as I told you once, and repeat again, the best little great good fellow that ever buckled on a sword? He took everything in good part, viewed every action in the most favorable light, was never in the least worried or shocked. To allow anything to upset or vex him, he believed, was tantamount to flying the divine coop of his reason. He knew well that everything heaven covers and earth bears, in all dimensions of height, depth, length and breadth, does not warrant our troubling our equanimity or perplexing our spirit.
(Book 3, Chapter 2)

Pantagruel's mythical and carnivalesque traits fade as he becomes more human and more heroic, but at the same time he acquires a certain abstract and rhetorical character. This transformation took place apparently under the influence of the Seigneur de Langey, whose image Rabelais wished to immortalize in his Pantagruel.[3]

However, the identification of Pantagruel with Guillaume du

[3] Georges Lote systematically identifies du Bellay with Pantagruel.

Bellay should not be exaggerated; this is but one of the elements of the image, which is mainly founded on folklore.

The Fourth Book is filled with allusions to contemporary political events and problems. We have seen that Pantagruel's itinerary combines the ancient Celtic route to the utopian land of death and regeneration with the very real colonial explorations of Jacques Cartier.

At the time of the writing of the Fourth Book, France's struggle against papal demands had become acute. This struggle is reflected in the chapters concerning the decretals. When these chapters were being written they corresponded to the king's Gallican policy, but when the book was published the conflict with the Pope had been almost completely solved. Thus Rabelais' political demonstration was somewhat belated.

Allusions to political events can also be found in such important episodes of the Fourth Book as the sausage war (the struggle of the Geneva Calvinists) and the picture of the storm (the Council of Trent).

We shall limit ourselves to these examples, which prove sufficiently how widely contemporary events and their problems were reflected in Rabelais' novel. His book is a "survey," reflecting the actual events of the day. But at the same time the problems posed by the Rabelaisian images are broader and deeper by far than the usual survey, reaching beyond the contemporary picture.

In the political conflicts of his time Rabelais took the most advanced and progressive positions. Royal power was in his eyes the expression of the new principle to which the immediate historic future belonged, the principle of the national state. Therefore, he was equally hostile to the claims of the papacy and to those of the empire seeking a supranational power. In the claims of both Pope and emperor he saw the dying past, whereas the national state reflected the new, youthful, popular and political historic life.

No less strong and sincere was Rabelais' view concerning science and culture; he was a convinced champion of humanism with its new methods and evaluations. In the field of medicine he demanded a return to the authentic sources of antiquity, to Hippocrates and Galen, and he was hostile to Arab medicine which had corrupted the ancient traditions. In the field of law he wanted to go back to the Roman legal system, unpolluted by the barbarian interpretation of ignorant medieval commentators. In military art, in all branches of technology, in education, architecture, sports, dress, customs and mores he was the defender of all the innovations that were flowing from Italy in a mighty, irrepressible stream. In all the fields that left a trace in his novel (which is a true encyclopedia) he was a man of the avant-garde. He had an extraordinary sense of the new, not of newfangled fashions but of that which was born from the death of the old and to which the future belonged. Rabelais possessed to the highest degree the gift to sense and demonstrate this world to be born.

The avant-garde positions in the field of politics, culture, science, and mores were directed and unambiguously expressed by Rabelais in various parts of his novel, for instance in the episodes of Gargantua's education, of the Abbey of Thélème, in Gargantua's letter to Pantagruel, in Pantagruel's speech concerning the medieval commentators of Roman law, of Grangousier's conversation with the pilgrims, and in the eulogy of Pantagruel's methods of military occupation. All these episodes have a more or less rhetorical character; the bookish and official language prevail in them. In these chapters we hear a direct and an almost entirely serious speech. It is a new form of speech, a progressive speech, the last word of the epoch and at the same time Rabelais' completely sincere opinion.

However, if the novel did not contain other episodes, other words, another language, Rabelais would be merely one of the progressive but commonplace humanists of his time, perhaps one of the foremost. He would be someone like Budé. But he would not be the man of genius, the unique Rabelais.

The last word of the epoch, sincerely and seriously asserted, was not Rabelais' last word. However progressive, our author knew the limits of this progressiveness. And although he spoke seriously of such things, he knew the limits of this seriousness. Rabelais' own last word is the gay, free, absolutely sober word of the people, which cannot be bribed with the help of the limited progressiveness accessible to the men of his time. This gay word of the people opened far wider future perspectives, even though the positive outlines of this future were still dimly utopian. All that was definite and completed within the epoch was in some way comic, insofar as it was limited. But laughter was gay, while all that was determined and finite was about to die and to open new possibilities.

We must therefore seek Rabelais' last word, not in the direct, rhetoricized episodes of the novel in which speech has in most cases only one single meaning and is nearly always completely serious. We must seek this last word in the popular-festive, elemental imagery in which these images are immersed. Here they never become entirely narrow and serious, for no matter how serious Rabelais may appear in these episodes, he always leaves a gay loophole—a loophole that opens on the distant future and that lends an aspect of ridicule to the relative progressiveness and relative truth accessible to the present or to the immediate future. Rabelais therefore never exhausts his resources in direct statements. This, of course, is not romantic irony; this is the broad, exacting spirit of the people which was transmitted to him with the entire system of the images of folk humor.

Thus contemporary reality, so widely and fully reflected in Rabelais' novel, is seen in the light of popular-festive images. And in this light even the best perspectives of reality appear limited and remote from the people's ideas and aspirations. However, contemporary reality did not lose its concreteness. On the contrary, in the sober light of folk imagery all objects and phenomena acquired a peculiar relief, a full, material nature. They were liberated from all narrow and dogmatic connotations and were disclosed in an absolutely free atmosphere. This determined the exceptional richness and variety of the forms drawn into the vortex of Rabelais' novel.

This novel, like all the great works of that period, is widely encyclopedic. There is no branch of knowledge or practical life which is not represented in these pages. Modern Rabelaisiana, especially that inspired by Sainéan, has shown by Rabelais' extra-

ordinary competence in all the fields he described. Thanks to special research it is possible to definitely prove our author's unerring
experience, not only in medicine and various branches of natural
science but also in law, architecture, military science, navigation,
culinary art, falconry, games, sports, and numismatics. The nomenclature in the novel of these various branches of scientific and practical knowledge is striking not merely for its richness and fullness
but also for the minute detail of technical terms and nuances,
known only to specialists. Whatever the expression used by Rabelais, he applied it with masterful precision. In the middle of the
last century certain doubts were raised concerning the correctness
of Rabelais' rich nautical vocabulary. But Sainéan proved that
this criticism was unfounded. In nautical affairs, also, Rabelais'
competence was substantial.

Rabelais' encyclopedic knowledge and the extraordinary richness of his world present one peculiar trait that Rabelais scholars
have not sufficiently appreciated: all that is new, fresh, or primary
prevails in the novel. This is the encyclopedia of a new world. It
was concrete and substantial, and much of this substance had entered for the first time the field of vision of Rabelais' contemporaries; it had acquired a name for the first time and had renewed
the old one by giving it another meaning. The world of objects and
the world of language were immensely broadened and enriched;
they had been essentially regenerated and regrouped according to
sharp and most unusual patterns.

We know that during the Renaissance a colossal and varied mass
of new objects entered this field of vision. These objects were somewhat late in making their appearance in France, but they poured
in a mighty stream from Italy and continued to increase during the
wars in that country. Rabelais lived precisely at the time when this
torrent was most unbridled. Since the close contact with Italy involved first the encounter of two armies, the first objects imported
belonged to military science and technology. Then came navigation and architecture, followed by industry, commerce, art, and
mores. We must stress that these were not merely isolated inventions or ideas; they had the power to renew and to reform the old

objects, forcing them to adapt to new conditions, for instance to technological discoveries. The new culture introduced new words too; French was flooded with Italian, Greek, and Latin words, as well as with neologisms.

Rabelais had a great love and awareness of the essential newness of objects and names. He not only never lagged behind his time, he was often ahead of it. His military terminology reflects (except for a few archaisms) the newest achievements of military technology, especially in engineering. Many words in this field were recorded for the first time in his novel.

Rabelais' architectural terminology also reflects new developments. This subject takes up considerable space in his novel. His architectural vocabulary is filled with new and renewed terms, many of which he was the first to use. The word "symmetry," which marked the renaissance of architecture, appeared almost for the first time in the novel. A number of other terms in the novel express something named for the first time: peristyle, portico, architrave, frieze. All these words were new; they had the power to renew and to reconstruct previously existing architectural conceptions. In the nomenclatures of all other fields of knowledge we can observe the same important role of regenerating words and objects. Rabelais' vocabulary, however, is also rich in old words and even contains some archaisms. Rabelais looked for fullness and variety in everything, but he constantly emphasized the new and used its power of rejuvenation and stimulation.

Let us now examine an important aspect of the stylistic life of the word in Rabelais's novel.

An enormous quantity of the elements of Rabelais' language was taken from oral sources; these are virginal words that emerged from the depths of the people's elemental life and entered the system of written and printed literature. Even the vocabularies of nearly all branches of science originally belonged, to a great extent, to speech and were being for the first time incorporated in the literary context, in systematic literary thought, intonation, and syntax. At the time of Rabelais science had obtained with the greatest difficulty the right to speak and write in the vernacular, and this right had not as yet been definitely consolidated, since neither the Church nor the universities and schools had recognized the popular media. Rabelais and Calvin were the creators of French literary prose. Rabelais was forced to lean on oral forms in all the branches of knowledge (in some of them more, and in others less); he had to draw upon the verbal wealth of the vernacular. The words taken from this source were still entirely fresh and unpolished by the literary context.

Let us take, for example, the nomenclature of fishes. It is extensive. The sixtieth chapter of the Fourth Book (the festive sacrifices of the Gastrolaters) contains more than sixty different names of fishes. We find here fresh-water, Mediterranean, and ocean species. Where did Rabelais collect this rich vocabulary? Certainly not in literary sources. The ichthyological works of the sixteenth century, composed by the French naturalists Guillaume Rondolet and Pierre Belon, were published in 1553–1554, after Rabelais' death. His source could only have been the vernacular. He learned about ocean fish in Brittany and Normandy, in the ports of Saint Malo, Dieppe, and Le Havre; he questioned the Breton and Norman fishermen for the names of these species. Mediterranean fish were named for him by the fishermen of Marseilles. All these were absolutely fresh words, as fresh as the fish Rabelais must have seen at the markets; they had never been used in written or printed form, they had not as yet been processed with an abstract, systematic context. They had not been in contact with the names of other species and were grouped only according to their own habitat; Breton fish were linked with Breton oaths and abuses, with the Breton storms and roaring ocean waves. Thus they were not named in ichthyological classifications but carried mere appellations of the local jargon. Only later were their names to acquire a definite form and character under the pen of Rondel and Belon, while in Rabelais' enumeration they have still something of the nature of proper nouns.

The crux of the matter is not the fact that Rabelais learned these words from an oral source but that they had never been used in a literary context. This determined their character in the consciousness of the author and of his contemporaries. The abstract, systematic classification was feebly developed; not only were their names unknown to the naturalist, but literary language did not as yet employ even general terms for them.

The same process can be observed more or less in Rabelais' vocabulary referring to other branches of knowledge. It is true of his medical nomenclature, for example. True, he widely used neologisms as well as Greek and Latin terms, but he also borrowed a great deal from oral sources of the vernacular. He often used side by side a scientific neologism and its popular equivalent (for example, *epiglotte* and *gargamelle*).

Popular names of diseases are of special interest in this connection. These words still contain a considerable element related to proper nouns and, simultaneously, to abusive expressions. Many names of diseases were linked with saints who were considered healers or sometimes the cause of the ailment. There was the *mal de Saint Antoine* and the *mal de Saint Vit*. But all names of diseases were personalized, that is, conceived as the names of living human beings. In the literature of that time we find such personalized diseases as *la Dame Vérolle* (syphilis) and *la Goutte* (gout). Diseases play a considerable role in oaths and curses and are sometimes turned into abusive nicknames. Persons are threatened with cholera, plague, pest, and are sometimes called by these names. The vernacular names of genitals acquire a similar character. In Rabelais' medical nomenclatures there are many such names, not sufficiently generalized and polished to become neutral expressions of literary or scientific terminology.

The virginal words of the oral vernacular which entered literary language for the first time are close, in a certain sense, to proper nouns. They are individualized and still contain a strong element of praise-abuse, which makes them similar to nicknames. They are as yet insufficiently neutral and generalized to become common nouns. Moreover, their very nature renders them infectious; their influence spreads to other words and affects the entire language.

We here touch upon a striking peculiarity of Rabelais' verbal style: his common and proper nouns are not sharply differentiated, as we are accustomed to find them in modern literary style. This softening of the dividing lines between proper and common nouns has the goal of expressing praise-abuse in a nickname. In other words, if a proper noun has a clear etymological meaning that characterizes its owner, it is no longer a name but a nickname. And a nickname can never be neutral, since its meaning always includes an element of evaluation, positive or negative. All real nicknames contain a nuance of praise-abuse.

The majority of the novel's proper nouns are nicknames. This is true not only of the names created by Rabelais himself but also of those that he inherited from tradition. Such are first of all the names of the main protagonists: Gargantua, Gargamelle, Pantagruel, Grangousier. These four names were handed down to the author by tradition. Two of them, Grangousier (big gullet) and Gargamelle (gullet), have a definite etymology clearly recognized by tradition as well as by Rabelais (and, of course, by his readers).

Gargantua's case is somewhat more complex. The etymology of this name is undertermined[4] and apparently not clear to Rabelais or to his contemporaries. In such cases the author had recourse to an artificial etymology of the name, even intentionally farfetched. This is the method used in the example of Gargantua. Gargantua was born shouting, "Drink, drink, drink!" and his father, Grangousier, exclaimed, *Que grand tu as le gousier!* ("What a big gullet you have!") From the father's first words, *que grand tu as,* came the name Gargantua. A similar artificial process (based on a different principle) was applied by Rabelais to the name Pantagruel, "the ever-thirsting one."

All four of these nicknames are ambivalent. Grangousier, Gargamelle, and Gargantua symbolize the gullet, not as a neutral anatomical term but as an abusive-laudatory image: gluttony, swallowing, devouring, banquetting. This is the gaping mouth, the

[4] In Spanish *gargantua* means the throat. The Provençal tongue has the word "gargantuan," meaning a glutton. Apparently, Gargantua's etymology is similar to that of the names of the other heroes : throat, gullet.

grave-womb, swallowing and generating. The etymology of Pantagruel has a similar connotation, the "ever-thirsting," disclosing the
traditional ambivalent image. The absence of roots in the national
language mollifies the ambivalence of this name.[5]

Thus the names transmitted to Rabelais by tradition either originally presented the character of nicknames suggesting praise-abuse
or acquired this character by study of their etymology.

Praise-abuse ambivalence is also found in the names created by
Rabelais himself. Typical are the names of the sixty-four cooks in
the Fourth Book, all of which are based on various words for
dishes, fish, salads, vegetables, dining ware, and various kitchen
utensils. For instance, soups produce a number of these names:
Clearbroth, Soupsnuffle, Pottagepiss. Meat also produces a few
names: Rotroast, Muttonshoulder, and others. Many of the names
are derived from lard. This enumeration is something like a talking kitchen, composed of proper nouns. Still another part of the
list is composed of nicknames of an abusive nature founded on
various physical disabilities, monstrosities, or signs of uncleanli-
ness. The stylistic form and imagery of these names are similar to
the abuses we saw hurled by the bakers at the shepherds.

The names of Picrochole's advisers and soldiers are also abusive
in character: Trepelu, Racquedenare, Merdaille (Smalltittle,
Swashbuckler, Krapp). The formation of proper names from abusive terms is one of the methods most frequently used by Rabelais
as well as by folk humor in general.

In contrast to Picrochole's retinue, Grangousier's soldiers have
Greek names: Sebaste (honorable), Tolmere (bold), Ithybole
(straightforward). The names of some of Rabelais' heroes, like
Ponocrates, Epistemon, and even Panurge, also contain elements
of praise-abuse (Panurge means "capable of doing everything," a
Jack-of-all-trades). All these Greek names are similar in form to
nicknames, but they are rhetorical and lack authentic ambivalence.

---

[5] It is possible that some roots in the national language and the dim
awareness of an etymological meaning were contained in this word.
This is Sainéan's supposition.

They resemble the separate groups of praise and abuse in the official parts of Rabelais' novel.

True ambivalence is inherent only in the abusive-laudatory names rooted in the soil of the vernacular and folk imagery linked with it. Let us limit ourselves to the examples analyzed previously. All Rabelais' names are in a way understood as nicknames of praise-abuse. The only exceptions are the names of historic persons or the author's friends (like Tiraqueau) or of those who remind us of real people, like Rondibilis instead of Rondelet. Other proper nouns, which do not belong to persons, also present these tendencies toward ambivalent forms of praise-abuse.

We have seen that a number of geographical names have a topographical bodily connotation, for example, *trou de Gibraltar, bondes de Hercule,* and others. In some cases Rabelais uses artificial comic etymology, as when he explains the origin of the name of "Paris" or "Beauce." Of course, we find special nuances, but the fundamental, rough interpretation of the names that have been turned into nicknames of praise-abuse remains identical.

Finally, the novel contains a number of chapters in which the theme of names and appellations is treated in a theoretical style. Thus the problem of the origin of the names of plants is treated in the Third Book, while the Fourth Book presents a carnivalesque game of names on the Isle of Ennasin; this book also contains a long commentary concerning the names of colonels Crushchitterling and Slicesausage.

Proper nouns in Rabelais' novel tend therefore to attain the limits of praise and abuse. But this is also true of the common nouns, which become more individual, less general. Names of animals, birds, fish, plants, organs, members and parts of the human body, of dishes and beverages, kitchen utensils and household wares, arms, clothing, and so forth, sound almost like the nicknames of the protagonists in a peculiar satirical drama of objects and bodies.

While analyzing the swab episode we observed the peculiar role played by objects, comparable to that of the protagonists of a comic drama. We must stress that many of the vulgar names of herbs and plants, as well as of some of the other materials figuring as swabs, were still fresh and unused in the literary context. These were nicknames rather than botanical terms. The unexpected role of the objects in the series of swabs still further contributed to their individualization. In this peculiar use they enter quite a new classification; they are removed from their initial weak general definition, and their individual character is strengthened thereby. Furthermore, in their dynamic abusive function as swabs their material and individual nature is sharply brought out. The name becomes almost like the nickname of a character in a farce.

The newness of the object and of its name, or the transfer of a known object to an unexpected use and place among other objects, individualizes it in a peculiar fashion, strengthens the special nature of the name, and brings it nearer to the nickname.

Also, the general saturation of the Rabelaisian text with proper nouns (personal or geographical) contributes to the individualization of names. We have already said that for his comparisons Rabelais uses historically individualized names (as when comparing pies to the bastion of Turin). He seeks to confer on every object a historical or topographical character.

Finally, an important role is played by the parodical distribution of obsolete ideological and conceptual links between objects and phenomena. Even elementary logical links are done away with, as in the illogicalities of *coq-à-l'âne*. Objects and names, freed from the chains of a dying philosophy and granted their independence, acquire a peculiar gay individuality; their names are brought nearer to appellations. The virginal words of oral folk language, as yet not disciplined by the literary context and its strict lexical differentiation and selection, its elaborate and limited meaning and tone, create a peculiar carnival freedom and individuality; they are easily changed into the names of characters of a comic drama.

To sum up: One of the essential traits of Rabelais' style is that all proper nouns on the one hand, and on the other hand all the names of objects and phenomena, tend to extremes in abusive-laudatory nicknames. Thanks to this process, all objects and phenomena of Rabelais' world acquire a peculiar individuality of praise-abuse. In this individualizing torrent of abusive-laudatory words the dividing lines between persons and objects are weakened; all of them become participants in the carnival drama of the simultaneous death of the old world and the birth of the new.

Let us turn our attention to another characteristic trait of Rabelais' style, the carnivalesque use of numbers.

Antique and medieval literature knows the symbolic, metaphysical, and mystical use of numbers. There were the sacred numbers: three, seven, nine, for example. The Hippocrates anthology contained a treatise concerning the number seven, considered the critical number of the whole world and especially of the human organism. But every number was sacred as such. Antiquity was pervaded with Pythagorean conceptions of the number as the foundation of all that exists, of every order, including the gods. The medieval symbolism and its mystic conception of numbers is well known. The sacred numbers were also considered the basis of artistic compositions, including that of literature. Let us recall Dante for whom these numbers determine not only the structure of the entire universe but also of his own poem.

If we somewhat simplify this conception, we may define the antique and medieval aesthetics of the number by saying that it must be determined, finite, rounded, symmetrical. Only such a number can be the basis of the completed (static) whole.

Rabelais tore off the sacred, symbolic robes of the numbers and uncrowned them. He profaned them. But this is not a nihilistic act; it is a gay, carnivalesque gesture that regenerates the numbers and renews them. It would seem that there is nothing more remote from laughter than a number. But Rabelais knew how to render a number comic and include it on equal rights in the carnivalesque world of his novel.

There are many numbers in Rabelais' novel; scarcely a single episode is described without them. All of them create a carnivalesque, grotesque character—an effect obtained by various means.

Sometimes Rabelais gives a parodical debasement of the sacred numbers: nine spits for venison inspired by the number of the nine muses; three triumphal pillars with carnivalesque decorations (in the episode of the destruction of the six hundred sixty-six knights, a number that is both parodical and apocalyptic per se). But such cases are relatively rare. The majority of grotesque numbers are striking and produce a comic effect through hyperbole (the quantity of food and wine absorbed, etc.). Generally speaking, all the quantitative definitions expressed in figures are vastly exaggerated; they transgress all limits. They are intentionally rendered immeasurable. Furthermore, the comic effect is obtained by a pretense at exactitude in situations where a precise count is impossible. For example, Gargantua drowned in his urine "two hundred sixty thousand four hundred and eighteen" Parisians. More important still is the grotesque structure of Rabelaisian numbers. The following example is taken from Panurge's story about his Turkish adventures (Book Two, Chapter 14). Escaping the blaze that had broken out in the town, Panurge turns to watch: ". . . six hundred, no, more than six, indeed, more than thirteen hundred and eleven dogs appeared on the horizon."

We have here a grotesque exaggeration with a sharp crescendo from six hundred to thirteen hundred and eleven all having to do with a trivial subject (dogs). Furthermore the count is quite unnecessarily precise, and its very impossibility is topped by the uncrowning exactness of the word "more." But most characteristic is the structure of the number. If we added one digit to obtain the figure thirteen hundred and twelve, this figure would be stabilized, rounded, completed, and the comic effect would be diminished. If we brought the figure to fifteen hundred and twelve, it would "calm down" entirely, would become static, would lose its asymmetry and openness, and would cease to be a grotesque Rabelaisian number.

Such is the structure of all the large numbers in the novel; they are all unbalanced and unstable figures. If we take the number of the Parisians drowned in Gargantua's urine, two hundred sixty thousand four hundred and eighteen, and change its aesthetic structure to two hundred fifty thousand five hundred twenty, the effect will be drastically transformed. And here is another example: The number of casualties in the monastery close was thirteen thousand six hundred twenty-two; if we slightly change this structure to twelve thousand five hundred twenty, we destroy the number's grotesque soul. We can be easily convinced of this by analyzing any large number quoted in the novel. If we do so, we find that it strictly supports its structural principle. All Rabelais' figures are unstable, ambiguous, and incomplete like the characters of the medieval diablerie. The structure of the number reflects, like a drop of water, the structure of the entire Rabelaisian world. It is impossible to build with such a number any harmonious and complete universe. In Rabelais the prevailing aesthetics of numbers is quite different from those of antiquity and of the high Middle Ages.

In conclusion, we shall touch upon the special attitude of Rabelais' time toward language and its philosophy.

The Renaissance is the only period in the history of European literature which marked the end of a dual language and a linguistic transformation. Much of what was possible at that exceptional time later became impossible.

It can be said of belles lettres, and especially of the modern novel, that they were born on the boundaries of two languages. Literary and linguistic life was concentrated on these confines. An intense interorientation, interaction, and mutual clarification of languages took place during that period. The two languages frankly and intensely peered into each other's faces, and each became more aware of itself, of its potentialities and limitations, in the light of the other. This line drawn between the languages was seen in relation to each object, each concept and point of view. For the two languages represent two philosophies.

We have already said, in Chapter One, that the line of demarcation between two cultures—the official and the popular—was drawn along the line dividing Latin from the vernacular. The vernacular invaded all the spheres of ideology and expelled Latin.

It brought new forms of thought (ambivalence) and new evaluations; this was the language of life, of material work and mores, of the "lowly," mostly humorous genres (*fabliaux, cris de Paris,* farces), the free speech of the marketplace (although popular language, of course, was not homogeneous and contained some elements of official speech). On the other hand, Latin was the medium of the official medieval world. Popular culture was but feebly reflected in it and was distorted, especially in the Latin branch of grotesque realism. But the picture was not limited to the vernacular and medieval Latin. Other languages were intersected at this point, and linguistic interorientation was complex and manifold.

The historian of the French language Ferdinand Brunot explained how the transfer to the vernacular had been performed during the Renaissance with its classical tendencies. Brunot correctly stated that the endeavor of the Renaissance to reestablish Latin in its classic antique purity transformed it into a dead language. It would have been impossible to maintain this classic purity and to use it at the same time in the everyday life of the sixteenth century. The defense of pure Latin was inevitably limited to stylization. Here, once again, we find the ambivalence of the Renaissance image; the other side of this phenomenon was death. The rebirth of Cicero's Latin made it a dead language. The contemporary world, the new times, broke the bonds of Cicero's language and its pretense at being a living idiom.

Thus we see that the interorientation of the vernacular and medieval Latin was complicated by intersection of the latter with classic Latin. One line cut through the other, and Cicero's Latin threw light upon the true nature of medieval Latin, whose character was actually perceived for the first time. Up to that moment medieval Latin had been used without awareness of its ugliness and limitations. Cicero's Latin could also offer the "mirror of comedy" to medieval Latin. The "Letters of Obscure People" was reflected in it.

The intersection of the classic and medieval forms took place against the background of the modern world, which could fit neither the one nor the other. This world with all that was new threw light upon the face of Cicero's Latin and disclosed a beautiful but dead face.[6]

The new social forces were most adequately expressed in the vernacular. Therefore, the process of interorientation of classical and medieval Latin took place in the light of the national popular languages. Three media interacted and defined their boundaries through one indissoluble development.

Rabelais could have compared this triple linguistic process to the *farce jouée à trois personnages* (a farce played by three characters), while the "Letters of Obscure People" and macaronic poetry could be represented as an exchange of marketplace abuse by three languages. The gay death of a language with senile lapses, wheezing, and coughing is pictured by Rabelais in Master Janotus de Bragmardo's speech.

In this process of mutual clarification, an exceptional self-awareness was developed by living reality, that is, by all that was new and had not existed formerly: new objects, new concepts, new points of view. The boundaries between periods in time and between philosophies were acutely realized. The flow of time could never have been so sharply and clearly felt within the confines of a single, gradually evolving language system. In medieval Latin, which levels all things, the marks of time were almost entirely effaced; here consciousness seemed to live on in an eternal, unchanging world. In such a system it was particularly difficult to look around in time and space, that is, to become aware of the peculiar traits of one's own nationality and homeland. But on the brink of the three languages this awareness was to acquire exceptionally sharp and varied forms. It saw the boundaries of epochs and philosophies and could for the first time embrace vast dimensions and

---

[6] The modern times also placed the "mirror of comedy" before the face of the stiff, stylized Latin of the Ciceronians. The Macaronics' Latin is a reaction against humanist purism. Not a parody of Kitchen Latin, the Macaronics' language presents a correct syntax, but it is filled with words of the vernacular given Latin endings. A world of modern objects and concepts, completely alien to classic antiquity, invades the Latin constructions.

measure the flow of time; it could realize the present, it could contrast "today" with "yesterday." This interorientation and mutual clarification of the three languages suddenly disclosed how much of the old was dead and how much of the new was born. The modern time became conscious of itself. It too could reflect its face in the "mirror of comedy."

But this process was not limited to the interorientation of the three languages. It also took place in the sphere of national folk idioms. A single national language did not exist as yet; it was being slowly formed. The process of transferring the whole of philosophy to the vernacular and of creating a new system of literary media led to an intense interorientation of dialects within this vernacular (but without concentration at a center). The naïve and peaceful coexistence of the dialects came to an end; they began to clarify each other, and their variety was gradually unveiled. We can also observe a scientific interest in the dialects and the artistic search of dialectalisms. Their role in Rabelais' novel is immense.[7]

This special interest of the sixteenth century in the peculiarities of dialects is exemplified in Claude Odde's book *Joyeuses recherches de la langue toulousaine*. This book was published in 1578 and reflects to a considerable extent Rabelais' influence.[8] But the author's approach to language and to the dialects is characteristic of the entire epoch. Odde analyzes the peculiar traits of the Toulouse dialect, comparing it to the general Provençal language from the point of view of the ambiguous allusions and with misinterpretations and misunderstandings. These blunders are used by the author for a merry linguistic game in the Rabelaisian spirit. The interplay of languages is here obviously developed as a linguistic farce.

The idea of "The Gay Grammar" is actually not new. We have already mentioned that the tradition of grammatical *facéties* can

---

[7] For instance, Rabelais was very fond of the Gascon dialect as the most dynamic and rich in abusive expressions, *jurons,* and curses. This love of Gascon was shared by his contemporaries. Montaigne wrote a eulogy of this dialect. (Montaigne, *Essays,* II, Chapter 16)

[8] This booklet was reprinted by F. Noulet in Toulouse in 1892.

be traced throughout the Middle Ages. The "Grammatical Virgil" that we described earlier started this parodical tradition in the seventh century. But this medieval genre has a somewhat formalistic character, concerns Latin only, and is in no way concerned with language as a whole, with its physiognomy, image, and comic aspect. Such an approach is, on the contrary, characteristic of the linguistic and grammatical *facéties* and travesties of the sixteenth century. The dialects become complete images and types of speech and thought; they are linguistic masks. The role of Italian dialects in the *commedia dell'arte* is well known. Each mask features a dialect of the Italian language. It must, however, be observed that the images of the dialects and their comic nature are offered somewhat primitively in this genre.

Rabelais gave a striking parody of the latinizers in the episode of the Limousin student in *Pantagruel* (Book Two, Chapter 6). The student's speech was full of uncrowning obscenities in high-flown Latin-based confections. Enraged by its tone, Pantagruel seized the student by the throat, and the unfortunate fellow was so scared that he began to speak in his pure Limousin tongue.[9]

If the interorientation and the mutual clarification of the major languages rendered the awareness of time and its changes more acute, it also stimulated the awareness of historic space in the dialects, which strengthened and expressed the local, provincial peculiarities. This awareness of space, whether of a specific land or of the entire world, is characteristic of that period and is strikingly featured in Rabelais' novel.

However, the process was not limited to the interorientation of dialects. The national language, having become the medium of

[9] The Middle Ages were familiar only with the comic nature of a foreign language. Thus the mysteries frequently contain speeches in nonexistent tongues that provoked laughter by their bizarre and meaningless character. A more substantial form of linguistic humor is found in the farce *Maître Pathelin*. The hero speaks in Breton, Flemish, Limousin, Lorrainese, Picardese, and Norman and finally uses Macaronic and the *Grimoire* (a nonexistent tongue). There is a similar parody in Rabelais in the episode in which Panurge answers Pantagruel in seven languages, two of which are fictitious.

ideology and literature, inevitably entered into contact with other national languages that had reached this stratum of development earlier and had already mastered the world of new objects and concepts. Italian was such a language in relation to French. Many Italianisms made their way into French, together with Italian culture and technology. As they flooded French speech they soon led to a reaction in the form of a struggle between purists and Italianizers. The latter affected such extremes of Italianism as to make themselves ridiculous and became the subject of parodies—for example, by Henri Éstienne.

The Italianization of the French language and the struggle against it are a new and important document in the history of linguistic interaction. We have here two national idioms, and their interorientation not only lends a new element to the awareness of language as a peculiar whole with its own limits and perspectives but also leads to the consciousness of concrete historic space.

It is important to stress the immense importance of translations in the above mutual clarification of languages. We know that translation played a considerable role in the linguistic and literary life of the sixteenth century. The translation of Homer by Salel was a great event. Even a greater one was Amyot's translation of Plutarch (1559). The numerous French versions of Italian authors were also significant. These works had to be translated into a language that had not been finally developed and formed. Indeed it had to be shaped in the very process of translation and had to master concomitantly a new world of high ideology and strange objects and concepts, disclosed for the first time in an alien medium.[10]

We see at what a complex intersection of languages, dialects,

[10] Étienne Dolet wrote a book concerning the principles of translation of the sixteenth century: "The Method of Translating Efficiently from One Language into Another" (1540). He also spoke at length of these principles in his "Defense and Eulogy of the French Language" (1540). See also P. Villey: *Les Sources d'idées au XVème siècle*. We also find a valuable analysis of the methods of translation in R. Sturel's *Amyot, traducteur de Plutarque*. Paris, 1909. This work analyzes the primary text of Amyot's translation and discloses the general methods of sixteenth-century translators.

idioms, and jargons the literary and linguistic consciousness of the Renaissance was formed. The primitive and naïve coexistence of languages and dialects had come to an end; the new consciousness was born not in a perfected and fixed linguistic system but at the intersection of many languages and at the point of their most intense interorientation and struggle. Languages are philosophies— not abstract but concrete, social philosophies, penetrated by a system of values inseparable from living practice and class struggle. This is why every object, every concept, every point of view, as well as every intonation found their place at this intersection of linguistic philosophies and was drawn into an intense ideological struggle. In these exceptional conditions, linguistic dogmatism or naïvety became impossible. The language of the sixteenth century, and especially the language of Rabelais, are sometimes described as naïve even today. In reality the history of European literature presents no language less naïve. Rabelais' exceptional frankness and ease are anything but that. The literary and linguistic consciousness of his time was aware of its media not only from the inside but also from the outside, in the light of other languages.

Such an active plurality of languages and the ability to see one's own media from the outside, that is, through the eyes of other idioms, led to exceptional linguistic freedom. Even formal grammatical construction became extremely plastic. The artistic and ideological plane demanded first of all an unwonted freedom of images and of their combination, a freedom from all speech norms.

The influence of the century-old hidden linguistic dogmatism on human thought, and especially on artistic imagery, is of great importance. If the creative spirit lives in one language only, or if several languages coexist but remain strictly divided without struggling for supremacy, it is impossible to overcome this dogmatism buried in the depths of linguistic consciousness. It is possible to place oneself outside one's own language only when an essential historic change of language occurs. Such precisely was the time of Rabelais. And only in such a period was the artistic and ideological radicalism of Rabelaisian images made possible.

In his remarkable book *Pulcinella* Dieterich speaks of the peculiar character of the antique comic art of southern Italy (mimes, farces, comic games, buffooneries, riddles, and improvisations). He asserts that all these forms are typical of a mixed culture. In this area Greek, Oscan, and Latin cultures and languages were interwoven. Three souls lived in all southern Italian media, as well as in the first Roman poet Ennius. The Attelanae with their comic culture are also situated at the center of Oscan-Greek and later Oscan-Latin mixed spheres.[11] Finally, the character of Pulcinella himself arose out of the depths of the peoples, at the very point where peoples and languages were constantly merged.

Dieterich's opinion can be summed up as follows: The peculiar and extremely free humorous language of Sicily and southern Italy, the similar media of the Attelanae and later of Pulcinella's own linguistic clownery were born on the confines of languages and cultures, which not only were in direct contact but were in a certain sense interwoven. We believe that their emergence and development on these linguistic boundaries had exceptional significance for the universalism of humor and radicalism represented by these forms. The link of these forms with a multilingual world, as pointed out by Dieterich, seems to us extremely important. In the sphere of literary and artistic creation it is impossible to overcome through abstract thought alone, within the system of a unique language, that deep dogmatism hidden in all the forms of this system. The completely new, self-criticizing, absolutely sober, fearless, and gay life of the image can start only on linguistic confines.

In the system of one language, closed to all others, the image is too strictly imprisoned to allow that "truly divine boldness and shamelessness," which Dieterich finds in the farce of southern Italy, in the Attelanae (as far as we can judge of them), and in Pulcinella's folk humor.[12] We repeat, another language means another philosophy and another culture but in their concrete and not fully translatable form. The exceptional freedom and pitiless gaiety of

[11] Albrecht Dieterich, *Pulcinella*, 1897, p. 82.
[12] "Only the truly divine boldness and shamelessness of Pulcinella," writes Dieterich, "can throw light on the character, tone, and atmosphere of the antique farce and the Attelanae." (*Ibid,* p. 266).

the Rabelaisian image were possible only on the confines of languages.

Thus we see that in Rabelais freedom of laughter, consecrated by the tradition of popular-festive forms, was raised to a higher level of ideological consciousness, thanks to the victory over linguistic dogmatism. The defeat of this most obstinate and secret element was possible only through the intense interorientation and mutual clarification of languages which took place at that time. Linguistic life enacted that same drama: simultaneous death and birth, the aging and renewal of separate forms and meanings as well as of entire philosophies.

We have examined all the aspects of Rabelais' work which are essential in our mind. We have tried to show that the exceptional originality of his work was determined by the ancient folk culture of humor, powerfully reflected in Rabelaisian imagery.

The main failure of contemporary West-European Rabelaisiana consists in the fact that it ignores folk culture and tries to fit François Rabelais' novel into the framework of official culture, to conceive it as following the stream of "great" French literature. Because of this misapprehension, Rabelais scholars are unable to master that which is most essential in this novel. We have tried to understand Rabelais precisely as part of the stream of folk culture, which at all stages of its development has opposed the official culture of the ruling classes and evolved its own conception of the world, its own forms and imagery.

Literary studies and aesthetics are usually based on the narrowed and diminished manifestations of humor in the writings of the three last centuries, in spite of the fact that these conceptions are inadequate even for the understanding of Molière. Rabelais inherited and brought to fulfillment thousands of years of folk humor. His work is the unique key for the understanding of this culture in its most powerful, deep, and original manifestations.

Our study is only a first step in the vast task of examining ancient folk humor and even as a first step possibly may not be sufficiently firm and correct. But we are profoundly convinced of the importance of this task. We cannot understand cultural and literary life and the struggle of mankind's historic past if we ignore that peculiar folk humor that always existed and was never merged with the official culture of the ruling classes. While analyzing past ages we are too often obliged to "take each epoch at its word," that is, to believe its official ideologists. We do not hear the voice of the people and cannot find and decipher its pure unmixed expression.

All the acts of the drama of world history were performed before a chorus of the laughing people. Without hearing this chorus we cannot understand the drama as a whole. Let us imagine Pushkin's *Boris Godunov* without the scenes involving the massed people; such a conception of Pushkin's drama would be not only incomplete but distorted. Each character in the play expresses a limited point of view. The authentic meaning of the epoch and its events is disclosed in these crowd scenes, where Pushkin lets the people have the last word.

Our example is not merely a metaphoric comparison. In all periods of the past there was the marketplace with its laughing people, that very marketplace that in Pushkin's drama appeared in the pretender's nightmare:

The people swarmed on the public square
And pointed laughingly at me,
And I was filled with shame and fear.

We repeat, every act of world history was accompanied by a laughing chorus. But not every period of history had Rabelais for coryphaeus. Though he led the popular chorus of only one time, the Renaissance, he so fully and clearly revealed the peculiar and difficult language of the laughing people that his work sheds its light on the folk culture of humor belonging to other ages.

Abel, 326–327, 330, 339
"Acts of the Apostles, The," 326, 347
Adam de la Halle, 15, 257–261, 262–263
Aeschylus, 125, 148
Agons, 434
Agrippa, Cornelius, 359
Agrippa of Nettesheim, 444
Albert the Great, 401
Allemann, Beda, 120 n
Amervalle, Eloi de, 193
Amyot, Jacques, 152 n, 470
Anarchus, 148, 182, 198, 199, 205–206, 209, 213, 279, 285, 333–334, 336–337, 352, 385–386, 449
Anissimov, I. I., 140
"Apocalypse of Peter," 388
Apuleius, 78, 209 n
Aquinas, Thomas, 378, 401
Ardillon, Abbot, 440, 441
Ariosto, Lodovico, 299
Aristophanes, 28 n, 92 n, 98 n, 330, 434
Aristotle, 68–69, 362
Artamonov, S. D., 140
Assouci, Charles d', 106, 297
Atellanae, 28 n, 148, 472–473
Athenaeus, 28 n, 70, 97, 284, 354
"Aucassin and Nicolette," 15, 297
Aulus Gellius, 408
Autos Sacramentalis, 230

Bafier, Jean, 342
Baïf, Jean-Antoine de, 64
Balzac, Honoré de, 52
Banquier, 429 n
Barclay, John, 116
Basché, Lord of, 200–207, 208, 264, 265, 267, 268, 269, 279, 370, 400
Basoche, Kingdom of, 97
Basochiens, 36, 97
Bede, 293 n

Beethoven, Ludwig van, 284 n
Belinski, V. G., 1
Bellay, Guillaume du, 73, 446, 447, 448–452
Bellay, Jean du, 73, 158, 448–449
Bellay, Joachim du, 64, 73
Bells, image of, 213–215
Belon, Pierre, 457
Benoît, 398
Bergk, Fr., 434 n
Bergson, Henri, 71
Berni, Francesco, 111, 299, 427 n
Bertrand, A., 130 n
Billingsgate, 15–17, 27–28, 87, 145–146, 150, 153, 164–167, 168, 171–172, 176, 187–195, 207, 348, 352, 373, 389, 458
Blazon, 426–430
Blok, Alexander, 78 n
Boccaccio, Giovanni, 18, 56, 65, 66, 72, 272–273, 340
Boeuf violles, 202
Bollnow, O. H. F., 277
Bonaventura, 38, 40, 41, 51
Bon Temps, 228 n
Bosch, Hieronymus, 27, 389 n
Boucher, Guillaume, 60, 89 n, 155
Boucher, Jean, 441
Boulenger, Jacques, 60 n, 61 n, 102 n, 129 n, 130
Bourquelot, F., 54, 75 n
Brantôme, Pierre de Bourdeille, 60
Brauer, Max, 36 n
Brecht, Bertold, 46
Breughel, Pieter, the Elder, 27, 298 n
Brewer, 287
Briève Déclaration, 110, 149
Bringuenarilles, 280, 298 n
Bruno, Giordano, 365
Brunot, Ferdinand, 188 n, 466
Budé, Guillaume, 168, 176, 453
Bumfondle, 279, 332, 372, 423, 424

Burckhardt, Jacob, 158
Burdach, Konrad, 56–58

Caillette, 385
Calderón, Pedro, 243
Callisthenes, 344–345
Calvin, Jean, 100–101, 269, 296–297, 350, 452, 457
"Cambridge song manuscript," 289–290
Campanella, Tommaso, 365
Canel, 429 n
Caquets, 105–106, 114
Cardano, G., 365
"Carefree Lads," 36, 97
Carême-prenant, figure in Rabelais, 323, 346, 400, 415, see also Shrovetide
Cartier, Jacques, 397–398, 400, 452
Castiglione, Baldassare, 242
Catchpoles, 196, 199–207, 211–213, 263, 264, 265, 269, 279, 283, 285, 400
Cervantes, Miguel de, 2, 3, 18, 22, 23, 37, 41, 52, 65, 66, 72, 99, 103, 124, 125, 143, 275, 306
Charles V, 113, 176, 232, 233, 446–447, 449
Chateaubriand, François-René de, 1, 123, 125
Chaulières, Nicolas de, 89 n
Choricius, 70 n
"Christmas laughter," 79
Chronos, 243
Chrysostom, John, 73
Cicero, 386, 466–467
Clouzot, H., 102 n, 129 n, 130, 155 n
Cocagne, 297
Coena Cypriani, 13–14, 20, 76, 84, 85, 286–289, 295
Collerye, Roger de, 189–190
Cologne, 218, 219

Comedy, Greek, 28 n, 31, 46
Sicillian, 28 n
"Comedy of Proverbs," 181
"Comedy of Songs," 181
Comestor, Pierre, 389
Commedia dell'arte, 34, 35, 36, 304, 315, 353, 374, 469
Copernicus, 359
Coq-à-l'âne, 372, 422–426, 462
Coquillart, 412
Corbeille, Pierre, 78
Cornford, F., 54
Corpus Christi, 229–230, 231, 343
Correggio, Antonio Allegri, 252, 322 n
"Council of Remiremont," 295
Council of Toledo, 77
Council of Trent, 452
Court spectacles, 102–103, 246
Ctesias, 344
Curtius, Ernst, 84 n
"Cyprian's supper," see Coena Cypriani
Cyrano de Bergerac, 43

Dante, 56, 123, 124, 125, 126, 301, 369 n, 370, 377, 389, 391, 402–403, 435, 463
Débats, 88, 153, 156, 434
Decameron, 65, 72, 219 n, 272–273
Dedekind, Friedrich, 63
Dek, P., 136
Democritus, 67–68, 111, 360–361
Descartes, René, 101
Des Périers, Bonaventure, 60, 62, 65 n, 233, 235
Devinière, La, 442–443, 444
Dickens, Charles, 52
Dict des Pays, 429
Diderot, Denis, 34, 118
Dieterich, A., 54, 121 n, 201 n, 220, 472–473
Dingdong, 149

Diogenes, 171, 174, 176, 177, 178–179
Dionysius the Areopagite, 400–401
Dits, 87, 153
Dobrolyubov, 274
Dolet, Étienne, 269, 360, 362, 470 n
Don Quixote, 20, 22, 201, 434
Don Quixote, 23, 65, 103, 104, 209 n, 275
Dorneaux, Paul, 129 n
Dostoevsky, Feodor Mikhailovich, 78 n, 236 n
Doumergue, Jean, 100-101
Drevs, 54
Driesen, O., 267, 348–349, 392 n
Drum, image of, 203–205
Dubouchet, 130 n
Dupont, Gratien, 239
Dürer, Albrecht, 51
Dzhivelegov, A. K., 139

Easter laughter, see Risus paschalis
Ebeling, Fr. W., 35 n, 80 n
Eckermann, J. P., 250, 252, 253, 322 n
Elysian mysteries, 369
Enfants sans soucis, see "Carefree Lads"
Engels, F., 64 n, 118, 213 n, 436 n
Enlightenment, 37, 116–118, 124, 152 n
Ennasin, 415, 423, 461
Ennius, 171, 284, 472
Entrapel, 89 n
Epics, 4, 15, 27, 85 n, 88, 194, 341–342, 354
Epistemon, 41, 69, 135, 209, 279, 338, 371, 379, 381–386, 460
Erasmus, Desiderius, 11, 14, 132, 134, 168–169, 198, 314 n, 447
Erigena, Johanes Scotus, 401
Erl-King, 214, 267, 391, 392, 393
Ermini, F., 293 n

Estienne, Henri, 60, 87 n, 100, 105 n, 163, 296
Estissac, Geoffroi de, 155, 440
Étampes, Madame d', 112
Euloges, 15
Euripides, 98 n, 122, 343
Evnina, E. M., 139–140
Existentialism, 46, 49–50
Expurgation, 118, 124, 145
"Extraordinary Chronicle," 150

Fabliaux, 15, 27, 41, 88, 240, 242, 297, 466
Facéties, 77, 104, 135, 155, 156, 179, 180–181, 240, 242, 451, 468–469
Fail, Noël du, 60, 62, 89 n
Fairy tales, 87, 153
Falstaff, 143
Farce, 27, 36, 97, 153, 156, 180, 184, 240, 242, 298, 374, 425, 466, 469 n
Fatrasie, 422–423
"Feast of the Achaeans, The," 148
"Feast of the ass," 5, 36, 42, 78, 90, 199 n
"Feast of beans," 219
"Feast of fools," 5, 14, 27, 36, 42, 54, 74, 77, 78, 81, 83, 90, 147, 154, 218–219, 220, 235, 260, 271
Febvre, Lucien, 131–136
Fevrial, see Triboulet
Ficino, Marsile, 365
Fischart, Johann, 11, 63–64, 161 n, 228 n, 231
Fischer, E. K., 44, 304
Flaubert, Gustave, 422 n
Fleury, Jean, 137 n
Flögel, 35–36, 304
Focht, Y., 137
Folengo, Teofilo, 150, 210 n, 299–300, 341
Fontenay-le-Comte, 154-155, 440
Francis I, 113–114, 189–190, 232, 233, 397, 446, 447, 448, 449

Francis of Assisi, 56, 57, 78
Franklin, Alfred, 181 n
Frazer, Sir James George, 54
Freidenberg, O., 54 n
French Revolution, 119–120
Friar John, 86, 87, 141, 143, 186,
    189, 193–194, 196–197, 201 n,
    208–209, 212, 228, 237–238, 243,
    293–294, 295, 296, 304, 310–312,
    316, 416–421, 430, 443, 445
Fulgosus, Baptista, 409 n
Funerals, 6, 70, 74, 283

Gaidoz, H., 429 n
Galen, 28 n, 162, 453
Galiani, Abbé, 146
Gallet, 443–444, 446
Games, 231–232, 235–239, 259
Garcia of Toledo, 290–291, 292,
    350
Gargamelle, 221, 223, 224, 225–
    226, 459–460
Gargantua, and bells, 213–214,
    215–217
  birth of, 163, 220–224, 225–227,
    228, 317, 323, 331, 407–408, 443
  education of, 30, 158–159, 169–
    170, 202, 231, 236, 237–238, 280,
    300, 415, 424, 453
  of folk lore, 292, 297, 342–344,
    350, 396
  as historical allusion, 113, 114
  interpretation of character of, 120,
    141
  letter to Pantagruel of, 98, 135,
    324, 367, 404–407, 453
  on marriage, 432
  name of, 459–460
  and pilgrims, 311–312
  and swabs, 371–377, 378, 380
  and urine, 112, 147, 150, 190–192,
    464–465

Gargantua, 63, 141–143, 168–179,
    228, 279–280, 284, 444–445, 446,
    449
Gaster, and Gastrolaters, 280, 298,
    300–301, 400, 457
Gautier, Léon, 74 n
Gautier, Théophile, 43
Gautier of Metz, 345
Genius, 123, 124, 125, 127
Genres, 64–65, 67, 101–102, 166
Giants, 298, 341–344
Ginguené, Pierre Louis, 119–120
Goethe, Johann Wolfgang, 50, 103,
    106, 220, 244–256, 261, 322 n,
    334, 433 n, 434
Goliards, 293 n
Golias Apocalisis, 293
Goliath, 293 n
Gordeyev, E. M., 140
Goshelin, 391–393, 399
Gospels, parodies of, 85
Gottsched, Johann Christoph, 35
"Grammatical Virgil Maro," 14,
    20, 469
Grangousier, 222–223, 228 n, 311–
    312, 442–443, 444, 446, 453, 459–
    460
"Great Chronicles, The," 150 n,
    157, 159–164, 213, 341–342, 343,
    396
Greene, Robert, 297
Grimmelshausen, Hans Jacob
    Christoph von, 11, 428 n
Grobianism, 63–64, 95 n, 228 n
Gros Guillaume, 292, 354
Guevara, Luis Velez de, 11
Guyon, Louis, 299 n
Guyon de Bordeaux, 297

Hagar, 288
Hamlet, 42
Hans Carvel, 243
Hanswurst, 8, 246 n, 298

Harlequin, 8, 35, 258–259, 260, 262, 267, 304, 305, 306, 308–309, 348–349, 353, 396–397
Hegel, Friedrich, 44
Heine, Heinrich, 252 n
Helius, 97
Heracles, 31, 148, 226, 391 392
Heraclitus, 82, 147, 435
Herder, Johann Gottfried von, 4, 406–407
Hermes Trismegistes, 369
Herr Trippa, 444
Herzen, A. I., 92 n
Heulhard, A., 130 n
Hippel, Theodor von, 37
Hippocrates, 28 n, 162, 179, 180, 286, 452–453; see also "Hippocratic anthology" and "Hippocratic novel"
"Hippocratic anthology," 67, 355–361, 463
"Hippocratic novel," 67, 360–361
Hippothadeus, 444
Hoffmann, Ernst Theodor Amadeus, 37, 41, 47
Holbein, Hans, 50
Holy Bottle, 368–369, 397, 403
Homer, 70, 123, 125, 128, 171, 184, 284, 354, 470
Horace, 100, 284
Houdenc, Raoul, 390
Hugo, Victor, 1, 18, 43, 52, 123, 125–128, 152, 184–185
Humanisme et Renaissance, 129
Hutten, Ulrich von, 14, 466–467

Id, 49
Ilvonen, E., 54, 84 n
"Indian Wonders," 344–347
Innocent III, Pope, 389
Isidore of Seville, 344
"Isle of Winds," 151 n, 280
Issoudun, François Habert d', 289 n

Ivan the Terrible, 270, 271

Jacobsen, J. P., 74 n
Jairus, daughter of, 381, 382 n
Janotus de Bragmardo, 206, 213, 215–217, 285, 408, 467
Jaquain, Clément, 181
Jarry, Alfred, 46
Jerome, 351
Joachim of Floris, 56, 57
Joca monacorum, 13, 85
John VIII, Pope, 289
Jolibois, Emile, 266 n
Joubert, Laurent, 68, 70, 316
Judge Bridlegoose, 232, 238
Julian the Apostate, 287

Kastner, J. G., 181 n
Kayser, Wolfgang, 46–52
Kerch terracottas, 25, 31
Kierkegaard, Sören, 120 n
King, image of, 5, 81, 197, 212, 219, 235, 242, 370, 387, 393
Kissarse, 279, 232, 372, 373, 423, 424–425
Klinger, Friedrich Maximilian, 37
Krzhevsky, B. A., 99, 139

La Bruyère, Jean de, 107–110, 117, 145
Laetebundus, 85
Langland, William, 340
Lapithae, 206–207
Lapôtre, 287
Last Supper, 290, 296, 379
Latini, Brunetto, 345
Lazarus, 381, 389, 390
Le Duchat, 110–111
Le Feurial, *see* Triboulet
Lefèvre d'Etaples, 444
Lefranc, Abel, 129, 131–133, 157, 171, 239, 269 n, 362, 379, 381, 438, 443, 444

Lehmann, P., 54, 84 n, 85 n, 287
Lemaire, Jean, 192, 385, 412, 445
Le Motteux, Pierre Antoine, 112, 113
Lent, 8, 78, 79, 86, 99, 202, 234, 251, 285, 298
Lenz, Jakob, 37
Leo XIII, Pope, 76
Léonicène, Nicolas, 236
Lermontov, Michaïl Iourievitch, 236 n, 429 n
Lessing, Gotthold Ephraim, 35
"Letters of Obscure People," 14, 466–467
Liturgy, parodies of, 14, 85
Liublinsky, V. S., 96 n
"Living Corpses, The," 298–299
Ljubimov, N. M., 140, 143–144
Lote, Georges, 130, 180 n, 360 n, 362 n, 398 n, 451
Lucian, 69–70, 92 n, 97, 161, 176, 206–207, 284, 310 n, 337, 343, 344, 386–388, 398
Lusignan, Geoffroi de, 440–441
Lycurgus, 71 n
Lyon, 156–157, 220, 231, 325

Macbeth, 244
Mâchecroûte, 156, 231, 325
Macrobius, 28 n, 70, 97, 198, 284, 354, 399
"Magister Golias," 293
Maillard, 135
"Malbrough theme," 47, 151 n, 173
Mâle, Emile, 27 n
Malherbe, François de, 305
Manardi, 361
Mandeville, Sir John, 345
Mann, Thomas, 46, 120 n
Manneken-Pis, 151
Mapes, Walter, 293
Marcus Aurelius, 66
Mardi gras, 8, 213, 220, 222, 223, 328. See also Shrovetide

Marguerite d'Angoulême, 138, 139
Marie of France, 389
Marot, Clément, 66 n, 107–108, 152 n, 423, 427, 429
Marsy, Abbé, 112, 118, 145
Martial, 70 n
Marx, Karl, 64 n, 101, 118 n, 213 n, 436 n
Masks, 31, 39–40
Massenet, Jules, 102 n
Masses, parodies of, 295
May Day, 257, 258, 259, 260, 262, 263
Medical elements, 159, 161–162, 167, 169–170, 173–174, 179–181, 186–187, 258, 260, 330, 355–362, 452–453, 458
Meister, Wilhelm, 106
Melander, 77
Meletinskii, E. M., 6 n
"Menippus, or the Descent into Hades," 69–70, 386–388
"Menippus Satire on the Virtues of the Spanish Catholikon," 60, 63, 186–187, 264 n
Menot, 135, 193
Méon, 297 n
Mère Folle, 228 n
Michelet, Jules, 2, 115, 124
Mime, 28 n, 31, 55, 70–71, 78, 82, 98, 179, 374
Miracle plays, 15
Moccoli, 248–251, 352, 393
Moland, L., 149 n, 157, 158 n
Molière, Jean-Baptiste Poquelin, 34, 116, 264 n, 474
Molinet, Jean, 298
Montaiglon, Anatole de, 233 n, 428 n
Montaigne, Michel Eyquem de, 65–66, 70, 98 n, 320, 468
Montpellier, 68, 155–156, 361
Moralities, 15, 97, 155, 156, 184, 187

More, Thomas, 446, 447
Morolf, 20, 350, 373 n
Möser, Justus, 35, 36
"Mule without a Bridle, The," 15
Musil, Robert, 120 n
Mysteries, 5, 15, 27, 41, 155, 177, 233, 266–267, 325–326, 335, 338, 347–349, 389, 390, 428, 431, 451
Myth, 4, 30, 44, 56, 392

Napoleon III, 306, 315
Narren-literatur, 11
Nash, Thomas, 297
Nemo, 413–415
Neri, F., 293 n
Neruda, Pablo, 46
Nietzsche, Friedrich Wilhelm, 120 n
Ninepins, image of, 205 n, 223, 232
Niort, 155, 231, 441
Nodier, Charles, 128
Noël, 79
Nopces à mitaines, 200–207, 219, 264, 265, 269
Nose, image of, 87, 306, 315–317
Novati, F., 54, 83, 84 n
Novel, comic, 34, 103, 106
  Gothic, 37
  Hippocratic, 67–68, 360–361
Nuremberg, 218, 219, 393

Odde, Claude, 468
Odet, Cardinal, 179, 180
Odysseus, 31, 148
"Odyssey, The," 386
Oedipus, 243
Olivétan, Pierre Robert, 100–101
Orderic Vital, 391, 392, 393
Orion, 150
Oudin, 264 n
Oulmont, Charles, 295 n
Ovid, 70 n, 150

"Palaver of the Potulent," 224–225, 296, 443

Pantagruel, and Anarchus, 196, 209–210, 214, 333–334, 336–337, 385, 445, 449–450,
birth of, 279, 329–331, 339, 352, 407, 439
on folly, 261, 360, 426
genealogy of, 326–328, 379, 440
as hero, 451
journeys, 196, 338, 370, 397–400, 440–442, 452
and "Pantagruelion," 366–367
and thirst, 267, 298, 325–340, 346, 347, 441, 459, 460
and urine, 150, 335, 338
Pantagruel, 61, 141–143, 150 n, 156, 157, 158–168, 172, 229, 279, 307, 325, 326–340, 349, 352, 396, 397, 439
Pantagrueline Prognostication, 157
"Pantagruelion," 186, 324, 374
"Pantagruel's Disciple," 343
Panurge, and Anarchus, 182, 199, 210, 385–386
and the ancestral body, 323–324
on folly, 426, 430
and Epistemon, 381–384
as historical character, 113, 439–440
as humorous character, 141
and "Malbrough theme," 173–174, 175
and name, 460
and Turks, 210–211, 279, 332, 379, 464
and women, 229, 231, 242–244, 304, 312–315, 323, 416–421, 430
Papimania, 400
Paracelsus, 359, 361–362, 365
Paris, 155, 176, 181–187, 190–192, 218, 219
Paschal laughter, *see Risus paschalis*
Pasquier, Etienne, 60, 105 n, 128
Pathelin, 180, 469 n

Patriotism, 178
Patrizzi, 365
Paul, Jean, (pseudonym of Jean Paul Friedrich Richter), 37, 41–42, 51
Pauli, Johannes, 77
Perraud, Abbé, 118, 145
Pertz, G. H., 85 n
Peter the Great, 218, 270–271
Petot, 264 n
Petrarch, Francesco, 56
Petronius, 299
Phaeton, 330
Physiologus, 344
Pickwick, Mr., 292
Pico della Mirandola, 364–365
Picrochole, 113, 147, 177, 198–199, 205–206, 227–228, 280, 285, 443–444, 446–448, 460
Pilgrims, 311–312, 444, 453
Pinsky, L. E., 32 n, 136 n, 140–143
Plato, 162, 168–169, 284, 286, 323, 386
Plattard, J., 98 n, 129, 130, 156, 171, 441
Plautus, 98 n
Pléiade, 64–65, 98 n, 101
Pliny, 28 n, 69, 186, 314, 327, 344, 354, 408
Plutarch, 28 n, 66, 97, 284, 330, 354, 398, 399, 451, 470
Poitou, 155, 440–442, 445
"Poliphila's Dream," 235–236
Polo, Marco, 345
Pomponazzi, 362, 365
Pomponius, 148
Ponocrates, 30, 158, 170, 189, 216, 236, 408, 460
Popefiggery, 400
Porta, Giambattista, 365
Prester John, 346, 396, 397
Prophecies, 231, 232–235, 236–238, 242–244, 260

Protestantism, 60, 63, 87 n, 99–101, 132, 137, 164, 183–184, 269, 291, 350
Pulci, Luigi, 194, 299, 341
Pulcinella, 247, 251–252, 256, 472
Pushkin, Alexander Sergeevich, 122 n, 199 n, 210, 474

Rabanus Maurus, 76, 289
Rabelais, Antoine, 442–443, 446
Radulfus Glaber, 413–414
Rafa, 202, 231
Raminagrobis, 377–378, 408, 444
Raphael, 32
Ravisius Textor, 328, 409
Régnier, Henri de, 53
Reich, H., 25, 54, 55–56, 70 n, 71 n, 73 n, 97
Reinach, S., 54, 71 n, 79 n, 343 n
Relics, 349–350
Revue des Etudes Rabelaisiennes, 60 n, 129
Revue du Seizième Siècle, 60 n, 129
Rhetoricians, 192, 385
Rienzo, Nicolas di, 56, 57
Rig-Veda, 351
Risus paschalis, 5, 14, 54, 78, 79, 83, 134, 146, 287
Rococo, 119
Roland 15, 111
Roman d'Alexandre, 345
Roman à clef, 62, 112–115, 116, 424 n
Roman du Fauvel, 147, 214, 267, 373 n, 411
Roman de la Rose, 66 n, 241, 369
Romanticism, 1, 3, 4, 36–45, 46, 47, 48, 51, 120 n, 123–128, 236, 252
Rome, 30, 158, 218, 219, 220, 244–245, 246–252, 254, 329, 334, 393, 434
Rondelet, Guillaume, 445, 457, 461
Rondibilis, 445, 461
Ronsard, Pierre de, 64, 68, 354

Rousseau, Jean-Jacques, 92 n
Rutebeuf, 185–186

Sachs, Hans, 11, 147 n, 245, 298 n, 316
Sainéan, Lazare, 60 n, 61, 129, 185 n, 193, 454–455, 460 n
Saint-Amant, Marc-Antoine Girard de, 43, 106, 297
St. Augustine, 293 n
St. Bonaventure of Beauvais, 369
Saint Brendan, 346, 398–399, 400, 451
St. Cyprian, 73, 286
Saint-Gelais, Mellin de, 232, 235, 237
St. Gregory, 389
St. John, 125, 250
Saint Louis, 326
Saint Maixent, 155, 200, 208, 263, 445, 446
Saint Patrick, 377, 388, 389, 398
St. Paul, 125, 227
St. Quentin, 347, 428
St. Valentine's day, 219, 231
Sainte-Marthe, Charles de, 296–297
Sainte-Marthe, Gauchet de, 443–444, 446
Salel, 470
Saltrais, Henri de, 388
Salut d'Enfer, 390
Sancho, 20 n, 22, 201, 434
Sand, George, 118 n, 145
Sardou, M. A. L., 112
Satires chrestiennes de la Cuisine Papale, 100, 183–184
Saturnalia, 6–8, 10, 13 n, 14, 70, 76, 79 n, 81, 82, 89, 138, 198–199, 246, 264 n, 287, 288, 387, 391, 392, 395, 399
"Satyric drama," 28 n, 31, 46, 88, 122, 230, 233

Scarron, Paul, 43, 103, 106–107, 200 n, 304, 305, 309, 315
Scheidt, Kasper, 63
Schlegel, Friedrich, 37, 41, 42, 120 n
Schmidt, J. P., 54, 79 n
Schneegans, G., 45–46, 130, 139, 304–312, 315–316
Schwänke, 27, 77, 88
Scudéry, Georges de, 43
Sebillet, Thomas, 233, 427
Sébillot, Paul, 342, 343, 396, 429 n
Second, Jean, 65
Seneca, 66, 151 n, 198
Sermons joyeux, 15, 85, 97 n
Sforza, Lodovico, 113, 446
Shakespeare, William, 1, 2, 3, 11, 18, 37, 41, 42, 43, 52, 66, 72, 122, 123, 124, 125, 127, 143, 275, 297, 306, 429 n
Shishmareff, V. F., 139
Shrovetide, 8, 36, 80, 99, 146, 177, 192 n, 213, 220, 222, 223–224, 294, 323, 328, 346, 400, 415
Sileni, 31, 168–170
Smirnov, A. A., 139
Societas cornardorum, 77, 220
Société des Etudes Rabelaisiennes, 129–131, 137
Socrates, 121, 168–169, 286
Solomon, 20, 227, 350, 373 n
Sophocles, 148
Sorbonne, 75, 86 n, 173, 205–206, 213, 215–217, 269
Sorel, Charles, 103–105, 107 n
Soties, 5, 15, 27, 28, 36, 97, 153, 180–181, 184, 187, 242, 298, 382, 425, 428, 431
Spinoza, Baruch, 141, 254
Spirituals, 56
Stapfer, Paul, 110, 130
Steinert, R., 37 n
Stendhal (pseudonym of Marie Henri Beyle), 52

Sterne, Laurence, 36, 37, 41, 42, 44, 47
Street cries, 153, 160, 181–187, 195, 260, 431, 466
Sturel, R., 470 n
Sturm und Drang, 37
Swabs, 105, 113, 114, 371–381, 383, 384, 396, 418, 461–462
Swift, Jonathan, 34, 308
Sybil of Panzoult, 240, 373, 377, 445
Symposium, 28 n, 168–169, 206, 207, 283–286, 289–292, 295–297, 323

Tabarin, 102, 397
Table talk, 89–90, 117, 280, 283–286, 354–355
Tahureau, Jacques, 60, 89 n
Terence, 98 n
Tersitus, 31
Tertullian, 73
Thaumastes, 279, 332
Thélème, 30, 135, 138–139, 280 n, 412, 415, 431, 453
Theophrastus, 110
Thou, Jacques Auguste de, 111
Ticklepecker, 206, 263–268, 270, 279, 285, 413, 445, 446
Tieck, Ludwig, 37
Tiraqueau, André, 98, 440–441, 461
Triboulet, 8, 177, 198, 261, 385, 426, 428, 429, 430
Tripe, image of, 162–164, 166, 221–222, 223, 224–225
Tropes, 74 n
Truque, 182, 183
Tungdal, 388, 389, 390, 391
Turlupin, 102, 292

Urquhart, Thomas, 112, 231

Vagantes, 293 n, 295
Vaiman, S. T., 140
Valerius, Julius, 344
Valerius Maximus, 409 n
Variorum, 112–113
Vasari, Giorgio, 33
Vega, Lope de, 11, 230
Vergilius Maro Grammaticus, see "Grammatical Virgil Maro"
Verrazano, Giovanni da, 397
Verville, Béroalde de, 60, 89 n
Verzmen, I. E., 139
Veselovsky, A. N., 85, 93, 137–139, 143, 146–147, 152
Vetruvius, 33
Viau, Théophile, 43, 106, 297
Villeneuve, Guillaume de, 181
Villetard, P., 54, 75 n
Villey, P., 98 n, 470 n
Villon, François, 43, 155, 174, 191, 200, 208, 214, 231, 263, 264, 265, 267, 268, 269, 400, 445
Vinci, Leonardo da, 50, 323
Viret, Pierre, 60, 100
Virgil, 354, 386
"Vision of Paul," 388, 389
Voltaire, François-Marie Arouet, 1, 34, 92 n, 113, 114, 116–118, 123, 124, 145, 152 n
Voulté, 296–297

Wetzel, 38
Wills, 14, 85, 351
Wirecker, Nigel, 85 n

Xenophon, 284, 286

Zeno, Bishop of Verona, 287, 295
Zeus, 243
Zhdanov, I. N., 85
Zola, Emile, 184
Zoroaster, 69